JOSEPH *Speaks*

JOSEPH
Speaks

Topical Quotes by the Prophet Joseph Smith

•••

Gleaned from the Prophet's numerous sermons, funeral talks, letters, and meetings during his dynamic ministry, as were recorded in such publications as the Documentary History of the Church *and other publications prominent during the life of the Prophet.*

In 1979, under the direction of Joseph Fielding Smith, historian for The Church of Jesus Christ of Latter-day Saints, Teachings of the Prophet Joseph Smith *was compiled. It is a fairly extensive and popular chronological text of many of the Prophet's more significant talks and writings. Now, from those textual pages, the book* Joseph Speaks *uncovers as gems thousands of quotes and topically organizes them for convenient access to what the eloquent Prophet Joseph Smith had to say on hundrends of topics.*

•••

Compiled by

Sterling H. Redd

Horizon Publishers

Springville, Utah

ISBN 13: 978-0-88290-830-4

Published by Horizon Publishers, an imprint of Cedar Fort, Inc., 2373 W. 700 S., Springville, UT, 84663
Distributed by Cedar Fort, Inc., www.cedarfort.com

LIBRARY OF CONGRESS CATALOGING-IN-PUBLICATION DATA

Smith, Joseph, 1805–1844.
 Topical quotes by the prophet Joseph Smith / [compiled by] Sterling H. Redd.
     p. cm.
  ISBN-13: 978-0-88290-830-4
  1. Smith, Joseph, 1805-1844—Quotations. 2. Church of Jesus Christ of Latter-day Saints—Doctrines—Quotations, maxims, etc. I. Redd, Sterling H., 1938- II. Title.
  BX8695.S6A25 2007
  289.3'2—dc22
                        2007031885

Cover design by Nicole Williams
Cover design © 2007 by Lyle Mortimer
Typeset by Kimiko M. Hammari

Printed in the United States of America

10 9 8 7 6 5 4 3 2 1

Printed on acid-free paper

INTRODUCTION

Of an earlier work on Joseph Smith's words compiled by an Edwin F. Parry, the Church Historian Joseph Fielding Smith wrote three quarters of a century later, "That little work filled an important mission, but left in the hearts and minds of all who were interested in the sayings of the great latter-day Prophet, a longing for more of his sayings, which longing was not satisfied." He continued with, "Many faithful members of the Church have expressed the desire that a more extensive work of this kind be published." Continuing further, he wrote, "The members of the Church quite generally desire to know what the prophet Joseph Smith may have said on important subjects, for they look upon his utterances as coming through divine inspiration" (Introduction, TPJS).

Subsequently, through the initiative of the Church Historian's Office at that time, a more arduous and comprehensive effort was made in gathering writings not only from the Documentary History of the Church, but from numerous scattered, some old, and some rather inaccessible publications. With the approval of the First Presidency, *Teachings of the Prophet Joseph Smith* was then written and published.

Joseph Fielding Smith explained in his Introduction: "It should be remembered that this compilation contains some discourses and statements from the minutes of council and priesthood meetings, which are not verbatim reports of the Prophet's remarks, but which have been approved in those meetings." He then acknowledged, "There has been no attempt to compile these sayings by subject, because frequently in the same article or discourse, several subjects are discussed." Consequently, his compilation follows a chronologically-formatted though rather in-depth text, accompanied by an exhaustive index and concordance at the end,—rather than an alphabetically-formatted text by subject.

Perhaps refreshingly, the primary focus in *Joseph Speaks* is presenting alphabetically by topic "what the Prophet Joseph Smith . . . said on important subjects" in the form of well over sixteen hundred carefully-selected quotes gleaned from the book *Teachings of the Prophet Joseph Smith*.

The editor has placed strong value on the ease of accessibility given to a reader in finding specific quotes or material sought for. Since certain original texts do contain many quotes—often on multiple topics; and since many of the quotes do fall appropriately under several subject or topic headings, therefore many quotes subsequently appear under more than one topic. Furthermore, in consideration of space, the equivalent of several pages of more in-depth discussion, somewhat historical matters, incidental or less important as well as non-quotable material are exchanged in favor of more space for expanded use of the chosen quotes.

Since this volume is presented in a topical form, recommendation is given for its use not so much as a book to be read straight through from cover to cover, but as a topical reference for easy access to powerful and insightful quotes of the Great Prophet of the Restoration.

—Sterling H. Redd

TOPICAL INDEX

JOSEPH AND BEGINNINGS

NEGATIVITY AND CONSEQUENCES

NEXT LIFE

PRINCIPLES

THIS LIFE

AARONIC PRIESTHOOD

The kingdom of God for a season seemed to rest with John alone. The Lord promised Zacharias that he should have a son who was a descendant of Aaron, the Lord having promised that the priesthood should continue with Aaron and his seed throughout their generations. Let no man take this honor upon himself, except he be called of God, as was Aaron; and Aaron received his call by revelation. (TPJS, 272)[91]

◆◆◆

An angel of God also appeared unto Zacharias while in the Temple, and told him that he should have a son, whose name should be John, and he should be filled with the Holy Ghost. Zacharias was a priest of God, and officiating in the Temple, and John was a priest after his father, and held the keys of the Aaronic Priesthood, and was called of God to preach the Gospel of the kingdom of God . . . and our Savior submitted to that authority Himself, by being baptized by John; therefore the kingdom of God was set up on earth, even in the days of John. (TPJS, 272)[91]

◆◆◆

The keys of the Aaronic Priesthood were committed unto . . . [John], and he was as the voice of one crying in the wilderness saying: "Prepare ye the way of the Lord and make his paths straight." (TPJS, 319)[117]

ABRAHAMIC PROMISE

If there is anything calculated to interest the mind of the Saints, to awaken in them the finest sensibilities, and arouse them to enterprise and exertion, surely it is the great and precious promises made by our heavenly Father to the children of Abraham; and those engaged in seeking the outcasts of Israel, and the dispersed of Judah, cannot fail to enjoy the spirit of the Lord and have the choicest blessings of heaven rest upon them in copious effusions. (TPJS, 163)[51]

ACCEPTANCE

[Joseph said that] it was the folly and nonsense of the human heart for a person to be aspiring to other stations than those to which they are appointed of God for them to occupy; that it was better for individuals to magnify their respective calling, and wait patiently till God shall say to them, "come up higher." (TPJS, 223)[75]

◆◆◆

Meddle not with any man for his religion; and all governments ought to permit every man to enjoy his religion unmolested. No man is authorized to take away life in consequence of difference in religion, which all laws and governments ought to tolerate and protect, right or wrong. (TPJS, 344)[130]

ACCOUNTABILITY
(*See also* PUNISHMENT;
CONSEQUENCES)

If others' blessings are not your blessings, others' curses are not your curses: you stand then in these last days, as all have stood before you, agents unto yourselves, to be judged according to your works. (TPJS, 12)[7]

◆◆◆

The eyes of my Maker are upon me, and . . . to Him I am accountable for every word I say, wishing nothing worse to my fellow-men than their eternal salvation. (TPJS, 17)[9]

◆◆◆

The Lord says that every man is to receive according to his works. Reflect for a moment, . . . and enquire whether you would consider yourselves worthy a seat at the marriage seat with Paul and others like him, if you had been unfaithful? Had you not fought the good fight, and kept the faith, could you expect to receive? (TPJS, 64)[21]

◆◆◆

Men not infrequently forget that they are dependent upon heaven for every blessing which they are permitted to enjoy, and that for every opportunity granted them they are to give an account. (TPJS, 68)[21]

◆◆◆

Our acts are recorded, and at a future day they will be laid before us, and if we should fail to judge right and injure our fellow-beings, they may there, perhaps, condemn us. (TPJS, 69)[22]

◆◆◆

Vengeance is mine, saith the Lord, and I will repay. (TPJS, 77)[29]

◆◆◆

Some have been uncharitable, and have manifested greediness because of their debts towards those who have been persecuted and dragged about with chains without cause, and imprisoned. Such characters God hates—and they shall have their turn of sorrow in the rolling of the great wheel, for it rolleth and none can hinder. (TPJS, 129)[46]

◆◆◆

Satan was generally blamed for the evils which we did, but if he was the cause of all our wickedness, men could not be condemned. The devil could not compel mankind to do evil; all was voluntary. Those who resisted the Spirit of God, would be liable to be led into temptation, and then the association of heaven would be withdrawn. (TPJS, 187)[60]

◆◆◆

[God] passes over no man's sins, but visits them with correction, and if His children will not repent of their sins He will discard them. (TPJS, 189)[60]

◆◆◆

The prayers of all the ministers in the world can never close the gates of hell against a murderer. (TPJS, 189)[60]

◆◆◆

All men have power to resist the devil. (TPJS, 189)[61]

◆◆◆

It is a desirable honor that you should so walk before our heavenly Father as to save yourselves; we are all responsible to God for the manner we improve the light and wisdom given by our Lord to enable us to save ourselves. (TPJS, 227)[75]

◆◆◆

"Fret not thyself because of evildoers." God will see to it. (TPJS, 239)[78]

◆◆◆

There will be wicked men on the earth during the thousand years. The heathen nations who will not come up to worship will be visited with the judgments of God, and must eventually be destroyed from the earth. (TPJS, 268)[88]

ADAM

[Adam] is the father of the human family, and presides over the spirits of all men. . . . Adam delivers up his stewardship to Christ, that which was delivered to him as holding the keys of the universe, but retains his standing as head of the human family. (TPJS, 157)[49]

•••

The Priesthood was first given to Adam. . . . He obtained it in the Creation, before the world was formed. . . . He had dominion given him over every living creature. He is Michael the Archangel, . . . then [the Priesthood was given] to Noah, who is Gabriel: he stands next in authority to Adam in the Priesthood; he was called of God to this office, and was the father of all living in this day, and to him was given the dominion. These men held keys first on earth, and then in heaven. (TPJS, 157)[49]

•••

Adam . . . was the first man . . . the "Ancient of Days" . . . [who] holds the keys of the dispensation of the fullness of times; i.e., the dispensation of all the times have been and will be revealed through him from the beginning to Christ, and from Christ to the end of the dispensations that are to be revealed. (TPJS, 167)[54]

ADMONISHMENT

(*See also* CHASTISEMENT)

I frequently rebuke and admonish my brethren, and that because I love them, not because I wish to incur their displeasure, or mar their happiness. Such a course of conduct is not calculated to gain the good will of all, but rather the ill will of many; . . . but these rebukes and admonitions become necessary, from the perverseness of the brethren, for their temporal as well as spiritual welfare. (TPJS, 113)[41]

ADVOCACY

I feel for my fellow men; I do it in the name of the Lord being moved upon by the Holy Spirit. Oh, that I could snatch them from the vortex of misery, into which I behold them plunging themselves, by their sins that I might be enabled by the warning voice, to be an instrument of bringing them to unfeigned repentance, that they might have faith to stand in the evil day! (TPJS, 87)[31]

•••

I am determined to do all that I can to uphold you, although I may do many things inadvertently that are not right in the sight of God. (TPJS, 90)[33]

•••

Be assured, brethren, I am willing to stem the torrent of all opposition, in storms and in tempests, in thunders and in lightnings, by sea and by land, in the wilderness or among false brethren, or mobs, or wherever God in His providence may call us. (TPJS, 106)[37]

•••

I have sometimes spoken too harshly from the impulse of the moment, and inasmuch as I have wounded your feelings, brethren, I ask your forgiveness, for I love you and will hold you up with all my heart in all righteousness, before the Lord, and before all men. (TPJS, 106)[37]

•••

"What greater love hath any man than that he lay down his life for his friend"; then why not fight for our friend until we die? (TPJS, 195)[66]

•••

He that will war the true Christian warfare against the corruptions of these last days will have wicked men and angels of devils, and all the infernal powers of darkness continually arrayed against him. (TPJS, 259)[84]

•••

When my enemies take away my rights, I will bear it and keep out of the way; but if they take away your rights, I will fight for you. (TPJS, 268)[87]

•••

If it has been demonstrated that I have been willing to die for a "Mormon," I am bold to declare before Heaven that I am just as ready to die in defending the rights of a Presbyterian, a Baptist, or a good man of any other denomination; for the same principle which would trample upon the rights of the Latter-day Saints would trample upon the rights of the Roman Catholics, or of any other denomination who may be unpopular and too weak to defend themselves. (TPJS, 313)[114]

•••

If I lose my life in a good cause I am willing to be sacrificed on the altar of virtue, righteousness and truth, in maintaining the laws and Constitution of the United States, if need be, for the general good of man. (TPJS, 332)[124]

•••

When I get hold of the Eastern papers, and see how popular I am, I am afraid myself that I shall be elected; but if I should be, I would not say, "*Your cause is just, but I can do nothing for you.*" (TPJS, 334)[127]

AFFECTION

When we lose a near and dear friend, upon whom we have set our hearts, it should be a caution unto us not to set our affections too firmly upon others, knowing that they may in like manner be taken from us. Our affections should be placed upon God and His work more intensely than upon our fellow beings. (TPJS, 216)[72]

•••

Let this [Relief] Society teach women how to behave towards their husbands, to treat them with mildness and affection. (TPJS, 228)[75]

AGENCY

(*See also* INDIVIDUALITY)

We deem it a just principle . . . that all men are created equal, and that all have the privilege of thinking for themselves upon all matters relative to conscience. Consequently, then, we are not disposed, had we the power, to deprive any one of exercising that free independence of mind which heaven has so graciously bestowed upon the human family as one of its choicest gifts. (TPJS, 49)[21]

•••

Satan was generally blamed for the evils which we did, but if he was the cause of all our wickedness, men could not be condemned. The devil could not compel mankind to do evil; all was voluntary. Those who resisted the Spirit of God, would be liable to be led into temptation, and then the association of heaven would be withdrawn from those who refused to be made partakers of such great glory. (TPJS, 187)[60]

•••

God would not exert any compulsory means, and the devil could not. (TPJS, 187)[60]

•••

[God] passes over no man's sins, but visits them with correction, and if His children will not repent of their sins He will discard them. (TPJS, 189)[60]

•••

The spirits of good men cannot interfere with the wicked beyond their prescribed bounds, for Michael, the Archangel, dared not bring a railing accusation against the devil, but said, "The Lord rebuke thee, Satan." (TPJS, 208)[71]

♦♦♦

Herein is the condemnation of the world; that light hath come into the world, and men choose darkness rather than light, because their deeds are evil. (TPJS, 96)[34]

♦♦♦

Men or women [can] not be compelled into the kingdom of God, but must be dealt with in long-suffering, and at last we shall save them. (TPJS, 241)[79]

♦♦♦

If I esteem mankind to be in error, shall I bear them down? No. I will lift them up, and in their own way too, if I cannot persuade them my way is better; and I will not seek to compel any man to believe as I do, only by the force of reasoning, for truth will cut its own way. (TPJS, 313)[114]

♦♦♦

It is one of the first principles of my life, and one that I have cultivated from my childhood, having been taught it by my father, to allow everyone the liberty of conscience. (TPJS, 326)[122]

♦♦♦

Did I ever exercise any compulsion over any man? Did I not give him the liberty of disbelieving any doctrine I have preached, if he saw fit? (TPJS, 341)[129]

♦♦♦

Meddle not with any man for his religion; and all governments ought to permit every man to enjoy his religion unmolested. No man is authorized to take away life in consequence of difference in religion, which all laws and governments ought to tolerate and protect, right or wrong. (TPJS, 344)[130]

AMBITION

[Joseph said that] it was the folly and nonsense of the human heart for a person to be aspiring to other stations than those to which they are appointed of God for them to occupy; that it was better for individuals to magnify their respective calling, and wait patiently till God shall say to them, "come up higher." (TPJS, 223)[75]

ANGELS

An angel of God never has wings. (TPJS, 162)[49]

♦♦♦

Jesus Christ became a ministering spirit [while His body was lying in the sepulcher] to the spirits in prison, to fulfill an important part of His mission, without which He could not have perfected His work, or entered into His rest. After His resurrection He appeared as an angel to His disciples. (TPJS, 191)[63]

♦♦♦

If you live up to your privileges, the angels cannot be restrained from being your associates. (TPJS, 226)[75]

♦♦♦

Gods have an ascendancy over the angels, who are ministering servants. In the resurrection, some are raised to be angels, others are raised to become Gods. (TPJS, 312)[113]

♦♦♦

Spirits can only be revealed in flaming fire and glory. Angels have advanced further, their light and glory being tabernacled; and hence they appear in bodily shape. . . . Angels have advanced higher in knowledge and power than spirits. (TPJS, 325)[121]

♦♦♦

When a corrupt man is chastened he gets angry and will not endure it. (TPJS, 195)[66]

•••

Many when they arrived here, were dissatisfied with the conduct of some of the Saints, because everything was not done perfectly right, and they get angry, and thus the devil gets advantage over them to destroy them. (TPJS, 268)[87]

ANIMALS

How will the serpent ever lose its venom, while the servants of God possess the same disposition, and continue to make war upon it? Men must become harmless before the brute creation, and when men lose their vicious dispositions and cease to destroy the animal race, the lion and the lamb can dwell together and the sucking child can play with the serpent in safety. (TPJS, 71)[24]

•••

John saw curious beasts in heaven; he saw every creature that was in heaven,— all the beasts, fowls and fish in heaven,— actually there, giving glory to God. . . . saying, Blessing and honor, and glory, and power, be unto Him that sitteth upon the throne, and unto the Lamb for ever and ever. (TPJS, 291)[101]

•••

I suppose John saw being there of a thousand forms, that had been saved from ten thousand times ten thousand earths like this,—strange beasts of which we have no conception: all might be seen in heaven. The grand secret was to show John what there was in heaven. John learned that God glorified Himself by saving all that His hands had made, whether beasts, fowls, fishes or men; and He will glorify Himself with them. (TPJS, 291)[101]

ANTICIPATION

Whenever the Lord revealed Himself to men in ancient days, and commanded them to offer sacrifices to Him, . . . it was done that they might look forward in faith to the time of His coming, and rely upon the power of that atonement for a remission of their sins. (TPJS, 60)[21]

•••

Those who have died in Jesus Christ may expect to enter into all that fruition of joy when they come forth, which they possessed or anticipated here. (TPJS, 295)[102]

•••

The expectation of seeing my friends in the morning of the resurrection cheers my soul and makes me bear up against the evils of life. It is like taking a long journey, and on their return we meet them with increased joy. (TPJS, 296)[102]

•••

God has revealed His Son from the heavens and the doctrine of the resurrection also; . . . . Let these truths sink down in our hearts, that we may even here begin to enjoy that which shall be in full hereafter. (TPJS, 296)[102]

•••

If I have no expectation of seeing my father, mother, brothers, sisters and friends again, my heart would burst in a moment, and I should go down to my grave. (TPJS, 296)[102]

•••

Those who have died in the faith are now in the celestial kingdom of God. . . . and your expectations and hopes are far above what man can conceive; Don't mourn, don't weep. I know it by the testimony of the Holy Ghost that is within me; and you may wait for your friends to come forth to meet you in the morn of the celestial world. (TPJS, 359)[130]

ANXIETY

Anxieties inexpressible crowd themselves continually upon my mind for the Saints, when I consider the many temptations to which we are subject, from the cunning and flattery of the great adversary of our souls. (TPJS, 29)[16]

♦♦♦

There is no pain so awful as that of suspense. This is the punishment of the wicked; their doubt, anxiety and suspense cause weeping, wailing and gnashing of teeth. (TPJS, 288)[101]

♦♦♦

I have had a good deal of anxiety about my safety since I left Nauvoo, which I never had before when I was under arrest. I could not help those feelings, and they have depressed me. (TPJS, 382)[140]

APATHY

(See also COMPLACENCE)

Some have been ordained in the ministry, and have never acted in that capacity, or magnified their calling at all. Such may expect to lose their appointment, except they awake and magnify their office. (TPJS, 42)[20]

♦♦♦

There are a great many wise men and women too in our midst who are too wise to be taught; therefore they . . . seal up the door of heaven by saying . . . God may reveal and I will believe. (TPJS, 309)[113]

♦♦♦

When things that are of the greatest importance are passed over by weak-minded men without even a thought, I want to see truth in all its bearings and hug it to my bosom. (TPJS, 374)[133]

♦♦♦

APOLOGY

The sound of the gathering, and of the doctrine, went abroad into the world; and many, having a zeal not according to knowledge, and not understanding the pure principles of the doctrine of the Church, have, no doubt, in the heat of enthusiasm, taught and said many things which are derogatory to the genuine character and principles of the Church; and for these things we are heartily sorry, and would apologize, if apology would do any good. (TPJS, 80)[30]

♦♦♦

I have sometimes spoken too harshly from the impulse of the moment, and inasmuch as I have wounded your feelings, brethren, I ask your forgiveness, for I love you and will hold you up with all my heart in all righteousness, before the Lord, and before all men. (TPJS, 106)[37]

APOSTASY

Christ said to His disciples, that these signs should follow them that believe:—"In my name shall they cast out devils; they shall speak with new tongues; they shall take up serpents; and if they drink any deadly thing, it shall not hurt them; they shall lay hands on the sick, and they shall recover"; . . . By the foregoing testimonies we may look at the Christian world and see the apostasy there has been from the apostolic platform; and who can look at this and not exclaim, in the language of Isaiah, "The earth also is defiled under the inhabitants thereof; because they have transgressed the laws, changed the ordinances, and broken the everlasting covenant"? (TPJS, 15)[9]

♦♦♦

It is reasonable to suppose that man departed from the first teachings, or instructions which he received from heaven in the first age, and refused by his disobedience to be governed by them. Consequently, he formed such laws as best suited his own mind, or as he supposed, were best adapted to his situation. But that God has influenced man more or less since that time in the formation of law for His benefit we have no hesitancy in believing . . . though man in his own supposed wisdom would not admit the influence of a power superior to his own . (TPJS, 57)[21]

♦♦♦

It was not until apostasy and rebellion against the things of God that the true knowledge of the universe as well as the knowledge of other truths, became lost among men. (TPJS, 119)[44]

♦♦♦

Behold the words of the Savior: "If the light which is in you become darkness, behold how great is that darkness." (TPJS, 124)[46]

♦♦♦

In all your trials, troubles, temptations, afflictions, bonds, imprisonments and death, see to it that you do not betray heaven; that you do not betray Jesus Christ; that you do not betray the brethren; that you do not betray the revelations of God, whether in Bible, Book of Mormon or Doctrine and Covenants, or any other . . . revealed unto man in this world . . . . Yea, in all your kickings and flounderings, see to it that you do not this thing, lest innocent blood be found upon your skirts, and you go down to hell. (TPJS, 156)[49]

♦♦♦

That man who rises up to condemn others, finding fault with the Church, saying that they are out of the way, while he himself is righteous, then know

assuredly that that man is in the high road to apostasy; and if he does not repent, will apostatize, as God lives. (TPJS, 156)[49]

♦♦♦

It was generally in consequence of the brethren disregarding or disobeying counsel that they became dissatisfied and murmured; . . . and thus the devil gets advantage over them to destroy them. (TPJS, 268)[87]

♦♦♦

Of the Twelve Apostles chosen in Kirtland, and ordained under the hands of Oliver Cowdery, David Whitmer and myself, there have been but two but what have lifted their heel against me—namely Brigham Young and Heber C. Kimball. (TPJS, 307)[112]

APOSTATES

(See also TRAITORS; BETRAYAL)

Respecting an apostate, or one who has been cut off from the Church, and who wishes to come in again, the law of our Church expressly says that such shall repent, and be baptized, and be admitted as at the first. (TPJS, 21)[12]

♦♦♦

The Messiah's kingdom on earth is of that kind of government, that there has always been numerous apostates, for the reason that it admits of no sins unrepented of without excluding the individual from its fellowship. (TPJS, 66)[21]

♦♦♦

Apostates after turning from the faith of Christ, unless they have speedily repented, have sooner or later fallen into the snares of the wicked one, and have been left destitute of the Spirit of God, to manifest their wickedness in the eyes of multitudes. (TPJS, 67)[21]

✦✦✦

From apostates the faithful have received the severest persecutions. (TPJS, 67)[21]

✦✦✦

Judas was rebuked and immediately betrayed his Lord into the hands of His enemies, because Satan entered into him. There is a superior intelligence bestowed upon such as obey the Gospel with full purpose of heart, which, if sinned against, the apostate is left naked and destitute of the Spirit of God, and he is, in truth, nigh unto cursing, and his end is to be burned. When once that light which was in them is taken from them, they become as much darkened as they were previously enlightened, and then, no marvel, if all their power should be enlisted against the truth, and they, like Judas, seek the destruction of those who were their greatest benefactors. (TPJS, 67)[21]

✦✦✦

What must a man do to commit the unpardonable sin? He must receive the Holy Ghost, have the heavens opened unto him, and know God, and then sin against Him. . . . He has got to say that the sun does not shine while he sees it; he has got to deny Jesus Christ when the heavens have been opened unto him, and to deny the Plan of Salvation with his eyes open to the truth of it; and from that time he begins to be an enemy. This is the case with many apostates of the Church of Jesus Christ of Latter-day Saints. (TPJS, 358)[130]

✦✦✦

The character of the old churches have always been slandered by all apostates since the world began. (TPJS, 375)[133]

✦✦✦

I testify again, as the Lord lives, God never will acknowledge any traitors or apostates. (TPJS, 375)[133]

✦✦✦

There should exist the greatest freedom and familiarity among the rulers in Zion. (TPJS, 24)[13]

✦✦✦

The Twelve Apostles . . . are called to the office of the Traveling High Council, who are to preside over the churches of the Saints, among the Gentiles, where there is no presidency established; and they are to travel and preach among the Gentiles, until the Lord shall command them to go to the Jews. They are to hold the keys to this ministry, to unlock the door of the Kingdom of heaven unto all nations, and to preach the Gospel to every creature. This is the power, authority, and virtue of their apostleship. (TPJS, 74)[27]

✦✦✦

The Twelve and the Seventy have particularly to depend upon their ministry for their support, and that of their families; and they have a right by virtue of their offices, to call upon the churches to assist them. (TPJS, 75)[28]

✦✦✦

I am well aware that you [of the Twelve] have to sustain my character against the vile calumnies and reproaches of this ungodly generation, and that you delight in doing so. (TPJS, 89)[33]

✦✦✦

The ordinance of washing of feet [of the twelve] . . . is necessary now, as much it was in the days of the Savior; and we must have a place prepared, that we may attend to this ordinance aside from the world. . . . It was never intended for any but official members. It is calculated to unite our hearts, that we may be one in feeling and sentiment, and that our faith may be strong, so that Satan cannot overthrow us, nor have any power over us here. (TPJS, 90)[33]

✦✦✦

The Twelve are not subject to any other than the First Presidency . . . and where I am not, there is no First Presidency over the Twelve. (TPJS, 106)[37]

• • •

I then called upon the quorums and congregation of Saints to acknowledge the Twelve Apostles, who were present, as Prophets, Seers, Revelators, and special witnesses to all the nations of the earth, holding the keys of the kingdom, to unlock it, or cause it to be done, among them, and uphold them by their prayers, which they assented to by rising. (TPJS, 109)[39]

• • •

The Twelve are at liberty to go wheresoever they will, and if . . . one will say, I wish to go to such a place, let all the rest say amen. (TPJS, 109)[40]

• • •

We [of the Twelve] are called to hold the keys of the mysteries of those things that have been kept hid from the foundation of the world until now. (TPJS, 137)[47]

APPEARANCE

Outward appearance is not always a criterion by which to judge our fellow man. (TPJS, 137)[47]

• • •

What many people call sin is not sin. (TPJS, 193)[64]

• • •

Handsome men are not apt to be wise and strong-minded men; but the strength of a strong-minded man will generally create coarse features, like the rough, strong bough of the oak. You will always discover in the first glance of a man, in the outlines of his features something of his mind. (TPJS, 299)[10]

APPRECIATION

When things that are of the greatest importance are passed over by weak-minded men without even a thought, I want to see truth in all its bearings and hug it to my bosom. (TPJS, 374)[133]

ARGUMENT
(See also CONTENTION)

Avoid contentions and vain disputes with men of corrupt minds, who do not desire to know the truth. (TPJS, 43)[20]

• • •

Sisters of the society, shall there be strife among you? I will not have it. You must repent, and get the love of God. Away with self-righteousness! (TPJS, 241)[79]

• • •

The evil of being puffed up with correct [though useless] knowledge is not so great as the evil of contention. (TPJS, 287)[101]

• • •

If we get puffed up by thinking that we have much knowledge, we are apt to get a contentious spirit, and correct knowledge is necessary to cast out that spirit. (TPJS, 287)[101]

ARROGANCE
(See also PRIDE)

Have not the pride, high-mindedness, and unbelief of the Gentiles, provoked the Holy One of Israel to withdraw His Holy Spirit from them, and send forth His judgments to scourge them for their wickedness? This is certainly the case. (TPJS, 15)[9]

• • •

Man in his own supposed wisdom would not admit the influence of a power superior to his own. (TPJS, 57)[21]

✦✦✦

The lips betray the haughty and overbearing imaginations of the heart; by his words and his deeds let him be judged. (TPJS, 137)[47]

✦✦✦

We ought at all times to be very careful that . . . high-mindedness shall never have place in our hearts; but condescend to men of low estate, and with all long-suffering bear the infirmities of the weak. (TPJS, 141)[47]

✦✦✦

The great designs of God in relation to the salvation of the human family, are very little understood by the professedly wise and intelligent generation in which we live. (TPJS, 217)[74]

✦✦✦

We are full of selfishness; the devil flatters us that we are very righteous, when [in fact] we are feeding on the faults of others. (TPJS, 241)[79]

✦✦✦

If we get puffed up by thinking that we have much knowledge, we are apt to get a contentious spirit, and correct knowledge is necessary to cast out that spirit. (TPJS, 287)[101]

✦✦✦

I hope sober-thinking and sound-reasoning people will sooner listen to the voice of truth, than be led astray by the vain pretensions of the self-wise. (TPJS, 299)[104]

✦✦✦

Paul said, "the world by wisdom know not God," so the world by speculation are destitute of revelation. (TPJS, 300)[104]

✦✦✦

There are a great many wise men and women too in our midst who are too wise to be taught; therefore they must die in their ignorance, and in the resurrection they will find their mistake. Many seal up the door of heaven by saying . . . God may reveal and I will believe. (TPJS, 309)[113]

✦✦✦

The government will not receive any advice or counsel from me; they are self-sufficient. But they must go to hell and work out their own salvation with fear and trembling. (TPJS, 334)[127]

✦✦✦

No man can limit the bounds or the eternal existence of eternal time. Hath he beheld the eternal world, and is he authorized to say that there is only one God? He makes himself a fool if he thinks or says so, and there is an end of his career or progress in knowledge. He cannot obtain all knowledge, for he has sealed up the gate to it. (TPJS, 371)[133]

✦✦✦

If we will but cleanse ourselves and covenant before God, to serve Him, it is our privilege to have an assurance that God will protect us at all times. (TPJS, 9)[3]

✦✦✦

"Be still, and know that I am God; all those who suffer for my name shall reign with me, and he that layeth down his life for my sake shall find it again." (TPJS, 34)[19]

✦✦✦

We . . . have an assurance of a better hope than that of our persecutors. Therefore God hath made broad our shoulders for the burden. We glory in our tribulation, because we know that God is with us, that He is our friend, and that He will save our souls. (TPJS, 123)[46]

✦✦✦

"My son, peace be unto thy soul; thine adversity and thine affliction shall be but a small moment; and then if thou endure it well, God shall exalt thee on high." (TPJS, 134)[47]

•••

Therefore . . . let us cheerfully do all things that lie in our power, and then may we stand still with the utmost assurance, to see the salvation of God, and for His arm to be revealed. (TPJS, 146)[47]

•••

Therefore, hold on thy way, and the Priesthood shall remain with thee, for their [persecution] bounds are set, they cannot pass. Thy days are known, and thy years shall not be numbered less; therefore, fear not what man can do, for God shall be with you forever and ever. (TPJS, 143)[47]

ATONEMENT

Man was not able himself to erect a system, or plan with power sufficient to free him from a destruction which awaited him. [This] is evident from the fact that God . . . prepared a sacrifice in the gift of His own Son who should be sent in due time, to prepare a way, or open a door through which man might enter into the Lord's presence, whence he had been cast out for disobedience. (TPJS, 58)[21]

•••

[In the days of Adam], sacrifice was instituted for a type, by which man was to discern the great Sacrifice which God had prepared; . . . Abel offered an acceptable sacrifice. . . . Certainly, the shedding of the blood of a beast could be beneficial to no man, except it was done in imitation, or as a type, or explanation of what was to be offered through the gift of God Himself . . . for a remission of sins. (TPJS, 58)[21]

•••

The mere shedding of the blood of beasts or offering anything else in sacrifice, could not procure a remission of sins, except it were performed in faith of something to come; if it could, Cain's offering must have been as good as Abel's. And if Abel was taught of the coming of the Son of God, was he not taught also of His ordinances? (TPJS, 59)[21]

•••

Whenever the Lord revealed Himself to men in ancient days, and commanded them to offer sacrifices to Him, . . . it was done that they might look forward in faith to the time of His coming, and rely upon the power of that atonement for a remission of their sins. (TPJS, 60)[21]

AUTHORITY

It is contrary to the economy of God for any member of the Church, or any one, to receive instruction for those in authority, higher than themselves; therefore you will see the impropriety of giving heed to them. (TPJS, 21)[12]

•••

Elijah was the last prophet that held the keys of the Priesthood, and who will, before the last dispensation, restore the authority and deliver the keys of the Priesthood, in order that all the ordinances may be attended to in righteousness. (TPJS, 172)[54]

•••

All the prophets had the Melchizedek Priesthood and were ordained by God himself. (TPJS, 181)[56]

•••

Everything that God gives us is lawful and right; and it is proper that we should enjoy His gifts and blessings whenever and wherever He is disposed to bestow; But if we should seize upon those same blessings and enjoyments without law, without revelation, without commandment, those blessings and enjoyments would prove cursings and vexations in the end, and we should have to lie down in sorrow and wailings of everlasting regret. (TPJS, 256)[83]

♦♦♦

Some say the kingdom of God was not set up on the earth until the day of Pentecost, and that John did not preach baptism of repentance for the remission of sins. But I say, in the name of the Lord, that the kingdom of God was set up on the earth from the days of Adam to the present time, whenever there has been a righteous man on earth unto whom God revealed His word and gave power and authority to administer in His name. And where there is a priest of God—a minister who has power and authority from God to administer in the ordinances of the gospel and officiate in the priesthood of God—there is the kingdom of God. (TPJS, 271)[91]

♦♦♦

Where there is a prophet, priest, or a righteous man unto whom God gives His oracles, there is the kingdom of God; and where the oracles of God are not, there the kingdom of God is not. (TPJS, 272)[91]

♦♦♦

There is a difference between the kingdom of God and the fruits and blessings that flow from the kingdom; because there were more miracles, gifts, visions, healings, tongues, etc., in the days of Jesus Christ and His apostles, and on the day of Pentecost, than under John's administration, it does not prove by any means that John had not the kingdom of God, any more than it would that a woman had not a milkpan because she had not a pan of milk, for while the pan might

be compared to the kingdom, the milk might be compared to the blessings of the kingdom. (TPJS, 273)[91]

♦♦♦

Whenever men can find out the will of God and find an administrator legally authorized from God, there is the kingdom of God. (TPJS, 274)[91]

♦♦♦

All the ordinances, systems and administrations on the earth are of no use to the children of men, unless they are ordained and authorized of God, for nothing will save a man but a legal administrator; for none others will be acknowledged either by God or angels. (TPJS, 274)[91]

♦♦♦

We never can comprehend the things of God and of heaven, but by revelation. We may spiritualize and express opinions to all eternity; but that is no authority. (TPJS, 292)[101]

♦♦♦

There is no salvation between the two lids of the Bible without a legal administrator. Jesus was then the legal administrator, and ordained His Apostles. (TPJS, 319)[117]

♦♦♦

I am going to enquire after God; for I want you all to know him, and to be familiar with him; . . . you will then know that I am his servant; for I speak as one having authority. (TPJS, 345)[130]

♦♦♦

Patriarch John Smith came from Macedonia to jail to see his nephews, Joseph and Hyrum. The road was thronged with mobbers. Three of them snapped their guns at him, and he was threatened by many others who recognized him. The guard at the jail refused him entrance.

Joseph saw him through the prison window, and said to the guard, "Let the old gentleman come in, he is my uncle." The guard replied they did not care who the hell he was uncle to, he should not go in.

Joseph replied, "You will not hinder so old and infirm a man as he is from coming in," and then said, "Come in, uncle," on which after searching him closely the guard let him pass into the jail, where he remained about an hour. (TPJS, 382)[141]

AWARENESS

Our circumstances are calculated to awaken our spirits to a sacred remembrance of everything. (TPJS, 130)[47]

• • •

Every honest man who has visited the city of Nauvoo since it existed, can bear record of better things, and place me in the front ranks of those who are known to do good for the sake of goodness, and show all liars, hypocrites and abominable creatures that, while vice sinks them down to darkness and woe, virtue exalts me and the Saints to light and immortality. (TPJS, 280)[96]

• • •

If men do not comprehend the character of God, they do not comprehend themselves. (TPJS, 343)[130]

BACKSLIDING

If you wish to go where God is, you must be like God, or possess the principles which God possesses; for if we are not drawing towards God in principle, we are going from Him and drawing towards the devil. (TPJS, 216)[73]

• • •

As far as we degenerate from God, we descend to the devil and lose knowledge, and without knowledge we cannot be saved, and while our hearts are filled with evil, and we are studying evil, there is no room in our hearts for good, or studying good. (TPJS, 217)[73]

• • •

There is now a day of salvation to such as repent and reform;—and they who repent not should be cast out from this society;

yet we should woo them to return to God, lest they escape not the damnation of hell! (TPJS, 238)[78]

• • •

I have tried a number of years to get the minds of the Saints prepared to receive the things of God; but we frequently see some of them, after suffering all they have for the work of God, will fly to pieces like glass as soon as anything comes that is contrary to their traditions: they cannot stand the fire at all. How many will be able to abide a celestial law, and go through and receive their exaltation, I am unable to say, as many are called, but few are chosen. (TPJS, 331)[123]

BAPTISM

Baptism is a holy ordinance preparatory to the reception of the Holy Ghost; it is the channel and key by which the Holy Ghost will be administered. (TPJS, 148)[48]

♦♦♦

Baptism is a sign to God, to angels, and to heaven that we do the will of God, and there is no other way beneath the heavens whereby God hath ordained for man to come to Him to be saved, and enter into the Kingdom of God, except faith in Jesus Christ, repentance, and baptism for the remission of sins, and any other course is in vain; then you have the promise of the gift of the Holy Ghost. (TPJS, 198)[68]

♦♦♦

Baptism is a sign ordained of God, for the believer in Christ to take upon himself in order to enter into the Kingdom of God, "for except ye are born of water and of the Spirit ye cannot enter into the Kingdom of God," said the Savior. It is a sign and a commandment which God has set for man to enter into His kingdom. Those who seek to enter in any other way will seek in vain; for God will not receive them . . . for they have not obeyed the ordinances, nor attended to the signs which God ordained for the salvation of man, to prepare him for, and give him a title to, a celestial glory. (TPJS, 198)[68]

♦♦♦

Upon looking over the sacred pages of the Bible, searching into the prophets and sayings of the apostles, we find no subject so nearly connected with salvation, as that of baptism. (TPJS, 262)[85]

♦♦♦

We can treat the subject [of baptism] as . . . inseparably connected with our eternal welfare; and . . . one of the only methods by which we can obtain a remission of sins in this world, and be prepared to enter into the joys of our Lord in the world to come. (TPJS, 262)[85]

♦♦♦

If God is the same yesterday, today, and forever: it is no wonder He is so positive in the great declaration: "he that believes and is baptized shall be saved, and he that believes not shall be damned!" (TPJS, 264)[85]

♦♦♦

If it became John and Jesus Christ, the Savior, to fulfill all righteousness to be baptized . . . so surely, then it will become every other person that seeks the kingdom of heaven to go and do likewise; for he is the door, and if any person climb up any other way, the same is a thief and a robber! (TPJS, 266)[85]

♦♦♦

In the former ages of the world, before the Savior came in the flesh, "the Saints" were baptized in the name of Jesus Christ to come, because there never was any other name whereby men could be saved; and after He came in the flesh and was crucified, then the Saints were baptized in the name of Jesus Christ, crucified, risen from the dead and ascended into heaven, that they might be buried in baptism like him, and be raised in glory like him, that as there was but one Lord, one faith, one baptism, and one God and father of us all, even so there was but one door to the mansions of bliss. Amen. (TPJS, 266)[85]

♦♦♦

All the ordinances, systems and administrations on the earth are of no use to the children of men, unless they are ordained and authorized of God, for nothing will save a man but a legal administrator; for none others will be acknowledged either by God or angels. (TPJS, 274)[91]

♦♦♦

Baptism by water is but half a baptism, and is good for nothing without the other half—that is, the baptism of the Holy Ghost. (TPJS, 314)[114]

•••

The gospel requires baptism by immersion for the remission of sins, which is the meaning of the word in the original language—namely, to bury or immerse. (TPJS, 314)[114]

•••

The baptism of water, without the baptism of fire and the Holy Ghost attending it, is of no use; they are necessarily and inseparably connected. An individual must be born of water and the Spirit in order to get into the kingdom of God. (TPJS, 360)[130]

•••

There is baptism for those to exercise who are alive, and baptism for the dead who die without the knowledge of the Gospel. (TPJS, 366)[132]

BAPTISM FOR THE DEAD

The Saints have the privilege of being baptized for those of their relatives who are dead, whom they believe would have embraced the Gospel, if they had been privileged with hearing it, and who have received the Gospel in the spirit, through the instrumentality of those who have been commissioned to preach to them while in prison. (TPJS, 179)[55]

•••

President Joseph Smith . . . presented baptism for the dead as the only way that men can appear as saviors on Mount Zion. (TPJS, 191)[63]

•••

The proclamation of the first principles of the Gospel was a means of salvation to men individually; and it was the truth, not men, that saved them; but men, by

actively engaging in rites of salvation substitutionally became instrumental in bringing multitudes of their kindred into the kingdom of God. (TPJS, 191)[63]

•••

This glorious truth [of baptism for the dead] is well calculated to enlarge the understanding, and to sustain the soul under troubles, difficulties and distresses. For illustration, suppose . . . [there are] two men, brothers, equally intelligent, learned, virtuous . . . walking in uprightness and in all good conscience, so far as they have been able to discern from the muddy stream of tradition, or from the blotted page of the book of nature.

One dies and is buried, having never heard the Gospel; . . . to the other the message of salvation is sent, he hears and embraces it, and is made the heir of eternal life. Shall the one become the partaker of glory and the other be consigned to hopeless perdition? Is there no chance for his escape? Sectarianism answers "none." Such an idea is worse than atheism. The truth shall break down . . . such bigot[ry]; the sects shall be sifted, the honest in heart brought out, and the priests left in the midst of their corruption. (TPJS, 192)[63]

•••

There is a way to release the spirits of the dead; that is by the power and authority of the Priesthood—by binding and loosing on earth. This doctrine appears glorious, inasmuch as it exhibits the greatness of divine compassion and benevolence in the extent of the plan of human salvation. (TPJS, 192)[63]

•••

If there is one word of the Lord that supports the doctrine of baptism for the dead, it is enough to establish it as a true doctrine. Again; if we can, by the authority of the priesthood of the Son of

God, baptize a man in the name of the Father, of the Son, and of the Holy Ghost, for the remission of sins, it is just as much our privilege to act as an agent, and be baptized for the remission of sins for and in behalf of our dead kindred, who have not heard the Gospel, or the fullness of it. (TPJS, 201)[69]

•••

What has become of our fathers? Will they all be damned for not obeying the Gospel when they never heard it? Certainly not. But they will possess the same privilege that we here enjoy, through the medium of the everlasting Priesthood, which not only administers on earth but also in heaven, and [in] the wise dispensations of the great Jehovah; hence will be visited by the Priesthood, and come out of their prison upon the same principle as those who were disobedient in the days of Noah were visited by our Savior . . . and had the Gospel preached to them by Him in prison; and in order that they might fulfill all the requisitions of God, living friends were baptized for their dead friends, and thus fulfilled the requirement of God which says, "Except a man be born of the water and of the Spirit, he cannot enter into the kingdom of God," they were baptized of course, not for themselves, but for their dead.

Paul, in speaking of the doctrine, says, "Else what shall they do which are baptized for the dead if the dead rise not at all? Why are they then baptized for the dead?" (1 Cor. 15:29). (TPJS, 221)[74]

•••

All persons baptized for the dead must have a recorder present, that he may be an eyewitness to record and testify of the truth and validity of his record. Therefore let [these things] be carefully attended to from this time forth. (TPJS, 260)[84]

•••

One of the ordinances of the house of the Lord is baptism for the dead. God decreed before the foundation of the world that that ordinance should be administered in a font prepared for that purpose in the house of the Lord. (TPJS, 308)[113]

•••

The doctrine of baptism for the dead is clearly shown in the New Testament; . . . it was the reason why Jesus said unto the Jews, "How oft would I have gathered thy children together, even as a hen gathereth her chickens under her wings, and ye would not!"—that they might attend to the ordinances of baptism for the dead as well as other ordinances of the priesthood, and receive revelations from heaven, and be perfected in the things of the kingdom of God—but they would not. (TPJS, 310)[113]

•••

Every man that has been baptized and belongs to the kingdom has a right to be baptized for those who have gone before; and as soon as the law of the Gospel is obeyed here by their friends who act as proxy for them, the Lord has administrators there to set them free. (TPJS, 367)[132]

BELIEF

Christ said to His disciples, that these signs should follow them that believe:—"In my name shall they cast out devils; they shall speak with new tongues; they shall take up serpents; and if they drink any deadly thing, it shall not hurt them; they shall lay hands on the sick, and they shall recover"; . . . By the foregoing testimonies we may look at the Christian world and see the apostasy there has been from the apostolic platform; and who can look at this and not exclaim, in the language of Isaiah, "The earth also is defiled under the inhabitants thereof; because they have transgressed the laws, changed the ordinances, and broken the everlasting covenant"? (TPJS, 15)[10]

• • •

In order to be benefited by the doctrine of repentance, we must believe in obtaining a remission of sins. And in order to obtain the remission of sins, we must believe in the doctrine of baptism in the name of the Lord Jesus Christ. (TPJS, 82)[30]

• • •

The very principle upon which the disciples were accounted blessed, was because [in their willingness,] they were permitted to see [the Lord] with their eyes and hear with their ears . . . [in contrast to] the multitude that received not His saying. (TPJS, 95)[34]

• • •

Why will not man learn wisdom by precept at this late age of the world, when we have such a cloud of witnesses and examples before us, and not be obliged to learn by sad experience everything we know. (TPJS, 155)[49]

Any man may believe that Jesus Christ is the Son of God, and be happy in that belief, and yet not obey his commandments, and at last be cut down for disobedience to the Lord's righteous requirements. (TPJS, 311)[113]

• • •

I believe all that God ever revealed, and I never hear of a man being damned for believing too much; but they are damned for unbelief. (TPJS, 374)[133]

BIBLE

From sundry revelations which had been received, it was apparent that many important points touching the salvation of men, had been taken from the Bible, or lost before it was compiled. (TPJS, 9)[5]

• • •

Nothing could be more pleasing to the Saints upon the order of the Kingdom of the Lord, than the light which burst upon the world through the foregoing vision. Every law, every commandment, every promise, every truth, and every point touching on the destiny of man, from Genesis to Revelation, where the purity of the Scriptures remain unsullied by the folly of men, go to show the perfection of the theory [of different degrees of glory in the future life] and witness the fact that the . . . [Bible] is a transcript from the records of the eternal world. The sublimity of the ideas; the purity of the language; the scope for action; the continued duration for completion, in order that the heirs of salvation may confess the Lord and bow the knee, are so much beyond the narrow-mindedness of men, that every man is constrained to exclaim: "It came from God." (TPJS, 11)[6]

• • •

Much instruction has been given to man since the beginning which we do not possess now. . . . Some . . . are bold to say that we have everything written in the Bible which God ever spoke to man since the world began, and that if He had ever said anything more we should certainly have received it. But we ask, does it remain for a people . . . [to be] indebted to the faith [solely] of another people who lived hundreds and thousands of years before them, does it remain for them to say how much God has spoken and how much He has not spoken? . . . To say that God never said anything more to man than is recorded, would be saying . . . that He would not . . . speak again. (TPJS, 61)[21]

• • •

I am now going to take exceptions to the present translation of the Bible in relation to [certain] matters. Our latitude and longitude can be determined in the original Hebrew with far greater accuracy than in the English version. (TPJS, 290)[101]

◆◆◆

There is no salvation between the two lids of the Bible without a legal administrator. Jesus was then the legal administrator, and ordained His Apostles. (TPJS, 319)[117]

◆◆◆

I believe the Bible as it read when it came from the pen of the original writers. Ignorant translators, careless transcribers, or designing and corrupt priests have committed many errors. (TPJS, 327)[122]

BLAMING

What many people call sin is not sin. . . . If you do not accuse each other, God will not accuse you. . . . If you will not accuse me, I will not accuse you. If you will throw a cloak of charity over my sins, I will over yours—for charity covereth a multitude of sins. . . . and if you will follow the revelations and instructions which God gives you through me, I will take you into heaven as my back load. (TPJS, 193][64]

BLESSEDNESS

The very principle upon which the disciples were accounted blessed, was because [in their willingness,] they were permitted to see [the Lord] with their eyes and hear with their ears . . . [in contrast to] the multitude that received not His saying. (TPJS, 95)[34]

BLESSINGS

Brother Joseph Smith, Jr. said . . . that the promise of God was that the greatest blessings which God had to bestow should be given to those who contributed to the support of his family while he was translating the fullness of the Scriptures. (TPJS, 9)[21]

◆◆◆

The law of heaven is presented to man, and as such guarantees to all who obey it a reward far beyond any earthly consideration; though it does not . . . exempt [one] from the afflictions and troubles arising from different sources in consequence of acts of wicked men on earth. Still in the midst of all this there is a promise predicated upon the fact that it is a law of heaven, which transcends the law of man, as far as eternal life [transcends] the temporal. (TPJS, 50)[21]

◆◆◆

The blessings which God is able to give, are greater than those which can be given by man. (TPJS, 50)[21]

◆◆◆

God ere long, will call all his servants before Him, and there from His own hand they will receive a just recompense and a righteous reward for all their labors. (TPJS, 57)[21]

◆◆◆

Live worthy of the blessings that shall follow, after much tribulation, to satiate the souls of them that hold out faithful to the end. (TPJS, 78)[29]

◆◆◆

Great blessings await us at this time, and will be soon poured out upon us, if we are faithful in all things, for we are even entitled to greater spiritual blessings than . . . [those during Christ's mortal ministry] because they had Christ in person with them. His personal presence we have not, therefore we have need of greater faith, on account of our peculiar circumstances. (TPJS, 90)[33]

◆ ◆ ◆

Let us realize that we are not to live to ourselves, but to God; by so doing the greatest blessings will rest upon us both in time and in eternity. (TPJS, 179)[55]

◆ ◆ ◆

The greatest temporal and spiritual blessings, which always come from faithfulness and concerted effort, never attended individual exertion or enterprise. (TPJS, 183)[58]

◆ ◆ ◆

They that turn many to righteousness shall shine as the stars for ever and ever. (TPJS, 253)[81]

◆ ◆ ◆

We are trying here to gird up our loins, and purge from our midst the workers of iniquity; . . . that as God's people, under His direction, and obedient to His law, we may grow up in righteousness and truth; and when His purposes shall be accomplished, we may receive an inheritance among those that are sanctified. (TPJS, 254)[81]

◆ ◆ ◆

In obedience there is joy and peace unspotted, unalloyed; and as God has designed our happiness—and the happiness of all His creatures, He never has—He never will institute an ordinance or give a commandment to His people that is not calculated in its nature to promote that happiness which He has designed, and which will not end in the greatest amount of good and glory to those who become the recipients of His law and ordinances. (TPJS, 256)[83]

◆ ◆ ◆

Everything that God gives us is lawful and right; and it is proper that we should enjoy His gifts and blessings whenever and wherever He is disposed to bestow; But if we should seize upon those same blessings and enjoyments without law, without revelation, without commandment, those blessings and enjoyments would prove cursings and vexations in the end, and we should have to lie down in sorrow and wailings of everlasting regret. (TPJS, 256)[83]

◆ ◆ ◆

Whatever God requires is right, no matter what it is, although we may not see the reason thereof till long after the events transpire. So with Solomon: first he asked wisdom, and God gave it him, and with it every desire of his heart, even things which might be considered abominable to all who understand the order of heaven only in part, but which in reality were right because God gave and sanctioned by special revelation. (TPJS, 256)[83]

◆ ◆ ◆

If we seek first the kingdom of God, all good things will be added. (TPJS, 256)[83]

◆ ◆ ◆

Our heavenly Father is more liberal in His views, and boundless in His mercies and blessings, than we are ready to believe or receive; and, at the same time, is more terrible to the workers of iniquity, more awful in the executions of His punishments, and more ready to detect every false way, than we are apt to suppose Him to be. (TPJS, 257)[83]

◆ ◆ ◆

"No good thing will I withhold from them who walk uprightly before me, and do my will in all things—who will listen to my voice and to the voice of my servant, whom I have sent; for I delight in those who seek diligently to know my precepts, and abide by the law of my kingdom; for all things shall be made known unto them in mine own due time, and in the end they shall have joy." (TPJS, 257)[83]

•••

Blessings offered, but rejected, are no longer blessings, but become like the talent hid in the earth by the wicked and slothful servant; the proffered good returns to the giver; the blessing is bestowed on those who will receive and occupy; for unto him that hath shall be given, and he shall have abundantly, but unto him that hath not, or will not receive, shall be taken away that which he hath, or might have had. (TPJS, 257)[83]

•••

It is a time-honored adage that love begets love. Let us pour forth love—show forth our kindness unto all mankind, and the Lord will reward us with everlasting increase; cast our bread upon the waters and we shall receive it after many days, increased to an hundredfold. (TPJS, 316)[115]

BOOK OF MORMON

I wish to mention here, that the title page of the Book of Mormon is a literal translation, taken from the very last leaf, on the left hand side of the collection or book of plates, which contained the record which has been translated, the language of the whole running the same as all Hebrew writing in general; and that said title page is not by any means a modern composition, either of mine or of any other man who has lived or does live in this generation. (TPJS, 7)[1]

•••

Brother Joseph Smith, Jr. said . . . that the promise of God was that the greatest blessings which God had to bestow should be given to those who contributed to the support of his family while he was translating the fullness of the Scriptures. (TPJS, 9)[4]

•••

The Book of Mormon is a record of the forefathers of our western tribes of Indians; having been found through the ministration of an holy angel, and translated into . . . [the English] language by the gift and power of God, after having been hid up in the earth for the last fourteen hundred years, containing the word of God which was delivered unto them. (TPJS, 17)[9]

•••

Take away the Book of Mormon and the revelations, and where is our religion? We have none; for without Zion, and a place of deliverance, we must fall. (TPJS, 71)[23]

•••

I told the brethren that the Book of Mormon was the most correct of any book on earth, and the keystone of our religion, and a man would get nearer to God by abiding by its precepts, than by any other book. (TPJS, 194)[65]

•••

[Moroni writes in the Book of Mormon:] "The Lord knoweth the things which we have written, and also, that none other people knoweth our [Reformed Egyptian] language, therefore he hath prepared means for the interpretation thereof." Therefore the Lord, and not man, had to interpret, after the people were all dead. And as Paul said, "the world by wisdom know not God," so the world by speculation are destitute of revelation; . . . [But] God in His superior wisdom, has always given his Saints . . . the same spirit, and that spirit, as John says, is the true spirit of prophecy, which is the testimony of Jesus. (TPJS, 300)[104]

BORN AGAIN

Every man lives for himself. . . . But except a man be born again, he cannot see the kingdom of God. . . . He may receive a glory like unto the moon, [i.e. of which the light of the moon is typical]. Or a star, [i.e. of which the light of the stars is typical] but he can never come unto Mount Zion, and unto the city of the living God . . . unless he becomes as a little child, and is taught by the Spirit of God. (TPJS, 12)[8]

♦♦♦

Any man may believe that Jesus Christ is the Son of God, and be happy in that belief, and yet not obey his commandments, and at last be cut down for disobedience to the Lord's righteous requirements. (TPJS, 311)[113]

♦♦♦

It is one thing to see the kingdom of God, and another thing to enter into it. We must have a change of heart to see the kingdom of God, and subscribe the articles of adoption to enter therein. (TPJS, 328)[122]

BROTHERHOOD

(See also UNITY)

Brother Joseph Smith, Jr. said . . . that the promise of God was that the greatest blessings which God had to bestow should be given to those who contributed to the support of his family while he was translating the fullness of the Scriptures. (TPJS, 9)[21]

♦♦♦

We remember your losses and sorrows [Bro. Peck]; our first ties are not broken; we participate with you in the evil as well as the good, in the sorrows as well as the joys; our union, we trust, is stronger than death, and shall never be severed. (TPJS, 79)[29]

♦♦♦

[Joseph said to the Twelve,] . . . I am determined that neither heights nor depths, principalities nor powers, things present or things to come, or any other creature, shall separate me from you. And I will now covenant with you before God, that I will not listen to or credit any derogatory report against any of you, nor condemn you upon any testimony beneath the heavens . . . until I can see you face to face and know of a surety; and I will place unremitted confidence in your word, for I believe you to be men of truth. And I ask the same of you, when I tell you anything, that you place equal confidence in my word, for I will not tell you I know anything that I do not know. (TPJS, 106)[37]

♦♦♦

[The] Priesthood . . . may be illustrated by the figure of the human body, which has different members, which have different offices to perform; all are necessary in their place, and the body is not complete without all the members. (TPJS, 112)[41]

♦♦♦

[Asked if "Joe" Smith professes to be Jesus Christ, Joseph answered:] No, but he professes to be His brother, as all other Saints have done and now do: Matt. 12:49–50, "And He stretched forth His hand toward His disciples and said, Behold my mother and my brethren; for whosoever shall do the will of my Father, which is in heaven, the same is my brother, and sister, and mother." (TPJS, 121)[45]

♦♦♦

We think . . . that every species of wickedness and cruelty practiced upon us will only tend to bind our hearts together and seal them together in love. . . . We are driven from our homes and smitten without cause. . . . We are compelled to hear nothing but blasphemous oaths, and witness a scene of blasphemy, and drunkenness and hypocrisy, and debaucheries of every description. (TPJS, 130)[47]

◆◆◆

How pleasing it is for the brethren to dwell together in unity! (TPJS, 174)[55]

◆◆◆

The greatest temporal and spiritual blessings which always come from faithfulness and concerted effort, never attended individual exertion or enterprise. (TPJS, 183)[58]

◆◆◆

The cause of God is one common cause, in which the Saints are alike all interested; we are all members of the one common body, and all partake of the same spirit, and are baptized into one baptism and possess alike the same glorious hope. (TPJS, 231)[76]

◆◆◆

The advancement of the cause of God and the building up of Zion is as much one man's business as another's. The only difference is, that one is called to fulfill one duty, and another another duty; "but if one member suffers, all the members suffer with it, and if one member is honored, all the rest rejoice with it, and the eye cannot say to the ear, I have no need of thee, nor the head to the foot, I have no need of thee"; party feelings, separate interests, exclusive designs should be lost sight of in the one common cause, in the interest of the whole. (TPJS, 231)[76]

◆◆◆

When our brethren . . . show a unity of purpose and design, and all put their shoulder to the wheel, our care, toil, labor and anxiety is materially diminished, our yoke is made easy and our burden is light. (TPJS, 231)[76]

◆◆◆

The Church is a compact body composed of different members, and [as] Paul . . . says, "now ye are the body of Christ and members in particular; and God hath set some in the Church, first Apostles, secondarily Prophets, thirdly Teachers, after miracles, then gifts of healing, helps, governments, diversities of tongues. Are all Teachers? Are all workers of miracles? Do all speak with tongues? Do all interpret? It is evident that they do not; yet they are all members of one body. All members of the natural [human] body are not the eye, the ear, the head or the hand— yet the eye cannot say to the ear, I have no need of thee, nor the head to the foot, I have no need of thee; they are all so many component parts in the perfect machine— the one body; and if one member suffer, the whole of the members suffer with it; and if one member rejoice, all the rest are honored with it." (TPJS, 244)[80]

◆◆◆

Many persons think a prophet must be a great deal better than anybody else. Suppose I would condescend—yes, I will call it condescend, to be a great deal better than any of you, I would be raised up to the highest heaven; and who should I have to accompany me? (TPJS, 303)[109]

◆◆◆

If a skillful mechanic . . . succeeds in welding together iron or steel more perfectly than any other mechanic, is he not deserving of praise? And if by the principles of truth I succeed in uniting men of all denominations in the bonds of love, shall I not have attained a good object? (TPJS, 313)[114]

◆◆◆

What would it profit us to come unto the spirits of the just men, but to learn and come up to the standard of their knowledge? (TPJS, 320)[118]

BUILDING THE KINGDOM

In regard to the building up of Zion, it has to be done by the counsel of Jehovah, by the revelations of heaven; and we should feel to say, "If the Lord go not with us, carry us not up hence." (TPJS, 254)[81]

BURIAL PLACE

I would esteem it one of the greatest blessings, if I am to be afflicted in this world, to have my lot cast where I can find brothers and friends all around me . . . to have the privilege of having our dead buried on the land where God has appointed to gather His Saints together, and . . . where they may have the privilege of laying their bodies where the Son of Man will make His appearance, and where they may hear the sound of the trump that shall call them forth to behold Him, that in the morn of the resurrection they may . . . come up out of their graves and strike hands immediately in eternal glory and felicity, rather than be scattered thousands of miles apart. There is something good and sacred to me in this thing. The place where a man is buried is sacred to me. . . . Even to the aborigines of this land, the burying places of their fathers are more sacred than anything else. (TPJS, 294)[102]

◆ ◆ ◆

I have said, Father, I desire to die here among the Saints. But if this is not Thy will, and I go hence and die, wilt Thou find some kind friend to bring my body back, and gather my friends who have fallen in foreign lands, and bring them up hither, that we may all lie together.

I will tell you what I want. If tomorrow I shall be called to lie in yonder tomb, in the morning of the resurrection let me strike hands with my father, and cry, "My father," and he will say, "My son, my son," as soon as the rock rends and before we come out of the graves.

And may we contemplate these things so? Yes, if we learn how to live and how to die. When we lie down we contemplate how we may rise in the morning; and it is pleasing for friends to lie down together, locked in the arms of love, to sleep and wake in each other's embrace and renew their conversation. (TPJS, 295)[102]

◆ ◆ ◆

One of the greatest curses the ancient prophets could put on any man, was that he should go without a burial. (TPJS, 295)[102]

CALLING AND ELECTION MADE SURE

(*See also* MORE SURE WORD OF PROPHECY)

After a person . . . receives the Holy Ghost . . . which is the first Comforter, then let him continue to humble himself before God, hungering and thirsting after righteousness, and living by every word of God, and the Lord will soon say unto him, Son, thou shalt be exalted. When the Lord has thoroughly proved him, and finds that the man is determined to serve Him at all hazards, then the man will find his calling and his election made sure, . . . then it will be his privilege to receive the other Comforter, which the Lord promised the Saints. . . . Now what is this other Comforter? It is no more nor less than the Lord Jesus Christ Himself; . . . when any man obtains this last Comforter, he will have the personage of Jesus Christ to attend him . . . from time to time, and even He will manifest the Father unto him, and they will take up their abode with him, and the Lord will teach him face to face, and he may have a perfect knowledge of the mysteries of the Kingdom of God. (TPJS, 150)[48]

•••

Though they might hear the voice of God and know that Jesus was the Son of God, this would be no evidence that their election and calling was made sure, that they had part with Christ, and were joint heirs with Him. They then would want that more sure word of prophecy, that they were sealed in the heavens and had the promise of eternal life in the kingdom of God. Then having this promise sealed unto them, it was an anchor to the soul, sure and steadfast. Though the thunders might roll and lightnings flash, and earthquakes bellow, and war gather thick around, yet this hope and knowledge would support the soul in every hour of trial, trouble and tribulation. Then knowledge through our Lord and Savior Jesus Christ is the grand key that unlocks the glories and mysteries of the kingdom of heaven.

Then I would exhort you to go on and continue to call upon God until you make your calling and election sure for yourselves, by obtaining this more sure word of prophecy, and wait patiently for the promise until you obtain it, etc. (TPJS, 298)[103]

•••

[Joseph quoted Peter:] "And add to your faith virtue," knowledge, temperance, patience, godliness, brotherly kindness, charity; "for if these things be in you, and abound, they make you that ye shall neither be barren, nor unfruitful in the knowledge of our Lord Jesus Christ." (TPJS, 305)[109]

•••

The anointing and sealing is to be called, elected and made sure. (TPJS, 323)[119]

•••

While the spirit of Elias is a forerunner, the power of Elijah is sufficient to make our calling and election made sure; and the same doctrine, where we are exhorted to go on to perfection. (TPJS, 338)[128]

CALLINGS

Some have been ordained in the ministry, and have never acted in that capacity, or magnified their calling at all. Such may expect to lose their appointment, except they awake and magnify their office. (TPJS, 42)[20]

•••

If . . . there is an importance in this respect [of obeying God's laws] is there not a responsibility of great weight resting upon those who are called to declare these truths to men? (TPJS, 57)[21]

•••

It is . . . the privilege of any officer in this Church to obtain revelations, so far as relates to his particular calling and duty in the Church. (TPJS, 111)[41]

•••

[Joseph said that] it was the folly and nonsense of the human heart for a person to be aspiring to other stations than those to which they are appointed of God for them to occupy; that it was better for individuals to magnify their respective calling, and wait patiently till God shall say to them, "come up higher." (TPJS, 223)[75]

•••

Every person should stand, and act in the place appointed. (TPJS, 225)[75]

•••

[To the Relief Society, Joseph] spoke of delivering the keys of the Priesthood to the Church . . . for according to his prayers, God had appointed him elsewhere. (TPJS, 226)[75]

•••

We are all responsible to God for the manner we improve the light and wisdom given by our Lord to enable us to save ourselves. (TPJS, 227)[75]

•••

Everyone should aspire only to magnify his own office and calling. (TPJS, 227)[75]

•••

The advancement of the cause of God and the building up of Zion is as much one man's business as another's. The only difference is, that one is called to fulfill one duty, and another another duty; "but if one member suffers, all the members suffer with it, and if one member is honored, all the rest rejoice with it, and the eye cannot say to the ear, I have no need of thee, nor the head to the foot, I have no need of thee"; party feelings, separate interests, exclusive designs should be lost sight of in the one common cause, in the interest of the whole. (TPJS, 231)[76]

•••

The Church is a compact body composed of different members, and [as] Paul . . . says, "now ye are the body of Christ and members in particular; and God hath set some in the Church, first Apostles, secondarily Prophets, thirdly Teachers, after miracles, then gifts of healing, helps, governments, diversities of tongues. Are all Teachers? Are all workers of miracles? Do all speak with tongues? Do all interpret? It is evident that they do not; yet they are all members of one body. All members of the natural body are not the eye, the ear, the head or the hand—yet the eye cannot say to the ear, I have no need of thee, nor the head to the foot, I have no need of thee; they are all so many component parts in the perfect machine—the one body; and if one member suffer, the whole of the members suffer with it; and if one member rejoice, all the rest are honored with it. (TPJS, 244)[80]

•••

If I had not actually got into this work and been called of God, I would back out. (TPJS, 286)[99]

•••

Every man who has a calling to minister to the inhabitants of the world was ordained to that very purpose in the Grand Council of heaven before this world was. I suppose I was ordained to this very office in that Grand Council. (TPJS, 365)[132]

CALMNESS

[On the way to Carthage, Joseph, Hyrum and others approached a Captain Dunn and about sixty mounted militia, on seeing which Joseph said:] Do not be alarmed, brethren, for they cannot do more to you than the enemies of truth did to the ancient Saints—they can only kill the body. . . . [He further said to the company that was with him] I am going like a lamb to the slaughter, but I am calm as a summer's morning. I have a conscience void of offence toward God and toward all men. (TPJS, 379)[137]

CAPTIVITY

A man is saved no faster than he gets knowledge, for if he does not get knowledge, he will be brought into captivity by some evil power in the other world, as evil spirits will have more knowledge, and consequently more power than many men who are on the earth. Hence it needs revelation to assist us, and give us knowledge of the things of God. (TPJS, 217)[73]

CAUTION

(*See also* PRECAUTION; PRUDENCE)

We must be wise as serpents and harmless as doves. (TPJS, 36)[19]

◆◆◆

I advise all of you to be careful what you do, or you may by-and-by find out that you have been deceived. Stay yourselves; do not give way; don't make any hasty moves, you may be saved. If a spirit of bitterness is in you, don't be in haste. You may say, that the man is a sinner. Well, if he repents, he shall be forgiven. Be cautious; await. (TPJS, 358)[130]

◆◆◆

It is the duty of all men to protect their lives and the lives of the household, whenever necessity requires, and no power has a right to forbid it, should the last extreme arrive, . . . caution is the parent of safety. (TPJS, 391)[144]

CELESTIAL

In order for you to receive your children to yourselves you must have a promise— some ordinance; some blessing, in order to ascend above principalities, or else it may be an angel. They must rise just as they died; we can there hail our lovely infants with the same glory—the same loveliness in the celestial glory, where they all enjoy alike. They differ in stature, in size, the same glorious spirit gives them the likeness of glory in bloom and beauty. The old man with his silvery hairs will glory in bloom and beauty. No man can describe it to you—no man can write it. (TPJS, 368)[132]

CELESTIAL GLORY

God has in reserve a time, or period appointed in His bosom, when He will bring all His subjects, who have obeyed His voice and kept His commandments, into His celestial rest. This rest is of such perfection and glory, that man has need of a preparation before he can, according to the laws of that kingdom, enter it and enjoy its blessings. This being the fact, God has given certain laws to the human family, which, if observed, are sufficient to prepare them to inherit this rest. This, then, we conclude, was the purpose of God in giving His laws to us. (TPJS, 54)[21]

◆◆◆

If . . . the grave has no victory, those who keep the sayings of Jesus and obey His teachings have not only a promise of a resurrection from the dead, but an assurance of being admitted into His glorious kingdom: for He Himself says, "Where I am, there shall also my servants be." (TPJS, 62)[21]

◆◆◆

I know a man that has been caught up to the third heavens and can say, with Paul, that we have seen and heard things that are not lawful to utter. (TPJS, 323)[119]

◆◆◆

Any person who is exalted to the highest mansion has to abide a celestial law, and the whole law too. (TPJS, 331)[123]

♦♦♦

Those who have died in the faith are now in the celestial kingdom of God. And hence is the glory of the sun. . . for at the resurrection . . . [they] will rise in perfect felicity and go to celestial glory, while many must wait myriads of years before they can receive the like blessings; and your expectations and hopes are far above what man can conceive.

Don't mourn, don't weep. I know it by the testimony of the Holy Ghost that is within me; and you may wait for your friends to come forth to meet you in the morn of the celestial world. (TPJS, 359)[130]

♦♦♦

Paul says, "There is one glory of the sun, and another glory of the moon, and another glory of the stars; for one star differeth from another star in glory. So also is the resurrection of the dead." They who obtain a glorious resurrection from the dead, are exalted far above principalities, powers, thrones, dominions and angels, and are expressly declared to be heirs of God and joint heirs with Jesus Christ, all having eternal power. (TPJS, 374)[133]

♦♦♦

Every man who reigns in celestial glory is a God to his dominions. (TPJS, 374)[133]

CELESTIAL HEIRS

God has in reserve a time, or period appointed in His own bosom, when He will bring all His subjects, who have obeyed His voice and kept His commandments, into His celestial rest. (TPJS, 54)[21]

♦♦♦

If . . . the grave has no victory, those who keep the sayings of Jesus and obey His teachings have not only a promise of a resurrection from the dead, but an assurance of being admitted into His glorious kingdom: for He Himself says, "Where I am, there shall also my servants be." (TPJS, 62)[21]

♦♦♦

All who have died without a knowledge of this Gospel, who would have received it if they had been permitted to tarry, shall be heirs of the celestial kingdom of God; also all that shall die henceforth without a knowledge of it, who would have received it with all their hearts, shall be heirs of that kingdom, "For I, the Lord, will judge all men according to their works, according to the desire of their hearts. And I also beheld that all children who die before they arrive at the years of accountability, are saved in the celestial kingdom of heaven. (TPJS, 106)[38]

♦♦♦

All men who become heirs of God and joint heirs of Jesus Christ will have to receive the fullness of the ordinances of his kingdom; and those who will not receive all the ordinances will come short of the fullness of that glory, if they do not lose the whole. (TPJS, 309)[113]

♦♦♦

To become a joint heir of the heirship of the Son, one must put away all his false traditions. (TPJS, 321)[119]

♦♦♦

Any person who is exalted to the highest mansion has to abide a celestial law, and the whole law too. (TPJS, 331)[123]

♦♦♦

Those who have died in the faith are now in the celestial kingdom of God. And hence is the glory of the sun. . . . For at the resurrection . . . [they] will rise in perfect felicity and go to celestial glory, while many must wait myriads of years before they can receive the like blessings; and your expectations and hopes are far above what man can conceive.

Don't mourn, don't weep. I know it by the testimony of the Holy Ghost that is within me; and you may wait for your friends to come forth to meet you in the morn of the celestial world. (TPJS, 359)[130]

•••

There are mansions for those who obey a celestial law, and there are other mansions for those who come short of the law[—]every man in his own order. (TPJS, 366)[131]

•••

Paul says, "There is one glory of the sun, and another glory of the moon, and another glory of the stars; for one star differeth from another star in glory. So also is the resurrection of the dead." They who obtain a glorious resurrection from the dead, are exalted far above principalities, powers, thrones, dominions and angels, and are expressly declared to be heirs of God and joint heirs with Jesus Christ, all having eternal power. (TPJS, 374)[133]

CELESTIAL LIFE

God has in reserve a time, or period appointed in His bosom, when He will bring all his subjects, who have obeyed his voice and kept His commandments, into His celestial rest. This rest is of such perfection and glory, that man has need of a preparation before he can, according to the laws of that kingdom, enter it and enjoy its blessings. This being the fact, God has given certain laws to the human family, which, if observed, are sufficient to prepare them to inherit this rest. This, then, we conclude, was the purpose of God in giving His laws to us. (TPJS, 54)[21]

CELESTIAL MARRIAGE

(*See also* ETERNAL INCREASE)

Except a man and his wife enter into an everlasting covenant and be married for eternity, while in this probation, by the power and authority of the Holy Priesthood, they will cease to increase when they die; that is, they will not have any children after the resurrection. But those who are married by the power and authority of the priesthood in this life, and continue without committing the sin against the Holy Ghost, will continue to increase and have children in the celestial glory. (TPJS, 300)[105]

CHALLENGE

The burdens which roll upon me are very great. . . . and I find that in the midst of business and care the spirit is willing, but the flesh is weak. (TPJS, 315)[115]

CHANCE

Time and chance happen to all men. (TPJS, 148)[47]

•••

"The firmament showeth His handiwork"; and a moment's reflection is sufficient to teach every man of common intelligence, that all these are not the mere productions of *chance,* nor could they be supported by any power less than an Almighty hand. (TPJS, 56)[21]

CHANGE

If we are not drawing towards God in principle, we are going from Him and drawing towards the devil. (TPJS, 216)[73]

CHARITY

Brother Joseph Smith, Jr. said . . . that the promise of God was that the greatest blessings which God had to bestow should be given to those who contributed to the support of his family while he was translating the fullness of the Scriptures. (TPJS, 9)[4]

•••

Now for a man to consecrate his property, wife and children, to the Lord, is nothing more nor less than to feed the hungry, clothe the naked, visit the widow and fatherless, the sick and afflicted, and do all he can to administer to their relief in their afflictions, and for him and his house to serve the Lord. In order to do this, he and all his house must be virtuous, and must shun the very appearance of evil. (TPJS, 127)[4]

•••

We ought at all times to be very careful that . . . high-mindedness shall never have place in our hearts; but condescend to men of low estate, and with all long-suffering bear the infirmities of the weak. (TPJS, 141)[47]

•••

A man filled with the love of God, is not content with blessing his family alone, but ranges through the whole world, anxious to bless the whole human race. (TPJS, 174)[54]

•••

If you will throw a cloak of charity over my sins, I will over yours—for charity covereth a multitude of sins . . . [then] if you will follow the revelations and instructions which God gives you through me, I will take you into heaven as my back load. (TPJS, 193)[64]

•••

This is a charitable [Relief] Society, and according to your natures; it is natural for females to have feelings of charity and benevolence. You are now placed in a situation in which you can act according to those sympathies which God has planted in your bosoms. (TPJS, 226)[75]

•••

Don't be limited in your views with regard to your neighbor's virtue, but beware of self-righteousness, and be limited in the estimate of your own virtues, and not think yourself more righteous than others. (TPJS, 228)[75]

•••

You [sisters of the Relief Society] will receive instructions through the order of the Priesthood which God had established, through the medium of those appointed to lead, guide and direct the affairs of the Church in this last dispensation; and I now turn the key in your behalf in the name of the Lord, and this Society shall rejoice, and knowledge and intelligence shall flow down from this time henceforth; this is the beginning of better days to the poor and needy, who shall be made to rejoice and pour forth blessings on your heads. (TPJS, 228)[75]

•••

I love that man better who swears a stream as long as my arm, yet deals justice to his neighbors and mercifully deals his substance to the poor, than the long, smooth-faced hypocrite. (TPJS, 303)[109]

•••

Charity, which is love, covereth a multitude of sins, and I have often covered up all the faults among you; but the prettiest thing is to have no faults at all. We should cultivate a meek, quiet and peaceable spirit. (TPJS, 316)[115]

•••

I never stole the value of a pin's head, or a picayune in my life; and when you are hungry don't steal. Come to me and I will feed you. (TPJS, 329)[122]

◆◆◆

Woe to ye rich men, who refuse to give to the poor, and then come and ask me for bread. Away with all your meanness, and be liberal. We need purging, purifying and cleansing. (TPJS, 329)[122]

CHASTISEMENT

(*See also* DISCIPLINE; PUNISHMENT)

I frequently rebuke and admonish my brethren, and that because I love them, not because I wish to incur their displeasure, or mar their happiness. Such a course of conduct is not calculated to gain the good will of all, but rather the ill will of many; . . . but these rebukes and admonitions become necessary, from the perverseness of the brethren, for their temporal as well as spiritual welfare. (TPJS, 112)[41]

◆◆◆

We have reproved in the gate, and men have laid snares for us. We have spoken words, and men have made us offenders. And notwithstanding all this, our minds are not yet darkened, but feel strong in the Lord. (TPJS, 124)[46]

◆◆◆

A frank and open rebuke provoketh a good man to emulation; and in the hour of trouble he will be your best friend. But on the other hand, it will draw out all the corruptions of corrupt hearts; and lying and the poison of asps is under their tongues; and they do cause the pure in heart to be cast into prison, because they want them out of their way. (TPJS, 137)[47]

◆◆◆

[God] passes over no man's sins, but visits them with correction, and if His children will not repent of their sins He will discard them. (TPJS, 189)[60]

◆◆◆

Some people say I am a fallen Prophet, because I do not bring forth more of the word of the Lord. Why do I not do it? Are we able to receive it? No! Not one in this room. [Joseph] then chastened the congregation for their wickedness and unbelief, "for whom the Lord loveth he chasteneth, and scourgeth every son and daughter whom he receiveth," and if we do not receive chastisements then we are bastards and not sons. (TPJS, 194)[66]

◆◆◆

When a corrupt man is chastened he gets angry and will not endure it. (TPJS, 195)[66]

◆◆◆

The object is to make those not so good reform and return to the path of virtue . . . [we] should chasten and reprove, and keep it all in silence, not even mention them again; then you will be established in power, virtue, and holiness, and the wrath of God will be turned away. (TPJS, 238)[78]

◆◆◆

We must use precaution in bringing sinners to justice, lest . . . we draw the indignation of a Gentile world upon us. . . . To the iniquitous show yourselves merciful. (TPJS, 239)[78]

◆◆◆

There should be no license for sin, but mercy should go hand in hand with reproof. (TPJS, 241)[79]

◆◆◆

I love you all; but I hate some of your deeds. I am your best friend, and if persons miss their mark it is their own fault. If I reprove a man, and he hates me, he is a fool; for I love all men, especially these my brethren and sisters. (TPJS, 361)[130]

CHEERFULNESS

Therefore . . . let us cheerfully do all things that lie in our power, and then may we stand still with the utmost assurance, to see the salvation of God, and for His arm to be revealed. (TPJS, 146)[47]

CHILDREN

"Children, obey your parents in all things, for this is well pleasing unto the Lord" (Colossians 3:20). (TPJS, 88–89)[31]

♦♦♦

Let honesty, and sobriety, and candor, and solemnity, and virtue, and pureness, and meekness, and simplicity crown our heads in every place; and in fine, become as little children, without malice, guile or hypocrisy. (TPJS, 137)[47]

♦♦♦

[If Jesus] comes to a little child, He will adapt himself to the language and capacity of a little child. (TPJS, 162)[49]

♦♦♦

All children are redeemed by the blood of Jesus Christ, and the moment that children leave this world, they are taken to the bosom of Abraham. The only difference between the old and young dying is, one lives longer in heaven and eternal light and glory than the other, and is freed a little sooner from this miserable wicked world. Notwithstanding all this glory, we for a moment lose sight of it, and mourn the loss, but we do not mourn as those without hope. (TPJS, 197)[68]

♦♦♦

Baptism is for remission of sins. Children have no sins. (TPJS, 314)[114]

CHRIST-CENTEREDNESS

The Son of Man is nigh, even at your doors. If our souls and our bodies are not looking forth for the coming of the Son of Man; and after we are dead, if we are not looking forth, we shall be among those who are calling for the rocks to fall upon them. (TPJS, 160)[49]

♦♦♦

When we lose a near and dear friend, upon whom we have set our hearts, it should be a caution unto us not to set our affections too firmly upon others, knowing that they may in like manner be taken from us. Our affections should be placed upon God and His work more intensely than upon our fellow beings. (TPJS, 216)[72]

♦♦♦

Jesus designs to save people out of their sins. Said Jesus, "Ye shall do the work, which ye see me do." These are the grand key-words for the society to act upon. (TPJS, 239)[78]

CHURCH GROWTH

(*See also* CHURCH PROGRESS)

The light of the latter-day glory begins to break forth through the dark atmosphere of sectarian wickedness. (TPJS, 16)[9]

♦♦♦

You must be aware in some measure of my feelings, when I contemplate the great work which is now rolling on, and the relation which I sustain to it, while it is extending to distant lands . . . I realize in some measure my responsibility, and the need I have for support from above, that I may be able to teach this people. (TPJS, 178)[55]

♦♦♦

I prophesied that . . . some of you will live to go and assist in making settlements and build cities and see the Saints become a mighty people in the midst of the Rocky Mountains. (TPJS, 255)[82]

◆◆◆

By seeing the blessings of the endowment rolling on, and the kingdom increasing and spreading from sea to sea, we shall rejoice that we were not overcome by these foolish [persecutions]. (TPJS, 259)[84]

◆◆◆

I do not know when I shall have the privilege of speaking in a house large enough to convene the people. I find my lungs are failing with continual preaching in the open air to large assemblies. (TPJS, 303)[109]

◆◆◆

I intend to lay a foundation that will revolutionize the whole world. (TPJS, 366)[132]

CHURCH MEMBERS

The Saints should be a select people, separate from all the evils of the world—choice, virtuous, and holy. (TPJS, 202)[70]

CHURCH OF JESUS CHRIST OF LATTER-DAY SAINTS

God has in reserve a time, or period appointed in His bosom, when He will bring all his subjects, who have obeyed his voice and kept His commandments, into His celestial rest. This rest is of such perfection and glory, that man has need of a preparation before he can, according to the laws of that kingdom, enter it and enjoy its blessings. This being the fact, God has given certain laws to the human family, which, if observed, are sufficient to prepare them to inherit this rest. This, then, we conclude, was the purpose of God

in giving His laws to us. (TPJS, 54)[21]

◆◆◆

It is very difficult for us to communicate to the churches all that God has revealed to us, in consequence of tradition; for we are differently situated from any other people that ever existed upon this earth. (TPJS, 70)[23]

◆◆◆

The Kingdom of Heaven is like unto a mustard seed. Behold, then is not this the Kingdom of Heaven that is raising its head in the last days in the majesty of its God, even the Church of the Latter-day Saints, like an impenetrable, immovable rock in the midst of the mighty deep, exposed to the storms and tempests of Satan, but has, thus far, remained steadfast, and is still braving the mountain waves of opposition . . . urged onward with redoubled fury by the enemy of righteousness, with his pitch fork of lies. (TPJS, 98)[34]

◆◆◆

In viewing the Church as a whole, we may strictly denominate it one Priesthood. (TPJS, 112)[41]

◆◆◆

"How long can rolling waters remain impure? What power shall stay the heavens? As well might man stretch forth his puny arm to stop the Missouri River in its decreed course, or to turn it up stream, as to hinder the Almighty from pouring down knowledge from heaven, upon the heads of the Latter-day Saints." (TPJS, 139)[47]

◆◆◆

The truth, like the sturdy oak, has stood unhurt amid the contending elements, which have beat upon it with tremendous force. The floods have rolled, wave after wave, in quick succession, and have not swallowed it up. . . . "The floods have lifted up their voice; but the Lord of Hosts is mightier than the mighty waves of the sea": nor have the flames of persecution, with all the influence of mobs, been able to destroy it; but like Moses' bush, it has stood unconsumed. (TPJS, 184)[59]

♦♦♦

[The Restored Church is] a work that is destined to bring about the destruction of the powers of darkness, the renovation of the earth, the glory of God, and the salvation of the human family. (TPJS, 232)[76]

♦♦♦

The Church is a compact body composed of different members, and [as] Paul . . . says, "now ye are the body of Christ and members in particular; and God hath set some in the Church, first Apostles, secondarily Prophets, thirdly Teachers, after miracles, then gifts of healing, helps, governments, diversities of tongues. Are all Teachers? Are all workers of miracles? Do all speak with tongues? Do all interpret? It is evident that they do not; yet they are all members of one body. All members of the natural body are not the eye, the ear, the head or the hand—yet the eye cannot say to the ear, I have no need of thee, nor the head to the foot, I have no need of thee; they are all so many component parts in the perfect machine—the one body; and if one member suffer, the whole of the members suffer with it; and if one member rejoice, all the rest are honored with it. (TPJS, 244)[80]

♦♦♦

My feelings at the present are that inasmuch as the Lord Almighty has preserved me until today, He will continue to preserve me, by the united faith and prayers of the Saints, until I have fully accomplished my mission in this life, and so firmly established the dispensation of

the fullness of the Priesthood in these last days, that all the powers of earth and hell can never prevail against it. (TPJS, 258)[84]

♦♦♦

Iniquity of any kind cannot be sustained in the Church, and it will not fare well where I am; for I am determined while I do lead the Church, to lead it right. (TPJS, 307)[111]

♦♦♦

One of the grand fundamental principles of "Mormonism" is to receive truth, let it come from whence it may. (TPJS, 313)[114]

♦♦♦

I see no faults in the Church, and therefore let me be resurrected with the Saints, whether I ascend to heaven or descend to hell, or go to any other place. And if we go to hell, we will turn the devils out of doors and make a heaven of it. (TPJS, 316)[115]

♦♦♦

Where this people are, there is good society. What do we care where we are, if the society be good. (TPJS, 316)[115]

♦♦♦

I calculate to be one of the instruments of setting up the kingdom of Daniel by the word of the Lord, and I intend to lay a foundation that will revolutionize the whole world. (TPJS, 366)[132]

♦♦♦

Did I build on any other man's foundation? I have got all the truth which the Christian world possessed, and an independent revelation in the bargain, and God will bear me off triumphant. (TPJS, 376)[133]

♦♦♦

So it is with the Church of Jesus Christ of Latter-day Saints; we have the revelation of Jesus, and the knowledge within us is sufficient to organize a righteous government upon the earth, and to give universal peace to all mankind, if they would receive it, but we lack the physical strength, as did our Savior when a child, to defend our principles, and we have of necessity to be afflicted, persecuted and smitten, and to bear it patiently until Jacob is of age, then he will take care of himself. (TPJS, 392)[145]

CHURCH PROGRESS

(*See also* CHURCH GROWTH)

Ignorance, superstition and bigotry . . . is oftentimes in the way of the prosperity of this Church; like the torrent rain in the mountains, that floods the most pure and crystal stream with mire, and dirt, and filthiness, and obscures everything that was clear before, and all rushes along in one general deluge; but time weathers tide; and notwithstanding we are rolled in the mire of the flood for the time being, the next surge peradventure, as time rolls on, may bring to us the fountain as clear as crystal, and as pure as snow; while the filthiness, flood-wood and rubbish is left and purged out by the way. (TPJS, 138)[47]

◆◆◆

"How long can rolling waters remain impure? What power shall stay the heavens? As well might man stretch forth his puny arm to stop the Missouri River in its decreed course, or to turn it up stream, as to hinder the Almighty from pouring down knowledge from heaven, upon the heads of the Latter-day Saints." (TPJS, 139)[47]

◆◆◆

Prejudice, with its attendant train of evil, is giving way before the force of truth whose benign rays are penetrating the nations afar off. (TPJS, 184)[59]

◆◆◆

I calculate to be one of the instruments of setting up the kingdom of Daniel by the word of the Lord, and I intend to lay a foundation that will revolutionize the whole world. . . . It will not be by sword or gun that this kingdom will roll on: the power of truth is such that all nations will be under the necessity of obeying the Gospel. (TPJS, 366)[132]

CLARITY

(*See also* LANGUAGE; SIMPLICITY; WORDS)

Be honest, open, and frank in all your intercourse with mankind. (TPJS, 156)[49]

◆◆◆

It will be well to study plainness and simplicity in whatever you publish, "for my soul delighteth in plainness." (TPJS, 164)[51]

◆◆◆

The world is full of technicalities and misrepresentation, which I calculate to overthrow, and speak of things as they actually exist. (TPJS, 292)[101]

◆◆◆

I will make every doctrine plain that I present, and it shall stand upon a firm basis, and I am at the defiance of the world, for I will take shelter under the broad cover of the wings of the work in which I am engaged. (TPJS, 339)[128]

◆◆◆

I do not intend to please your ears with superfluity of words or oratory, or with much learning; but I intend to edify you with the simple truths from heaven. (TPJS, 342)[130]

CLEANLINESS

(*See also* PURITY)

Strive to be prepared in your hearts, be faithful in all things. . . . We must be clean every whit. (TPJS, 91)[33]

CO-ETERNAL BEINGS

The mind or the intelligence which man possesses is co-[eternal] with God himself. . . . When I talk to . . . mourners, what have they lost? Their relatives and friends are only separated from their bodies for a short season: their spirits which existed with God have left the tabernacle of clay only for a little moment, as it were; and they now exist in a place where they converse together the same as we do on the earth. (TPJS, 353)[130]

COMFORT

(*See also* CONSOLATION)

"My son, peace be unto thy soul; thine adversity and thine affliction shall be but a small moment; and then if thou endure it well, God shall exalt thee on high." (TPJS, 134)[47]

◆◆◆

There are two Comforters spoken of. One is the Holy Ghost . . . that all Saints receive after faith, repentance, and baptism. This first Comforter or the Holy Ghost has no other effect than pure intelligence. It is more powerful in expanding the mind, enlightening the understanding and storing the intellect with present knowledge. (TPJS, 149)[48]

◆◆◆

The Lord takes many away even in infancy, that they may escape the envy of man, and the sorrows and evils of this present world; they were too pure, too lovely, to live on earth; therefore, if rightly considered, instead of mourning we have reason to rejoice as they are delivered from evil, and we shall soon have them again. (TPJS, 196)[68]

◆◆◆

All children are redeemed by the blood of Jesus Christ, and the moment that children leave this world, they are taken to the bosom of Abraham. The only difference between the old and young dying is, one lives longer in heaven and eternal light and glory than the other, and is freed a little sooner from this miserable wicked world. Notwithstanding all this glory, we for a moment lose sight of it, and mourn the loss, but we do not mourn as those without hope. (TPJS, 197)[68]

◆◆◆

When a man is born down with trouble, when he is perplexed with care and difficulty, if he can meet a smile instead of an argument or a murmur—if he can meet with mildness, it will calm down his soul and soothe his feelings; when the mind is going to despair, it needs a solace of affection and kindness. (TPJS, 228)[75]

◆◆◆

[Joseph said that] it was according to revelation that the sick should be nursed with herbs and mild food, and not by the hand of an enemy. Who are better qualified to administer than our faithful and zealous sisters, whose hearts are full of faith, tenderness, sympathy and compassion. No one. (TPJS, 229)[75]

◆◆◆

I would esteem it one of the greatest blessings, if I am to be afflicted in this world, to have my lot cast where I can find brothers and friends all around me. (TPJS, 294)[102]

♦♦♦

All your losses will be made up to you in the resurrection, provided you continue faithful. By the vision of the Almighty I have seen it. (TPJS, 296)[102]

♦♦♦

God has revealed His Son from the heavens and the doctrine of the resurrection also; and we have a knowledge that those we bury here God will bring up again, clothed upon and quickened by the Spirit of the great God. . . . Let these truths sink down in our hearts, that we may even here begin to enjoy that which shall be in full hereafter. (TPJS, 296)[102]

♦♦♦

How consoling to the mourners when they are called to part with a husband, wife, father, mother, child, or dear relative, to know that, although the earthly tabernacle is laid down and dissolved, they shall rise again to dwell in everlasting burnings in immortal glory, not to sorrow, suffer, or die any more; but they shall be heirs of God and joint heirs with Jesus Christ. (TPJS, 347)[130]

COMMANDMENTS

If the Church knew all the commandments, one-half they would condemn through prejudice and ignorance. (TPJS, 112)[41]

♦♦♦

God…never has—He never will institute an ordinance or give a commandment to His people that is not calculated in its nature to promote that happiness which he has designed, and which will not end in the greatest amount of good and glory to those who become the recipients of His law and ordinances. (TPJS, 256)[83]

♦♦♦

To get salvation we must not only do some things, but everything which God has commanded. (TPJS, 332)[125]

COMMON CAUSE

The advancement of the cause of God and the building up of Zion is as much one man's business as another's. The only difference is, that one is called to fulfill one duty, and another another duty; "but if one member suffers, all the members suffer with it, and if one member is honored, all the rest rejoice with it, and the eye cannot say to the ear, I have no need of thee, nor the head to the foot, I have no need of thee"; party feelings, separate interests, exclusive designs should be lost sight of in the one common cause, in the interest of the whole. (TPJS, 231)[76]

COMMUNICATION

It is very difficult for us to communicate to the churches all that God has revealed to us, in consequence of tradition; for we are differently situated from any other people that ever existed upon this earth. (TPJS, 70)[23]

♦♦♦

Be honest, open, and frank in all your intercourse with mankind. (TPJS, 156)[49]

♦♦♦

It will be well to study plainness and simplicity in whatever you publish, "for my soul delighteth in plainness." (TPJS, 164)[51]

♦♦♦

The Lord deals with this people as a tender parent with a child, communicating light and intelligence and the knowledge of His ways as they can bear it. (TPJS, 305)[109]

♦ ♦ ♦

I will make every doctrine plain that I present, and it shall stand upon a firm basis, and I am at the defiance of the world, for I will take shelter under the broad cover of the wings of the work in which I am engaged. (TPJS, 339)[128]

COMPASSION

(*See also* KINDNESS)

I feel for my fellow men; I do it in the name of the Lord being moved upon by the Holy Spirit. Oh, that I could snatch them from the vortex of misery, into which I behold them plunging themselves, by their sins that I might be enabled by the warning voice, to be an instrument of bringing them to unfeigned repentance, that they might have faith to stand in the evil day! (TPJS, 87)[31]

♦ ♦ ♦

"Oh God! Where art Thou? And where is the pavilion that covereth Thy hiding place? How long shall Thy hand be stayed, and Thine eye, yea Thy pure eye, behold from the eternal heavens, the wrongs of Thy people, and of Thy servants, and Thy ear be penetrated with their cries? Yea, O Lord, how long shall they suffer these wrongs and unlawful oppressions, before Thine heart shall be softened towards them?" (TPJS, 131)[47]

♦ ♦ ♦

"O Lord God Almighty, Maker of Heaven, Earth and Seas, and of all things that in them are, and who controllest and subjectest the devil, and the dark and benighted dominion of Sheol! Stretch forth Thy hand, let Thine eye pierce; let

Thy pavilion be taken up; let Thy hiding place no longer be covered; let Thine ear be inclined; let Thine heart be softened, and Thy bowels moved with compassion towards us; let Thine anger be kindled against our enemies; and in the fury of Thine heart, with Thy sword avenge us of our wrongs; remember Thy suffering Saints, O our God! And Thy servants will rejoice in Thy name forever." (TPJS, 132)[47]

♦ ♦ ♦

We ought at all times to be very careful that . . . high-mindedness shall never have place in our hearts; but condescend to men of low estate, and with all long-suffering bear the infirmities of the weak. (TPJS, 141)[47]

♦ ♦ ♦

A man filled with the love of God, is not content with blessing his family alone, but ranges through the whole world, anxious to bless the whole human race. (TPJS, 174)[55]

♦ ♦ ♦

As you increase in innocence and virtue, as you increase in goodness, let your heart expand, let them be enlarged toward others; be long-suffering, and bear with the faults and errors of mankind. (TPJS, 228)[75]

♦ ♦ ♦

[Joseph said that] it was according to revelation that the sick should be nursed with herbs and mild food, and not by the hand of an enemy. Who are better qualified to administer than our faithful and zealous sisters, whose hearts are full of faith, tenderness, sympathy and compassion. No one. (TPJS, 229)[75]

♦ ♦ ♦

I want the innocent to go free—rather spare ten iniquitous among you, than condemn one innocent one. . . . "Fret not thyself because of evildoers." God will see to it. (TPJS, 239)[78]

♦♦♦

Nothing is so much calculated to lead people to forsake sin as to take them by the hand, and watch over them with tenderness. When persons manifest the least kindness and love to me, O, what power it has over my mind, while the opposite course has a tendency to harrow up all the harsh feelings and depress the human mind. (TPJS, 240)[79]

♦♦♦

God does not look on sin with allowance, but when men have sinned, there must be allowance made for them. (TPJS, 240)[79]

♦♦♦

The nearer we get to our heavenly Father, the more we are disposed to look with compassion on perishing souls; we feel that we want to take them upon our shoulders, and cast their sins behind our backs . . . if you would have God have mercy on you, have mercy on one another. (TPJS, 241)[79]

♦♦♦

The best measure or principle to bring the poor to repentance is to administer to their wants. (TPJS, 241)[79]

♦♦♦

The Ladies' Relief Society is not only to relieve the poor, but to save souls. (TPJS, 242)[79]

♦♦♦

Remember that he that gives a cup of cold water in the name of a disciple to one of the Saints in prison, or secluded from friends by reason of vexatious law suits, intended for persecution, shall in no wise lose his reward. (TPJS, 261)[85]

♦♦♦

We should cultivate sympathy for the afflicted among us. . . . and although a stranger and afflicted when he arrives, he [should find] a brother and a friend ready to administer to his necessities. (TPJS, 294)[102]

♦♦♦

If there is a place on earth where men should cultivate the spirit and pour in the oil and wine in the bosoms of the afflicted, it is in this [funeral service]. (TPJS, 294)[102]

♦♦♦

I would esteem it one of the greatest blessings, if I am to be afflicted in this world, to have my lot cast where I can find brothers and friends all around me. (TPJS, 294)[102]

♦♦♦

I love that man better who swears a stream as long as my arm, yet deals justice to his neighbors and mercifully deals his substance to the poor, than the long, smooth-faced hypocrite. (TPJS, 303)[109]

COMPLACENCE

Men are in the habit, when the truth is exhibited by the servants of God, of saying, All is mystery; they have spoken in parables, and therefore, are not to be understood. It is true they have eyes to see, and see not, but none are so blind as those who will not see. (TPJS, 96)[34]

♦♦♦

Men who have no principle of righteousness in themselves, and whose hearts are full of iniquity, and have no desire for the principles of truth, do not understand the word of truth when they hear it. The devil taketh away the word of truth out of their hearts, because there is no desire of righteousness in them. (TPJS, 96)[34]

COMPLAINING

Remember not to murmur at the dealings of God with his creatures. (TPJS, 31)[18]

COMPULSION

God would not exert any compulsory means, and the devil could not. (TPJS, 187)[60]

•••

Men or women [can] not be compelled into the kingdom of God, but must be dealt with in long-suffering, and at last we shall save them. (TPJS, 241)[78]

•••

Did I ever exercise any compulsion over any man? Did I not give him the liberty of disbelieving any doctrine I have preached, if he saw fit? (TPJS, 341)[129]

•••

In relation to the power over the minds of mankind which I hold, I would say, It is in consequence of the power of truth in the doctrines which I have been an instrument in the hands of God of presenting unto them, and not because of any compulsion on my part. (TPJS, 341)[129]

CONDEMNATION

Herein is the condemnation of the world; that light hath come into the world, and men choose darkness rather than light, because their deeds are evil. (TPJS, 96)[34]

•••

The principle of knowledge is the principle of salvation. . . . Everyone that does not obtain knowledge to be saved will be condemned. The principle of salvation is given us through the knowledge of Jesus Christ. (TPJS, 297)[103]

CONFERENCES

The general affairs of the Church . . . should be transacted by a general conference of the most faithful and the most respectable of the authorities of the Church, and a minute of those transactions may be kept and forwarded from time to time, to your humble servant. (TPJS, 136)[47]

CONFESSION

Let the Twelve and all Saints be willing to confess all their sins and not keep back a part; and let the Twelve be humble and not be exalted, and beware of pride. (TPJS, 155)[49]

•••

Let not any man publish his own righteousness, for others can see that for [themselves]; sooner let him confess his sins, and then he will be forgiven, and he will bring forth more fruit. (TPJS, 194)[66]

•••

If [you] have done anything . . . that [you] are sorry for, or that [you] would not like to meet and answer for at the bar of God . . . let it prove as a warning to all to deal justly before God, and with all mankind, then we shall be clear in the day of judgment. (TPJS, 216)[72]

CONFIDENCE

"Therefore, hold on thy way, and the Priesthood shall remain with thee, for their [persecution] bounds are set, they cannot pass. Thy days are known, and thy years shall not be numbered less; therefore, fear not what man can do, for God shall be with you forever and ever." (TPJS, 143)[47]

•••

As God governed Abraham, Isaac and Jacob as families, and the children of Israel as a nation; so we, as a Church, must be under His guidance if we are prospered, preserved and sustained. Our only confidence can be in God; our only wisdom obtained from Him; and He alone must be our protector and safeguard, spiritually and temporally, or we fall. (TPJS, 253)[81]

♦ ♦ ♦

I know what I say; I understand my mission and business. God Almighty is my shield; and what can man do if God is my friend? I shall not be sacrificed until my time comes; then I shall be offered freely. (TPJS, 274)[91]

♦ ♦ ♦

The way I know in whom to confide—God tells me in whom I may place confidence. (TPJS, 301)[105]

♦ ♦ ♦

I will make every doctrine plain that I present, and it shall stand upon a firm basis, and I am at the defiance of the world, for I will take shelter under the broad cover of the wings of the work in which I am engaged. It matters not to me if all hell boils over; I regard it only as I would the crackling of the thorns under a pot. (TPJS, 339)[128]

CONFIDENTIALITY

Let us be faithful and silent, brethren, and if God gives you a manifestation, keep it to yourselves; be watchful and prayerful, and you shall have a prelude of those joys that God will pour out on that day. (TPJS, 91)[33]

♦ ♦ ♦

The reason we do not have the secrets of the Lord revealed unto us, is because we do not keep them but reveal them; we do not keep our own secrets, but reveal our difficulties to the world, even to our enemies, then how would we keep the secrets of the Lord? I can keep a secret till Doomsday. (TPJS, 195)[66]

♦ ♦ ♦

Put a double watch over the tongue; no organized body can exist without this at all. . . . The object is to make those not so good reform and return to the path of virtue—[you] should chasten and reprove, and keep it all in silence, not even mention them again; then you will be established in power, virtue, and holiness, and the wrath of God will be turned away. (TPJS, 238)[78]

♦ ♦ ♦

Search yourselves—the tongue is an unruly member—hold your tongues about things of no moment—a little tale will set the world on fire. At [certain] time[s] the truth on the guilty should not be told openly. . . . We must use precaution in bringing sinners to justice, lest . . . we draw the indignation of a Gentile world upon us. (TPJS, 239)[78]

♦ ♦ ♦

I could explain a hundred fold more than I ever have of the glories of the kingdoms manifested to me in the vision, were I permitted, and were the people prepared to receive them. (TPJS, 305)[109]

♦ ♦ ♦

I know a man that has been caught up to the third heavens, and can say, with Paul, that we have seen and heard things that are not lawful to utter. (TPJS, 323)[119]

♦ ♦ ♦

I know much that I do not tell. I have had bribes offered me, but I have rejected them. (TPJS, 334)[127]

CONFRONTATION

It is your privilege to use every lawful means in your power to seek redress for your grievances from your enemies, and prosecute them to the extent of the law. (TPJS, 32)[18]

•••

Be not afraid of your adversaries; contend earnestly against mobs, and the unlawful works of dissenters and of darkness. And the very God of peace shall be with you, and make a way for your escape from the adversary of your souls. (TPJS, 129)[46]

•••

Several of the officers of the troops in Carthage, and other gentlemen, curious to see the prophet, visited Joseph in his room. General Smith asked them if there was anything in his appearance that indicated he was the desperate character his enemies represented him to be; and he asked them to give him their honest opinion on the subject. The reply was, "No, Sir. Your appearance would indicate the very contrary, General Smith; but we cannot see what is in your heart, neither can we tell what are your intentions." To which Joseph replied, "Very true, gentlemen, you cannot see what is in my heart, and you are therefore unable to judge me or my intentions; but I can see what is in your hearts, and will tell you what I see. I can see that you thirst for blood, and nothing but my blood will satisfy you. It is not for crime of any description that I and my brethren are thus continually persecuted and harassed by our enemies, but there are other motives, and some of them I have expressed, so far as relates to myself; and inasmuch as you and the people thirst for blood, I prophesy, in the name of the Lord, that you shall witness scenes of blood and sorrow to your entire satisfaction. Your souls shall be perfectly satiated with blood, and many of you who are now present shall have an opportunity to face the cannon's mouth from sources you think not of; and those people that desire this great evil

upon me and my brethren, shall be filled with regret and sorrow because of the scenes of desolation and distress that await them. They shall seek for peace, and shall not be able to find it. Gentlemen, you will find what I have told you to be true. (TPJS, 381)[139]

CONFUSION

The world has always mistook false prophets for true ones, and those that were sent of God, they considered to be false prophets, and hence they killed, stoned, punished and imprisoned the true prophets . . . and though the most honorable men of the earth, they banished them from their society as vagabonds, whilst they cherished, honored and supported knaves, vagabonds, hypocrites, imposters, and the basest of men. (TPJS, 206)[71]

•••

Various and conflicting are the opinions of men concerning the plan of salvation, the requisitions of the Almighty, the necessary preparations for heaven, the state and condition of departed spirits, and the happiness or misery that is consequent upon the practice of righteousness or iniquity according to several notions of virtue and vice. [And one sect tends to condemn the other sect.] (TPJS, 217)[74]

•••

There has been a great difficulty in getting anything into the heads of this generation. . . . Even the Saints are slow to understand. (TPJS, 331)[123]

CONSCIENCE

We have great need to live near to God, and always be in strict obedience to all His commandments, that we may have a conscience void of offense toward God and man. (TPJS, 32)[18]

◆◆◆

If [you] have done anything . . . that [you] are sorry for, or that [you] would not like to meet and answer for at the bar of God . . . let it prove as a warning to all to deal justly before God, and with all mankind, then we shall be clear in the day of judgment. (TPJS, 216)[72]

◆◆◆

It is one of the first principles of my life, and one that I have cultivated from my childhood, having been taught it by my father, to allow everyone the liberty of conscience. (TPJS, 326)[122]

◆◆◆

Never afflict thy soul for what an enemy hath put it out of thy power to do, if thy desires are ever so just. (TPJS, 317)[116]

◆◆◆

[On the way to Carthage, Joseph said to the company that was with him:] I am going like a lamb to the slaughter, but I am calm as a summer's morning. I have a conscience void of offence toward God and toward all men. If they take my life I shall die an innocent man, and my blood shall cry from the ground for vengeance, and it shall be said of me, "He was murdered in cold blood"! (TPJS, 379)[137]

CONSECRATION

The matter of consecration must be done by the mutual consent of both parties; . . . The fact is, there must be a balance or equilibrium of power, between the bishop and the people; and thus harmony and good-will may be preserved among you. (TPJS, 23)[13]

◆◆◆

Now for a man to consecrate his property, wife and children, to the Lord, is nothing more nor less than to feed the hungry, clothe the naked, visit the widow and fatherless, the sick and afflicted, and do all he can to administer to their relief in their afflictions, and for him and his house to serve the Lord. In order to do this, he and all his house must be virtuous, and must shun the very appearance of evil. (TPJS, 127)[46]

CONSEQUENCES

Repent, repent, is the voice of God to Zion; and strange as it may appear, yet it is true, mankind will persist in self-justification until all their iniquity is exposed, and their character past being redeemed, and that which is treasured up in their hearts be exposed to the gaze of mankind. I say to you [and what I say to you I say to all] hear the warning voice of God, lest Zion fall, and the Lord swear in His wrath the inhabitants of Zion shall not enter into His rest. (TPJS, 18)[10]

◆◆◆

God has respect to the feelings of His Saints, and He will not suffer them to be tantalized with impunity. (TPJS, 19)[10]

◆◆◆

The law of heaven is presented to man, and as such guarantees to all who obey it a reward far beyond any earthly consideration; though it does not . . . exempt [one] from the afflictions and troubles arising from different sources in consequence of acts of wicked men on earth. Still in the midst of all this there is a promise predicated upon the fact that it is a law of heaven, which transcends the law of man, as far as eternal life [transcends] the temporal; and as the blessings which God is able to give, are greater than those which can be given by man. (TPJS, 50)[21]

◆◆◆

Our acts are recorded, and at a future day they will be laid before us, and if we should fail to judge right and injure our fellow beings, they may there, perhaps, condemn us. (TPJS, 69)[22]

◆◆◆

I say unto you, that those who have thus vilely treated us . . . shall be hanged upon their own gallows; or, in other words, shall fall into their own gin, and snare, and ditch, and trap, which they have prepared for us, and shall go backwards and stumble and fall, and their name shall be blotted out, and God shall reward them according to all their abominations. (TPJS, 123)[46]

◆◆◆

It must needs be that offences come, but woe unto them by whom they come. (TPJS, 131)[47]

◆◆◆

No murderer hath eternal life. Even David must wait for those times of refreshing, before he can come forth and his sins be blotted out . . . for such . . . cannot be forgiven, until they have paid the last farthing. (TPJS, 188)[60]

◆◆◆

[God] passes over no man's sins, but visits them with correction, and if His children will not repent of their sins He will discard them. (TPJS, 189)[60]

◆◆◆

"Fret not thyself because of evildoers." God will see to it. (TPJS, 239)[78]

◆◆◆

The earth is groaning under corruption, oppression, tyranny and bloodshed; and God is coming out of His hiding place. (TPJS, 253)[81]

◆◆◆

Our heavenly Father is more liberal in His views, and boundless in His mercies and blessings, than we are ready to believe or receive; and, at the same time, is more terrible to the workers of iniquity, more awful in the executions of His punishments, and more ready to detect every false way, than we are apt to suppose Him to be. (TPJS, 257)[83]

◆◆◆

All those that rise up against me will surely feel the weight of their iniquity upon their own heads. (TPJS, 258)[84]

◆◆◆

Remember, brethren, he that offends one of the least of the Saints, would be better off with a millstone tied to his neck and he and the stone plunged into the depth of the sea! (TPJS, 261)[85]

◆◆◆

And, in consequence of rejecting the Gospel of Jesus Christ and the Prophets whom God hath sent, the judgments of God have rested upon people, cities, and nations, in various ages of the world, which was the case with the cities of Sodom and Gomorrah, that were destroyed for rejecting the prophets. (TPJS, 271)[91]

◆◆◆

There is no pain so awful as that of suspense. This is the punishment of the wicked; their doubt, anxiety and suspense cause weeping, wailing and gnashing of teeth. (TPJS, 288)[101]

◆◆◆

The disappointment of hopes and expectations at the resurrection would be indescribably dreadful. (TPJS, 325)[121]

◆◆◆

Beware, O earth, how you fight against the saints of God and shed innocent blood; for in the days of Elijah, his enemies came upon him, and fire was called down from heaven and destroyed them. (TPJS, 340)[128]

◆◆◆

I am the voice of one crying in the wilderness, "Repent ye of your sins and prepare the way for the coming of the Son of Man; for the kingdom of God has come unto you, and henceforth the axe is laid unto the root of the tree; and every tree that bringeth not forth good fruit, God Almighty . . . shall hew it down and cast it into the fire." (TPJS, 341)[129]

◆◆◆

Rejoice, O Israel! Your friends who have been murdered for the truth's sake in the persecutions shall triumph gloriously in the celestial world, while their murderers shall welter for ages in torment, even until they shall have paid the uttermost farthing. (TPJS, 359)[130]

◆◆◆

Those who have done wrong always have that wrong gnawing them. Immortality dwells in everlasting burnings. (TPJS, 367)[132]

◆◆◆

So long as men are under the law of God, they have no fears. . . . When men open their lips against these truths they do not injure me, but injure themselves. (TPJS, 373)[133]

CONSIDERATION
(*See also* THOUGHTFULNESS)

It is an insult to a meeting for persons to leave just before its close. If they must go out, let them go half an hour before. No gentlemen will go out of a meeting just at closing. (TPJS, 287)[100]

◆◆◆

As president of this house, I forbid any man leaving just as we are going to close the meeting. He is no gentleman who will do it. I don't care who does it, even if it were the king of England. I forbid it. (TPJS, 297)[102]

CONSOLATION
(*See also* COMFORT)

All your losses will be made up to you in the resurrection, provided you continue faithful. By the vision of the Almighty I have seen it. (TPJS, 296)[102]

◆◆◆

How consoling to the mourners when they are called to part with a husband, wife, father, mother, child, or dear relative, to know that, although the earthly tabernacle is laid down and dissolved, they shall rise again to dwell in everlasting burnings in immortal glory, not to sorrow, suffer, or die any more; but they shall be heirs of God and joint heirs with Jesus Christ. (TPJS, 347)[130]

◆◆◆

We have reason to have the greatest hope and consolations for our dead of any people on the earth; for we have seen them walk worthily in our midst, and seen them sink asleep in the arms of Jesus. (TPJS, 359)[130]

◆◆◆

Those who have died in the faith are now in the celestial kingdom of God. And hence is the glory of the sun. . . . For at the resurrection . . . [they] will rise in perfect felicity and go to celestial glory, while many must wait myriads of years before they can receive the like blessings; and your expectations and hopes are far above what man can conceive; Don't mourn, don't weep. I know it by the testimony of the Holy Ghost that is within me; and you may wait for your friends to come forth to meet you in the morn of the celestial world. (TPJS, 359)[130]

♦♦♦

When we depart, we shall hail our mothers, fathers, friends, and all whom we love, who have fallen asleep in Jesus. There will be no fear of mobs, persecutions, or malicious lawsuits and arrests; but it will be an eternity of felicity. (TPJS, 360)[130]

CONSTITUTION

The Constitution of the United States is a glorious standard; it is founded in the wisdom of God. It is a heavenly banner; it is to all those who are privileged with the sweets of liberty, like the cooling shades and refreshing waters of a great rock in a thirsty and weary land. It is like a great tree under whose branches men from every climb can be shielded from the burning rays of the sun. (TPJS, 147)[47]

♦♦♦

The Constitution is not a law, but it empowers the people to make laws. For instance, the Constitution governs the land of Iowa, but it is not a law for the people. (TPJS, 278)[95]

♦♦♦

The Constitution is not law to us, but it makes provision for us whereby we can make laws. Where it provides that no one shall be hindered from worshiping God according to his own conscience, is a law. No legislature can enact a law to prohibit it. The Constitution provides to regulate bodies of men and not individuals. (TPJS, 279)[95]

♦♦♦

The different states, and even Congress itself, have passed many laws diametrically contrary to the Constitution of the United States. (TPJS, 279)[95]

♦♦♦

The Constitution acknowledges that the people have all power not reserved to itself. (TPJS, 279)[95]

♦♦♦

It is contrary to [a governor's] oath of office, to send a man to [a state] where he is proscribed in his religious opinions; for he is sworn to support the Constitution of the United States and also to the State, and these constitutions guarantee religious as well as civil liberty to all religious societies whatever. (TPJS, 317)[115]

♦♦♦

I am the greatest advocate of the Constitution of the United States there is on the earth. In my feelings I am always ready to die for the protection of the weak and oppressed in their just rights. The only fault I find with the Constitution is, it is not broad enough to cover the whole ground.

Although it provides that all men shall enjoy religious freedom, yet it does not provide the manner by which that freedom can be preserved, nor for the punishment of government officers who refuse to protect the people in their religious rights, or punish those mobs, states or communities who interfere with the rights of the people on account of their religion. Its sentiments are good, but it provides no means of enforcing them. It has but this one fault. Under its provision, a man or a people who are able to protect themselves can get along well enough; but those who have the misfortune to be weak or unpopular are left to the merciless rage of popular fury. (TPJS, 326)[122]

♦♦♦

The Constitution should contain a provision that every officer of the government who should neglect or refuse to extend the protection guaranteed in the Constitution should be subject to capital punishment; and then the president of the United States would not say, "Your cause is just, but I can do nothing for you." Executive writs could be issued when they ought to be, and not be made instruments of cruelty to oppress the innocent, and persecute men whose religion is unpopular. (TPJS, 327)[122]

◆◆◆

I would not have suffered my name to have been used by my friends on anywise as President of the United States, or candidate for that office, if I and my friends could have had the privilege of enjoying our religious and civil rights as American citizens, even those rights which the Constitution guarantees unto all her citizens alike. But this as a people we have been denied from the beginning. (TPJS, 331)[124]

◆◆◆

If I lose my life in a good cause I am willing to be sacrificed on the altar of virtue, righteousness and truth, in maintaining the laws and Constitution of the United States, if need be, for the general good of man. (TPJS, 332)[124]

CONSULTATION

The way to get along in any important matter is to gather unto yourselves wise men, experienced and aged men, to assist in council in all times of trouble. (TPJS, 299)[103]

CONTENTION

Avoid contentions and vain disputes with men of corrupt minds, who do not desire to know the truth. (TPJS, 43)[20]

◆◆◆

The Elders . . . [are] to go in all meekness, in sobriety, and preach Jesus Christ and Him crucified; not to contend with others

on account of their faith. (TPJS, 109)[40]

◆◆◆

Sisters of the [Relief] Society, shall there be strife among you? I will not have it. You must repent, and get the love of God. Away with self-righteousness! (TPJS, 241)[79]

◆◆◆

The little foxes spoil the vines—little evils do the most injury to the Church. If you have evil feelings, and speak of them to one another, it has a tendency to do mischief. (TPJS, 258)[84]

◆◆◆

The evil of being puffed up with correct [though useless] knowledge is not so great as the evil of contention. (TPJS, 287)[101]

◆◆◆

If we get puffed up by thinking that we have much knowledge, we are apt to get a contentious spirit, and correct knowledge is necessary to cast out that spirit. (TPJS, 287)[101]

◆◆◆

Christians should cease wrangling and contending with each other, and cultivate the principles of union and friendship in their midst . . . before the millennium can be ushered in and Christ takes possession of His kingdom. (TPJS, 314)[114]

CONVICTION

Our light speeches, which may have escaped our lips from time to time . . . have nothing to do with the fixed purposes of our hearts; therefore it sufficeth us to say, that our souls were vexed from day to day. (TPJS, 124)[46]

◆◆◆

As well might we argue that water is not water, because the mountain torrents send down mire and roil the crystal stream, although afterwards render it more pure than before; or that fire is not fire, because it is of a quenchable nature, by pouring on the flood; as to say that our cause is down because renegades, liars, priests, thieves and murderers, who are all alike tenacious of their crafts and creeds, have poured down from their spiritual wickedness in high places, and from their strongholds of the devil, a flood of dirt and mire and filthiness and vomit upon our heads. (TPJS, 139)[47]

COOPERATION

The greatest temporal and spiritual blessings which always come from faithfulness and concerted effort, never attended individual exertion or enterprise. (TPJS, 183)[58]

♦♦♦

From the interest which is generally manifested by the Saints at large, we hope to accomplish much by a combination of effort, and a concentration of action, and erect the Temple and other buildings. (TPJS, 186)[59]

COPING

(*See also* RESILIENCE)

Our light speeches, which may have escaped our lips from time to time . . . have nothing to do with the fixed purposes of our hearts; therefore it sufficeth us to say, that our souls were vexed from day to day. (TPJS, 124)[46]

♦♦♦

Evil spirits will have more knowledge, and consequently more power than many men who are on the earth. Hence it needs revelation to assist us, and give us knowledge of the things of God. (TPJS, 217)[73]

♦♦♦

I am like a huge, rough stone rolling down from a high mountain; and the only polishing I get is when some corner gets rubbed off by coming in contact with something else, striking with accelerating force against religious bigotry, priest-craft, lawyer-craft, doctor-craft, lying editors, suborned judges and jurors, and the authority of perjured executives, backed by mobs, blasphemers, licentious and corrupt men and women—all hell knocking off a corner here and a corner there. Thus I will become a smooth and polished shaft in the quiver of the Almighty, who will give me dominion over all and every one of them, when their refuge of lies shall fail, and their hiding place shall be destroyed, while these smooth-polished stones with which I come in contact become marred. (TPJS, 304)[109]

CORRUPTION

(*See also* WICKEDNESS)

A frank and open rebuke provoketh a good man to emulation; and in the hour of trouble he will be your best friend. But on the other hand, it will draw out all the corruptions of corrupt hearts; and lying and the poison of asps is under their tongues; and they do cause the pure in heart to be cast into prison, because they want them out of their way. (TPJS, 137)[47]

♦♦♦

When a corrupt man is chastened he gets angry and will not endure it. (TPJS, 195)[66]

♦♦♦

The greatest acts of the mighty men have been to depopulate nations and to overthrow kingdoms; and whilst they have exalted themselves and become glorious, it has been at the expense of the lives of the innocent, the blood of the oppressed, the moans of the widow, and the tears of the orphans. (TPJS, 248)[80]

♦♦♦

The earth is groaning under corruption, oppression, tyranny and bloodshed; and God is coming out of His hiding place. (TPJS, 253)[81]

♦♦♦

Everything that God gives us is lawful and right; and it is proper that we should enjoy His gifts and blessings whenever and wherever He is disposed to bestow; but if we should seize upon those same blessings and enjoyments without law, without revelation, without commandment, those blessings and enjoyments would prove cursings and vexations in the end, and we should have to lie down in sorrow and wailings of everlasting regret. (TPJS, 256)[83]

♦♦♦

The world is full of technicalities and misrepresentation, which I calculate to overthrow, and speak of things as they actually exist. (TPJS, 292)[101]

♦♦♦

This generation is as corrupt as the generation of the Jews that crucified Christ; and if He were here today, and should preach the same doctrine He did then, they would put Him to death. (TPJS, 328)[122]

♦♦♦

All ye doctors who are fools, not well read, and do not understand the human constitution, stop your practice. And all ye lawyers who have no business, only as you hatch it up, would to God you would go to work or run away. (TPJS, 329)[122]

COUNCIL IN HEAVEN

At the first organization in heaven we were all present, and saw the Savior chosen and appointed and the Plan of Salvation made, and we sanctioned it. (TPJS, 181)[56]

♦♦♦

In the beginning, the head of the Gods called a council of the Gods; and they came together and concocted a plan to create the world and people it. (TPJS, 349)[130]

COURAGE

I am bold to declare I have taught all the strong doctrines publicly, and always teach stronger doctrines in public than in private. (TPJS, 370)[133]

♦♦♦

[On the way to Carthage, Joseph, Hyrum and others approached a Captain Dunn and about sixty mounted militia, on which seeing Joseph said:] Do not be alarmed, brethren, for they cannot do more to you than the enemies of truth did to the ancient Saints—they can only kill the body. (TPJS, 379)[137]

COURTESY

(*See also* MANNERS)

As president of this house, I forbid any man leaving just as we are going to close the meeting. He is no gentleman who will do it. I don't care who does it, even if it were the king of England. I forbid it. (TPJS, 297)[102]

COVENANTS

It requires two parties to make a covenant, and those two parties must be agreed, or no covenant can be made. (TPJS, 14)[9]

COVETING

(See also ENVY)

God had often sealed up the heavens because of covetousness in the Church. (TPJS, 9)[4]

CREATION

"The firmament showeth His handiwork"; and a moment's reflection is sufficient to teach every man of common intelligence, that all these are not the mere productions of *chance,* nor could they be supported by any power less than an Almighty hand. (TPJS, 56)[21]

◆◆◆

The organization of the spiritual and heavenly worlds, and of spiritual and heavenly beings, was agreeable to the most perfect order and harmony: their limits and bounds were fixed irrevocably, and voluntarily subscribed to in their heavenly estate by themselves, and were by our first parents subscribed to upon the earth. Hence the importance of embracing and subscribing to principles of eternal truth by all men upon the earth that expect eternal life. (TPJS, 325)[121]

◆◆◆

The spirit of man is not a created being; it existed from eternity and will exist to eternity. Anything created cannot be eternal; and earth, water, etc., had their existence in an elementary state, from eternity. . . . The Father called all spirits before Him at the creation of man, and organized them. (TPJS, 158)[49]

◆◆◆

The elements are eternal. That which has a beginning will surely have an end. . . . If the soul of man had a beginning it will surely have an end. . . . The word created should be formed, or organized. . . . "The

first step in salvation of man is the laws of eternal and self-existent principles. Spirits are eternal. At the first organization in heaven we were all present, and saw the Savior chosen and appointed and the plan of salvation made, and we sanctioned it." (TPJS, 181)[56]

◆◆◆

Now, I ask all who hear me, why the learned men who are preaching salvation, say that God created the heavens and the earth out of nothing? The reason is, that they are unlearned in the things of God, and have not the gift of the Holy Ghost; they account it blasphemy in any one to contradict their idea. If you tell them that God made the world out of something, they will call you a fool. But I am learned, and know more than all the world put together. The Holy Ghost does, anyhow, and He is within me, and comprehends more than all the world; and I will associate myself with Him. (TPJS, 350)[130]

◆◆◆

You ask the learned doctors why they say the world was made out of nothing; and they will answer, "Doesn't the Bible say he *created* the world"? And they infer, from the word create, that it must have been made out of nothing. Now, the word create came from the word *baurau* which does not mean to create out of nothing; it means to organize; the same as a man would organize materials and build a ship. Hence, we infer that God had materials to organize the world out of chaos— chaotic matter, which is element, and in which dwells all the glory. Elements had an existence from the time He had. The pure principles of element are principles which can never be destroyed; they may be organized and re-organized, but not destroyed. They had no beginning, and can have no end. (TPJS, 350)[130]

•••

Another subject . . . calculated to exalt man . . . I shall therefore just touch upon . . . is associated with the subject of the resurrection of the dead—namely, the soul—the mind of man—the immortal spirit. Where did it come from? All learned men and doctors of divinity say that God created it in the beginning; But it is not so. . . . Hear it, all ye ends of the world; for God has told me so . . . . I am going to tell of things more noble.

We say that God himself is a self-existent being. Who told you so? It is correct enough; but how did it get into your heads? Who told you that man did not exist in like manner upon the same principles? Man does exist upon the same principles. God made a tabernacle and put a spirit into it, and it became a living soul. . . . It does not say in the Hebrew [Bible] that God created the spirit of man. It says "God made man out of the earth and put into him Adam's spirit, and so became a living body." (TPJS, 352)[130]

•••

God never had the power to create the spirit of man at all. God himself could not create himself.

Intelligence is eternal and exists upon a self-existent principle. It is a spirit from age to age, and there is no creation about it. (TPJS, 354)[130]

CRITICISM

Do not watch for iniquity in each other; if you do you will not get an endowment, for God will not bestow it on such. (TPJS, 91)[33]

•••

Every man, before he makes an objection to any item that is brought before a council for consideration, should be sure that he can throw light upon the subject rather than spread darkness, and that his objection be founded in righteousness. (TPJS, 94)[36]

•••

We are full of selfishness; the devil flatters us that we are very righteous, when [in fact] we are feeding on the faults of others. (TPJS, 241)[79]

•••

Notwithstanding my weaknesses, I am under the necessity of bearing the infirmities of others, who, when they get into difficulty, hang on to me tenaciously to get them out, and wish me to cover their faults. On the other hand, the same characters, when they discover a weakness in Brother Joseph, endeavor to blast his reputation, and publish it to all the world, and thereby aid my enemies in destroying the Saints. (TPJS, 315)[114]

D

DAMNATION

God had decreed that all who will not obey His voice shall not escape the damnation of hell. What is the damnation of hell? To go with that society who have not obeyed His commands. (TPJS, 198)[68]

♦♦♦

I know that all men will be damned if they do not come in the way which He hath opened. (TPJS, 199)[68]

♦♦♦

When God offers a blessing or knowledge to a man, and he refuses to receive it, he will be damned. (TPJS, 322)[119]

♦♦♦

All spirits who have not obeyed the Gospel in the flesh must either obey it in the spirit or be damned. (TPJS, 355)[130]

♦♦♦

Hear it, all ye ends of the earth—all ye priests, all ye sinners, and all men. Repent! Repent! Obey the gospel. Turn to God; for your religion won't save you, and you will be damned. I do not say how long. (TPJS, 361)[130]

♦♦♦

I believe all that God ever revealed, and I never hear of a man being damned for believing too much; but they are damned for unbelief. (TPJS, 374)[133]

DAVID

No murderer hath eternal life. Even David must wait for those times of refreshing, before he can come forth and his sins be blotted out . . . for such . . . cannot be forgiven, until they have paid the last farthing. (TPJS, 188)[60]

♦♦♦

A murderer . . . that sheds innocent blood cannot have forgiveness. David sought repentance at the hand of God carefully with tears, for the murder of Uriah; but he could only get it through hell; he got a promise that his soul should not be left in hell.

Although David was a king, he never did obtain the spirit and power of Elijah and the fullness of the Priesthood; and the priesthood that he received, and the throne and kingdom of David is to be taken from him and given to another by the name of David in the last days, raised up out of his lineage. (TPJS, 339)[128]

DEATH

We believe that due respect ought to be had to the memory of the dead, . . . [as well as] the feelings of both friends and children. (TPJS, 120)[45]

♦♦♦

The Lord takes many away even in infancy, that they may escape the envy of man, and the sorrows and evils of this present world; they were too pure, too lovely, to live on earth; therefore, if rightly considered, instead of mourning we have reason to rejoice as they are delivered from evil, and we shall soon have them again. (TPJS, 196)[68]

♦♦♦

Blessed are the dead who die in the Lord, for they rest from their labors and their works do follow them. (TPJS, 200)[68]

❖❖❖

It will be but a short time before we shall all in like manner be called [to die]. . . . Some have supposed that Brother Joseph could not die; but this is a mistake: it is true there have been times when I have had the promise of my life to accomplish such and such things, but, having now accomplished those things, I have not at present any lease of my life, I am as liable to die as other men. (TPJS, 216)[72]

❖❖❖

If there is a place on earth where men should cultivate the spirit and pour in the oil and wine in the bosoms of the afflicted, it is in this [funeral] place; and this spirit is manifest here; and although a stranger and afflicted when he arrives, he finds a brother and a friend ready to administer to his necessities. (TPJS, 294)[102]

❖❖❖

This [passing of Brother Barnes] has been a warning voice to us all to be sober and diligent and lay aside mirth, vanity and folly, and to be prepared to die tomorrow. (TPJS, 296)[102]

❖❖❖

Salvation is for a man to be saved from all his enemies; for until a man can triumph over death, he is not saved. A knowledge of the priesthood alone will do this. (TPJS, 305)[109]

❖❖❖

[Our departed brother] . . . has gone to a more important work. When men are prepared, they are better off to go hence. (TPJS, 326)[121]

❖❖❖

The spirits of the just are exalted to a greater and more glorious work; hence they are blessed in their departure to the world of spirits. Enveloped in flaming fire,

they are not far from us, and know and understand our thoughts, and emotions, and are often pained therewith. (TPJS, 326)[121]

❖❖❖

When we depart, we shall hail our mothers, fathers, friends, and all whom we love, who have fallen asleep in Jesus. There will be no fear of mobs, persecutions, or malicious lawsuits and arrests; but it will be an eternity of felicity. (TPJS, 360)[130]

❖❖❖

All men are born to die, and all men must rise; all must enter eternity. (TPJS, 367)[132]

DEBT

Let thy hand never fail to hand out that that thou owest while it is yet within thy grasp to do so. (TPJS, 317)[116]

DECEPTION

(*See also* LYING)

I have learned in my travels that man is treacherous and selfish, but few excepted. (TPJS, 30)[17]

❖❖❖

I have been drawn into this course of proceeding by persecution, that is brought upon us from false rumors and misrepresentations concerning my sentiments. (TPJS, 83)[31]

❖❖❖

Those who cry transgression do it because they are the servants of sin and are the children of disobedience themselves; and those who swear falsely against my servants, that they might bring them into bondage and death; wo unto them; because they have offended my little ones;

they shall be severed from the ordinances of mine house. (TPJS, 135)[47]

◆ ◆ ◆

"There are many yet on the earth among all sects, parties, denominations, who are blinded by the subtle craftiness of men, whereby they lie in wait to deceive, and who are only kept from the truth because they know not where to find it." (TPJS, 145)[47]

◆ ◆ ◆

Pure friendship always becomes weakened the very moment you undertake to make it stronger by penal oaths and secrecy. (TPJS, 146)[47]

◆ ◆ ◆

Not every spirit, or vision, or singing, is of God. The devil is an orator; he is powerful; he took our Savior on to a pinnacle of the Temple, and kept Him in the wilderness for forty days. (TPJS, 162)[49]

◆ ◆ ◆

The devil can speak in tongues; the adversary will come with his work; he can tempt all classes; can speak in English or Dutch. (TPJS, 162)[49]

◆ ◆ ◆

If Satan could not speak in tongues, he could not tempt a Dutchman, or any other nation, but the English, for he can tempt the Englishman, for he has tempted me, and I am an Englishman. (TPJS, 195)[67]

◆ ◆ ◆

The world has always mistook false prophets for true ones, and those that were sent of God, they considered to be false prophets, and hence they killed, stoned, punished and imprisoned the true prophets . . . and though the most honorable men of the earth, they banished them from their society as vagabonds, whilst they cherished, honored and supported knaves, vagabonds, hypocrites, imposters, and the basest of men. (TPJS, 206)[71]

◆ ◆ ◆

We must be as particular with regard to the character of members now, as when the [Relief] Society started; . . . sometimes persons wish to crowd themselves into a society of this kind when they do not intend to pursue the ways of purity and righteousness, as if the society would be a shelter to them in their iniquity. (TPJS, 240)[79]

◆ ◆ ◆

What is it that inspires professors of Christianity generally with a hope of salvation? It is that smooth, sophisticated influence of the devil, by which he deceives the whole world. (TPJS, 270)[90]

◆ ◆ ◆

The world is full of technicalities and misrepresentation, which I calculate to overthrow, and speak of things as they actually exist. (TPJS, 292)[101]

◆ ◆ ◆

My only trouble at the present time is concerning ourselves, that the Saints *will be divided, broken up, and scattered,* before we get our salvation secure; for there are so many fools in the world for the devil to operate upon, it gives him the advantage oftentimes. (TPJS, 331)[123]

◆ ◆ ◆

I advise all of you to be careful what you do, or you may by-and-by find out that you have been deceived. Stay yourselves; do not give way; don't make any hasty moves, you may be saved. If a spirit of bitterness is in you, don't be in hast. You may say, that the man is a sinner. Well, if he repents, he shall be forgiven. Be cautious; await. (TPJS, 358)[130]

◆◆◆

False prophets always arise to oppose the true prophets and they will prophesy so very near the truth that they will deceive almost the very chosen ones. (TPJS, 365)[132]

◆◆◆

Woe, woe be to that man or set of men who lift up their hands against God and His witness in these last days: for they shall deceive almost the very chosen ones! (TPJS, 365)[132]

DECISIONS

We frequently are so filled with prejudice, or have a beam in our own eye, that we are not capable of passing right decisions. (TPJS, 69)[22]

◆◆◆

I preached to the Saints, setting forth the evils that existed, and that would exist, by reason of hasty judgment, or decisions upon any subject given by any people, or in judging before they had heard both sides of a question. (TPJS, 118)[44]

DEDICATION

Hasten the work in the Temple, renew your exertions to forward all the work of the last days, and walk before the Lord in soberness and righteousness. (TPJS, 326)[121]

◆◆◆

I have tried a number of years to get the minds of the Saints prepared to receive the things of God; but we frequently see some of them, after suffering all they have for the work of God, will fly to pieces like glass as soon as anything comes that is contrary to their traditions: they cannot stand the fire at all. How many will be able to abide a celestial law, and go through

and receive their exaltation, I am unable to say, as many are called, but few are chosen. (TPJS, 331)[123]

◆◆◆

I cannot lie down until all my work is finished. (TPJS, 361)[130]

DEFENSE

He that arms himself with gun, sword, or pistol, except in the defense of truth, will sometime be sorry for it. I never carry any weapon with me bigger than my penknife. When I was dragged before the cannon and muskets in Missouri, I was unarmed. God will always protect me until my mission is fulfilled. (TPJS, 365)[132]

◆◆◆

The prediction is that army will be against army; it may be that the Saints will have to beat their ploughs into swords, for it will not do for men to sit down patiently and see their children destroyed. (TPJS, 366)[132]

◆◆◆

It is the duty of all men to protect their lives and the lives of the household, whenever necessity requires, and no power has a right to forbid it, should the last extreme arrive . . . caution is the parent of safety. (TPJS, 391)[144]

DEMOCRACY

Exalt the standard of Democracy! Down with that of priestcraft, and let all the people say Amen! That the blood of our fathers may not cry from the ground against us. Sacred is the memory of that blood which bought for us our liberty. (TPJS, 117)[42]

◆◆◆

It is a love of liberty which inspires my soul—civil and religious liberty to the whole of the human race. Love of liberty was diffused into my soul by my grandfathers while they dandled me on their knees; and shall I want friends? No. (TPJS, 313)[114]

DESIRE

The man who willeth to do well, we should extol his virtues, and speak not of his faults behind his back. (TPJS, 31)[17]

•••

I find that in the midst of business and care the spirit is willing, but the flesh is weak. (TPJS, 315)[114]

•••

Never afflict thy soul for what an enemy hath put it out of thy power to do, if thy desires are ever so just. (TPJS, 317)[116]

•••

Out of the abundance of the heart of man the mouth speaketh. (TPJS, 358)[130]

DESTINY

Every man lives for himself . . . but except a man be born again, he cannot see the kingdom of God . . . he may receive a glory like unto the moon, [i.e. of which the light of the moon is typical] or a star, [i.e. of which the light of the stars is typical] but he can never come unto Mount Zion, and unto the city of the living God . . . unless he becomes as a little child, and is taught by the Spirit of God. (TPJS, 12)[8]

•••

"How long can rolling waters remain impure? What power shall stay the heavens? As well might man stretch forth his puny arm to stop the Missouri River in its decreed course, or to turn it up stream, as to hinder the Almighty from pouring down knowledge from heaven, upon the heads of the Latter-day Saints." (TPJS, 139)[47]

•••

The blessings of the Most High will rest upon our tabernacles, and our name will be handed down to future ages; our children will rise up and call us blessed; and generations yet unborn will dwell with peculiar delight upon the scenes that we have passed through, the privations that we have endured; the untiring zeal that we have manifested; the all but insurmountable difficulties that we have overcome in laying the foundation of a work that brought about the glory and blessing which they will realize; a work that God and angels have contemplated with delight for generations past; that fired the souls of the ancient patriarchs and prophets. (TPJS, 232)[76]

•••

[The Restored Church is] a work that is destined to bring about the destruction of the powers of darkness, the renovation of the earth, the glory of God, and the salvation of the human family. (TPJS, 232)[76]

•••

It has been the design of Jehovah, from the commencement of the world, and is His purpose now, to regulate the affairs of the world in His own hand. When that is done, judgment will be administered in righteousness; anarchy and confusion will be destroyed, and "nations will learn war no more." It is for want of this great governing principle, that all this confusion has existed; "for it is not in man that walketh, to direct his steps"; this we have fully shown. (TPJS, 250)[81]

•••

My feelings at the present are that, inasmuch as the Lord Almighty has preserved me until today, He will continue to preserve me, by the united faith and prayers of the Saints, until I have fully accomplished my mission in this life, and so firmly established the dispensation of the fullness of the Priesthood in these last days, that all the powers of earth and hell can never prevail against it. (TPJS, 258)[84]

◆◆◆

All men are born to die, and all men must rise; all must enter eternity. (TPJS, 367)[132]

DEVOTION

I know that Zion, in the due time of the Lord, will be redeemed; but how many will be the days of her purification, tribulation, and affliction, the Lord has kept hid from my eyes; and when I enquire concerning this subject, the voice of the Lord is: Be still, and know that I am God; all those who suffer for my name shall reign with me, and he that layeth down his life for my sake shall find it again. (TPJS, 34)[19]

◆◆◆

The great Plan of Salvation is a theme which ought to occupy our strict attention, and be regarded as one of heaven's best gifts to mankind. No consideration whatever ought to deter us from showing ourselves approved in the sight of God. (TPJS, 68)[21]

◆◆◆

Let us realize that we are not to live to ourselves, but to God; by so doing the greatest blessings will rest upon us both in time and in eternity. (TPJS, 179)[55]

◆◆◆

Our affections should be placed upon God and His work more intensely than upon our fellow beings. (TPJS, 216)[72]

DIGNITY

How much more dignified and noble are the thoughts of God, than the vain imaginations of the human heart! None but fools will trifle with the souls of men. (TPJS, 137)[47]

◆◆◆

How vain and trifling have been our spirits, our councils, our meetings, our private as well as public conversations— too low, too mean, too vulgar, too condescending for the dignified characters of the called and chosen of God. (TPJS, 137)[47]

◆◆◆

Let every word be seasoned with grace. (TPJS, 156)[49]

◆◆◆

This [passing of Brother Barnes] has been a warning voice to us all to be sober and diligent and lay aside mirth, vanity and folly, and to be prepared to die tomorrow. (TPJS, 296)[102]

DILIGENCE

Everyone should aspire only to magnify his own office and calling. (TPJS, 227)[75]

◆◆◆

We have no new commandment to give, but admonish Elders and members to live by every word that proceedeth forth from the mouth of God, lest they come short of the glory that is reserved for the faithful. (TPJS, 306)[110]

DIPLOMACY

(*See also* TACT)

Search yourselves—the tongue is an unruly member—hold your tongues about things of no moment—a little tale will set the world on fire. At [certain] time[s] the truth on the guilty should not be told openly. . . . We must use precaution in bringing sinners to justice, lest . . . we draw the indignation of a Gentile world upon us. . . . It is necessary to hold an influence in the world, and thus spare ourselves an extermination; and also accomplish our end in spreading the Gospel, or holiness, in the earth. (TPJS, 239)[78]

◆◆◆

To the iniquitous show yourselves merciful. . . . beware, be still, be prudent, repent, reform, but do it in a way not to destroy all around you. I do not want to cloak iniquity—all things contrary to the will of God, should be cast from us, but don't do more hurt than good, with your tongues—be pure in heart. Jesus designs to save people out of their sins. Said Jesus, "Ye shall do the work, which ye see me do." These are the grand key-words for the society to act upon. (TPJS, 239)[78]

◆◆◆

Friendship is one of the grand fundamental principles of "Mormonism"; to revolutionize and civilize the world, and cause wars and contentions to cease and men to become friends and brothers. (TPJS, 316)[115]

DIRECTION

Trusting in that God who has said that these things are hid from the wise and prudent and revealed unto babes, I step forth into the field to tell you what the Lord is doing, and what you must do, to enjoy the smiles of your Savior in these last days. (TPJS, 14)[9]

◆◆◆

All men are naturally disposed to walk in their own paths as they are pointed out by their own fingers, and we are not willing to consider and walk in the path which is pointed out by another, saying, This is the way, walk ye in it, although he should be an unerring director, and the Lord his God sent him. (TPJS, 26)[15]

◆◆◆

Though there were different dispensations, yet all things which God communicated to His people were calculated to draw their minds to the great object, and to teach them to rely upon God alone as the author of their salvation, as contained in His law. (TPJS, 61)[21]

◆◆◆

Righteousness must be the aim of the Saints in all things, and . . . great things must be expected of them. (TPJS, 77)[29]

◆◆◆

There are many yet on the earth among all sects, parties, denominations, who are blinded by the subtle craftiness of men, whereby they lie in wait to deceive, and who are only kept from the truth because they know not where to find it. (TPJS, 145)[47]

◆◆◆

A very large ship is benefited very much by a very small helm in the time of a storm, by being kept workways with the wind and the waves. (TPJS, 146)[47]

◆◆◆

The Son of Man is nigh, even at your doors. If our souls and our bodies are not looking forth for the coming of the Son of Man; and after we are dead, if we are not looking forth, we shall be among those who are calling for the rocks to fall upon them. (TPJS, 160)[49]

◆◆◆

Look to the Presidency and receive instruction. (TPJS, 161)[49]

✦ ✦ ✦

Let us realize that we are not to live to ourselves, but to God; by so doing the greatest blessings will rest upon us both in time and in eternity. (TPJS, 179)[55]

✦ ✦ ✦

[Some men] . . . intelligent, learned, virtuous and lovely, walking in uprightness and in all good conscience, so far as they have been able . . . [are left to] discern duty from the muddy stream of tradition, or from the blotted page of the book of nature. (TPJS, 192)[63]

✦ ✦ ✦

Is not God good? Then you be good; if He is faithful, then you be faithful. Add to your faith virtue, to virtue knowledge, and seek for every good thing. (TPJS, 217)[73]

✦ ✦ ✦

Jesus designs to save people out of their sins. Said Jesus, "Ye shall do the work, which ye see me do." These are the grand key-words for the society to act upon. (TPJS, 239)[78]

✦ ✦ ✦

Be virtuous and pure; be men of integrity and truth; keep the commandments of God; and then you will be able more perfectly to understand the difference between right and wrong—between the things of God and the things of men; and your path will be like that of the just, which shineth brighter and brighter unto the perfect day. (TPJS, 247)[80]

✦ ✦ ✦

It has been the design of Jehovah, from the commencement of the world, and is His purpose now, to regulate the affairs of the world in His own hand. When that is done, judgment will be administered in righteousness; anarchy and confusion will be destroyed, and "nations will learn war no more," It is for want of this great governing principle, that all this confusion has existed; "for it is not in man that walketh, to direct his steps"; this we have fully shown. (TPJS, 250)[81]

✦ ✦ ✦

The world itself presents one great theater of misery, woe, and "distress of nations and perplexity." All, all, speak with a voice of thunder, that man is not able to govern himself, to legislate for himself, to protect himself, to promote his own good, nor the good of the world. (TPJS, 250)[81]

✦ ✦ ✦

If we seek first the kingdom of God, all good things will be added. (TPJS, 256)[83]

✦ ✦ ✦

I know what I say; I understand my mission and business. God Almighty is my shield; and what can man do if God is my friend? I shall not be sacrificed until my time comes; then I shall be offered freely. (TPJS, 274)[91]

✦ ✦ ✦

I hope sober-thinking and sound-reasoning people will sooner listen to the voice of truth, than be led astray by the vain pretensions of the self-wise. (TPJS, 299)[104]

✦ ✦ ✦

If we start right, it is easy to go right all the time; but if we start wrong, we may go wrong, and it be a hard matter to get right. (TPJS, 343)[130]

✦ ✦ ✦

My first object is to find out the character of the only wise and true God, and what kind of being he is. (TPJS, 344)[130]

✦ ✦ ✦

A good man will speak good things and holy principles, and an evil man evil things. I feel, in the name of the Lord, to rebuke all such bad principles, liars, etc., and I warn all of you to look out whom you are going after. (TPJS, 367)[132]

DIRECTNESS

Your humble servant or servants, intend from henceforth to [morally disapprove] everything that is not in accordance with the fullness of the Gospel of Jesus Christ, and is not of a bold, and frank, and upright nature. (TPJS, 146)[47]

DISAPPOINTMENT

If men would acquire salvation, they have got to be subject, before they leave this world, to certain rules and principles, which were fixed by an unalterable decree before the world was.

The disappointment of hopes and expectations at the resurrection would be indescribably dreadful. (TPJS, 324)[121]

◆◆◆

A man is his own tormenter and his own condemner.... The torment of disappointment in the mind of man is as exquisite as a lake burning with fire and brimstone. (TPJS, 357)[130]

DISBELIEF

Have not the pride, high-mindedness, and unbelief of the Gentiles, provoked the Holy One of Israel to withdraw His Holy Spirit from them, and send forth His judgments to scourge them for their wickedness? This is certainly the case. (TPJS, 15)[9]

◆◆◆

All men are naturally disposed to walk in their own paths as they are pointed out by their own fingers, and we are not willing to consider and walk in the path which is pointed out by another, saying, This is the way, walk ye in it, although he should be an unerring director, and the Lord his God sent him. (TPJS, 26)[15]

◆◆◆

It is reasonable to suppose that man departed from the first teachings, or instructions which he received from heaven in the first age, and refused by his disobedience to be governed by them. Consequently, he formed such laws as best suited his own mind, or as he supposed, were best adapted to his situation. But that God has influenced man more or less since that time in the formation of law for His benefit we have no hesitancy in believing . . . though man in his own supposed wisdom would not admit the influence of a power superior to his own. (TPJS, 57)[21]

◆◆◆

Men are in the habit, when the truth is exhibited by the servants of God, of saying, All is mystery; they have spoken in parables, and therefore, are not to be understood. It is true they have eyes to see, and see not, but none are so blind as those who will not see. (TPJS, 96)[34]

◆◆◆

Men who have no principle of righteousness in themselves, and whose hearts are full of iniquity, and have no desire for the principles of truth, do not understand the word of truth when they hear it. The devil taketh away the word of truth out of their hearts, because there is no desire of righteousness in them. (TPJS, 96)[34]

◆◆◆

Why will not man learn wisdom by precept at this late age of the world, when we have such a cloud of witnesses and examples before us, and not be obliged to learn by sad experience everything we know. (TPJS, 155)[49]

• • •

In the earlier ages of the world a righteous man, and a man of God and intelligence, had a better chance to do good, to be believed and received than at the present day; but in these days, such a man is much opposed and persecuted by most of the inhabitants of the earth, and he has much sorrow to pass through here. (TPJS, 196)[68]

• • •

Blessings offered, but rejected, are no longer blessings, but become like the talent hid in the earth by the wicked and slothful servant; the proffered good returns to the giver; the blessing is bestowed on those who will receive and occupy; for unto him that hath shall be given, and he shall have abundantly, but unto him that hath not, or will not receive, shall be taken away that which he hath, or might have had. (TPJS, 257)[83]

• • •

I could explain a hundred fold more than I ever have of the glories of the kingdoms manifested to me in the vision, were I permitted, and were the people prepared to receive them. (TPJS, 305)[109]

• • •

All men who become heirs of God and joint heirs of Jesus Christ will have to receive the fullness of the ordinances of his kingdom; and those who will not receive all the ordinances will come short of the fullness of that glory, if they do not lose the whole. (TPJS, 309)[113]

• • •

There are a great many wise men and women too in our midst who are too wise to be taught; therefore they must die in their ignorance, and in the resurrection they will find their mistake. Many seal up the door of heaven by saying . . . God may reveal and I will believe. (TPJS, 309) [113]

• • •

Many things are insoluble to the children of men in the last days; for instance, that God should raise the dead, and forgetting that things have been hid from before the foundation of the world, which are to be revealed to babes in the last days. (TPJS, 309)[113]

• • •

Many men will say, "I will never forsake you, but will stand by you all the times," But the moment you teach them some of the mysteries of the kingdom of God that are retained in the heavens and are to be revealed to the children of men when they are prepared for them they will be the first to stone you and put you to death. (TPJS, 309)[113]

• • •

It always has been when a man was sent of God with the priesthood and he began to preach the fullness of the gospel, that he was thrust out by his friends, who are already to butcher him if he teaches things which they imagine to be wrong; and Jesus was crucified upon this principle. (TPJS, 310)[113]

• • •

When God offers a blessing or knowledge to a man, and he refuses to receive it, he will be damned. (TPJS, 322)[119]

• • •

There has been a great difficulty in getting anything into the heads of this generation. . . . Even the Saints are slow to understand. (TPJS, 331)[123]

♦♦♦

The salvation of Jesus Christ was wrought out for all men, in order to triumph over the devil; for if it did not catch him in one place, it would in another; for he stood up as a Savior. All will suffer [however] until they obey Christ himself. (TPJS, 357)[130]

♦♦♦

When men open their lips against these truths they do not injure me, but injure themselves. (TPJS, 373)[133]

♦♦♦

I believe all that God ever revealed, and I never hear of a man being damned for believing too much; but they are damned for unbelief. (TPJS, 374)[133]

♦♦♦

DISCERNING OF SPIRITS

The Egyptians were not able to discover the difference between the miracles of Moses and those of the magicians until they came to be tested together; and if Moses had not appeared in their midst, they would unquestionably have thought that the miracles of the magicians were performed through the mighty power of God. (TPJS, 202)[71]

♦♦♦

There always did, in every age, seem to be a lack of intelligence pertaining to this subject [of discerning spirits]. Spirits of all kinds have been manifested, in every age, and almost among all people. (TPJS, 203)[71]

♦♦♦

One great evil is, that men are ignorant of the nature of spirits; their power, laws, government, intelligence, etc., and imagine that when there is anything like power, revelation, or vision manifested,

that it must be of God. . . . [But ask:] Is there any intelligence communicated? Are the curtains of heaven withdrawn, or the purposes of God developed? Have they seen and conversed with an angel— or have the glories of futurity burst upon their view? No! but their body has been inanimate, the operation of their spirit suspended, and all the intelligence that can be obtained from them when they arise, is a shout of "glory," or "hallelujah," or some incoherent expression; but they [say they] have had "the power." (TPJS, 203)[71]

♦♦♦

No man can [develop the hidden mysteries of the false spirits] . . . without the Priesthood, and having a knowledge of the laws by which spirits are governed; for as no man knows the things of God, but by the Spirit of God, so no man knows the spirit of the devil, and his power and influence, but by possessing intelligence which is more than human. (TPJS, 204)[71]

♦♦♦

A man must have the discerning of spirits . . . to understand [the things of God or of the devil] and how is he to obtain this gift if there are no gifts of the spirit? And how can these gifts be obtained without revelation? "Christ" ascended into heaven, and gave gifts to men; . . . He gave some Apostles, and some Prophets, and some Evangelists, and some Pastors and Teachers . . . chosen [by] prophesy [revelation] and by laying on of hands—by a divine communication, and a divinely appointed ordinance through the medium of the Priesthood, organized according to the order of God by divine appointment. (TPJS, 206)[71]

♦♦♦

No man nor sect of men without the regular constituted authorities, the

Priesthood and discerning of spirits, can tell true from false spirits. (TPJS, 213)[71]

•••

The Church of Jesus Christ of Latter-day Saints has also had its false spirits; and as it is made up of all those different sects professing every variety of opinion, and having been under the influence of so many kinds of spirits, it is not to be wondered at if there should be found among us false spirits. (TPJS, 213)[71]

•••

No person through the discerning of spirits can bring a charge against another, they must be proven guilty by positive evidence, or they stand clear. (TPJS, 214)[71]

•••

[One way that a spirit may be] known to be a bad angel . . . [is] by his contradicting a former revelation. (TPJS, 214)[71]

DISCERNMENT

[Some men] . . . intelligent, learned, virtuous and lovely, walking in uprightness and in all good conscience, so far as they have been able . . . [are left to] discern duty from the muddy stream of tradition, or from the blotted page of the book of nature. (TPJS, 192)[63]

•••

Be virtuous and pure; be men of integrity and truth; keep the commandments of God; and then you will be able more perfectly to understand the difference between right and wrong—between the things of God and the things of men; and your path will be like that of the just, which shineth brighter and brighter unto the perfect day. (TPJS, 247)[80]

DISCIPLINE

(*See* CHASTISEMENT; PUNISHMENT)

DISCRETION

I do not want to cloak iniquity—all things contrary to the will of God, should be cast from us, but don't do more hurt than good. (TPJS, 239)[78]

DISHONESTY

Lying spirits are going forth in the earth. There will be great manifestations of spirits, both false and true. (TPJS, 161)[49]

•••

Everything that God gives us is lawful and right; and it is proper that we should enjoy His gifts and blessings whenever and wherever He is disposed to bestow; But if we should seize upon those same blessings and enjoyments without law, without revelation, without commandment, those blessings and enjoyments would prove cursings and vexations in the end, and we should have to lie down in sorrow and wailings of everlasting regret. (TPJS, 256)[83]

DISOBEDIENCE

It is reasonable to suppose that man departed from the first teachings, or instructions which he received from heaven in the first age, and refused by his disobedience to be governed by them. Consequently, he formed such laws as best suited his own mind, or as he supposed, were best adapted to his situation. (TPJS, 57)[21]

•••

The law [of Moses] . . . was added [to the Gospel already being preached,] because of transgression. (TPJS, 60)[21]

•••

All who will not obey His voice shall not escape the damnation of hell. What is the damnation of hell? To go with that society who have not obeyed His commands. (TPJS, 198)[68]

•••

We have been chastened by the hand of God heretofore for not obeying His commands, although we never violated any human law, . . . yet we have treated lightly His commands, and departed from His ordinances, and the Lord has chastened us sore, and we have felt His arm and kissed the rod; let us be wise in time to come and ever remember that "to obey is better than sacrifice, and to hearken than the fat of rams." (TPJS, 253)[81]

•••

It was generally in consequence of the brethren disregarding or disobeying counsel that they became dissatisfied and murmured; . . . and thus the devil gets advantage over them to destroy them. (TPJS, 268)[8]

•••

Any man may believe that Jesus Christ is the Son of God, and be happy in that belief, and yet not obey his commandments, and at last be cut down for disobedience to the Lord's righteous requirements. (TPJS, 311)[113]

•••

All spirits who have not obeyed the Gospel in the flesh must either obey it in the spirit or be damned. (TPJS, 355)[130]

•••

So long as a man will not give heed to the commandments, he must abide without salvation. If a man has knowledge, he can be saved; although, if he has been guilty of great sins, he will be punished for them.

But when he consents to obey the Gospel, whether here or in the world of spirits, he is saved. (TPJS, 357)[130]

DISPENSATION OF THE FULLNESS OF TIMES

We are called to hold the keys of the mysteries of those things that have been kept hid from the foundation of the world until now. (TPJS, 137)[47]

•••

And now, brethren, after your tribulations, if you do these things ". . . let honesty, and sobriety, and candor, and solemnity, and virtue, and pureness, and meekness, and simplicity crown our heads in every place; and in fine, become as little children, without malice, guile or hypocrisy," and exercise fervent prayer and faith in the sight of God always, "He shall give unto you knowledge by His Holy Spirit, yea by the unspeakable gift of the Holy Ghost, that has not been revealed since the world was until now; which our forefathers have waited with anxious expectation to be revealed in the last times, which their minds were pointed to by the angels, as held in reserve for the fullness of their glory; a time to come in the which nothing shall be withheld, whether there be one God or many Gods, they shall be manifest; all thrones and dominions, principalities and powers, shall be revealed and set forth upon all who have endured valiantly for the Gospel of Jesus Christ." (TPJS, 138)[47]

•••

Paul spoke of the dispensation of the fullness of times, when God would gather together all things in one . . . and those men to whom these keys have been given, will have to be there. (TPJS, 159)[49]

•••

Adam . . . was the first man . . . the "Ancient of Days" . . . [who] holds the keys of the dispensation of the fullness of times; i.e., the dispensation of all the times have been and will be revealed through him from the beginning to Christ, and from Christ to the end of the dispensations that are to be revealed. (TPJS, 167)[54]

◆◆◆

"In the dispensation of the fullness of times . . . [Christ will] gather together in one all things in Christ, both which are in heaven, and which are on earth; even in Him."

Now the purpose in Himself in the winding up scene of the last dispensation is that all things pertaining to that dispensation should be conducted precisely in accordance with the preceding dispensations. (TPJS, 168)[54]

◆◆◆

God purposed in Himself that there should not be an eternal fullness until every dispensation should be fulfilled and gathered together in one, and that all things whatsoever, that should be gathered together in one in those dispensations unto the same fullness and eternal glory, should be in Christ Jesus. (TPJS, 168)[54]

◆◆◆

There are many things which belong to the powers of the Priesthood and the keys thereof, that have been kept hid from before the foundation of the world; they are hid from the wise and prudent to be revealed in the last times. (TPJS, 170)[54]

◆◆◆

All the ordinances and duties that ever have been required by the Priesthood, under the directions and commandments of the Almighty in any of the dispensations, shall all be had in the last dispensation, therefore all things had under the authority of the Priesthood at any former period, shall be had again, bringing to pass the restoration spoken of by the mouth of all the Holy Prophets. (TPJS, 171)[54]

◆◆◆

Elijah was the last prophet that held the keys of the Priesthood, and who will, before the last dispensation, restore the authority and deliver the keys of the Priesthood, in order that all the ordinances may be attended to in righteousness. (TPJS, 172)[54]

◆◆◆

The dispensation of the fullness of times will bring to light the things that have been revealed in all former dispensations; also other things that have not been before revealed. (TPJS, 193)[63]

◆◆◆

The building up of Zion is a cause that interested the people of God in every age; it is a theme upon which prophets, priests and kings have dwelt with peculiar delight; they have looked forward with joyful anticipation to the day in which we live; and fired with heavenly and joyful anticipations they have sung and written and prophesied of this our day; but they died without the sight; We are the favored people that God has made choice of to bring about the Latter-day glory; it is left for us to see, participate in and help to roll forward the Latter-day glory, "the dispensation of the fullness of times, when God will gather together all things that are in heaven, and all things that are upon the earth." (TPJS, 231)[76]

◆◆◆

The blessings of the Most High will rest upon our tabernacles, and our name will be handed down to future ages; our children will rise up and call us blessed; and generations yet unborn will dwell with peculiar delight upon the scenes that we have passed through, the privations that we have endured; the untiring zeal that we have manifested; the all but insurmountable difficulties that we have overcome in laying the foundation of a work that brought about the glory and blessing which they will realize; a work that God and angels have contemplated with delight for generations past; that fired the souls of the ancient patriarchs and prophets; a work that is destined to bring about the destruction of the powers of darkness, the renovation of the earth, the glory of God, and the salvation of the human family. (TPJS, 232)[76]

•••

This is the only thing that can bring about the "restitution of all things spoken of by all the holy Prophets since the world was"—"the dispensation of the fullness of times, when God shall gather together all things in one." Other attempts to promote universal peace and happiness in the human family have proved abortive; every effort has failed; every plan and design has fallen to the ground; it needs the wisdom of God, the intelligence of God, and the power of God to accomplish this. (TPJS, 252)[81]

•••

My feelings at the present are that, inasmuch as the Lord Almighty has preserved me until today, He will continue to preserve me, by the united faith and prayers of the Saints, until I have fully accomplished my mission in this life, and so firmly established the dispensation of the fullness of the Priesthood in these last days, that all the powers of earth and hell can never prevail against it. (TPJS, 258)[84]

•••

Although I was called of my heavenly Father to lay the foundation of this great work and kingdom in this dispensation,

and testify of His revealed will to scattered Israel, I am subject to like passions as other men, like the prophets of olden times. (TPJS, 315)[114]

•••

That which hath been hid from before the foundation of the world is revealed to babes and sucklings in the last days. (TPJS, 321)[118]

•••

The fullness of the dispensation of times [is]—a dispensation to meet the promises made by Jesus Christ before the foundation of the world for the salvation of man. (TPJS, 356)[130]

DISPENSATIONS

Adam holds the keys of the dispensation of the fullness of times; i.e., the dispensation of all the times have been and will be revealed through him from the beginning to Christ, and from Christ to the end of the dispensations that are to be revealed. (TPJS, 167)[54]

•••

What would it profit us to come unto the spirits of the just men, but to learn and come up to the standard of their knowledge? (TPJS, 320)[118]

•••

It is in the order of heavenly things that God should always send a new dispensation into the world when men have apostatized from the truth and lost the priesthood, but when men come out and build upon other men's foundations, they do it on their own responsibility, without authority from God; and when the floods come and the winds blow, their foundations will be found to be sand, and their whole fabric will crumble to dust. (TPJS, 375)[133]

DOCTRINE AND COVENANTS

The Book of revelations, [is] now to be printed, being the foundation of the Church in these last days, and a benefit to the world, showing that the keys of the mysteries of the kingdom of our Savior are again entrusted to man; and the riches of eternity within the compass of those who are willing to live by every word that proceedeth out of the mouth of God—therefore the conference voted that they prize the revelations to be worth to the Church the riches of the whole earth, speaking temporally. (TPJS, 7)[2]

DOCTRINES

In relation to the power over the minds of mankind which I hold, I would say, It is in consequence of the power of truth in the doctrines which I have been an instrument in the hands of God of presenting unto them, and not because of any compulsion on my part. (TPJS, 341)[129]

◆◆◆

I am bold to declare I have taught all the strong doctrines publicly, and always teach stronger doctrines in public than in private. (TPJS, 370)[133]

DOCUMENTATION

(*See also* RECORD KEEPING)

An item thus decided may appear, at the time, of little or no worth, but should it be published, and one of you lay hands on it after, you will find it of infinite worth, not only to your brethren, but it will be a feast to your own souls. (TPJS, 73)[26]

◆◆◆

And again, we would suggest for your consideration the propriety of all the Saints gathering up a knowledge of all the facts and sufferings and abuses put upon them by the people of this state; and also of all the property and amount of damages which they have sustained, both of character and personal injuries, as well as real property; and also the names of all persons that have had a hand in their oppressions, as far as they can get hold of them and find them out; and perhaps a committee can be appointed to find out these things, and to take statements, and affidavits, and also to gather up the libelous publications that are afloat, and all that are in the magazines, and in the encyclopaedias, and all the libelous histories that are published and are writing, and by whom, and present the whole concatenation of diabolical rascality, and nefarious and murderous impositions that have been practiced upon this people, that we may not only publish to all the world, but present them to the heads of government in all their dark and hellish hue, as the last effort which is enjoined on us by our heavenly Father, before we can fully and completely claim that promise which shall call him forth from His hiding place, and also that the whole nation may be left without excuse before He can send forth the power of His mighty arm. (TPJS, 144)[47]

◆◆◆

[The documentation of persecutions] is an imperative duty that we owe to God, to angels, with whom we shall be brought to stand, and also to ourselves, to our wives and children, who have been made to bow down with grief, sorrow, and care, under the most damning hand of murder, tyranny and oppressions, supported and urged on and upheld by the influence of that spirit which has so strongly riveted the creeds of the fathers, who have inherited lies, upon the hearts of the children, and filled the world with confusion, and has been growing stronger and stronger, and is now the very main-spring of all corruption, and the whole earth groans under the weight of its iniquity.

It is an iron yoke, it is a strong band; they are the very handcuffs, and chains, and shackles, and fetters of hell.

Therefore, it is an imperative duty that we owe [also] to the widows and fatherless, whose husbands and fathers have been murdered under its iron hand; which darkened and blackening deeds are enough to make hell itself shudder, and to stand aghast and pale, and the hands of the very devil to tremble and palsy. And also it is an imperative duty that we owe to all the rising generation, and to all the pure in heart, "for there are many yet on the earth among all sects, parties, denominations, who are blinded by the subtle craftiness of men, whereby they lie in wait to deceive, and who are only kept from the truth because they know not where to find it"; wherefore that we should waste and wear out our lives in bringing to light all the hidden things of darkness, wherein we know them; and they are truly manifest from heaven.

These should then be attended to with great earnestness. . . . For there is much which lieth in futurity, pertaining to the Saints, which depends upon these things. You know . . . that a very large ship is benefited very much by a very small helm in the time of a storm, by being kept workways with the wind and the waves.

Therefore . . . let us cheerfully do all things that lie in our power, and then may we stand still with the utmost assurance, to see the salvation of God, and for His arm to be revealed. (TPJS, 145)[47]

EARLY DEATH

The Lord takes many away even in infancy, that they may escape the envy of man, and the sorrows and evils of this present world; they were too pure, too lovely, to live on earth; therefore, if rightly considered, instead of mourning we have reason to rejoice as they are delivered from evil, and we shall soon have them again. (TPJS, 196)[68]

◆◆◆

All children are redeemed by the blood of Jesus Christ, and the moment that children leave this world, they are taken to the bosom of Abraham. The only difference between the old and young dying is, one lives longer in heaven and eternal light and glory than the other, and is freed a little sooner from this miserable wicked world. Notwithstanding all this glory, we for a moment lose sight of it, and mourn the loss, but we do not mourn as those without hope. (TPJS, 197)[68]

◆◆◆

It has been hard for me to live on earth and see these young men upon whom we have leaned for support and comfort taken from us in the midst of their youth. . . . I have sometimes thought that I should have felt more reconciled to have been called away myself if it had been the will of God; yet I know we ought to be still and know it is of God, and be reconciled to His will. (TPJS, 215)[71]

EARLY SAINTS

Our circumstances are calculated to awaken our spirits to a sacred remembrance of everything, and we think . . . that nothing therefore can separate us from the love of God and fellowship one with another; and that every species of wickedness and cruelty practiced upon us will only tend to bind our hearts together and seal them together in love. (TPJS, 130)[47]

♦♦♦

We contemplate a people who have embraced a system of religion, unpopular, and the adherence to which has brought upon them repeated persecutions. A people who for their love of God, and attachment to His cause, have suffered hunger, nakedness, perils, and almost every privation. A people who, for the sake of their religion have had to mourn the premature death of parents, husbands, wives, and children. A people, who have preferred death to slavery and hypocrisy, and have honorably maintained their characters, and stood firm and immovable, in times that have tried men's souls. . . . Your names will be handed down to posterity as Saints of God and virtuous men. (TPJS, 185)[59]

EARTH

This earth will be rolled back into the presence of God, and crowned with celestial glory. (TPJS, 181)[56]

ELDERS

All the Elders of the Church are bound to travel in the world to preach the gospel, with all their might, mind, and strength, when their circumstances will admit of it; . . . the door is now opened. (TPJS, 75)[28]

ELECTION MADE SURE

(See CALLING AND ELECTION MADE SURE)

ELEMENTS

(*See also* MATTER)

The elements are eternal. That which has a beginning will surely have an end; take a ring, it is without beginning or end—cut it for a beginning place and at the same time you have an ending place. (TPJS, 181)[56]

♦♦♦

There is no such thing as immaterial matter. All spirit is matter, but is more fine or pure, and can only be discerned by purer eyes. We cannot see it, but when our bodies are purified, we shall see that it is all matter. (TPJS, 301)[107]

♦♦♦

You ask the learned doctors why they say the world was made out of nothing; and they will answer, "Doesn't the Bible say he *created* the world"? And they infer, from the word create, that it must have been made out of nothing. Now, the word create came from the word *baurau* which does not mean to create out of nothing; it means to organize; the same as a man would organize materials and build a ship. Hence, we infer that God had materials to organize the world out of chaos—chaotic matter, which is element, and in which dwells all the glory. Elements had an existence from the time He had. The pure principles of element are principles which can never be destroyed; they may be organized and re-organized, but not destroyed. They had no beginning, and can have no end. (TPJS, 350)[130]

EMPATHY

I feel for my fellow men; I do it in the name of the Lord being moved upon by the Holy Spirit. Oh, that I could snatch them from the vortex of misery, into which I behold them plunging themselves, by their sins that I might be enabled by the warning voice, to be an instrument of bringing them to unfeigned repentance, that they might have faith to stand in the evil day! (TPJS, 87)[31]

• • •

O that I had the language of the archangel to express my feelings once to my friends! But I never expect to in this life. When others rejoice, I rejoice; when they mourn, I mourn. (TPJS, 296)[102]

• • •

Never afflict thy soul for what an enemy hath put it out of thy power to do, if thy desires are ever so just. (TPJS, 317)[116]

ENCOURAGEMENT

(*See also* PERSUASION)

Bear with those who do not feel themselves more worthy than yourselves. (TPJS, 137)[47]

END OF THE WORLD

The end of the world is the destruction of the wicked. (TPJS, 101)[34]

• • •

The harvest and the end of the world have an allusion directly to the human family in the last days, instead of the earth, as many have imagined. . . . And the angels are the reapers. . . . As the servants of God go forth warning the nations . . . and as they harden their hearts and reject the light of truth, these first being delivered over to the buffetings of Satan, and the law and the testimony being closed up . . . , they are left in darkness, and delivered over unto the day of burning; thus being bound up by their creeds. . . . "There shall be wailing and gnashing of teeth" . . . after the day of burnings, the righteous shall shine forth like the sun, in the Kingdom of their Father. Who hath ears to hear, let him hear. (TPJS, 101)[34]

ENDOWMENT

(*See also* EXALTING ORDINANCE)

You need an endowment . . . in order that you may be prepared and able to overcome all things. (TPJS, 91)[33]

• • •

I spent the day in the upper part of the store, that is in my private office . . . in council with General James Adams, of Springfield, Patriarch Hyrum Smith, Bishops Newel K. Whitney and George Miller, and President Brigham Young and Elders Heber C. Kimball and Willard Richards, instructing them in the principles and order of the Priesthood, attending to washings, anointings, endowments and the communication of keys pertaining to the Aaronic Priesthood, and so on to the highest order of the Melchizedek Priesthood, setting forth the order pertaining to the Ancient of Days, and all those plans and principles by which anyone is enabled to secure the fullness of those blessings which have been prepared for the Church of the Firstborn and come up and abide in the presence of the Eloheim in the eternal worlds. In this council was instituted the ancient order of things for the first time in these last days. And the communications I made to this council were of things spiritual, and to be received only by the spiritual minded: and there was nothing made known to these men but what will be made known to all the Saints of the last days, so soon as they are prepared to receive . . . them, even to the weakest of the Saints. (TPJS, 237)[77]

ENDURANCE

Those who cannot endure persecution, and stand in the day of affliction, cannot stand in the day when the Son of God shall burst the veil, and appear in all the glory of His Father, with all the holy angels. (TPJS, 42)[20]

•••

"My son, peace be unto thy soul; thine adversity and thine affliction shall be but a small moment; and then if thou endure it well, God shall exalt thee on high." (TPJS, 134)[47]

•••

In His Almighty name we are determined to endure tribulation as good soldiers unto the end. (TPJS, 139)[47]

•••

I have tried a number of years to get the minds of the Saints prepared to receive the things of God; but we frequently see some of them, after suffering all they have for the work of God, will fly to pieces like glass as soon as anything comes that is contrary to their traditions: they cannot stand the fire at all. How many will be able to abide a celestial law, and go through and receive their exaltation, I am unable to say, as many are called, but few are chosen. (TPJS, 331)[123]

ENVY

Don't envy the finery and fleeting show of sinners, for they are in a miserable situation; but as far as you can, have mercy on them, for in a short time God will destroy them, if they will not repent and turn unto him. (TPJS, 229)[75]

EQUALITY

(See also FAIRNESS)

Fellow sojourners upon the earth, it is your privilege to purify yourselves and come up to the same glory, and see

for yourselves, and know for yourselves. (TPJS, 13)[8]

•••

I will proceed to tell you what the Lord requires of all people, high and low, rich and poor, male and female, ministers and people, professors of religion and non-professors, in order that they may enjoy the Holy Spirit of God to a fullness, and escape the judgments of God, which are almost ready to burst upon the nations of the earth. Repent of all your sins, and be baptized in water for the remission of them, in the name of the Father, and of the Son, and of the Holy Ghost, and receive the ordinance of the laying on of the hands of him who is ordained and sealed unto this power, that ye may receive the Holy Spirit of God; and this is according to the Holy Scriptures, and the Book of Mormon; and the only way that man can enter into the celestial kingdom. (TPJS, 16)[9]

•••

The Lord says that every man is to receive according to his works. Reflect for a moment, . . . and enquire whether you would consider yourselves worthy a seat at the marriage seat with Paul and others like him, if you had been unfaithful? Had you not fought the good fight, and kept the faith, could you expect to receive? (TPJS, 64)[21]

•••

In every nation, he that feareth God and worketh righteousness, is acceptable with Him. (TPJS, 66)[21]

•••

All those who have not had an opportunity of hearing the Gospel, and being administered unto by an inspired man in the flesh, must have it hereafter, before they can be finally judged. (TPJS, 121)[45]

•••

Even the least Saint may know all things as fast as he is able to bear them. (TPJS, 149)[48]

•••

The Gospel net gathers of every kind. (TPJS, 160)[49]

•••

God will deal with all the human family equally; and . . . those characters referred to by Isaiah, [will] have their time of visitation and deliverance; after having been many days in prison. (TPJS, 219)[74]

•••

Many of our orthodox preachers . . . suppose that if a man is not what they call converted, if he dies in that state, he must remain eternally in hell without any hope. Infinite years in torment must he spend, and never, never, never have an end; and yet this eternal misery is made frequently to rest upon the merest casualty [of circumstances]. The plans of Jehovah are not so unjust, the statements of holy writ so visionary, nor the Plan of Salvation for the human family so incompatible with common sense; at such proceedings God would frown with indignant, angels would hide their heads in shame, and every virtuous, intelligent man would recoil. (TPJS, 220)[74]

•••

If human laws award to each man his deserts, and punish all delinquents according to their several crimes, surely the Lord will not be more cruel than man, for He is a wise legislator, and His laws are more equitable, His enactments more just, and His decisions more perfect than those of man; and as man judges his fellow man by law, and punishes him according to the penalty of the law, so does God of heaven judge "according to the deeds done

in the body." . . . The hearer cannot believe without he hear a "sent" preacher, and cannot be condemned for what he has not heard, and being without law, will have to be judged without law. (TPJS, 221)[74]

•••

What has become of our fathers? Will they all be damned for not obeying the Gospel when they never heard it? Certainly not. But they will possess the same privilege that we here enjoy, through the medium of the everlasting Priesthood, which not only administers on earth but also in heaven, and [in] the wise dispensations of the great Jehovah; hence [they] will be visited by the Priesthood, and come out of their prison upon the same principle as those who were disobedient in the days of Noah were visited by our Savior . . . and had the Gospel preached to them by Him in prison; and in order that they might fulfill all the requisitions of God, living friends were baptized for their dead friends, and thus fulfilled the requirement of God which says, "Except a man be born of the water and of the Spirit, he cannot enter into the kingdom of God," they were baptized of course, not for themselves, but for their dead. . . . Paul, in speaking of the doctrine, says, "Else what shall they do which are baptized for the dead if the dead rise not at all? Why are they then baptized for the dead"? 1 Cor. 15:29 (TPJS, 222)[74]

•••

A view of . . . [the principle of salvation for the dead] reconciles the Scriptures of truth, justifies the ways of God to man, places the human family upon equal footing, and harmonizes with every principle of righteousness, justice and truth. We will conclude with the words of Peter: "For the time past of our life may suffice us to have wrought the will of the Gentiles." "For, for this cause was the Gospel preached also to them that are dead, that they might be judged according to men in the flesh, but live according to God in the Spirit." (TPJS, 223)[74]

◆◆◆

There was nothing made known to . . . [the council of Church leaders regarding the temple ordinances about to be initiated] but what will be made known to all the Saints of the last days, so soon as they are prepared to receive . . . them, even to the weakest of the Saints. (TPJS, 237)[77]

◆◆◆

If there was sin among men, repentance was as necessary at one time or age of the world as another. (TPJS, 265)[85]

◆◆◆

Ordinances instituted in the heavens before the foundation of the world, in the priesthood, for the salvation of men, are not to be altered or changed. All must be saved on the same principles. (TPJS, 308)[113]

◆◆◆

The salvation of Jesus Christ was wrought out for all men, in order to triumph over the devil; for if it did not catch him in one place, it would in another; for he stood up as a Savior. All will suffer [however,] until they obey Christ himself. (TPJS, 357)[130]

ETERNAL

The order of the house of God has been, and ever will be, the same, even after Christ comes; and after the termination of the thousand years it will be the same; and we shall finally enter into the celestial kingdom of God, and enjoy it forever. (TPJS, 91)[33]

◆◆◆

Water, fire, truth and God are all realities. (TPJS, 139)[47]

◆◆◆

The Priesthood is an everlasting principle, and existed with God from eternity, and will to eternity, without beginning of days or end of years. The keys have to be brought from heaven whenever the Gospel is sent. When they are revealed, it is by Adam's authority. (TPJS, 157)[49]

◆◆◆

The elements are eternal. That which has a beginning will surely have an end. . . . Every principle proceeding from God is eternal and any principle which is not eternal is of the devil. (TPJS, 181)[56]

◆◆◆

The gospel has always been the same; the ordinances to fulfill its requirements, the same; and the officers to officiate, the same; and the signs and fruits resulting from the promises, the same. (TPJS, 264)[85]

◆◆◆

The Melchizedek Priesthood holds the right from the eternal God . . . and . . . is as eternal as God Himself, having neither beginning of days nor end of life . . . and is by an oath and covenant. (TPJS, 323)[119]

◆◆◆

No man can limit the bounds or the eternal existence of eternal time. Hath he beheld the eternal world, and is he authorized to say that there is only one God? He makes himself a fool if he thinks or says so, and there is an end of his career or progress in knowledge. He cannot obtain all knowledge, for he has sealed up the gate to it. (TPJS, 371)[133]

ETERNAL INCREASE

(See also CELESTIAL MARRIAGE;
ETERNAL LIFE; ETERNAL
PROGRESSION)

Except a man and his wife enter into an everlasting covenant and be married for eternity, while in this probation, by the power and authority of the Holy Priesthood, they will cease to increase when they die; that is, they will not have any children after the resurrection. But those who are married by the power and authority of the priesthood in this life, and continue without committing the sin against the Holy Ghost, will continue to increase and have children in the celestial glory. (TPJS, 300)[105]

ETERNAL LIFE

We have no claim in our eternal compact, in relation to eternal things, unless our actions and contracts and all things tend to this. (TPJS, 306)[109]

• • •

The power of the Melchizedek Priesthood is to have the power of "endless lives": for the everlasting covenant cannot be broken. (TPJS, 322)[119]

• • •

The organization of the spiritual and heavenly worlds, and of spiritual and heavenly beings, was agreeable to the most perfect order and harmony: their limits and bounds were fixed irrevocably, and voluntarily subscribed to in their heavenly estate by themselves, and were by our first parents subscribed to upon the earth. Hence the importance of embracing and subscribing to principles of eternal truth by all men upon the earth that expect eternal life. (TPJS, 325)[121]

• • •

Here, then, is eternal life—to know the only wise and true God; and you have got to learn how to be Gods yourselves, and to be kings and priests to God, the same as all Gods have done before you, namely, by going from one small degree

to another, and from a small capacity to a great one; from grace to grace, from exaltation to exaltation, until you attain to the resurrection of the dead, and are able to dwell in everlasting burnings, and to sit in glory, as do those who sit enthroned in everlasting power. And I want you to know that God, in the last days, while certain individuals are proclaiming his name, is not trifling with you or me. (TPJS, 346)[130]

• • •

The Savior has the words of eternal life. Nothing else can profit us. (TPJS, 364)[132]

ETERNAL PROGRESSION

(See also PERFECTION)

If you wish to go where God is, you must be like God, or possess the principles which God possesses; for if we are not drawing towards God in principle, we are going from Him and drawing towards the devil. (TPJS, 216)[73]

• • •

Except a man and his wife enter into an everlasting covenant and be married for eternity, while in this probation, by the power and authority of the Holy Priesthood, they will cease to increase when they die; that is, they will not have any children after the resurrection. But those who are married by the power and authority of the priesthood in this life, and continue without committing the sin against the Holy Ghost, will continue to increase and have children in the celestial glory. (TPJS, 301)[105]

• • •

Here, then, is eternal life—to know the only wise and true God; and you have got to learn how to be Gods yourselves, and to be kings and priests to God, the same as all Gods have done before you, namely, by going from one small degree to another, and from a small capacity to a great one; from grace to grace, from exaltation to exaltation, until you attain to the resurrection of the dead, and are able to dwell in everlasting burnings, and to sit in glory, as do those who sit enthroned in everlasting power. And I want you to know that God, in the last days, while certain individuals are proclaiming his name, is not trifling with you or me. [Elder B. H. Roberts writes in a footnote, "The argument here made by the Prophet is very much strengthened by the following passage: "The Son can do nothing of himself, but what he seeth the Father do; for what things soever he doeth, these also doeth the Son likewise" St. John 5:19. Elder Roberts further wrote, "Whatever happened to him (Christ) . . . whether within our individual reach or not, is assuredly within reach of humanity. That is what he (Christ) urged again and again, "Be born again." "Be ye perfect." "Ye are the sons of God." "My Father and your Father, my God and your God."] (TPJS, 346)[130]

♦♦♦

But they shall be heirs of God and joint heirs with Jesus Christ. What is it? To inherit the same power, the same glory and the same exaltation, until you arrive at the station of a God, and ascend the throne of eternal power, the same as those who have gone before. What did Jesus do? Why, I do the things I saw my Father do when worlds came rolling into existence. My Father worked out his kingdom with fear and trembling, and I must do the same; and when I get my kingdom, I shall present it to my Father, so that he may obtain kingdom upon kingdom, and it will exalt Him in glory. He will then take a higher exaltation, and I will take his place, and thereby become exalted myself. So that Jesus treads in the tracks of his Father, and inherits what God did before; and God is thus glorified and exalted in the salvation and exaltation of all his children. (TPJS, 347)[130]

♦♦♦

When you climb up a ladder, you must begin at the bottom, and ascend step by step, until you arrive at the top; and so it is with the principles of the Gospel—you must begin with the first, and go on until you learn all the principles of exaltation. But it will be a great while after you have passed through the veil before you will have learned them. It is not all to be comprehended in this world; it will be a great work to learn our salvation and exaltation even beyond the grave. I suppose I am not allowed to go into an investigation of anything that is not contained in the Bible. If I do, I think there are so many ever-wise men here, that they would cry, "treason" and put me to death. So I will go to the old Bible and turn commentator today. (TPJS, 348)[130]

♦♦♦

No man can limit the bounds or the eternal existence of eternal time. Hath he beheld the eternal world, and is he authorized to say that there is only one God? He makes himself a fool if he thinks or says so, and there is an end of his career or progress in knowledge. He cannot obtain all knowledge, for he has sealed up the gate to it. (TPJS, 371)[133]

ETERNAL REWARDS

The law of heaven is presented to man, and as such guarantees to all who obey it a reward far beyond any earthly consideration. (TPJS, 50)[21]

♦♦♦

God ere long, will call all his servants before Him, and there from His own hand they will receive a just recompense and a righteous reward for all their labors. (TPJS, 57)[21]

There is to be a day when all will be judged of their works, and rewarded according to the same; . . . those who have kept the faith will be crowned with a crown of righteousness; be clothed in white raiment; be admitted to the marriage feast; be free from every affliction, and reign with Christ on the earth, where, according to the ancient promise, they will partake of the fruit of the vine new in the glorious kingdom with Him. (TPJS, 66)[21]

♦♦♦

In obedience there is joy and peace unspotted, unalloyed; and as God has designed our happiness—and the happiness of all His creatures, he never has—He never will institute an ordinance or give a commandment to His people that is not calculated in its nature to promote that happiness which He has designed, and which will not end in the greatest amount of good and glory to those who become the recipients of His law and ordinances. (TPJS, 256)[83]

♦♦♦

Our heavenly Father is more liberal in His views, and boundless in His mercies and blessings, than we are ready to believe or receive; and, at the same time, is more terrible to the workers of iniquity, more awful in the executions of His punishments, and more ready to detect every false way, than we are apt to suppose Him to be. (TPJS, 257)[83]

♦♦♦

There are mansions for those who obey a celestial law, and there are other mansions for those who come short of the law[—]every man in his own order. (TPJS, 366)[132]

♦♦♦

Paul says, "There is one glory of the sun, and another glory of the moon, and another glory of the stars; for one star differeth from another star in glory. So also is the resurrection of the dead." They who obtain a glorious resurrection from the dead, are exalted far above principalities, powers, thrones, dominions and angels, and are expressly declared to be heirs of God and joint heirs with Jesus Christ, all having eternal power. (TPJS, 374)[133]

ETERNAL SPIRITS

Without attempting to describe this mysterious connection, and the laws that govern the body and the spirit of man, their relationship to each other, and the design of God in relation to the human body and spirit, I would just remark that the spirits of men are eternal, that they are governed by the same Priesthood that Abraham, Melchizedek and the Apostles were; that they are organized according to the Priesthood which is everlasting, "without beginning of days or end of years,"—that they all move in their respective spheres, and are governed by the law of God; that when they appear upon the earth they are in a probationary state, and are preparing, if righteous, for a future and greater glory; that the spirits of good men cannot interfere with the wicked beyond their prescribed bounds. (TPJS, 208)[71]

♦♦♦

The intelligence of spirits had no beginning, neither will it have an end. . . . That which has a beginning may have an end. There never was a time when there were not spirits; for they are co-[eternal] with our Father in Heaven. (TPJS, 353)[130]

♦♦♦

[On the way to Carthage, Joseph, Hyrum and others met a] Captain Dunn with a company of about sixty mounted militia, on seeing which Joseph said, "Do not be alarmed, brethren, for they cannot do more to you than the enemies of truth did to the ancient Saints—they can only kill the body." (TPJS, 379)[137]

ETERNITY

The Great Jehovah contemplated the whole of the events connected with the earth, pertaining to the Plan of Salvation, before it rolled into existence, or ever, "the morning stars sang together" for joy; the past, the present, and the future were and are, with Him, one eternal "now." (TPJS, 220)[74]

◆◆◆

Ordinances instituted in the heavens before the foundation of the world, in the priesthood, for the salvation of men, are not to be altered or changed. All must be saved on the same principles. (TPJS, 308)[113]

◆◆◆

When . . . [God's] commandments teach us, it is in view of eternity; for we are looked upon by God as though we were in eternity. God dwells in eternity, and does not view things as we do. (TPJS, 356)[130]

EVIL

(*See also* CORRUPTION; WICKEDNESS)

I have learned in my travels that man is treacherous and selfish, but few excepted. (TPJS, 30)[17]

◆◆◆

A frank and open rebuke provoketh a good man to emulation; and in the hour of trouble he will be your best friend. But on the other hand, it will draw out all the corruptions of corrupt hearts; and lying and the poison of asps is under their tongues; and they do cause the pure in heart to be cast into prison, because they want them out of their way. (TPJS, 137)[47]

◆◆◆

Evil spirits will have more knowledge, and consequently more power than many men who are on the earth. Hence it needs revelation to assist us, and give us knowledge of the things of God. (TPJS, 217)[73]

◆◆◆

The little foxes spoil the vines—little evils do the most injury to the Church. If you have evil feelings, and speak of them to one another, it has a tendency to do mischief. (TPJS, 258)[84]

◆◆◆

He that will war the true Christian warfare against the corruptions of these last days will have wicked men and angels of devils, and all the infernal powers of darkness continually arrayed against him. (TPJS, 259)[84]

◆◆◆

Iniquity of any kind cannot be sustained in the Church, and it will not fare well where I am; for I am determined while I do lead the Church, to lead it right. (TPJS, 307)[111]

◆◆◆

Concerning [the death of] Brother James Adams, it should appear strange that so good and so great a man was hated. . . . But so it was. Whenever light shone, it stirred up darkness. Truth and error, good and evil cannot be reconciled. (TPJS, 325)[121]

EXALTATION

Live in strict obedience to the commandments of God, and walk humbly before Him, and He will exalt thee in His own due time. (TPJS, 27)[15]

◆◆◆

The world has had a fair trial for six thousand years; the Lord will try the seventh thousand Himself; "He whose right it is, will possess the kingdom, and reign until He has put all things under His feet"; iniquity will hide its hoary head, Satan will be bound, and the works of darkness destroyed; righteousness will be put to the line, and judgment to the plummet, and "he that fears the Lord will alone be exalted in that day." (TPJS, 252)[81]

◆ ◆ ◆

Any person who is exalted to the highest mansion has to abide a celestial law, and the whole law too. (TPJS, 331)[123]

◆ ◆ ◆

Here, then, is eternal life—to know the only wise and true God; and you have got to learn how to be Gods yourselves, and to be kings and priests to God, the same as all Gods have done before you, namely, by going from one small degree to another, and from a small capacity to a great one; from grace to grace, from exaltation to exaltation, until you attain to the resurrection of the dead, and are able to dwell in everlasting burnings, and to sit in glory, as do those who sit enthroned in everlasting power. And I want you to know that God, in the last days, while certain individuals are proclaiming his name, is not trifling with you or me. [Elder B. H. Roberts writes in a footnote, "The argument here made by the Prophet is very much strengthened by the following passage: "The Son can do nothing of himself, but what he seeth the Father do; for what things soever he doeth, these also doeth the Son likewise." (St. John 5:19)] [Elder Roberts further writes, "Whatever happened to him (Christ) . . . whether within our individual reach or not, is assuredly within reach of humanity. That is what he (Christ) urged again and again, "Be born again." "Be ye perfect." "Ye are the sons of God." "My Father and your Father, my God and your God."] (TPJS, 346)[130]

◆ ◆ ◆

But they shall be heirs of God and joint heirs with Jesus Christ. What is it? To inherit the same power, the same glory and the same exaltation, until you arrive at the station of a God, and ascend the throne of eternal power, the same as those who have gone before. What did Jesus do? Why, I do the things I saw my Father do when worlds came rolling into existence. My Father worked out his kingdom with fear and trembling, and I must do the same; and when I get my kingdom, I shall present it to my Father, so that he may obtain kingdom upon kingdom, and it will exalt him in glory. He will then take a higher exaltation, and I will take his place, and thereby become exalted myself. So that Jesus treads in the tracks of his Father, and inherits what God did before; and God is thus glorified and exalted in the salvation and exaltation of all his children. (TPJS, 347)[130]

◆ ◆ ◆

If a man has knowledge, he can be saved. (TPJS, 357)[130]

◆ ◆ ◆

In the world of spirits no man can be exalted but by knowledge. (TPJS, 357)[130]

◆ ◆ ◆

Every man who reigns in celestial glory is a God to his dominions (TPJS, 374)[133]

EXALTING ORDINANCES

You need an endowment . . . in order that you may be prepared and able to overcome all things. (TPJS, 91)[33]

◆ ◆ ◆

I spent the day in the upper part of the store, that is in my private office . . . in council with General James Adams, of Springfield, Patriarch Hyrum Smith, Bishops Newel K. Whitney and George Miller, and President Brigham Young and

Elders Heber C. Kimball and Willard Richards, instructing them in the principles and order of the Priesthood, attending to washings, anointings, endowments and the communication of keys pertaining to the Aaronic Priesthood, and so on to the highest order of the Melchizedek Priesthood, setting forth the order pertaining to the Ancient of Days, and all those plans and principles by which anyone is enabled to secure the fullness of those blessings which have been prepared for the Church of the Firstborn and come up and abide in the presence of the Eloheim in the eternal worlds. In this council was instituted the ancient order of things for the first time in these last days. And the communications I made to this council were of things spiritual, and to be received only by the spiritual minded: and there was nothing made known to these men but what will be made known to all the Saints of the last days, so soon as they are prepared to receive . . . them, even to the weakest of the Saints. (TPJS, 237)[77]

EXAMPLE

Let honesty, and sobriety, and candor, and solemnity, and virtue, and pureness, and meekness, and simplicity crown our heads in every place; and in fine, become as little children, without malice, guile or hypocrisy. (TPJS, 137)[47]

♦♦♦

There are many teachers, but, perhaps, not many fathers. (TPJS, 144)[47]

♦♦♦

Inasmuch as long-suffering, patience, and mercy have ever characterized the dealings of our heavenly Father towards the humble and penitent, I feel disposed to copy the example, cherish the same principles, and by so doing being a savior of my fellow men. (TPJS, 165)[53]

♦♦♦

You need not be teasing your husbands because of their deeds, but let the weight of your innocence, kindness and affection be felt, which is more mighty than a millstone hung about the neck; not war, not jangle, not contradiction or dispute, but meekness, love, purity—these are the things that should magnify you in the eyes of all good men. (TPJS, 227)[75]

♦♦♦

Jesus designs to save people out of their sins. Said Jesus, "Ye shall do the work, which ye see me do." These are the grand key-words for the society to act upon. (TPJS, 239)[78]

♦♦♦

Search yourselves—the tongue is an unruly member—hold your tongues about things of no moment—a little tale will set the world on fire. At [certain] time[s] the truth on the guilty should not be told openly. . . . We must use precaution in bringing sinners to justice, lest . . . we draw the indignation of a Gentile world upon us. . . . It is necessary to hold an influence in the world, and thus spare ourselves an extermination; and also accomplish our end in spreading the Gospel, or holiness, in the earth. . . . To the iniquitous show yourselves merciful. (TPJS, 239)[78]

♦♦♦

It is the object of this [Relief] Society to reform persons, not to take those that are corrupt and foster them in their wickedness; but if they repent, we are bound to take them, and by kindness sanctify and cleanse them from all unrighteousness by our influence in watching over them. Nothing will have such influence over people as the fear of being disfellowshipped by so goodly a society as this. (TPJS, 240)[79]

EXCLUSIVENESS

Party feelings, separate interests, exclusive designs should be lost sight of in the one common cause, in the interest of the whole. (TPJS, 231)[76]

EXCOMMUNICATION

The Messiah's kingdom on earth is of that kind of government, that there has always been numerous apostates, for the reason that it admits of no sins unrepented of without excluding the individual from its fellowship. (TPJS, 66)[21]

•••

If one member becomes corrupt, and you know it, you must immediately put it away, or it will either injure or destroy the whole body. The sympathies of the heads of the Church have induced them to bear a long time with those who were corrupt until they were obliged to cut them off, lest all become contaminated. (TPJS, 226)[75]

•••

It is the object of this society to reform persons, not to take those that are corrupt and foster them in their wickedness; but if they repent, we are bound to take them, and by kindness sanctify and cleanse them from all unrighteousness by our influence in watching over them. Nothing will have such influence over people as the fear of being disfellowshipped by so goodly a society as this. (TPJS, 240)[79]

EXPERIENCE

"If thou art called to pass through tribulations; if thou art in perils among false brethren; if thou art in perils among robbers; if thou art in perils by land or by sea; if thou art accused with all manner of false accusations; if thine enemies fall upon thee; if they tear thee from the society from thy father and mother and brethren and sisters; and if with a drawn sword thine enemies tear thee from the bosom of thy wife, and thine offspring, and thine elder son, although but six years of age, shall cling to thy garments, and shall say, My father, my father, why can't you stay with us? O my father, what are the men going to do with you? And if then he shall be thrust from thee by the sword, and thou be dragged to prison, and thine enemies prowl around thee like wolves for the blood of the lamb; and if thou shouldst be cast into the pit, or into the hands of murderers, and the sentence of death passed upon thee; if thou be cast into the deep, if the billowing surge conspire against thee; if fierce winds become thine enemy; if the heavens gather blackness, and all the elements combine to hedge up the way; and above all, if the very jaws of hell shall gape open the mouth wide after thee, know thou, my son, that all these things shall give thee experience, and shall be for thy good. The Son of Man hath descended below them all; art thou greater than he?" (TPJS, 143)[47]

•••

Why will not man learn wisdom by precept at this late age of the world, when we have such a cloud of witnesses and examples before us, and not be obliged to learn by sad experience everything we know? (TPJS, 155)[49]

•••

I am like a huge, rough stone rolling down from a high mountain; and the only polishing I get is when some corner gets rubbed off by coming in contact with something else, striking with accelerating force against religious bigotry, priest-craft, lawyer-craft, doctor-craft, lying editors, suborned judges and jurors, and the authority of perjured executives, backed by mobs, blasphemers, licentious and corrupt men and women—all hell knocking off a corner here and a corner there. Thus I will become a smooth and polished shaft in the quiver of the Almighty, who will give me dominion over all and every one of them, when their refuge of lies shall fail, and their hiding place shall be destroyed, while these smooth-polished stones with which I come in contact become marred. (TPJS, 304)[109]

FAIRNESS

(See also EQUALITY)

If God rewarded everyone according to the deeds done in the body, the term "Heaven" as intended for the Saints' eternal home, must include more kingdoms than one. (TPJS, 10)[5]

♦♦♦

The Lord says that every man is to receive according to his works. Reflect for a moment . . . and enquire whether you would consider yourselves worthy a seat at the marriage seat with Paul and others like him, if you had been unfaithful? Had you not fought the good fight, and kept the faith, could you expect to receive? (TPJS, 64)[21]

♦♦♦

In every nation, he that feareth God and worketh righteousness, is acceptable with Him. (TPJS, 66)[21]

♦♦♦

There is to be a day when all will be judged of their works, and rewarded according to the same. (TPJS, 66)[21]

♦♦♦

Our acts are recorded, and at a future day they will be laid before us, and if we should fail to judge right and injure our fellow-beings, they may there, perhaps, condemn us. (TPJS, 69)[22]

♦♦♦

All who have died without a knowledge of this Gospel, who would have received it if they had been permitted to tarry, shall be heirs of the celestial kingdom of God; also all that shall die henceforth without a knowledge of it, who would have received it with all their hearts, shall be heirs of that kingdom, "For I, the Lord, will judge all men according to their works, according to the desire of their hearts." And I also beheld that all children who die before they arrive at the years of accountability, are saved in the celestial kingdom of heaven. (TPJS, 106)[38]

♦♦♦

All those who have not had an opportunity of hearing the Gospel, and being administered unto by an inspired man in the flesh, must have it hereafter, before they can be finally judged. (TPJS, 121)[45]

♦♦♦

Even the least Saint may know all things as fast as he is able to bear them (TPJS, 149)[48]

♦♦♦

The [High] Council should try no case without both parties being present, or having had an opportunity to be present; neither should they hear one person's complaint before his case is brought up for trial; neither should they suffer the character of any one to be exposed before the High Council without the person being present and ready to defend him or herself; that the minds of the councilors be not prejudiced for or against any one whose case they may possibly have to act upon. (TPJS, 165)[52]

◆◆◆

[Jehovah] . . . holds the reins of judgment in His hands; He is a wise Lawgiver, and will judge all men, not according to the narrow, contracted notions of men, but, "according to the deeds done in the body whether they be good or evil," or whether these deeds were done in England, America, Spain, Turkey, or India. He will judge them, "not according to what they have not, but according to what they have," those who have lived without law, will be judged without law, and those who have a law, will be judged by the law. We need not doubt the wisdom and intelligence of the Great Jehovah; He will award judgment or mercy to all nations according to their several deserts, their means of obtaining intelligence, the laws by which they are governed, the facilities afforded them of obtaining correct information, and His inscrutable designs in relation to the human family; and when the designs of God shall be made manifest, and the curtain of futurity be withdrawn, we shall all of us have to confess that the Judge of all the earth has done right. (TPJS, 218)[74]

◆◆◆

If human laws award to each man his deserts, and punish all delinquents according to their several crimes, surely the Lord will not be more cruel than man, for He is a wise legislator, and His laws are more equitable, His enactments more just, and His decisions more perfect than those of man; and as man judges his fellow man by law, and punishes him according to the penalty of the law, so does God of heaven judge "according to the deeds done in the body." . . . The hearer cannot believe without he hear a "sent" preacher, and cannot be condemned for what he has not heard, and being without law, will have to be judged without law. (TPJS, 221)[74]

◆◆◆

God judges men according to the use they make of the light which He gives them. (TPJS, 303)[109]

◆◆◆

The Lord deals with this people as a tender parent with a child, communicating light and intelligence and the knowledge of His ways as they can bear it. (TPJS, 305)[109]

◆◆◆

When I get hold of the Eastern papers, and see how popular I am, I am afraid myself that I shall be elected; but if I should be, I would not say, "*Your cause is just, but I can do nothing for you.*" (TPJS, 334)[127]

FAITH

Though there were different dispensations, yet all things which God communicated to His people were calculated to draw their minds to the great object, and to teach them to rely upon God alone as the author of their salvation, as contained in His law. (TPJS, 61)[21]

◆◆◆

Great blessings await us at this time, and will be soon poured out upon us, if we are faithful in all things, for we are even entitled to greater spiritual blessings than . . . [those during Christ's mortal ministry] because they had Christ in person with them. His personal presence we have not, therefore we have need of greater faith, on account of our peculiar circumstances. (TPJS, 90)[33]

◆◆◆

In His Almighty name we are determined to endure tribulation as good soldiers unto the end. (TPJS, 139)[47]

◆◆◆

Faith comes by hearing the word of God; that testimony is always attended by the spirit of prophesy and revelation. (TPJS, 148)[48]

◆◆◆

Faith comes not by signs, but by hearing the word of God. (TPJS, 149)[48]

◆◆◆

[Joseph] . . . called upon the assembly before him to humble themselves in faith before God, and in mighty prayer and fasting to call upon the name of the Lord, until the elements were purified over our heads, and the earth sanctified under our feet, that the inhabitants of this city may escape the power of disease and pestilence, and the destroyer that rideth upon the face of the earth, and that the Holy Spirit of God may rest upon this vast multitude. (TPJS, 200)[68]

◆◆◆

By faith the worlds were made. (TPJS, 270)[90]

◆◆◆

Faith has been wanting, not only among the heathen, but in professed Christendom, also, so that . . . all the gifts and blessings have been wanting. (TPJS, 270)[90]

◆◆◆

The present generation, if they were going to battle, if they got any assistance from God, they would have to obtain it by faith. (TPJS, 299)[103]

◆◆◆

We have no new commandment to give, but admonish Elders and members to live by every word that proceedeth forth from the mouth of God, lest they come short of the glory that is reserved for the faithful. (TPJS, 306)[110]

FAITHFULNESS

I pray . . . that you all may be kept in the faith unto the end: let your sufferings be what they may, it is better in the eyes of God that you should die, than that you should give up the land of Zion, the inheritances which you have purchased with your monies; for every man that giveth not up his inheritance, though he should die, yet, when the Lord shall come, he shall stand upon it, and with Job, in his flesh he shall see God. Therefore, this is my counsel, that you retain your lands. (TPJS, 35)[19]

◆◆◆

The great Plan of Salvation is a theme which ought to occupy our strict attention, and be regarded as one of heaven's best gifts to mankind. No consideration whatever ought to deter us from showing ourselves approved in the sight of God. (TPJS, 68)[21]

◆◆◆

After having suffered so great sacrifice and having passed through so great a season of sorrow, we trust that a ram may be caught in the thicket speedily, to relieve the sons and daughters of Abraham from their great anxiety, and to light up the lamp of salvation upon their countenances, that they may hold on now, after having gone so far unto everlasting life. (TPJS, 136)[47]

◆◆◆

As well might the devil seek to dethrone Jehovah, as overthrow an innocent soul that resists everything which is evil. (TPJS, 226)[75]

♦♦♦

In His Almighty name we are determined to endure tribulation as good soldiers unto the end. (TPJS, 139)[47]

♦♦♦

All your losses will be made up to you in the resurrection, provided you continue faithful. By the vision of the Almighty I have seen it. (TPJS, 296)[102]

♦♦♦

I have tried a number of years to get the minds of the Saints prepared to receive the things of God; but we frequently see some of them, after suffering all they have for the work of God, will fly to pieces like glass as soon as anything comes that is contrary to their traditions: they cannot stand the fire at all. How many will be able to abide a celestial law, and go through and receive their exaltation, I am unable to say, as many are called, but few are chosen. (TPJS, 331)[123]

FALSE DOCTRINE

Many of our orthodox preachers . . . suppose that if a man is not what they call converted, if he dies in that state, he must remain eternally in hell without any hope. Infinite years in torment must he spend, and never, never, never have an end; and yet this eternal misery is made frequently to rest upon the merest casualty [of circumstances]. (TPJS, 220)[74]

♦♦♦

It is often the case that . . . [new] members of this Church for want of better information, carry along with them their old notions of things, and sometimes fall into egregious errors. (TPJS, 242)[80]

♦♦♦

To become a joint heir of the heirship of the Son, one must put away all his false

traditions. (TPJS, 321)[119]

FALSE PROPHETS

The world has always mistook false prophets for true ones, and those that were sent of God, they considered to be false prophets, and hence they killed, stoned, punished and imprisoned the true prophets . . . and though the most honorable men of the earth, they banished them from their society as vagabonds, whilst they cherished, honored and supported knaves, vagabonds, hypocrites, imposters, and the basest of men. (TPJS, 206)[71]

♦♦♦

God never had any prophets that acted in this way [strange fits, trembling, fainting, swooning or in trances]; there was nothing indecorous in the proceedings of the Lord's prophets in any age; neither had the apostles nor prophets in the apostles" day anything of this kind. . . . Paul says, "Let everything be done decently and in order," but here we find the greatest disorder and indecency in the conduct of both men and women. The same would apply to . . . many of our modern revivalists. (TPJS, 209)[71]

♦♦♦

My enemies say that I have been a true prophet. Why, I had rather be a fallen true prophet than a false prophet. When a man goes about prophesying, and commands men to obey his teachings, he must either be a true or false prophet. (TPJS, 365)[132]

♦♦♦

Woe, woe be to that man or set of men who lift up their hands against God and His witness in these last day. . . . False prophets always arise to oppose the true prophets and they will prophesy so very near the truth that they will deceive almost the very chosen ones. (TPJS, 365)[132]

All men are liars who say they are of the true Church without the revelations of Jesus Christ and the Priesthood of Melchizedek, which is after the order of the Son of God. (TPJS, 375)[133]

FALSE SPIRITS

Lying spirits are going forth in the earth. There will be great manifestations of spirits, both false and true. (TPJS, 161)[49]

◆◆◆

It is evident from the Apostles' writings, that many false spirits existed in their day, and had "gone forth into the world," and that it needed intelligence which God alone could impart to detect false spirits, and to prove which spirits were of God. (TPJS, 202)[71]

◆◆◆

Nothing is a greater injury to the children of men than to be under the influence of a false spirit when they think they have the Spirit of God. Thousands have felt the influence of its terrible power and baneful effects. . . . Pain, misery and ruin have followed in their train; nations have been convulsed, kingdoms overthrown, provinces laid waste, and blood, carnage and desolation are habiliments in which it has been clothed. (TPJS, 205)[71]

FALSE TEACHERS

Any man who says he is a teacher or a preacher of righteousness, and denies the spirit of prophecy, is a liar, and the truth is not in him; and by this key false teachers and imposters may be detected. (TPJS, 269)[89]

◆◆◆

If any man is authorized to take away my life because he thinks and says I am a false teacher, then, upon the same principle, we should be justified in taking away the life of every false teacher, and where would be the end of blood? And who would not be the sufferer? (TPJS, 344)[130]

FAMILY

It becomes . . . Elder[s] when . . . traveling through the world . . . [to] commence their labor with parents, or guardians; and their teachings should be such as are calculated to turn the hearts of the fathers to the children, and the hearts of children to the fathers; and no influence should be used with children, contrary to the consent of their parents or guardians; but all such as can be persuaded in a lawful and righteous manner, and with common consent, we should feel it our duty to influence them to gather with the people of God. But otherwise let the responsibility rest upon the heads of parents or guardians. (TPJS, 86)[31]

◆◆◆

And if children embrace the Gospel, and their parents or guardians are unbelievers, teach them to stay at home and be obedient to their parents or guardians, if they require it; but if they consent to let them gather with the people of God, let them do so, and there shall be no wrong; and let all things be done carefully and righteously, and God will extend to all such His guardian care. (TPJS, 87)[30]

◆◆◆

We send our respects to fathers, mothers, wives and children, brothers and sisters; we hold them in the most sacred remembrance. (TPJS, 139)[47]

◆◆◆

There are many teachers, but, perhaps, not many fathers. (TPJS, 144)[47]

◆◆◆

The Kingdom of Heaven is like a grain of mustard seed . . . small, but brings forth a large tree, and the fowls lodge in the branches. The fowls are the angels [which] come down, combine together [and] gather their children. . . . We cannot be made perfect without them, nor they without us. (TPJS, 159)[49]

•••

The Great Parent of the universe looks upon the whole of the human family with a fatherly care and a paternal regard; He views them as his offspring, and without any of those contracted feelings that influence the children of men, causes "His sun to rise on the evil and on the good, and sendeth rain on the just and on the unjust." (TPJS, 218)[74]

•••

So plain was the vision, that I actually saw men, before they had ascended from the tomb, as though they were getting up slowly. They took each other by the hand and said to each other, "My father, my son, my mother, my daughter, my brother, my sister." And when the voice calls for the dead to arise, suppose I am laid by the side of my father, what would be the first joy of my heart? To meet my father, my mother, my brother, my sister; and when they are by my side, I embrace them and they me. (TPJS, 295)[102]

•••

If I have no expectation of seeing my father, mother, brothers, sisters and friends again, my heart would burst in a moment, and I should go down to my grave. (TPJS, 296)[102]

•••

When a seal is put upon the father and mother, it secures their posterity, so that they cannot be lost, but will be saved by virtue of the covenant of their father and mother. (TPJS, 321)[118]

•••

In order to receive your children to yourselves you must have a promise—some ordinance; some blessing, in order to ascend above principalities, or else it may be an angel. They must rise just as they died; we can there hail our lovely infants with the same glory—the same loveliness in the celestial glory, where they all enjoy alike. They differ in stature, in size, the same glorious spirit gives them the likeness of glory in bloom and beauty. The old man with his silvery hairs will glory in bloom and beauty. No man can describe it to you—no man can write it. (TPJS, 368)[132]

FASTING

If we would be sober and watch in fasting and prayer, God would turn away sickness from our midst. (TPJS, 326)[121]

FATHERS

"Fathers, provoke not your children to anger, lest they be discouraged" (Colossians 3:21). (TPJS, 89)[31]

•••

There are many teachers, but, perhaps, not many fathers. (TPJS, 144)[47]

FAULTS

Although I do wrong, I do not the wrongs that I am charged with doing; the wrong that I do is through the frailty of human nature, like other men. No man lives without fault. (TPJS, 258)[84]

•••

I do not dwell upon your faults, and you shall not upon mine. (TPJS, 316)[115]

FINAL DISPENSATION

(See DISPENSATION OF THE FULLNESS OF TIMES)

FIRST PRESIDENCY

Revelations of the mind and will of God to the Church, are to come through the presidency. This is the order of heaven, and the power and privilege of this priesthood. (TPJS, 111)[41]

• • •

I will proceed to tell you what the Lord requires of all people, high and low, rich and poor, male and female, ministers and people, professors of religion and non-professors, in order that they may enjoy the Holy Spirit of God to a fullness, and escape the judgments of God, which are almost ready to burst upon the nations of the earth. Repent of all your sins, and be baptized in water for the remission of them, in the name of the Father, and of the Son, and of the Holy Ghost, and receive the ordinance of the laying on of the hands of him who is ordained and sealed unto this power, that ye may receive the Holy Spirit of God; and this is according to the Holy Scriptures, and the Book of Mormon; and the only way that man can enter into the celestial kingdom. (TPJS, 16)[9]

FIRST PRINCIPLES

The Doctrines of the Resurrection of the Dead and the Eternal Judgment are necessary to preach among the first principles of the Gospel of Jesus Christ. (TPJS, 149)[48]

• • •

The proclamation of the first principles of the Gospel was a means of salvation to men individually; and it was the truth, not men, that saved them; but men, by actively engaging in rites of salvation substitutionally became instrumental in bringing multitudes of their kindred into the kingdom of God. (TPJS, 191)[63]

• • •

Declare the first principles, and let the mysteries alone, lest ye be overthrown. (TPJS, 292)[101]

FLATTERY

Anxieties inexpressible crowd themselves continually upon my mind for the Saints, when I consider the many temptations to which we are subject, from the cunning and flattery of the great adversary of our souls. (TPJS, 29)[16]

• • •

Flattery is . . . a deadly poison. (TPJS, 137)[47]

• • •

The devil flatters us that we are very righteous, when [in fact] we are feeding on the faults of others. (TPJS, 241)[79]

FLEXIBILITY

The things of God are of deep import; and time, and experience, and careful and ponderous and solemn thoughts can only find them out. Thy mind, O man! If thou will lead a soul unto salvation, must stretch as high as the utmost heavens, and search into and contemplate the darkest abyss and the broad expanse of eternity. (TPJS, 137)[47]

• • •

[If Jesus] comes to a little child, He will adapt himself to the language and capacity of a little child. (TPJS, 162)[49]

• • •

Be faithful, let your love and moderation be known unto all men; be patient, be mindful to observe all the commandments of your heavenly Father, and the God of all grace shall bless you. Even so. Amen. (TPJS, 187)[59]

•••

It mattereth not whether we live long or short on the earth after we come to a knowledge of [Gospel] principles and obey them unto the end. (TPJS, 199)[68]

•••

As females possess refined feelings and sensitiveness, they are also subject to overmuch zeal, which must ever prove dangerous, and cause them to be rigid in a religious capacity—[they] should be armed with mercy, notwithstanding the iniquity among us. (TPJS, 238)[78]

•••

We must be merciful to one another, and overlook small things. (TPJS, 240)[79]

•••

That which is wrong under one circumstance, may be, and often is, right under another.

God said, "Thou shalt not kill"; at another time He said, "Thou shalt utterly destroy." (TPJS, 256)[83]

•••

Whatever God requires is right, no matter what it is, although we may not see the reason thereof till long after the events transpire. So with Solomon: first he asked wisdom, and God gave it him, and with it every desire of his heart, even things which might be considered abominable to all who understand the order of heaven only in part, but which in reality were right because God gave and sanctioned by special revelation. (TPJS, 256)[83]

•••

The Lord deals with this people as a tender parent with a child, communicating light and intelligence and the knowledge of His ways as they can bear it. (TPJS, 305)[109]

•••

The Saints need not think because I am familiar with them and am playful and cheerful, that I am ignorant of what is going on. (TPJS, 307)[111]

•••

Never exact of a friend in adversity what you would require in prosperity. (TPJS, 317)[116]

FORCE

Did I ever exercise any compulsion over any man? Did I not give him the liberty of disbelieving any doctrine I have preached, if he saw fit? (TPJS, 341)[129]

FOREORDINATION

Every man who has a calling to minister to the inhabitants of the world was ordained to that very purpose in the Grand Council of heaven before this world was. I suppose I was ordained to this very office in that Grand Council. (TPJS, 365)[132]

FORGIVENESS

(*See also* MERCY)

The time has at last arrived when the God of Abraham, of Isaac, and of Jacob, has set his hand again the second time to recover the remnants of his people. . . . Their unbelief has not rendered the promise of God of none effect for there was another day limited . . . which was the day of His power; and then His people, Israel, should be a willing people;—and He would write His law in their hearts, and print it in their thoughts; their sins and their iniquities He would remember no more. (TPJS, 14)[9]

•••

Meekly persuade and urge every one to forgive one another all their trespasses, offenses and sins, that they may work out their own salvation with fear and trembling. (TPJS, 77)[29]

◆◆◆

Ever keep in exercise the principle of mercy, and be ready to forgive our brother on the first intimation of repentance, and asking forgiveness; and should we ever forgive our brother, or even our enemy, before he repent or ask forgiveness, our heavenly Father would be equally as merciful unto us. (TPJS, 155)[49]

◆◆◆

Inasmuch as long-suffering, patience, and mercy have ever characterized the dealings of our heavenly Father towards the humble and penitent, I feel disposed to copy the example, cherish the same principles, and by so doing being a savior of my fellow men. (TPJS, 165)[53]

◆◆◆

Believing your confession to be real, and your repentance genuine, I shall be happy once again to give you the right hand of fellowship, and rejoice over the returning prodigal, "Come on, dear brother, since the war is past, For friends at first, are friends again at last." (TPJS, 166)[53]

◆◆◆

There is never a time when the spirit is too old to approach God. All are within the reach of pardoning mercy, who have not committed the unpardonable sin, which hath no forgiveness. (TPJS, 191)[63]

◆◆◆

There are sins which may be forgiven in the world to come, although the sin of blasphemy [against the Holy Ghost] cannot be forgiven. (TPJS, 219)[74]

◆◆◆

The object is to make those not so good reform and return to the path of virtue— chasten and reprove, and keep it all in silence, not even mention them again; then you will be established in power, virtue, and holiness, and the wrath of God will be turned away. (TPJS, 238)[78]

◆◆◆

[Joseph said] it was a melancholy thought and awful that so many should place themselves under the condemnation of the devil, and going to perdition . . . they are fellow mortals, we loved them once, shall we not encourage them to reformation? We have not yet forgiven them seventy times seven, as our Savior directed; perhaps we have not forgiven them once. There is now a day of salvation to such as repent and reform;—and they who repent not should be cast out from this society; yet we should woo them to return to God, lest they escape not the damnation of hell! Where there is a mountain top there is also a valley—we should act in all things on a proper medium to every immortal spirit. Notwithstanding the unworthy are among us, the virtuous should not, from self-importance, grieve and oppress needlessly, those unfortunate ones—even these should be encouraged to hereafter live to be honored by this society. (TPJS, 238)[78]

◆◆◆

God does not look on sin with allowance, but when men have sinned, there must be allowance made for them. (TPJS, 240)[79]

◆◆◆

The unpardonable sin is to shed innocent blood, or be accessory thereto. All other sins will be visited with judgment in the flesh, and the spirit being delivered to the buffetings of Satan until the day of the Lord Jesus. (TPJS, 301)[105]

◆◆◆

Joseph remarked that all was well between him and the heavens; that he had no enmity against any one; and as the prayer of Jesus, or his pattern, so prayed

Joseph—Father, forgive me my trespasses as I forgive those who trespass against me, for I freely forgive all men. If we would secure and cultivate the love of others, we must love others, even our enemies as well as friends. (TPJS, 312)[114]

• • •

All sin, and all blasphemies, and every transgression, except one, that man can be guilty of, may be forgiven; and there is a salvation for all men, either in this world or the world to come, who have not committed the unpardonable sin, there being a provision either in this world or the world of spirits. (TPJS, 356)[130]

• • •

God hath made a provision that every spirit in the eternal world can be ferreted out and saved unless he has committed that unpardonable sin. (TPJS, 357)[130]

• • •

All sins shall be forgiven, except the sin against the Holy Ghost. (TPJS, 358)[130]

FREEDOM

There should exist the greatest freedom and familiarity among the rulers in Zion. (TPJS, 24)[13]

• • •

The Constitution of the United States is a glorious standard; it is founded in the wisdom of God. It is a heavenly banner; it is to all those who are privileged with the sweets of liberty, like the cooling shades and refreshing waters of a great rock in a thirsty and weary land. It is like a great tree under whose branches men from every climb can be shielded from the burning rays of the sun. (TPJS, 147)[47]

• • •

If it has been demonstrated that I have been willing to die for a "Mormon," I am bold to declare before Heaven that I am just as ready to die in defending the rights of a Presbyterian, a Baptist, or a good man of any other denomination; for the same principle which would trample upon the rights of the Latter-day Saints would trample upon the rights of the Roman Catholics, or of any other denomination who may be unpopular and too weak to defend themselves. (TPJS, 313)[114]

FRIENDS

"Come on, dear brother, since the war is past, For friends at first, are friends again at last." (TPJS, 166)[53]

• • •

I would esteem it one of the greatest blessings, if I am to be afflicted in this world, to have my lot cast where I can find brothers and friends all around me. (TPJS, 294)[102]

• • •

If I have no expectation of seeing my father, mother, brothers, sisters and friends again, my heart would burst in a moment, and I should go down to my grave. (TPJS, 296)[102]

• • •

I don't care what a man's character is; if he's my friend—a true friend, I will be a friend to him, and preach the Gospel of salvation to him, and give him good counsel, helping him out of his difficulties. (TPJS, 316)[115]

• • •

If my life is of no value to my friends it is of none to myself. (TPJS, 377)[136]

FRIENDSHIP

We remember your losses and sorrows [Bro. Peck]; our first ties are not broken; we participate with you in the evil as well as the good, in the sorrows as well as the joys; our union, we trust, is stronger than death, and shall never be severed. (TPJS, 79)[29]

•••

We received some letters last evening— one from Emma, one from Don C. Smith, and one from Bishop Partridge—all breathing a kind and consoling spirit. We were much gratified with their contents. We had been a long time without information; and when we read those letters they were to our souls as the gentle air is refreshing, but our joy was mingled with grief, because of the sufferings of the poor and much injured Saints. . . . The floodgates of our hearts were lifted and our eyes were a fountain of tears, but those who have not been enclosed in the walls of prison without cause of provocation, can have but little idea how sweet the voice of a friend is; one token of friendship from any source whatever awakens and calls into action every sympathetic feeling; it brings up in an instant everything that is passed; it seizes the present with the avidity of lightning; it grasps after the future with the fierceness of a tiger; it moves the mind backward and forward, from one thing to another, until finally all enmity, malice and hatred, and past differences, misunderstandings and mismanagements are slain victorious at the feet of hope; and when the heart is sufficiently contrite, then the voice of inspiration steals along and whispers. (TPJS, 134)[47]

•••

Pure friendship always becomes weakened the very moment you undertake to make it stronger by penal oaths and secrecy. (TPJS, 146)[47]

•••

What greater love hath any man than that he lay down his life for his friend; then why not fight for our friend until we die?

(TPJS, 195)[66]

•••

O that I had the language of the archangel to express my feelings once to my friends! But I never expect to in this life. When others rejoice, I rejoice; when they mourn, I mourn. (TPJS, 296)[102]

•••

Christians should cease wrangling and contending with each other, and cultivate the principles of union and friendship in their midst . . . before the millennium can be ushered in and Christ takes possession of His kingdom. (TPJS, 314)[114]

•••

It is a time-honored adage that love begets love. Let us pour forth love—show forth our kindness unto all mankind, and the Lord will reward us with everlasting increase; cast our bread upon the waters and we shall receive it after many days, increased to an hundredfold. (TPJS, 316)[115]

•••

Friendship is one of the grand fundamental principles of "Mormonism"; [it is designed] to revolutionize and civilize the world, and cause wars and contentions to cease and men to become friends and brothers. (TPJS, 316)[115]

•••

Friendship is like Brother Turley in his blacksmith shop welding iron to iron; it unites the human family with its happy influence. (TPJS, 316)[115]

•••

I love you all; but I hate some of your deeds. I am your best friend, and if persons miss their mark it is their own fault. If I reprove a man, and he hates me, he is a fool; for I love all men, especially these my brethren and sisters. (TPJS, 361)[130]

•••

If my life is of no value to my friends it is of none to myself. (TPJS, 377)[136]

FRIENDSHIPPING

The Saints ought to lay hold of every door that shall seem to be opened to them, to obtain foothold on the earth, and be making all the preparation that is within their power for the terrible storms that are now gathering in the heavens. (TPJS, 141)[47]

FRUSTRATION

Our light speeches, which may have escaped our lips from time to time . . . have nothing to do with the fixed purposes of our hearts; therefore it sufficeth us to say, that our souls were vexed from day to day. (TPJS, 124)[46]

FUNDAMENTAL PRINCIPLES

The fundamental principles of our religion are the testimonies of the Apostles and Prophets, concerning Jesus Christ, that He died, was buried, and rose again the third day, and ascended into heaven; and all other things which pertain to our religion are only appendages to it. But in connection with these, we believe in the gift of the Holy Ghost, the power of faith, the enjoyment of the spiritual gifts according to the will of God, the restoration of the house of Israel, and the final triumph of truth. (TPJS, 121)[45]

GATHERING

The time has at last arrived when the God of Abraham, of Isaac, and of Jacob, has set his hand again the second time to recover the remnants of his people. . . . Their unbelief has not rendered the promise of God of none effect for there was another day limited . . . which was the day of His power; and then His people, Israel, should be a willing people;—and He would write His law in their hearts, and print it in their thoughts; their sins and their iniquities He would remember no more. (TPJS, 14)[9]

•••

[God's] work will go on until Israel is gathered; and they who will not hear His voice, must expect to feel His wrath. (TPJS, 18)[10]

•••

All that the prophets have written, from the days of the righteous Abel, down to the last man that has left any testimony on record for our consideration, in speaking of the salvation of Israel in the last days . . . show that it consists in the work of the gathering. (TPJS, 83)[31]

•••

We should feel it our duty to influence . . . [families] to gather with the people of God. But otherwise let the responsibility rest upon the heads of parents or guardians. (TPJS, 86)[31]

•••

One of the most important points in the faith of the Church of the Latter-day Saints, through the fullness of the everlasting Gospel, is the gathering of Israel . . . that happy time . . . when every man may sit under his own vine and fig tree, and there will be none to molest or make afraid; when He will turn to them a pure language, and the earth will be filled with sacred knowledge, as the waters cover the great deep; when it shall no longer be said, the Lord lives that brought up the children of Israel out of the land of Egypt, but the Lord lives that brought up the children of Israel from the land of the north, and from all the lands whither He has driven them. That day is one, all important to all men. (TPJS, 92)[35]

•••

The Book of Mormon has made known who Israel is, upon this continent. And while we behold the government of the United States gathering the [Native Americans] and locating them upon lands to be their own, how sweet it is to think that they may one day be gathered by the Gospel. (TPJS, 93)[35]

•••

We want all honest men to have a chance to gather and build up a city of righteousness, when even upon the bells of the horses shall be written *Holiness to the Lord.* (TPJS, 93)[35]

•••

The Kingdom of Heaven is like a grain of mustard seed . . . small, but brings forth a large tree, and the fowls lodge in the branches. The fowls are the angels [which] come down, combine together [and] gather their children. . . . We cannot be made perfect without them, nor they without us. (TPJS, 159)[49]

•••

The Gospel net gathers of every kind. (TPJS, 160)[49]

•••

If there is anything calculated to interest the mind of the Saints, to awaken in them the finest sensibilities, and arouse them to enterprise and exertion, surely it the great and precious promises made by our heavenly Father to the children of Abraham; and those engaged in seeking the outcasts of Israel, and the dispersed of Judah, cannot fail to enjoy the spirit of the Lord and have the choicest blessings of heaven rest upon them in copious effusions. (TPJS, 163)[51]

•••

He who has scattered Israel has promised to gather them. (TPJS, 163)[51]

•••

It is also the concurrent testimony of all the prophets, that this gathering together of all the Saints, must take place before the Lord comes to "take vengeance upon the ungodly," and "to be glorified and admired by all those who obey the Gospel." (TPJS, 183)[58]

•••

The greatest temporal and spiritual blessings, which always come from faithfulness and concerted effort, never attended individual exertion or enterprise. (TPJS, 183)[58]

•••

There is now a day of salvation to such as repent and reform;—and they who repent not should be cast out from this society; yet we should woo them to return to God, lest they escape not the damnation of hell! (TPJS, 238)[78]

•••

The Saints have not too much time to save and redress their dead, and gather together their living relatives, that they may be saved also, before the earth will be smitten, and the consumption decreed falls upon the world. (TPJS, 330)[122]

GIFT OF THE HOLY GHOST

The Gift of the Holy Ghost by the laying on of hands, cannot be received through the medium of any other principle of righteousness, for if the proposals are not complied with, it is of no use, but withdraws. (TPJS, 148)[48]

•••

We believe in [the gift of the Holy Ghost] in all its fullness, and power, and greatness, and glory; but whilst we do this, we believe in it rationally, consistently, and scripturally, and not according to the wild vagaries, foolish notions and traditions of men. (TPJS, 243)[80]

GIFT OF TONGUES

(*See also* SPEAKING IN TONGUES)

The devil can speak in tongues; the adversary will come with his work; he can tempt all classes; can speak in English or Dutch. (TPJS, 162)[49]

•••

The gift of tongues by the power of the Holy Ghost in the Church, is for the benefit of the servants of God to preach to unbelievers, as on the day of Pentecost. (TPJS, 195)[67]

•••

If you have a matter to reveal, let it be in your own tongue; do not indulge too much in the exercise of the gift of tongues, or the devil will take advantage of the innocent and unwary. You may speak in tongues for your own comfort, but I lay this down for a rule, that if anything is taught by the gift of tongues, it is not to be received for doctrine. (TPJS, 229)[75]

•••

Be not so curious about tongues, do not speak in tongues except there be an interpreter present; the ultimate design of tongues is to speak to foreigners, and if persons are very anxious to display their intelligence, let them speak to such in their own tongues. (TPJS, 247)[80]

GIFTS

The gifts of God are all useful in their place, but when they are applied to that which God does not intend, they prove an injury, a snare and a curse instead of a blessing. (TPJS, 248)[80]

•••

Faith has been wanting, not only among the heathen, but in professed Christendom, also, so that . . . all the gifts and blessings have been wanting. (TPJS, 270)[90]

GIFTS OF THE SPIRIT

All the gifts of the Spirit are not visible to the natural vision, or understanding of men; indeed very few of them are. (TPJS, 244)[80]

•••

There are only two gifts [of the Spirit] that could be made visible—the gift of tongues and the gift of prophecy. . . . The gift of tongues is the smallest gift perhaps of the whole, and yet it is one that is most sought after.

The greatest, the best, and the most useful gifts would be known nothing about by an observer. . . . We shall finally have to come to the same conclusion that Paul did—"No man knows the things of God but by the Spirit of God." (TPJS, 246)[80]

•••

While [Paul] gazed upon the glories of the eternal world, saw an innumerable company of angels and heard the voice of God—it was in the Spirit, on the

Lord's day, unnoticed and [subsequently] unobserved by the world. (TPJS, 247)[80]

♦♦♦

[Gifts of the Spirit in the ancient days] were in the Church, but not enjoyed by all in their outward manifestations . . . for all the gifts of the Spirit are not visible to the natural vision, or understanding of men; indeed very few of them are. (TPJS, 244)[80]

GLORY

He who has scattered Israel has promised to gather them; therefore inasmuch as you are to be instrumental in this great work, He will endow you with power, might, wisdom and intelligence, and every qualification necessary; while your minds will expand wider and wider, until you can circumscribe the earth and the heavens, reach forth into eternity, and contemplate the mighty acts of Jehovah in all their variety and glory. (TPJS, 163)[51]

♦♦♦

I could explain a hundred fold more than I ever have of the glories of the kingdoms manifested to me in the vision, were I permitted, and were the people prepared to receive them. (TPJS, 305)[109]

♦♦♦

In order to receive your children to yourselves you must have a promise—some ordinance; some blessing, in order to ascend above principalities, or else it may be an angel. They must rise just as they died; we can there hail our lovely infants with the same glory—the same loveliness in the celestial glory, where they all enjoy alike. They differ in stature, in size, the same glorious spirit gives them the likeness of glory in bloom and beauty. The old man with his silvery hairs will glory in bloom and beauty. No man can describe it to you—no man can write it. (TPJS, 368)[132]

GLORY OF GOD

But they shall be heirs of God and joint heirs with Jesus Christ. What is it? To inherit the same power, the same glory and the same exaltation, until you arrive at the station of a God, and ascend the throne of eternal power, the same as those who have gone before. What did Jesus do? Why, I do the things I saw my Father do when worlds came rolling into existence. My Father worked out his kingdom with fear and trembling, and I must do the same; and when I get my kingdom, I shall present it to my Father, so that he may obtain kingdom upon kingdom, and it will exalt him in glory. He will then take a higher exaltation, and I will take his place, and thereby become exalted myself. So that Jesus treads in the tracks of his Father, and inherits what God did before; and God is thus glorified and exalted in the salvation and exaltation of all his children. (TPJS, 347)[130]

GOD

[God] . . . passes over no man's sins, but visits them with correction, and if His children will not repent of their sins He will discard them. (TPJS, 189)[60]

♦♦♦

In knowledge there is power. God has more power than all other beings, because he has knowledge; and hence he knows how to subject all other beings to Him. He has power over all. (TPJS, 288)[101]

♦♦♦

The Lord deals with this people as a tender parent with a child, communicating light and intelligence and the knowledge of His ways as they can bear it. (TPJS, 305)[109]

♦♦♦

As the Father hath power in Himself, so hath the Son power in Himself, to lay down His life and take it again, so He has a body of His own. The Son doeth what He hath seen the Father do; then the Father hath some day laid down His life and taken it again; so He has a body of His own; each one will be in His own body. (TPJS, 312)[113]

•••

Now, what I am after is the knowledge of God, and I take my own course to obtain it. (TPJS, 337)[128]

•••

There are but a very few beings in the world who understand rightly the character of God. The great majority of mankind do not comprehend anything, either that which is past, or that which is to come, as it respects their relationship to God. . . . and consequently they know but little above the brute beast, or more than to eat, drink and sleep. . . . unless it is given by the inspiration of the Almighty. (TPJS, 343)[130]

•••

If men do not comprehend the character of God, they do not comprehend themselves. (TPJS, 343)[130]

•••

My first object is to find out the character of the only wise and true God, and what kind of being he is. (TPJS, 344)[130]

•••

I am going to enquire after God; for I want you all to know him, and to be familiar with him. . . . You will then know that I am his servant; for I speak as one having authority. (TPJS, 345)[130]

•••

God himself was once as we are now, and is an exalted man, and sits enthroned in yonder heavens! That is the great secret. If the veil were rent today, and the great God who holds this world in its orbit, and who upholds all worlds and all things by his power, was to make himself visible,—I say, if you were to see him today, you would see him like a man in form—like yourselves in all the person, image, and very form as a man; for Adam was created in the very fashion, image and likeness of God, and received instruction from, and walked, talked and conversed with him, as one man talks and communes with another. (TPJS, 345)[130]

•••

I am going to tell you how God came to be God. We have imagined and supposed that God was God from all eternity. I will refute that idea, and take away the veil, so that you may see.

These are incomprehensible ideas to some, but they are simple. *It is the first principle of the Gospel to know for a certainty the Character of God, and to know that we may converse with him as one man converses with another, and that he was once a man like us; yea, that God himself, the Father of us all, dwelt on an earth, the same as Jesus Christ himself did; and I will show it from the Bible.*

I wish . . . that I had the trump of an archangel, so that I could tell the story in such a manner that persecution would cease for ever. The scriptures inform us that Jesus said, "As the Father hath power in Himself, even so hath the Son power . . . to lay down His body and take it up again." The Scriptures say it, and I defy all the learning and wisdom and all the combined powers of earth and hell together to refute it. (TPJS, 345)[130]

•••

But they shall be heirs of God and joint heirs with Jesus Christ. What is it? To inherit the same power, the same glory and the same exaltation, until you arrive at the station of a God, and ascend the throne of eternal power, the same as those who have gone before. What did Jesus do? Why, I do the things I saw my Father do when worlds came rolling into existence. My Father worked out his kingdom with fear and trembling, and I must do the same; and when I get my kingdom, I shall present it to my Father, so that he may obtain kingdom upon kingdom, and it will exalt him in glory. He will then take a higher exaltation, and I will take his place, and thereby become exalted myself. So that Jesus treads in the tracks of his Father, and inherits what God did before; and God is thus glorified and exalted in the salvation and exaltation of all his children. (TPJS, 347)[130]

♦♦♦

[Learning of the council in heaven] . . . we begin to learn the only true God, and what kind of a being we have got to worship. Having a knowledge of God, we begin to know how to approach him, and how to ask so as to receive an answer. When we understand the character of God, and know how to come to him, he begins to unfold the heavens to us, and to tell us all about it. When we are ready to come to him, he is ready to come to us. (TPJS, 350)[130]

♦♦♦

I say there are Gods many and Lords many, but to us only one, and we are to be in subjection to that one. (TPJS, 371)[133]

GODHEAD

Everlasting covenant was made between three personages before organization of this earth; these personages, according to Abraham's record, are called God the first, the Creator; God the second, the Redeemer; and God the third, the witness or Testator. (TPJS, 190)[61]

♦♦♦

I have always declared God to be a distinct personage, Jesus Christ a separate and distinct personage from God the Father, and that the Holy Ghost was a distinct personage and a Spirit; and these three constitute three distinct personages and three Gods. If this is in accordance with the New Testament, lo and behold! We have three Gods anyhow, and they are plural; and who can contradict it? . . . The doctrine of a plurality of Gods is as prominent in the Bible as any other doctrine. It is all over the face of the Bible. It stands beyond the power of controversy. A wayfaring man, though a fool, need not err therein.

Paul says there are Gods many and Lords many. I want to set forth in a plain and simple manner; but to us there is but one God—that is pertaining to us; and he is in all and through all. But if Joseph Smith says there are Gods many and Lords many, they cry, "Away with him! Crucify him! Crucify him!" (TPJS, 370)[133]

GODLINESS

(*See also* PERFECTION)

[To the] first principles of the Gospel of Christ: . . . Add to your faith, virtue; and to virtue, knowledge; and to knowledge, temperance; and to temperance, patience; and to patience, godliness; and to godliness, brotherly kindness; and to brotherly kindness, charity [or love]; for if these things be in you, and abound, they make you that ye shall neither be barren nor unfruitful, in the knowledge of our Lord Jesus Christ. (TPJS, 16)[9]

♦♦♦

We know not what we shall be called to pass through before Zion is delivered and established; therefore, we have great need to live near to God, and always be in strict obedience to all His commandments, that we may have a conscience void of offense toward God and man. (TPJS, 32)[18]

◆◆◆

God has created man with a mind capable of instruction, and a faculty which may be enlarged in proportion to the heed and diligence given to the light communicated from heaven to the intellect; and that the nearer man approaches perfection, the clearer are his views, and the greater his enjoyments, till he has overcome the evils of his life and lost every desire for sin; and like the ancients, arrives at that point of faith where he is wrapped in the power and glory of his Maker and is caught up to dwell with Him. (TPJS, 51)[21]

◆◆◆

God ere long, will call all his servants before Him, and there from His own hand they will receive a just recompense and a righteous reward for all their labors. (TPJS, 57)[21]

◆◆◆

If the Saints are not to reign, for what purpose are they crowned? . . . By His servant John [the Lord said] . . . "Behold, I come quickly: hold that fast which thou hast, that no man take thy crown." And again, "To him that overcometh will I grant to sit with Me in My throne, even as I also overcame, and am set down with My Father in His throne. (TPJS, 64)[21]

◆◆◆

It is a duty which every Saint ought to render to his brethren freely—to always love them, and ever succor them. To be justified before God we must love one another; we must overcome evil; we must visit the fatherless and the widow in their affliction, and we must keep ourselves unspotted from the world; for such virtues flow from the great fountain of pure religion, strengthening our faith by adding every good quality that adorns the children of the blessed Jesus, we can pray in the season of prayer; we can love our neighbor as ourselves, and be faithful in tribulation, knowing that the reward of such is greater in the kingdom of heaven. What a consolation! What a joy! Let me live the life of the righteous, and let my reward be like his! (TPJS, 76)[29]

◆◆◆

Let honesty, and sobriety, and candor, and solemnity, and virtue, and pureness, and meekness, and simplicity crown our heads in every place; and in fine, become as little children, without malice, guile or hypocrisy. (TPJS, 137)[47]

◆◆◆

There is a love from God that should be exercised toward those of our faith, who walk uprightly, which is peculiar to itself; but it is without prejudice; it also gives scope to the mind, which enables us to conduct ourselves with greater liberality towards all that are not of our faith, than what they exercise towards one another. These principles approximate nearer to the mind of God, because it is like God, or Godlike. (TPJS, 147)[47]

◆◆◆

Inasmuch as long-suffering, patience, and mercy have ever characterized the dealings of our heavenly Father towards the humble and penitent, I feel disposed to copy the example, cherish the same principles, and by so doing being a savior of my fellow men. (TPJS, 165)[53]

◆◆◆

Love is one of the chief characteristics of Deity, and ought to be manifested by those who aspire to be the sons of God. (TPJS, 174)[54]

◆◆◆

Be on the alert to concentrate our energies, . . . the best feelings should exist in our midst; and then, by the help of the Almighty, we shall go on from victory to victory, and from conquest to conquest; our evil passions will be subdued, our prejudices depart; we shall find no room in our bosoms for hatred; vice will hide its deformed head, and we shall stand approved in the sight of Heaven, and be acknowledged the sons of God. (TPJS, 179)[54]

• • •

Be faithful, let your love and moderation be known unto all men; be patient, be mindful to observe all the commandments of your heavenly Father, and the God of all grace shall bless you. Even so. Amen. (TPJS, 187)[59]

• • •

I told the brethren that the Book of Mormon was the most correct of any book on earth, and the keystone of our religion, and a man would get nearer to God by abiding by its precepts, than by any other book. (TPJS, 194)[65]

• • •

If we keep the commandments of God, we should bring forth fruit and be the friends of God, and know what the Lord did. (TPJS, 194)[66]

• • •

The Saints should be a select people, separate from all the evils of the world—choice, virtuous, and holy. (TPJS, 202)[70]

• • •

Search your hearts, and see if you are like God. I have searched mine, and feel to repent of all my sins. (TPJS, 216)[73]

• • •

If you wish to go where God is, you must be like God, or possess the principles which God possesses; for if we are not drawing towards God in principle, we are going from Him and drawing towards the devil. (TPJS, 216)[73]

• • •

Is not God good? Then you be good; if He is faithful, then you be faithful. Add to your faith virtue, to virtue knowledge, and seek for every good thing. (TPJS, 217)[73]

• • •

As well might the devil seek to dethrone Jehovah, as overthrow an innocent soul that resists everything which is evil. (TPJS, 226)[75]

• • •

If you live up to your privileges, the angels cannot be restrained from being your associates. (TPJS, 226)[75]

• • •

If we would come before God, we must keep ourselves pure, as He is pure. (TPJS, 227)[75]

• • •

The nearer we get to our heavenly Father, the more we are disposed to look with compassion on perishing souls; we feel that we want to take them upon our shoulders, and cast their sins behind our backs . . . if you would have God have mercy on you, have mercy on one another. (TPJS, 241)[79]

• • •

Be virtuous and pure; be men of integrity and truth; keep the commandments of God; and then you will be able more perfectly to understand the difference between right and wrong—between the things of God and the things of men; and your path will be like that of the just, which shineth brighter and brighter unto the perfect day. (TPJS, 247)[80]

•••

Here, then, is eternal life—to know the only wise and true God; and you have got to learn how to be Gods yourselves, and to be kings and priests to God, the same as all Gods have done before you, namely, by going from one small degree to another, and from a small capacity to a great one; from grace to grace, from exaltation to exaltation, until you attain to the resurrection of the dead, and are able to dwell in everlasting burnings, and to sit in glory, as do those who sit enthroned in everlasting power. And I want you to know that God, in the last days, while certain individuals are proclaiming his name, is not trifling with you or me. [Elder B.H. Roberts writes in a footnote, "The argument here made by the Prophet is very much strengthened by the following passage: "The Son can do nothing of himself, but what he seeth the Father do; for what things soever he doeth, these also doeth the Son likewise" St. John 5:19. Elder Roberts further wrote, "Whatever happened to (Christ) . . . whether within our individual reach or not, is assuredly within reach of humanity. That is what he urged again and again, "Be born again." "Be ye perfect." "Ye are the sons of God." "My Father and your Father, my God and your God."] (TPJS, 346)[130]

•••

I advise all to go on to perfection, and search deeper and deeper into the mysteries of Godliness. (TPJS, 364)[132]

GOD'S BASIC REQUIREMENTS

I will proceed to tell you what the Lord requires of all people, high and low, rich and poor, male and female, ministers and people, professors of religion and non-professors, in order that they may enjoy the Holy Spirit of God to a fullness, and escape the judgments of God, which are almost ready to burst upon the nations of the earth. Repent of all your sins, and be baptized in water for the remission of them, in the name of the Father, and of the Son, and of the Holy Ghost, and receive the ordinance of the laying on of the hands of him who is ordained and sealed unto this power, that ye may receive the Holy Spirit of God; and this is according to the Holy Scriptures, and the Book of Mormon; and the only way that man can enter into the celestial kingdom. (TPJS, 16)[9]

GOD'S GOVERNMENT

The Almighty is a lover of order and good government. (TPJS, 187)[59]

•••

The government of the Almighty [whether religious or over nations] has always been very dissimilar to the government of men. . . . The government of God has always tended to promote peace, unity, harmony, strength, and happiness; while that of man has been productive of confusion, disorder, weakness, and misery. (TPJS, 248)[81]

•••

The designs of God, [in contrast to the governments of man] have been to promote the universal good of the . . . world; to establish peace and good will among men; to promote the principles of eternal truth; to bring about a state of things that shall unite man to his fellow man; cause the world to "beat their swords into plowshares, and their spears into pruning hooks," [and to] make the nations of the earth dwell in peace. (TPJS, 248)[81]

•••

It has been the design of Jehovah, from the commencement of the world, and is His purpose now, to regulate the affairs of the world in His own hand. When that is done, judgment will be administered in righteousness; anarchy and confusion will be destroyed, and "nations will learn war no more." It is for want of this great governing principle, that all this confusion has existed; "for it is not in man that walketh, to direct his steps"; this we have fully shown. (TPJS, 250)[81]

♦♦♦

Wisdom to govern the house of Israel was given to Solomon, and the judges of Israel; and if he had always been their king, and they subject to his mandate, and obedient to his laws, they would still have been a great and mighty people-—the rulers of the universe, and the wonder of the world. (TPJS, 251)[81]

♦♦♦

[Several ancient governments were set up by God.] If, then, God puts up one, and sets down another at His pleasure, and made instruments of kings, unknown to themselves, to fulfill His prophecies, how much more was He able, if man would have been subject to His mandate, to regulate the affairs of this world, and promote peace and happiness among the human family. (TPJS, 251)[81]

♦♦♦

The world has had a fair trial for six thousand years; the Lord will try the seventh thousand Himself; "He whose right it is, will possess the kingdom, and reign until He has put all things under His feet"; iniquity will hide its hoary head, Satan will be bound, and the works of darkness destroyed; righteousness will be put to the line, and judgment to the plummet, and "he that fears the Lord will alone be exalted in that day." (TPJS, 252)[81]

♦♦♦

When the children of Israel were chosen with Moses at their head. . . . Their motto was: "The Lord is our lawgiver; the Lord is our Judge; the Lord is our King; and He shall reign over us." While in this state they might truly say, "Happy is that people, whose God is the Lord." (TPJS, 252)[81]

♦♦♦

Moses received the word of the Lord from God Himself; he was the mouth of God to Aaron, and Aaron taught the people, in both civil and ecclesiastical affairs; they were both one, there was no distinction; so will it be when the purposes of God shall be accomplished: when "the Lord shall be King over the whole earth" and "Jerusalem His throne." "The law shall go forth from Zion, and the word of the Lord from Jerusalem." (TPJS, 252)[81]

♦♦♦

As God governed Abraham, Isaac and Jacob as families, and the children of Israel as a nation; so we, as a Church, must be under His guidance if we are prospered, preserved and sustained. Our only confidence can be in God; our only wisdom obtained from Him; and He alone must be our protector and safeguard, spiritually and temporally, or we fall. (TPJS, 253)[81]

GOD'S HELP

The inhabitants of the [American] continent anciently were so constituted, and were so determined and persevering, either in righteousness or wickedness, that God visited them, immediately either with great judgments or blessings. But the present generation, if they were going to battle, if they got any assistance from God, they would have to obtain it by faith. (TPJS, 299)[103]

GOD'S JUDGMENT

[Jehovah] . . . holds the reins of judgment in His hands; He is a wise Lawgiver, and will judge all men, not according to the narrow, contracted notions of men, but, "according to the deeds done in the body whether they be good or evil," or whether these deeds were done in England, America, Spain, Turkey, or India. He will judge them, "not according to what they have not, but according to what they have," those who have lived without law, will be judged without law, and those who have a law, will be judged by the law. We need not doubt the wisdom and intelligence of the Great Jehovah; He will award judgment or mercy to all nations according to their several deserts, their means of obtaining intelligence, the laws by which they are governed, the facilities afforded them of obtaining correct information, and His inscrutable designs in relation to the human family; and when the designs of God shall be made manifest, and the curtain of futurity be withdrawn, we shall all of us have to confess that the Judge of all the earth has done right. (TPJS, 218)[74]

GOD'S LAW

(*See also* LAW OF HEAVEN)

All well established and properly organized governments have certain fixed and prominent laws for the regulation and management of the same. If man has grown to wisdom and is capable of discerning the propriety of laws to govern nations, what less can be expected from the Ruler and Upholder of the universe? Can we suppose that He has a kingdom without laws? Or do we believe that it is composed of an innumerable company of beings who are entirely beyond all law? . . . Would it not be asserting that man had found out a secret beyond Deity? That he had learned that it was good to have laws, while God after existing from eternity and having power to create man, had not found out that it was proper to have laws for His

government? . . . We admit that God is the great source and fountain from whence proceeds all good; . . . and if man is benefited by law, then certainly, law is good; and if law is good, then law, or the principle of it emanated from God; for God is the source of all good; consequently, then, He was the first Author of law, or the principle of it, to mankind. (TPJS, 55)[21]

◆◆◆

For a moment reflect: what could have been the purpose of our Father in giving to us a law? Was it that it might be obeyed, or disobeyed? And think further . . . of the importance of attending to His laws in every particular. (TPJS, 56)[21]

◆◆◆

That which is wrong under one circumstance, may be, and often is right under another. God said, "Thou shalt not kill": at another time He said, "Thou shalt utterly destroy." This is the principle on which the government of heaven is conducted—by revelation adapted to the circumstances in which the children of the kingdom are placed. (TPJS, 256)[83]

◆◆◆

Whatever God requires is right, no matter what it is, although we may not see the reason thereof till long after the events transpire. (TPJS, 256)[83]

◆◆◆

So with Solomon: first he asked wisdom, and God gave it him, and with it every desire of his heart, even things which might be considered abominable to all who understand the order of heaven only in part, but which in reality were right because God gave and sanctioned by special revelation. (TPJS, 256)[83]

◆◆◆

All the ordinances, systems and administrations on the earth are of no use to the children of men, unless they are ordained and authorized of God, for nothing will save a man but a legal administrator; for none others will be acknowledged either by God or angels. (TPJS, 274)[91]

◆ ◆ ◆

We have no claim in our eternal compact, in relation to eternal things, unless our actions and contracts and all things tend to this. (TPJS, 306)[109]

◆ ◆ ◆

Those holding the fullness of the Melchizedek Priesthood are kings and priests of the Most High God, holding the keys of power and blessings. In fact, that Priesthood is a perfect law of theocracy, and stands as God to give law unto the people, administering endless lives to the sons and daughters of Adam. (TPJS, 322)[119]

◆ ◆ ◆

The organization of the spiritual and heavenly worlds, and of spiritual and heavenly beings, was agreeable to the most perfect order and harmony: their limits and bounds were fixed irrevocably, and voluntarily subscribed to in their heavenly estate by themselves, and were by our first parents subscribed to upon the earth. Hence the importance of embracing and subscribing to principles of eternal truth by all men upon the earth that expect eternal life. (TPJS, 325)[121]

GOD'S LOVE

May God grant that notwithstanding your great afflictions and sufferings, there may not anything separate us from the love of Christ. (TPJS, 35)[19]

◆ ◆ ◆

Some people say I am a fallen Prophet, because I do not bring forth more of the word of the Lord. Why do I not do it? Are we able to receive it? No! Not one in this room. [Joseph] then chastened the congregation for their wickedness and unbelief, "for whom the Lord loveth he chasteneth, and scourgeth every son and daughter whom he receiveth," and if we do not receive chastisements then we are bastards and not sons. (TPJS, 194)[66]

◆ ◆ ◆

The Great Parent of the universe looks upon the whole of the human family with a fatherly care and a paternal regard; He views them as his offspring, and without any of those contracted feelings that influence the children of men, causes "His sun to rise of the evil and on the good, and sendeth rain on the just and on the unjust." (TPJS, 218)[74]

◆ ◆ ◆

[The Lord] knows the situation of both the living and the dead, and has made ample provision for their redemption, according to their several circumstances, and the laws of the kingdom of God, whether in this world, or in the world to come. (TPJS, 220)[74]

GOD'S OMNIPOTENCE

This is the only thing that can bring about the "restitution of all things spoken of by all the holy Prophets since the world was"—"the dispensation of the fullness of times, when God shall gather together all things in one." Other attempts to promote universal peace and happiness in the human family have proved abortive; every effort has failed; every plan and design has fallen to the ground; it needs the wisdom of God, the intelligence of God, and the power of God to accomplish this. (TPJS, 252)[81]

GOD'S OMNISCIENCE

[The Lord] knows the situation of both the living and the dead, and has made ample provision for their redemption, according to their several circumstances, and the laws of the kingdom of God, whether in this world, or in the world to come. (TPJS, 220)[74]

◆◆◆

The Great Jehovah contemplated the whole of the events connected with the earth, pertaining to the Plan of Salvation, before it rolled into existence, or ever, "the morning stars sang together" for joy; the past, the present, and the future were and are, with Him, one eternal "now". (TPJS, 220)[74]

◆◆◆

[The Lord] knew of the fall of Adam, the iniquities of the Antediluvians, of the depth of iniquity that would be connected with the human family, their weakness and strength, their power and glory, apostasies, their crimes, their righteousness and iniquity; He comprehended the fall of man, and his redemption; He knew the Plan of Salvation and pointed it out; He was acquainted with the situation of all nations and with their destiny; He ordered all things according to the council of His will; He knows the situation of both the living and the dead, and has made ample provision for their redemption, according to their several circumstances, and the laws of the kingdom of God, whether in this world, or in the world to come. (TPJS, 220)[74]

◆◆◆

You cannot go anywhere but where God can find you out. (TPJS, 367)[132]

GOD'S PHYSICAL NATURE

"That which is without body, parts and passions is nothing. There is no other God in heaven but that God who has flesh and bones. (TPJS, 181)[56]

GOD'S RESPECT FOR MAN

God has respect to the feelings of His Saints, and He will not suffer them to be tantalized with impunity. (TPJS, 19)[10]

GOD'S REWARDS

God has in reserve a time, or period appointed in His own bosom, when He will bring all His subjects, who have obeyed His voice and kept His commandments, into His celestial rest. (TPJS, 54)[21]

GOD'S THOUGHTS

How much more dignified and noble are the thoughts of God, than the vain imaginations of the human heart! (TPJS, 137)[47]

GOOD

If there was anything great or good in the world, it came from God. The construction of the first vessel was given to Noah by revelation. The design of the ark was given by God, "a pattern of heavenly things." The learning of the Egyptians, and their knowledge of astronomy was no doubt taught them by Abraham and Joseph, as their records testify, who received it from the Lord. The art of working in brass, silver, gold, and precious stones, was taught by revelation, in the wilderness. The architectural designs of the Temple at Jerusalem, together with its ornaments and beauty, were given of God. Wisdom to govern the house of Israel was given to Solomon, and the judges of Israel; and if he had always been their king, and they subject to his mandate, and obedient to his laws, they would still have been a great and mighty people—the rulers of the universe, and the wonder of the world. (TPJS, 251)[81]

•••

If we seek first the kingdom of God, all good things will be added. (TPJS, 256)[83]

•••

Our heavenly Father is more liberal in His views, and boundless in His mercies and blessings, than we are ready to believe or receive; and, at the same time, is more terrible to the workers of iniquity, more awful in the executions of His punishments, and more ready to detect every false way, than we are apt to suppose Him to be, " . . . No good thing will I withhold from them who walk uprightly before me, and do my will in all things—who will listen to my voice and to the voice of my servant, whom I have sent; for I delight in those who seek diligently to know my precepts, and abide by the law of my kingdom; for all things shall be made known unto them in mine own due time, and in the end they shall have joy." (TPJS, 257)[83]

•••

When I do the best I can—when I am accomplishing the greatest good, then the most evil and wicked surmisings are got up against me. (TPJS, 259)[84]

•••

I thank God for preserving me from my enemies; I have no enemies but for the truth's sake. I have no desire but to do all men good. I feel to pray for all men. (TPJS, 275)[91]

•••

Every honest man who has visited the city of Nauvoo since it existed, can bear record of better things, and place me in the front ranks of those who are known to do good for the sake of goodness, and

show all liars, hypocrites and abominable creatures that, while vice sinks them down to darkness and woe, virtue exalts me and the Saints to light and immortality. (TPJS, 280)[96]

•••

It will not be beyond the common use of terms, to say that good is among the most important [words] in use, and though known by various names in different languages, still its meaning is the same, and is ever in opposition to "bad." (TPJS, 300)[104]

•••

There have been many good men on the earth since the days of Adam; but there was one good man and his name was Jesus. (TPJS, 303)[109]

•••

Sectarian priests cry out concerning me, and ask, "Why is it this babbler gains so many followers, and retains them?" I answer, It is because I possess the principle of love. All I can offer the world is a good heart and a good hand. (TPJS, 313)[113]

•••

We should gather all the good and true principles in the world and treasure them up, or we shall not come out true "Mormons." (TPJS, 316)[115]

•••

Concerning [the death of] Brother James Adams, it should appear strange that so good and so great a man was hated. . . . But so it was. Whenever light shone, it stirred up darkness. Truth and error, good and evil cannot be reconciled. (TPJS, 325)[121]

•••

I calculate to be one of the instruments of setting up the kingdom of Daniel by the word of the Lord, and I intend to lay a foundation that will revolutionize the whole world. (TPJS, 366)[132]

GOOD WORKS

The man who willeth to do well, we should extol his virtues, and speak not of his faults behind his back. (TPJS, 31)[17]

•••

Let the Twelve and all Saints be willing to confess all their sins and not keep back a part; and let the Twelve be humble and not be exalted, and beware of pride, and not seek to excel one above another, but act for each other's good, and pray for one another, and honor our brother or make honorable mention of his name, and not backbite and devour our brother. (TPJS, 155)[49]

•••

If I lose my life in a good cause I am willing to be sacrificed on the altar of virtue, righteousness and truth, in maintaining the laws and Constitution of the United States, if need be, for the general good of man. (TPJS, 332)[124]

•••

The best men bring forth the best works. The man who tells you words of life is the man who can save you. (TPJS, 358)[130]

GOSPEL OF JESUS CHRIST

The law of heaven is presented to man, and as such guarantees to all who obey it a reward far beyond any earthly consideration. (TPJS, 50)[21]

•••

God has in reserve a time, or period appointed . . . when He will bring all his subjects, who have obeyed his voice and kept His commandments, into His celestial rest. This rest is of such perfection and glory, that man has need of a preparation before he can, according to the laws of that kingdom, enter it and enjoy its blessings. This being the fact, God has given certain laws to the human family, which, if observed, are sufficient to prepare them to inherit this rest. This, then, we conclude, was the purpose of God in giving His laws to us. (TPJS, 54)[21]

•••

Is not the Gospel the news of the redemption? (TPJS, 59)[21]

•••

The Book of Mormon has made known who Israel is, upon this continent. . . . How sweet it is to think that [Israel] may one day be gathered by the Gospel. (TPJS, 93)[35]

•••

We have reason to be truly humble before the God of our fathers, that He hath left . . . [scriptures] on record for us, so plain . . . if we will but open our eyes, and read with candor, for a moment. (TPJS, 96)[34]

•••

One of the grand fundamental principles of "Mormonism" is to receive truth, let it come from whence it may. (TPJS, 313)[114]

•••

All the testimony is that the Lord in the last days would commit the keys of the Priesthood to a witness over all people. Has the Gospel of the kingdom commenced in the last days? And will God take it from the man until He takes him Himself? (TPJS, 364)[132]

•••

So long as men are under the law of God, they have no fears. . . . When men open their lips against these truths they do not injure me, but injure themselves. (TPJS, 373)[133]

•••

Did I build on any other man's foundation? I have got all the truth which the Christian world possessed, and an independent revelation in the bargain, and God will bear me off triumphant. (TPJS, 376)[133]

GOSPEL BLESSINGS

The gospel has always been the same; the ordinances to fulfill its requirements, the same; and the officers to officiate, the same; and the signs and fruits resulting from the promises, the same: (TPJS, 264)[85]

GOSPEL DESTINY

The Lord will have a place whence His word will go forth, in these last days, in purity; for if Zion will not purify herself, so as to be approved of in all things, in His sight, He will seek another people; for His work will go on until Israel is gathered, and they who will not hear His voice, must expect to feel His wrath. Let me say unto you, seek to purify yourselves . . . lest the Lord's anger be kindled to fierceness. (TPJS, 18)[10]

GOSSIP

The man who willeth to do well, we should extol his virtues, and speak not of his faults behind his back. (TPJS, 31)[17]

•••

Rumor with her ten thousand tongues is diffusing her uncertain sounds in almost every ear; but in these times of sore trial, let the Saints be patient and see the salvation of God. (TPJS, 42)[20]

•••

False and wicked misrepresentations, . . . have caused . . . thousands to think they were doing God's service, when they were persecuting the children of God. (TPJS, 80)[30]

•••

Let the Twelve and all Saints be . . . humble and not be exalted, and beware of pride, and not seek to excel one above another, but act for each other's good, and pray for one another, and honor our brother or make honorable mention of his name, and not backbite and devour our brother. (TPJS, 155)[49]

•••

Put a double watch over the tongue; no organized body can exist without this at all. . . . The object is to make those not so good reform and return to the path of virtue—[you] should chasten and reprove, and keep it all in silence, not even mention them again; then you will be established in power, virtue, and holiness, and the wrath of God will be turned away. (TPJS, 238)[78]

•••

Search yourselves the tongue is an unruly member—hold your tongues about things of no moment—a little tale will set the world on fire. At [certain] time[s] the truth on the guilty should not be told openly. . . . We must use precaution in bringing sinners to justice, lest . . . we draw the indignation of a Gentile world upon us. (TPJS, 239)[78]

•••

We are full of selfishness; the devil flatters us that we are very righteous, when [in fact] we are feeding on the faults of others. (TPJS, 241)[79]

•••

Sisters of the [Relief] Society, shall there be strife among you? I will not have it. You must repent, and get the love of God. Away with self-righteousness! (TPJS, 241)[79]

◆◆◆

The little foxes spoil the vines—little evils do the most injury to the Church. If you have evil feelings, and speak of them to one another, it has a tendency to do mischief. (TPJS, 258)[84]

◆◆◆

If you know anything calculated to disturb the peace or injure the feelings of your brother or sister, hold your tongues and the least harm will be done. (TPJS, 259)[84]

◆◆◆

There is no salvation in believing an evil report against our neighbor. (TPJS, 364)[132]

GRATITUDE

The kindness of a man should never be forgotten. (TPJS, 31)[17]

◆◆◆

O brethren, let us be thankful that it is as well with us as it is, and we are yet alive and peradventure, God hath laid up in store great good for us in this generation, and may grant that we may yet glorify His name. (TPJS, 35)[19]

◆◆◆

Men not infrequently forget that they are dependent upon heaven for every blessing which they are permitted to enjoy, and that for every opportunity granted them they are to give an account. (TPJS, 68)[21]

◆◆◆

We received some letters last evening—one from Emma, one from Don C. Smith, and one from Bishop Partridge—all breathing a kind and consoling spirit. We were much gratified with their contents. We had been a long time without information; and when we read those letters they were to our souls as the gentle air is refreshing, but our joy was mingled with grief, because of the sufferings of the poor and much injured Saints. . . . The floodgates of our hearts were lifted and our eyes were a fountain of tears, but those who have not been enclosed in the walls of prison without cause of provocation, can have but little idea how sweet the voice of a friend is; one token of friendship from any source whatever awakens and calls into action every sympathetic feeling; it brings up in an instant everything that is passed; it seizes the present with the avidity of lightning; it grasps after the future with the fierceness of a tiger; it moves the mind backward and forward, from one thing to another, until finally all enmity, malice and hatred, and past differences, misunderstandings and mismanagements are slain victorious at the feet of hope; and when the heart is sufficiently contrite, then the voice of inspiration steals along and whispers. (TPJS, 134)[47]

◆◆◆

Hosanna, hosanna, hosanna to Almighty God, that rays of light begin to burst forth upon us even now. I cannot find words in which to express myself. I am not learned, but I have as good feelings as any man. (TPJS, 296)[102]

GREED

The Elders . . . are combating the prejudices of a crooked and perverse generation, by having in their possession . . . religious principles, which are misrepresented by almost all those whose crafts are in danger by the same. (TPJS, 83)[31]

♦♦♦

Some have been uncharitable, and have manifested greediness because of their debts towards those who have been persecuted and dragged about with chains without cause, and imprisoned. Such characters God hates—and they shall have their turn of sorrow in the rolling of the great wheel, for it rolleth and none can hinder. (TPJS, 129)[46]

♦♦♦

If there are any among you who aspire after their own aggrandizement, and seek their own opulence, while their brethren are groaning in poverty, and are under sore trials and temptations, they cannot be benefited by the intercession of the Holy Spirit. (TPJS, 141)[47]

♦♦♦

"Behold, there are many called, but few are chosen. And why are they not chosen? Because their hearts are so set upon the things of this world, and aspire to the honors of men, that they do not learn this one lesson—that the rights of the Priesthood are inseparably connected with the powers of heaven, and that the powers of heaven cannot be controlled nor handled only upon the principles of righteousness. That they may be conferred upon us, it is true; but when we undertake to cover our sins, or to gratify our pride, our vain ambition, or to exercise control, or dominion, or compulsion, upon the souls of the children of men in any degree of unrighteousness, behold, the heavens withdraw themselves, the Spirit of the Lord is grieved; and when it is withdrawn, Amen to the Priesthood, or the authority of that man. Behold! Ere he is aware, he is left to himself to kick against the pricks, to persecute the saints, and to fight against God.

"We have learned by sad experience that it is the nature and disposition of almost all men, as soon as they get a little authority, as they suppose, they will immediately begin to exercise unrighteous dominion. Hence, many are called, but few are chosen." (TPJS, 142)[47]

♦♦♦

Now, in this world, mankind are naturally selfish, ambitious and striving to excel one above another; yet some are willing to build up others as well as themselves. (TPJS, 297)[103]

♦♦♦

Never exact of a friend in adversity what you would require in prosperity. (TPJS, 317)[116]

♦♦♦

Woe to ye rich men, who refuse to give to the poor, and then come and ask me for bread. Away with all your meanness, and be liberal. We need purging, purifying and cleansing. (TPJS, 329)[122]

HABIT

If we start right, it is easy to go right all the time; but if we start wrong, we may go wrong, and it be a hard matter to get right. (TPJS, 343)[130]

•••

HAPPINESS

The great principle of happiness consists in having a body. . . . All beings who have bodies have power over those who have not. (TPJS, 181)[56]

•••

[Several ancient governments were set up by God]. If, then, God puts up one, and sets down another at His pleasure, and made instruments of kings, unknown to themselves, to fulfill His prophecies, how much more was He able, if man would have been subject to His mandate, to regulate the affairs of this world, and promote peace and happiness among the human family. (TPJS, 251)[81]

•••

When the children of Israel were chosen with Moses at their head. . . . Their motto was: "The Lord is our lawgiver; the Lord is our Judge; the Lord is our King; and He shall reign over us." While in this state they might truly say, "Happy is that people, whose God is the Lord." (TPJS, 252)[81]

•••

Happiness is the object and design of our existence; and will be the end thereof, if we pursue the path that leads to it; and this path is virtue, uprightness, faithfulness, holiness, and keeping all the commandments of God. (TPJS, 255)[83]

•••

Everything that God gives us is lawful and right; and it is proper that we should enjoy His gifts and blessings whenever and wherever He is disposed to bestow; But if we should seize upon those same blessings and enjoyments without law, without revelation, without commandment, those blessings and enjoyments would prove cursings and vexations in the end, and we should have to lie down in sorrow and wailings of everlasting regret. (TPJS, 256)[83]

•••

But in obedience there is joy and peace unspotted, unalloyed; and as God has designed our happiness—and the happiness of all His creatures, he never has—He never will institute an ordinance or give a commandment to His people that is not calculated in its nature to promote that happiness which he has designed, and which will not end in the greatest amount of good and glory to those who become the recipients of His law and ordinances. (TPJS, 256)[83]

HEALING

(*See also* LAYING ON OF HANDS)

When a man designedly provokes a serpent to bite him, the principle is the same as when a man drinks deadly poison knowing it to be such. In that case no man has any claim on the promises of God to be healed. (TPJS, 72)[25]

♦♦♦

[In response to the question: "Can the Mormons raise the dead?"] Joseph responded: No, nor can any other people that now lives, or ever did live. But God can raise the dead, through man as an instrument. (TPJS, 120)[45]

♦♦♦

After having suffered so great sacrifice and having passed through so great a season of sorrow, we trust that a ram may be caught in the thicket speedily, to relieve the sons and daughters of Abraham from their great anxiety, and to light up the lamp of salvation upon their countenances, that they may hold on now, after having gone so far unto everlasting life. (TPJS, 136)[47]

♦♦♦

What is the sign of the healing of the sick? The laying on of hands is the sign or way marked out by James, and the custom of the ancient Saints as ordered by the Lord, and we cannot obtain the blessings by pursuing any other course except the way marked out by the Lord. (TPJS, 198)[68]

♦♦♦

No matter who believeth, these signs, such as healing the sick, casting out devils, etc., should follow all that believe, whether male or female. (TPJS, 224)[75]

♦♦♦

If God gave His sanction by healing . . . there could be no more sin in any female laying hands on and praying for the sick, than in wetting the face with water; it is no sin for anybody to administer that has faith, or if the sick have faith to be healed by their administration. (TPJS, 225)[75]

♦♦♦

[Joseph said that] it was according to revelation that the sick should be nursed

with herbs and mild food, and not by the hand of an enemy. Who are better qualified to administer than our faithful and zealous sisters, whose hearts are full of faith, tenderness, sympathy and compassion. No one. (TPJS, 229)[75]

♦♦♦

Elder Jedediah M. Grant enquired of me the cause of my turning pale and losing strength last night while blessing children. I told him that I saw that Lucifer would exert his influence to destroy the children that I was blessing, and I strove with all the faith and spirit that I had to seal upon them a blessing that would secure their lives upon the earth; and so much virtue went out of me into the children, that I became weak . . . and I referred to the case of the woman touching the hem of the garment of Jesus. [Luke. 8th chapter]. The virtue here referred to is the spirit of life; and a man who exercises great faith in administering to the sick, blessing little children, or confirming, is liable to become weakened. (TPJS, 281)[97]

♦♦♦

If we would be sober and watch in fasting and prayer, God would turn away sickness from our midst. (TPJS, 326)[121]

HEALTH

I preached to . . . persuade the Saints to trust in God when sick, and not in an arm of flesh, and live by faith and not by medicine, or poison; and when they were sick, and had called for the Elders to pray for them, and they were not healed, to use herbs and mild food. (TPJS, 190)[62]

♦♦♦

[Joseph said that] it was according to revelation that the sick should be nursed with herbs and mild food, and not by the hand of an enemy. Who are better qualified to administer than our faithful and zealous sisters, whose hearts are full of faith, tenderness, sympathy and compassion. No one. (TPJS, 229)[75]

•••

If God gave His sanction by healing . . . there could be no more sin in any female laying hands on and praying for the sick, than in wetting the face with water; it is no sin for anybody to administer that has faith, or if the sick have faith to be healed by their administration. (TPJS, 225)[75]

•••

If we would be sober and watch in fasting and prayer, God would turn away sickness from our midst. (TPJS, 326)[121]

HEAVEN

If God rewarded everyone according to the deeds done in the body, the term "Heaven" as intended for the Saints' eternal home, must include more kingdoms than one. (TPJS, 10)[5]

•••

The law of heaven is presented to man, and as such guarantees to all who obey it a reward far beyond any earthly consideration; though it does not . . . exempt [one] from the afflictions and troubles arising from different sources in consequence of acts of wicked men on earth. Still in the midst of all this there is a promise predicated upon the fact that it is a law of heaven, which transcends the law of man, as far as eternal life [transcends] the temporal; and as the blessings which God is able to give, are greater than those which can be given by man. (TPJS, 50)[21]

•••

God has created man with a mind capable of instruction, and a faculty which may be enlarged in proportion to the heed and diligence given to the light communicated from heaven to the intellect; and that the nearer man approaches perfection, the clearer are his views, and the greater his enjoyments, till he has overcome the evils of his life and lost every desire for sin; and like the ancients, arrives at that point of faith where he is wrapped in the power and glory of his Maker and is caught up to dwell with Him. (TPJS, 51)[21]

•••

Men of the present time testify of heaven and hell, and have never seen either; and I will say that no man knows these things without this [testimony]. (TPJS, 160)[49]

•••

If you wish to go where God is, you must be like God, or possess the principles which God possesses; for if we are not drawing towards God in principle, we are going from Him and drawing towards the devil. (TPJS, 216)[73]

•••

Could you gaze into heaven five minutes you would know more than you would by reading all that ever was written on the subject. (TPJS, 324)[121]

•••

We have reason to have the greatest hope and consolations for our dead of any people on the earth; for we have seen them walk worthily in our midst, and seen them sink asleep in the arms of Jesus; and those who have died in the faith are now in the celestial kingdom of God. And hence is the glory of the sun. (TPJS, 359)[130]

HEAVENLY POWER

Beware, O earth, how you fight against the Saints of God and shed innocent blood; for in the days of Elijah, his enemies came upon him, and fire was called down from heaven and destroyed them. (TPJS, 340)[128]

HELL

All who will not obey His voice shall not escape the damnation of hell. What is the damnation of hell? To go with that society who have not obeyed His commands. (TPJS, 198)[68]

◆◆◆

There is no pain so awful as that of suspense. This is the punishment of the wicked; their doubt, anxiety and suspense cause weeping, wailing and gnashing of teeth. (TPJS, 288)[101]

◆◆◆

What is hell? It is [a] modern term, and is taken from hades. . . . Hades, Sheol, paradise, spirits in prison, are all one: it is a world of spirits.
The righteous and the wicked all go to the same world of spirits until the resurrection.
The great misery of departed spirits in the world of spirits, where they go after death, is to know that they come short of the glory that others enjoy and that they might have enjoyed themselves, and they are their own accusers. (TPJS, 310)[113]

◆◆◆

If I had time, I would dig into hell, Hades, Sheol, and tell what exists there. (TPJS, 311)[113]

◆◆◆

A man is his own tormenter and his own condemner. . . . The torment of disappointment in the mind of man is as exquisite as a lake burning with fire and brimstone. (TPJS, 357)[130]

◆◆◆

Those who have done wrong always have that wrong gnawing them. Immortality

dwells in everlasting burnings. (TPJS, 367)[132]

HELPFULNESS

Every man, before he makes an objection to any item that is brought before a council for consideration, should be sure that he can throw light upon the subject rather than spread darkness, and that his objection be founded in righteousness. (TPJS, 94)[36]

HIGH COUNCILS

No man is capable of judging a matter, in council, unless his own heart is pure; . . . we frequently are so filled with prejudice, or have a beam in our own eye, that we are not capable of passing right decisions. (TPJS, 69)[22]

◆◆◆

The [High] Council should try no case without both parties being present, or having had an opportunity to be present; neither should they hear one person's complaint before his case is brought up for trial; neither should they suffer the character of any one to be exposed before the High Council without the person being present and ready to defend him or herself; that the minds of the councilors be not prejudiced for or against any one whose case they may possibly have to act upon. (TPJS, 165)[52]

◆◆◆

In all our councils, especially while on trial of any one, we should see and observe all things appertaining to the subject, and discern the spirit by which either party was governed. We should be in a situation to understand every spirit and judge righteous judgment and not be asleep. We should keep order and not let the council be imposed upon by unruly conduct. (TPJS, 307)[111]

•••

Every man, before he makes an objection to any item that is brought before a council for consideration, should be sure that he can throw light upon the subject rather than spread darkness, and that his objection be founded in righteousness. (TPJS, 94)[36]

HIGH PRIESTS

The duty of a High Priest is to administer in spiritual and holy things, and to hold communion with God. (TPJS, 21)[12]

HOLY GHOST

All are to preach the Gospel, by the power and influence of the Holy Ghost; and no man can preach the Gospel without the Holy Ghost. (TPJS, 112)[41]

•••

Faith comes by hearing the word of God; that testimony is always attended by the spirit of prophesy and revelation. (TPJS, 148)[48]

•••

Any man that has the Holy Ghost, can speak of the things of God in his own tongue as well as to speak in another. (TPJS, 149)[48]

•••

There are two Comforters spoken of. One is the Holy Ghost . . . that all Saints receive after faith, repentance, and baptism. This first Comforter or the Holy Ghost has no other effect than pure intelligence. It is more powerful in expanding the mind, enlightening the understanding and storing the intellect with present knowledge. (TPJS, 149)[48]

•••

Various and conflicting are the opinions of men in regard to the gift of the Holy

Ghost. . . . It is not to be wondered at that men should be ignorant . . . of the nature . . . of the Holy Ghost, when we consider that the human family have been enveloped in gross darkness and ignorance for many centuries past, without revelation. (TPJS, 242)[80]

•••

We believe that the holy men of old spake as they were moved upon by the Holy Ghost, and that holy men in these days speak by the same principle; we believe in its being a comforter and a witness bearer, that it brings things past to our remembrance, leads us into all truth, and shows us of things to come; we believe that "no man can know that Jesus is the Christ, but by the Holy Ghost," We believe in it in all its fullness, and power, and greatness, and glory; but whilst we do this, we believe in it rationally, consistently, and scripturally, and not according to the wild vagaries, foolish notions and traditions of men. (TPJS, 243)[80]

•••

We believe in the gift of the Holy Ghost being enjoyed now, as much as it was in the Apostles' days; we believe that it is necessary . . . to organize the Priesthood, that no man can be called to fill any office in the ministry without it; we also believe in prophecy, in tongues, in visions, and in revelations, in gifts, and in healings; and that these things cannot be enjoyed without the gift of the Holy Ghost. (TPJS, 243)[80]

•••

We believe that the Holy Ghost is imparted by the laying on of hands of those in authority. (TPJS, 243)[80]

•••

The Holy Ghost is a personage, and is in the form of a personage. It does not confine itself to the form of the dove, but in sign of the dove; but the sign of a dove was given to John to signify the truth of the deed, as the dove is an emblem or token of truth and innocence. (TPJS, 276)[93]

• • •

The Holy Ghost is God's messenger to administer in all priesthoods. (TPJS, 323)[119]

• • •

No man can receive the Holy Ghost without receiving revelation. The Holy Ghost is a revelator. (TPJS, 328)[122]

• • •

I have got this old [Latin, Hebrew, German and Greek New Testament] book; but I thank [God] . . . more for the gift of the Holy Ghost. I have got the oldest book in the world; but I [also] have the oldest book in my heart, even the gift of the Holy Ghost. (TPJS, 349)[130]

• • •

I am learned, and know more than all the world put together. The Holy Ghost does, anyhow, and He is within me, and comprehends more than all the world; and I will associate myself with Him. (TPJS, 350)[130]

HONESTY

We want all honest men to have a chance to gather and build up a city of righteousness, when even upon the bells of the horses shall be written *Holiness to the Lord.* (TPJS, 93)[35]

• • •

Your humble servant or servants, intend from henceforth to [morally disapprove] everything that is not in accordance with the fullness of the Gospel of Jesus Christ, and is not of a bold, and frank, and upright nature. (TPJS, 146)[47]

• • •

Be honest, open, and frank in all your intercourse with mankind. (TPJS, 156)[49]

• • •

Let it prove as a warning to all to deal justly before God, and with all mankind, then we shall be clear in the day of judgment. (TPJS, 216)[72]

• • •

Let thy hand never fail to hand out that that thou owest while it is yet within thy grasp to do so. (TPJS, 317)[116]

• • •

I never stole the value of a pin's head, or a picayune in my life; and when you are hungry don't steal. Come to me and I will feed you. (TPJS, 329)[122]

• • •

It mattereth not whether the principle is popular or unpopular, I will always maintain a true principle, even if I stand alone in it. (TPJS, 332)[125]

• • •

I know much that I do not tell. I have had bribes offered me, but I have rejected them. (TPJS, 334)[127]

HONOR

That person who never forsaketh his trust should ever have the highest place of regard in our hearts. (TPJS, 31)[17]

• • •

Remember not to murmur at the dealings of God with His creatures. You are not as yet brought into as trying circumstances as were the ancient Prophets and Apostles . . . of whom the world was not worthy. . . . Amidst all their afflictions they rejoiced that they were counted worthy to receive persecution for Christ's sake. (TPJS, 32)[18]

◆ ◆ ◆

If they receive not your testimony in one place, flee to another, remembering to cast no reflections, nor throw out any bitter sayings. If you do your duty, it will be just as well with you, as though all men embraced the Gospel. (TPJS, 43)[20]

◆ ◆ ◆

Ignorance, superstition and bigotry . . . is oftentimes in the way of the prosperity of this Church; like the torrent rain in the mountains, that floods the most pure and crystal stream with mire, and dirt, and filthiness, and obscures everything that was clear before, and all rushes along in one general deluge; but time weathers tide; and notwithstanding we are rolled in the mire of the flood for the time being, the next surge peradventure, as time rolls on, may bring to us the fountain as clear as crystal, and as pure as snow; while the filthiness, flood-wood and rubbish is left and purged out by the way. (TPJS, 138)[47]

◆ ◆ ◆

We contemplate a people who have embraced a system of religion, unpopular, and the adherence to which has brought upon them repeated persecutions. A people who for their love of God, and attachment to His cause, have suffered hunger, nakedness, perils, and almost every privation. A people who, for the sake of their religion have had to mourn the premature death of parents, husbands, wives, and children. A people, who have preferred death to slavery and hypocrisy, and have honorably maintained their characters, and stood firm and immovable, in times that have tried men's souls. . . . Your names will be handed down to posterity as Saints of God and virtuous men. (TPJS, 185)[59]

◆ ◆ ◆

Never . . . let us hear of those who profess to be governed by the law of God,

and make their garments clean in the blood of the Lamb, shrinking from the assistance of those who bear the ark of the Lord—in the hour of danger! (TPJS, 261)[85]

◆ ◆ ◆

If I lose my life in a good cause I am willing to be sacrificed on the altar of virtue, righteousness and truth, in maintaining the laws and Constitution of the United States, if need be, for the general good of man. (TPJS, 332)[124]

◆ ◆ ◆

It mattereth not whether the principle is popular or unpopular, I will always maintain a true principle, even if I stand alone in it. (TPJS, 332)[125]

HOPE

After having suffered so great sacrifice and having passed through so great a season of sorrow, we trust that a ram may be caught in the thicket speedily, to relieve the sons and daughters of Abraham from their great anxiety, and to light up the lamp of salvation upon their countenances, that they may hold on now, after having gone so far unto everlasting life. (TPJS, 136)[47]

◆ ◆ ◆

There seems to be a whispering that the angels of heaven . . . have taken counsel together; and . . . have taken cognizance of the testimony of those who were murdered at Haun's Mills, and also those who were martyred . . . elsewhere, and have passed some decisions peradventure in favor of the Saints, and those who were called to suffer without cause. (TPJS, 141)[47]

◆ ◆ ◆

Notwithstanding their vanity, men look forward with hope to the time of their deliverance. (TPJS, 187)[60]

◆ ◆ ◆

God has revealed His Son from the heavens and the doctrine of the resurrection also; and we have a knowledge that those we bury here God will bring up again, clothed upon and quickened by the Spirit of the great God. . . . Let these truths sink down in our hearts, that we may even here begin to enjoy that which shall be in full hereafter. (TPJS, 296)[102]

•••

All your losses will be made up to you in the resurrection, provided you continue faithful. By the vision of the Almighty I have seen it. (TPJS, 296)[102]

•••

We have reason to have the greatest hope and consolations for our dead of any people on the earth; for we have seen them walk worthily in our midst, and seen them sink asleep in the arms of Jesus; and those who have died in the faith are now in the celestial kingdom of God. And hence is the glory of the sun. (TPJS, 359)[130]

•••

Those who have died in the faith are now in the celestial kingdom of God. . . . Don't mourn, don't weep. I know it by the testimony of the Holy Ghost that is within me; and you may wait for your friends to come forth to meet you in the morn of the celestial world. (TPJS, 359)[130]

•••

Your expectations and hopes are far above what man can conceive. (TPJS, 359)[130]

HUMILITY

Live in strict obedience to the commandments of God, and walk humbly before Him, and He will exalt thee in His own due time. (TPJS, 27)[15]

•••

Humble [yourselves] in a peculiar manner that God may open the eyes of [your] understanding. (TPJS, 78)[29]

•••

When the heart is sufficiently contrite, then the voice of inspiration steals along and whispers. (TPJS, 134)[47]

•••

A frank and open rebuke provoketh a good man to emulation; and in the hour of trouble he will be your best friend. But on the other hand, it will draw out all the corruptions of corrupt hearts; and lying and the poison of asps is under their tongues; and they do cause the pure in heart to be cast into prison, because they want them out of their way. (TPJS, 137)[47]

•••

We ought at all times to be very careful that . . . high-mindedness shall never have place in our hearts; but condescend to men of low estate, and with all long-suffering bear the infirmities of the weak. (TPJS, 141)[47]

•••

We believe that . . . the Saints . . . will from henceforth be always ready to obey the truth without having men's persons in admiration because of advantage. (TPJS, 146)[47]

•••

Why will not man learn wisdom by precept at this late age of the world, when we have such a cloud of witnesses and examples before us, and not be obliged to learn by sad experience everything we know. (TPJS, 155)[49]

•••

When the Twelve or any other witnesses stand before the congregation of the earth, and they preach in the power and demonstration of the Spirit of God, and the people are astonished and confounded at the doctrine, and say, "That man has preached a powerful discourse, a great sermon," then let that man or those men take care that they do not ascribe the glory unto themselves, but be careful that they are humble, and ascribe the praise and glory to God and the Lamb; for it is by the power of the Holy Priesthood and the Holy Ghost that they have power to speak. What art thou, O man, but dust? And from whom receivest thou thy power and blessings, but from God? (TPJS, 155)[49]

•••

Let the Twelve and all Saints be willing to confess all their sins and not keep back a part; and let the Twelve be humble and not be exalted, and beware of pride, and not seek to excel one above another, but act for each other's good, and pray for one another, and honor our brother or make honorable mention of his name, and not backbite and devour our brother. (TPJS, 155)[49]

•••

Let not any man publish his own righteousness, for others can see that for him; sooner let him confess his sins, and then he will be forgiven, and he will bring forth more fruit. (TPJS, 194)[66]

•••

When a corrupt man is chastened he gets angry and will not endure it. (TPJS, 195)[66]

•••

[Joseph said that] it was the folly and nonsense of the human heart for a person to be aspiring to other stations than those to which they are appointed of God for them to occupy; that it was better for individuals to magnify their respective calling, and wait patiently till God shall say to them, "come up higher." (TPJS, 223)[75]

•••

Don't be limited in your views with regard to your neighbor's virtue, but beware of self-righteousness, and be limited in the estimate of your own virtues, and not think yourself more righteous than others. (TPJS, 228)[75]

•••

I do not want you to think that I am very righteous, for I am not. God judges men according to the use they make of the light which He gives them. (TPJS, 303)[109]

•••

In relation to the power over the minds of mankind which I hold, I would say, It is in consequence of the power of truth in the doctrines which I have been an instrument in the hands of God of presenting unto them, and not because of any compulsion on my part. (TPJS, 341)[129]

HUSBANDS

Wives, submit yourselves unto your own husbands, as it is fit in the Lord. Husbands, love your wives, and be not bitter against them. (TPJS, 88)[31]

HYMNS

I entirely approve of . . . the hymn book, as a new edition, containing a greater variety of hymns . . . which I think will be a standard work. (TPJS, 164)[51]

HYPOCRISY

I love that man better who swears a stream as long as my arm, yet deals justice to his neighbors and mercifully deals his substance to the poor, than the long, smooth-faced hypocrite. (TPJS, 303)[109]

•••

Notwithstanding my weaknesses, I am under the necessity of bearing the infirmities of others, who, when they get into difficulty, hang on to me tenaciously to get them out, and wish me to cover their faults. On the other hand, the same characters, when they discover a weakness in Brother Joseph, endeavor to blast his reputation, and publish it to all the world, and thereby aid my enemies in destroying the Saints. (TPJS, 315)[114]

◆◆◆

Woe to ye rich men, who refuse to give to the poor, and then come and ask me for bread. Away with all your meanness, and be liberal. We need purging, purifying and cleansing. (TPJS, 329)[122]

IDENTITY

"If we keep the commandments of God, we should bring forth fruit and be the friends of God, and know what the Lord did." (TPJS, 194)[66]

◆◆◆

If men do not comprehend the character of God, they do not comprehend themselves. (TPJS, 343)[130]

◆◆◆

My first object is to find out the character of the only wise and true God, and what kind of being he is. (TPJS, 344)[130]

◆◆◆

I am going to enquire after God; for I want you all to know him, and to be familiar with him. . . . You will then know that I am his servant; for I speak as one having authority. (TPJS, 345)[130]

◆◆◆

[Learning of the council in heaven] . . . we begin to learn the only true God, and what kind of a being we have got to worship. Having a knowledge of God, we begin to know how to approach him, and how to ask so as to receive an answer. When we understand the character of God, and know how to come to him, he begins to unfold the heavens to us, and to tell us all about it. (TPJS, 350)[130]

◆◆◆

When we are ready to come to him, he is ready to come to us. (TPJS, 350)[130]

◆◆◆

Such is the darkness and ignorance of this generation, that they look upon it as incredible that a man should have any intercourse with his Maker. (TPJS, 89)[32]

◆◆◆

Darkness prevails at this time as it did at the time Jesus Christ was about to be crucified. The powers of darkness strove to obscure the glorious Sun of righteousness, that began to dawn upon the world, and was soon to burst in great blessings upon the heads of the faithful. (TPJS, 90)[33]

◆◆◆

Men are in the habit, when the truth is exhibited by the servants of God, of saying, All is mystery; they have spoken in parables, and therefore, are not to be understood. It is true they have eyes to see, and see not, but none are so blind as those who will not see. (TPJS, 96)[34]

•••

If the Church knew all the commandments, one-half they would condemn through prejudice and ignorance. (TPJS, 112)[41]

IGNORANCE

It was not until apostasy and rebellion against the things of God that the true knowledge of the universe as well as the knowledge of other truths, became lost among men. (TPJS, 119)[44]

•••

Ignorance, superstition and bigotry . . . is oftentimes in the way of the prosperity of this Church; like the torrent rain in the mountains, that floods the most pure and crystal stream with mire, and dirt, and filthiness, and obscures everything that was clear before, and all rushes along in one general deluge; but time weathers tide; and notwithstanding we are rolled in the mire of the flood for the time being, the next surge peradventure, as time rolls on, may bring to us the fountain as clear as crystal, and as pure as snow; while the filthiness, flood-wood and rubbish is left and purged out by the way. (TPJS, 138)[47]

•••

Unless some person or persons have a communication, or revelation from God, unfolding to them the operation of the spirit, they must eternally remain ignorant of these principles; for if one man cannot understand these things but by the Spirit of God, ten thousand men cannot; it is alike out of the reach of the wisdom of the learned, the tongue of the eloquent, [or] the power of the mighty. And we shall at last have to come to this conclusion, whatever we may think of revelation, that without it, we can neither know nor understand anything of God, or of the devil; and

however unwilling the world may be to acknowledge this principle, it is evident from the multifarious creeds . . . that they understand nothing of this principle, and it is as equally as plain that without a divine communication they must remain in ignorance. (TPJS, 205)[71]

•••

The great designs of God in relation to the salvation of the human family, are very little understood by the professedly wise and intelligent generation in which we live. (TPJS, 217)[74]

•••

The great designs of God in relation to the salvation of the human family, are very little understood by the professedly wise and intelligent generation in which we live. (TPJS, 218)[74]

•••

Various and conflicting are the opinions of men in regard to the gift of the Holy Ghost. . . . It is not to be wondered at that men should be ignorant . . . of the nature . . . of the Holy Ghost, when we consider that the human family have been enveloped in gross darkness and ignorance for many centuries past, without revelation. (TPJS, 242)[80]

•••

The earth is groaning under the corruption, oppression, tyranny and bloodshed; . . . none of the wicked shall understand; but the wise shall understand, and they that turn many to righteousness shall shine as the stars for ever and ever. (TPJS, 253)[81]

•••

Knowledge does away with darkness, suspense and doubt; for these cannot exist where knowledge is. (TPJS, 287)[101]

•••

There is no pain so awful as that of suspense. This is the punishment of the wicked; their doubt, anxiety and suspense cause weeping, wailing and gnashing of teeth. (TPJS, 288)[101]

♦♦♦

It is impossible for a man to be saved in ignorance. (TPJS, 301)[106]

♦♦♦

The inhabitants of the earth are asleep; they know not the day of their visitation. (TPJS, 305)[109]

♦♦♦

Many things are insoluble to the children of men in the last days; for instance, that God should raise the dead, and forgetting that things have been hid from before the foundation of the world, which are to be revealed to babes in the last days. (TPJS, 309)[113]

♦♦♦

There are a great many wise men and women too in our midst who are too wise to be taught; therefore they must die in their ignorance, and in the resurrection they will find their mistake. Many seal up the door of heaven by saying . . . God may reveal and I will believe. (TPJS, 309)[113]

♦♦♦

[There are] nonsensical teachings of hireling priests, whose object and aim were to keep the people in ignorance for the sake of filthy lucre; or as the prophet says, to feed themselves, not the flock. (TPJS, 315)[114]

♦♦♦

There are but a very few beings in the world who understand rightly the character of God. The great majority of mankind do not comprehend anything, either that which is past, or that which is to come, as it respects their relationship to God. . . . And consequently they know but little above the brute beast, or more than to eat, drink and sleep . . . unless it is given by the inspiration of the Almighty. (TPJS, 343)[130]

♦♦♦

Now, I ask all who hear me, why the learned men who are preaching salvation, say that God created the heavens and the earth out of nothing? The reason is, that they are unlearned in the things of God, and have not the gift of the Holy Ghost; they account it blasphemy in any one to contradict their idea. If you tell them that God made the world out of something, they will call you a fool. But I am learned, and know more than all the world put together. The Holy ghost does, anyhow, and He is within me, and comprehends more than all the world; and I will associate myself with Him. (TPJS, 350)[130]

ILLNESS

It is an unhallowed principle to say that such and such have transgressed because they have been preyed upon by disease or death, for all flesh is subject to death. (TPJS, 162)[50]

IMMORTALITY

All men who are immortal dwell in everlasting burnings. You cannot go anywhere but where God can find you out. (TPJS, 367)[132]

♦♦♦

[On the way to Carthage, Joseph, Hyrum and others met a] Captain Dunn and a company of about sixty mounted militia, on seeing which Joseph said, Do not be alarmed, brethren, for they cannot do more to you than the enemies of truth did to the ancient Saints—they can only kill the body. (TPJS, 379)[137]

INDEPENDENCE

(*See also* AGENCY)

Selfishness and independence of mind . . . too often manifested [in an authority] destroy the confidence of those who would [otherwise] lay down their lives for [the man]. (TPJS, 30)[17]

◆◆◆

If others' blessings are not your blessings, others' curses are not your curses: you stand then in these last days, as all have stood before you, agents unto yourselves, to be judged according to your works. (TPJS, 12)[7]

INDIVIDUALITY

Every man lives for himself. . . . But except a man be born again, he cannot see the kingdom of God. . . . He may receive a glory like unto the moon, [i.e. of which the light of the moon is typical]. Or a star, [i.e. of which the light of the stars is typical] but he can never come unto Mount Zion, and unto the city of the living God . . . unless he becomes as a little child, and is taught by the Spirit of God. (TPJS, 12)[8]

◆◆◆

All men are naturally disposed to walk in their own paths as they are pointed out by their own fingers, and we are not willing to consider and walk in the path which is pointed out by another, saying, This is the way, walk ye in it, although he should be an unerring director, and the Lord his God sent him. (TPJS, 26)[15]

◆◆◆

Let us realize that we are not to live to ourselves, but to God; by so doing the greatest blessings will rest upon us both in time and in eternity. (TPJS, 179)[55]

◆◆◆

The greatest temporal and spiritual blessings, which always come from faithfulness and concerted effort, never attended individual exertion or enterprise. (TPJS, 183)[58]

◆◆◆

Every person should stand, and act in the place appointed. (TPJS, 225)[75]

◆◆◆

Now, what I am after is the knowledge of God, and I take my own course to obtain it. (TPJS, 337)[128]

◆◆◆

I have always declared God to be a distinct personage, Jesus Christ a separate and distinct personage from God the Father, and that the Holy Ghost was a distinct personage and a Spirit; and these three constitute three distinct personages and three Gods. If this is in accordance with the New Testament, lo and behold! We have three Gods anyhow, and they are plural; and who can contradict it? . . . The doctrine of a plurality of Gods is as prominent in the Bible as any other doctrine. It is all over the face of the Bible. It stands beyond the power of controversy. A wayfaring man, though a fool, need not err therein.

Paul says there are Gods many and Lords many. I want to set forth in a plain and simple manner; but to us there is but one God—that is pertaining to us; and he is in all and through all. But if Joseph Smith says there are Gods many and Lords many, they cry, "Away with him! Crucify him! Crucify him!" (TPJS, 370)[133]

INFANT BAPTISM

Baptism is for remission of sins. Children have no sins. (TPJS, 314)[114]

INFANT DEATH

The Lord takes many away even in

infancy, that they may escape the envy of man, and the sorrows and evils of this present world; they were too pure, too lovely, to live on earth; therefore, if rightly considered, instead of mourning we have reason to rejoice as they are delivered from evil, and we shall soon have them again. (TPJS, 196)[68]

♦♦♦

All children are redeemed by the blood of Jesus Christ, and the moment that children leave this world, they are taken to the bosom of Abraham. The only difference between the old and young dying is, one lives longer in heaven and eternal light and glory than the other, and is freed a little sooner from this miserable wicked world. Notwithstanding all this glory, we for a moment lose sight of it, and mourn the loss, but we do not mourn as those without hope. (TPJS, 197)[68]

INHERITANCE IN ZION

I pray . . . that you all may be kept in the faith unto the end: let your sufferings be what they may, it is better in the eyes of God that you should die, than that you should give up the land of Zion, the inheritances which you have purchased with your monies; for every man that giveth not up his inheritance, though he should die, yet, when the Lord shall come, he shall stand upon it, and with Job, in his flesh he shall see God. Therefore, this is my counsel, that you retain your lands. (TPJS, 35)[19]

INITIATIVE

We believe that . . . the Saints . . . will from henceforth be always ready to obey the truth without having men's persons in admiration because of advantage. (TPJS, 146)[47]

INNOCENCE

I am aware that I ought not to murmur, and do not murmur, only in this, that those who are innocent are compelled to suffer for the iniquities of the guilty. (TPJS, 34)[19]

♦♦♦

Females, if they are pure and innocent, can come in the presence of God; for what is more pleasing to God than innocence? . . . If we would come before God, we must keep ourselves pure, as He is pure. (TPJS, 227)[75]

♦♦♦

I do not want to cloak iniquity—all things contrary to the will of God, should be cast from us, but don't do more hurt than good. . . . I want the innocent to go free—rather spare ten iniquitous among you, than condemn one innocent one. . . , "Fret not thyself because of evildoers." God will see to it. (TPJS, 239)[78]

♦♦♦

No man knows my history. I cannot tell it; I shall never undertake it. I don't blame any one for not believing my history. If I had not experienced what I have, I could not have believed it myself. I never did harm any man since I was born in the world. My voice is always for peace. (TPJS, 361)[130]

♦♦♦

[On the way to Carthage, Joseph, Hyrum and others met a] Captain Dunn and a company of about sixty mounted militia, on seeing which Joseph said, Do not be alarmed, brethren, for they cannot do more to you than the enemies of truth did to the ancient Saints—they can only kill the body. . . . [Joseph said to the company that was with him] I am going like a lamb to the slaughter, but I am calm as a summer's morning. I have a conscience void of offence toward God and toward all men. (TPJS, 379)[137]

INSENSITIVITY

Some have been uncharitable, and have manifested greediness because of their debts towards those who have been persecuted and dragged about with chains without cause, and imprisoned. Such characters God hates—and they shall have their turn of sorrow in the rolling of the great wheel, for it rolleth and none can hinder. (TPJS, 129)[46]

•••

If there are any among you who aspire after their own aggrandizement, and seek their own opulence, while their brethren are groaning in poverty, and are under sore trials and temptations, they cannot be benefited by the intercession of the Holy Spirit. (TPJS, 141)[47]

•••

Blessings offered, but rejected, are no longer blessings, but become like the talent hid in the earth by the wicked and slothful servant; the proffered good returns to the giver; the blessing is bestowed on those who will receive and occupy; for unto him that hath shall be given, and he shall have abundantly, but unto him that hath not, or will not receive, shall be taken away that which he hath, or might have had. (TPJS, 257)[83]

•••

It is an insult to a meeting for persons to leave just before its close. If they must go out, let them go half an hour before. No gentlemen will go out of a meeting just at closing. (TPJS, 287)[100]

•••

As president of this house, I forbid any man leaving just as we are going to close

the meeting. He is no gentleman who will do it. I don't care who does it, even if it were the king of England. I forbid it. (TPJS, 296)[102]

INSPIRATION

Fellow sojourners upon the earth, it is your privilege to purify yourselves and come up to the same glory, and see for yourselves, and know for yourselves. (TPJS, 13)[8]

•••

Let us be faithful and silent, brethren, and if God gives you a manifestation, keep it to yourselves; be watchful and prayerful, and you shall have a prelude of those joys that God will pour out on that day. (TPJS, 91)[33]

•••

When the heart is sufficiently contrite, then the voice of inspiration steals along and whispers. (TPJS, 134)[47]

•••

There are two Comforters spoken of. One is the Holy Ghost . . . that all Saints receive after faith, repentance, and baptism. This first Comforter or the Holy Ghost has no other effect than pure intelligence. It is more powerful in expanding the mind, enlightening the understanding and storing the intellect with present knowledge. (TPJS, 149)[48]

•••

No man knows the things of God, but by the Spirit of God, so no man knows the spirit of the devil, and his power and influence, but by possessing intelligence which is more than human. (TPJS, 205)[71]

•••

That which is wrong under one circumstance, may be, and often is, right under another.

God said, "Thou shalt not kill"; at another time He said, "Thou shalt utterly destroy." (TPJS, 256)[83]

◆◆◆

Knowledge does away with darkness, suspense and doubt; for these cannot exist where knowledge is. (TPJS, 287)[101]

◆◆◆

The way I know in whom to confide— God tells me in whom I may place confidence. (TPJS, 301)[105]

◆◆◆

I am not like other men. My mind is continually occupied with the business of the day, and I have to depend entirely upon the living God for everything I say on such [funeral] occasions as these. (TPJS, 320)[118]

◆◆◆

There are but a very few beings in the world who understand rightly the character of God. The great majority of mankind do not comprehend anything, either that which is past, or that which is to come, as it respects their relationship to God . . . and consequently they know but little above the brute beast, or more than to eat, drink and sleep . . . unless it is given by the inspiration of the Almighty. (TPJS, 343)[130]

INTEGRITY

That person who never forsaketh his trust should ever have the highest place of regard in our hearts. (TPJS, 31)[17]

◆◆◆

We believe that . . . the Saints . . . will from henceforth be always ready to obey the truth without having men's persons in admiration because of advantage. (TPJS, 146)[47]

◆◆◆

In all your trials, troubles, temptations, afflictions, bonds, imprisonments and death, see to it that you do not betray heaven; that you do not betray Jesus Christ; that you do not betray the brethren; that you do not betray the revelations of God, whether in Bible, Book of Mormon, or Doctrine and Covenants, or any other . . . revealed unto man. . . . Yea, in all your kickings and flounderings, see to it that you do not this thing, lest innocent blood be found upon your skirts, and you go down to hell. All other sins are not to be compared to sinning against the Holy Ghost, and proving a traitor to the brethren. (TPJS, 156)[49]

◆◆◆

We contemplate a people who have embraced a system of religion, unpopular, and the adherence to which has brought upon them repeated persecutions. A people who for their love of God, and attachment to His cause, have suffered hunger, nakedness, perils, and almost every privation. A people who, for the sake of their religion have had to mourn the premature death of parents, husbands, wives, and children. A people, who have preferred death to slavery and hypocrisy, and have honorably maintained their characters, and stood firm and immovable, in times that have tried men's souls. . . . Your names will be handed down to posterity as Saints of God and virtuous men. (TPJS, 185)[59]

◆◆◆

As well might the devil seek to dethrone Jehovah, as overthrow an innocent soul that resists everything which is evil. (TPJS, 226)[75]

◆◆◆

If you live up to your privileges, the angels cannot be restrained from being your associates. (TPJS, 226)[75]

◆◆◆

We have no claim in our eternal compact, in relation to eternal things, unless our actions and contracts and all things tend to this. (TPJS, 306)[109]

◆◆◆

We should gather all the good and true principles in the world and treasure them up, or we shall not come out true "Mormons." (TPJS, 316)[115]

◆◆◆

It mattereth not whether the principle is popular or unpopular, I will always maintain a true principle, even if I stand alone in it. (TPJS, 332)[125]

◆◆◆

I know much that I do not tell. I have had bribes offered me, but I have rejected them. (TPJS, 334)[127]

INTELLIGENCE

God has created man with a mind capable of instruction, and a faculty which may be enlarged in proportion to the heed and diligence given to the light communicated from heaven to the intellect; and ... the nearer man approaches perfection, the clearer are his views, and the greater his enjoyments, till he has overcome the evils of his life and lost every desire for sin; and like the ancients, arrives at that point of faith where he is wrapped in the power and glory of his Maker and is caught up to dwell with Him. (TPJS, 51)[21]

◆◆◆

There is a superior intelligence bestowed upon such as obey the Gospel with full purpose of heart, which, if sinned against, the apostate is left naked and destitute of the Spirit of God, and he is, in truth, nigh unto cursing, and his end is to be burned. When once that light which was

in them is taken from them, they become as much darkened as they were previously enlightened, and then, no marvel, if all their power should be enlisted against the truth ... they, like Judas, seek the destruction of those who were their greatest benefactors. (TPJS, 67)[21]

◆◆◆

The things of God are of deep import; and time, and experience, and careful and ponderous and solemn thoughts can only find them out. Thy mind, O man! If thou will lead a soul unto salvation, must stretch as high as the utmost heavens, and search into and contemplate the darkest abyss and the broad expanse of eternity. (TPJS, 137)[47]

◆◆◆

There are two Comforters spoken of. One is the Holy Ghost ... that all Saints receive after faith, repentance, and baptism. This first Comforter or the Holy Ghost has no other effect than pure intelligence. It is more powerful in expanding the mind, enlightening the understanding and storing the intellect with present knowledge. (TPJS, 149)[48]

◆◆◆

We cannot keep all the commandments without first knowing them, and we cannot expect to know all, or more than we now know unless we comply with or keep those we have already received. (TPJS, 256)[83]

◆◆◆

God never had the power to create the spirit of man at all. God himself could not create himself.

Intelligence is eternal and exists upon a self-existent principle. It is a spirit from age to age, and there is no creation about it. All the minds and spirits that God ever sent into the world are susceptible of enlargement. (TPJS, 354)[130]

•••

The intelligence of spirits had no beginning, neither will it have an end. . . . That which has a beginning may have an end. There never was a time when there were not spirits; for they are co-[eternal] with our Father in Heaven. (TPJS, 353)[130]

INTERPRETATION OF SCRIPTURE

I have a key by which I understand the scriptures. . . . To ascertain [a scripture's] meaning, we must dig up the root and ascertain what it was that drew the saying out of Jesus. (TPJS, 276)[93]

•••

It is not very essential for the Elders to have knowledge in relation to the meaning of beasts, and heads and horns, and other figures made use of in the revelations. . . . If we get puffed up by thinking that we have much knowledge, we are apt to get a contentious spirit, and correct knowledge is necessary to cast out that spirit. (TPJS, 287)[101]

•••

When God made use of a beast in visions to the prophets He did it to represent those kingdoms which had degenerated and become corrupt, savage and beast-like in their dispositions, even the degenerate kingdoms of the wicked world; but He never made use of the figure of a beast nor any of the brute kind to represent His kingdom. (TPJS, 289)[101]

•••

Whenever God gives a vision of an image, or beast, or figure of any kind, He always holds Himself responsible to give a revelation or interpretation of the meaning thereof, otherwise we are not responsible or accountable for our belief in it. Don't be afraid of being damned for not knowing the meaning of a vision or figure, if God has not given a revelation or interpretation of the subject. (TPJS, 291)[101]

•••

[Moroni writes in the Book of Mormon] "the Lord knoweth the things which we have written, and also, that none other people knoweth our [Reformed Egyptian] language, therefore he hath prepared means for the interpretation thereof."

Therefore the Lord, and not man, had to interpret, after the people were all dead. And as Paul said, "the world by wisdom know not God," so the world by speculation are destitute of revelation; . . . [But] God in His superior wisdom, has always given his Saints . . . the same spirit, and that spirit, as John says, is the true spirit of prophecy, which is the testimony of Jesus. (TPJS, 300)[104]

•••

All things whatsoever God in his infinite wisdom has seen fit and proper to reveal to us, while we are dwelling in mortality, in regard to our mortal bodies . . . are revealed to our spirits precisely as though we had no bodies at all; and those revelations which will save our spirits will save our bodies. God reveals them to us in view of no eternal dissolution of the body, or tabernacle. (TPJS, 355)[130]

INTERVIEWS WITH OFFICIALS

Several of the officers of the troops in Carthage, and other gentlemen, curious to see the prophet, visited Joseph in his room. General Smith asked them if there was anything in his appearance that indicated he was the desperate character his enemies represented him to be; and he asked them to give him their honest opinion on the subject. The reply was, "No, Sir. Your appearance would indicate the very contrary, General Smith; but we cannot see what is in your heart, neither can we tell what are your intentions." To which Joseph replied, "Very true, gentlemen, you cannot see what is in my heart, and you are therefore unable to judge me or my intentions; but I can see what is in your hearts, and will tell you what I see. I can see that you thirst for blood, and nothing but my blood will satisfy you. It is not for crime of any description that I and my brethren are thus continually persecuted and harassed by our enemies, but there are other motives, and some of them I have expressed, so far as relates to myself; and inasmuch as you and the people thirst for blood, I prophesy, in the name of the Lord, that you shall witness scenes of blood and sorrow to your entire satisfaction. Your souls shall be perfectly satiated with blood, and many of you who are now present shall have an opportunity to face the cannon's mouth from sources you think not of; and those people that desire this great evil upon me and my brethren, shall be filled with regret and sorrow because of the scenes of desolation and distress that await them. They shall seek for peace, and shall not be able to find it. Gentlemen, you will find what I have told you to be true. (TPJS, 381)[139]

• • •

This account [of an interview with Governor Ford of Illinois] was written by [Elder] John Taylor subsequent to the events here portrayed.

Governor—General Smith, I believe you have given me a general outline of the difficulties that have existed in the country, in the documents forwarded to me by Dr. Bernhisel and Mr. Taylor; but, unfortunately, there seems to be a discrepancy between your statements and those of your enemies. It is true that you are substantiated by evidence and affidavit, but for such an extraordinary excitement as that which is now in the country, there must be some cause, and I attribute the last outbreak to the destruction of the Expositor, and to your refusal to comply with the writ issued by Esq. Morrison. The press in the United States is looked upon as the great bulwark of American freedom, and its destruction in Nauvoo was represented and looked upon as a high-handed measure, and manifests to the people a disposition on your part to suppress the liberty of speech and of the press; this, with your refusal to comply with the requisition of a writ, I conceive to be the principal cause of this difficulty, and you are, moreover, represented to me as turbulent and defiant of the laws and institutions of your country.

Gen. Smith—Governor Ford, you, sir, as Governor of this state, are aware of the prosecutions and persecutions that I have endured. You know well that our course has been peaceable and law-abiding, for I have furnished this state, ever since our settlement here, with sufficient evidence of my pacific intentions, and those of the people with whom I am associated, by the endurance of every conceivable indignity and lawless outrage perpetrated upon me and upon this people since our settlement here, and you yourself know that I have kept you well posted in relation to all matters associated with the late difficulties. If you have not got some of my communications, it has not been my fault.

Agreeably to your orders, I assembled the Nauvoo Legion for the protection of Nauvoo and the surrounding country against an armed band of marauders, and ever since they have been mustered I have almost daily communicated with you in regard to all the leading events that have transpired; and whether in the capacity of mayor of the city, or lieutenant-general of the Nauvoo Legion, I have striven to preserve the peace and administer even-handed justice to all; but my motives are impugned, my acts are misconstrued, and I am grossly and wickedly misrepresented. I suppose I am indebted for my incarceration here to the oath of a worthless man that was arraigned before me and fined for abusing and maltreating his lame, helpless brother.

That I should be charged by you, sir, who know better, of acting contrary to law, is to me a matter of surprise. Was it the Mormons or our enemies who first commenced these difficulties? You know well it was not us; and when this turbulent, outrageous people commenced their insurrectionary movements, I made you acquainted with them, officially, asked your advice, and have followed strictly your counsel in every particular.

Who ordered out the Nauvoo Legion? I did, under your direction. For what purpose? To suppress these insurrectionary movements. It was at your instance, sir, that I issued a proclamation calling upon the Nauvoo legion to be in readiness, at a moment's warning, to guard against the incursions of mobs, and gave an order to Jonathan Dunham, acting major-general, to that effect. Am I then to be charged for the acts of others; and because lawlessness and mobocracy abound, am I when carrying out your instructions, to be charged with not abiding the law? Why is it that I must be held accountable for other men's acts? If there is trouble in the country, neither I nor my people made it, and all that we have ever done, after much endurance on our part, is to maintain and uphold the Constitution and institutions of our country, and to protect an injured, innocent, and persecuted people against misrule and mob violence.

Concerning the destruction of the press to which you refer, men may differ somewhat in their opinions about it; but can it be supposed that after all the indignities to which we have been subjected outside, that this people could suffer a set of worthless vagabonds to come into our city, and right under our own eyes and protection, vilify and calumniate not only ourselves, but the character of our wives and daughters, as was impudently and unblushingly done in that infamous and filthy sheet? There is not a city in the United States that would have suffered such an indignity for twenty-four hours.

Our whole people were indignant, and loudly called upon our city authorities for redress of their grievances, which, if not attended to they themselves would have taken the matter into their own hands, and have summarily punished the audacious wretches, as they deserved.

The principles of equal rights that have been instilled into our bosoms from our cradles, as American citizens, forbid us from submitting to every foul indignity, and succumbing and pandering to wretches so infamous as these. But, independent of this, the course that we pursued we considered to be strictly legal; for notwithstanding the insult we were anxious to be governed strictly by law, and therefore convened the City Council; and being desirous in our deliberations to abide law, summoned legal counsel to be present on the occasion.

Upon investigating the matter, we found that our City Charter gave us power to remove all nuisances; and, furthermore, upon consulting Blackstone upon what might be considered a nuisance, that distinguished lawyer, who is considered authority, I believe, in all our courts, states, among other things, that a libelous and filthy press may be considered a nuisance, and abated as such.

Here, then, one of the most eminent English barristers, whose works are considered standard with us, declares that a libelous press may be considered a nuisance, we conceived that we were acting strictly in accordance with law. We made that order in our corporate capacity, and the City Marshall carried it out. It is possible there may have been a better way, but I must confess that I could not see it.

In relation to the writ served upon us, we were willing to abide the consequences of our own acts, but were unwilling, in answering a writ of that kind, to submit to legal exactions sought to be imposed upon us under the pressure of law, when we knew they were in open violation of it.

When that document was presented to me by Mr. Bettisworth, I offered, in the presence of more than twenty persons, to go to any other magistrate, either in our city or Appanoose, or any other place where we should be safe, but we all refused to put ourselves into the power of a mob.

What right had that constable to refuse our request? He had none according to law; for you know, Governor Ford, that the state law in Illinois is, that the parties served with the writ shall go before him who issued it, or some other justice of the peace. Why, then, should we be dragged to Carthage, where the law does not compel us to go? Does this not look like many others of our prosecutions with which you are acquainted? And had we not a right to expect foul play?

This very act was a breach of law on his part—an assumption of power that did not belong to him, and an attempt, at least, to deprive us of our legal and constitutional rights and privileges. What could we do under the circumstances different from what we did do? We sued for, and obtained a writ of habeas corpus from the Municipal Court, by which we were delivered from the hands of Constable Bettisworth,

and brought before and acquitted by the Municipal Court.

After our acquittal, in a conversation with Judge Thomas, although he considered the acts of the party illegal, he advised, that to satisfy the people, we had better go before another magistrate who was not in the Church.

In accordance with his advice we went before Esq. Wells, with whom you are well acquainted; both parties were present, witnesses were called on both sides, the case was fully investigated, and we were again dismissed.

And what is this intended desire to enforce the law, and these lying, base rumors put into circulation for, but to seek, through mob influence, under pressure of law, to make us submit to requisitions that are contrary to law, and subversive of every principle of justice?

And when you, sir, required us to come out here, we came, not because it was legal, but because you required it of us, and we were desirous of showing to you and to all men that we shrunk not from the most rigid investigation of our acts.

We certainly did expect other treatment than to be immured in a jail at the instance of these men, and I think, from your plighted faith, we had a right to, after disbanding our own forces, and putting ourselves entirely in your hands; and now, after having fulfilled my part, sir, as a man and an American citizen, I call upon you, Governor Ford, and think I have a right to do so, to deliver us from this place, and rescue us from this outrage that is sought to be practiced upon us by a set of infamous scoundrels.

Gov. Ford—But you have placed men under arrest, detained men as prisoners, and given passes to others, some of which I have seen.

John P. Green, City Marshall—Perhaps I can explain. Since these difficulties have commenced, you are aware that we have been placed under very peculiar circumstances, our city has been placed under a very rigid police guard; in addition to this, frequent guards have been placed outside the city to prevent any sudden surprise, and those guards have questioned suspected or suspicious persons as to their business.

To strangers, in some instances, passes have been given, to prevent difficulty in passing those guards. It is some of those passes you have seen. No person, sir, has been imprisoned without a legal cause in our city.

Gov.—Why did you not give a more speedy answer to the posse that I sent out?

Gen. Smith.—We had matters of importance to consult upon. Your letter showed anything but an amicable spirit. We have suffered immensely in Missouri from mobs, in loss of property, imprisonment and otherwise.

It took some time for us to weigh duly these matters. We could not decide upon the matters of such importance immediately, and your *posse* were too hasty in returning. We were consulting for a large people, and vast interests were at stake. We had been outrageously imposed upon, and knew not how far we could trust anyone; besides, a question necessarily arose, how shall we come? Your request was that we should come unarmed. It became a matter of serious importance to decide how far promises could be trusted, and how far we were safe from mob violence.

Geddes—It certainly did look from all I have heard, from the general spirit of violence and mobocracy that here prevails, that it was not safe for you to come unprotected.

Gov.—I think that sufficient time was not allowed by the posse for you to consult and get ready. They were too hasty; but I suppose they found themselves bound by

their orders. I think, too, there is a great deal of truth in what you say, and your reasoning is plausible; yet, I must beg leave to differ from you in relation to the acts of the city council. That council, in my opinion, had no right to act in a legislative capacity, and in that of the judiciary.

They should have passed a law in relation to the matter, and then the Municipal Court, upon complaint, could have removed it; but for the City Council to take upon themselves the law-making and the execution of the laws, in my opinion, was wrong; besides, these men ought to have had a hearing before their property was destroyed; to destroy it without was an infringement of their rights; besides, it is so contrary to the feelings of the American people to interfere with the press.

And furthermore, I cannot but think that it would have been more judicious for you to have gone with Mr. Bettisworth to Carthage, notwithstanding the law did not require it. Concerning your being in jail, I am sorry for that. I wish it had been otherwise. I hope you will soon be released, but I cannot interfere.

Joseph Smith—Governor Ford, allow me, sir, to bring one thing to your mind, that you seem to have overlooked. You state that you think it would have been better for us to have submitted to the requisition of Constable Bettisworth, and to have gone to Carthage.

Do you not know, sir, that that writ was served at the instance of an anti-Mormon mob, who had passed resolutions and published them to the effect that they would exterminate the Mormon leaders; and are you not informed that Captain Anderson was not only threatened when coming to Nauvoo, but had a gun fired at his boat by this said mob at Warsaw, when coming up to Nauvoo, and that this very thing was made use of as a means to get us into their hands, and we could not, without taking an armed force with us, go there without, according to their published declarations, going into the jaws of death?

To have taken a force would only have fanned the excitement, as they would have stated that we wanted to use intimidation, therefore we thought it the most judicious to avail ourselves of the protection of the law.

Gov.—I see, I see.

Joseph Smith.—Furthermore, in relation to the press, you say that you differ with me in opinion; be it so, the thing after all is a legal difficulty, and the courts I should judge competent to judge on the matter.

If our act was illegal, we are willing to meet it; and although I cannot see the distinction that you draw about the acts of the city council, and what difference it could have made in point of fact, law, or justice, between the City Council's acting together or separate, or how much more legal it would have been for the Municipal Court, who were a part of City Council, to act separate, instead of with the councilors.

Yet, if it is deemed that we did a wrong in destroying that press, we refuse not to pay for it. We are desirous to fulfill the law in every particular, and are responsible for our acts.

You say that the parties ought to have had a hearing. Had it been a civil suit, this of course would have been proper; but there was a flagrant violation of every principle of right, a nuisance, and it was abated on the same principle that any nuisance, stench, or putrified carcass would have been removed.

Our first step, therefore, was to stop the foul, noisome, filthy sheet, and then the next, in our opinion, would have been to have prosecuted the men for a breach of public decency.

And furthermore, again, let me say, Governor Ford, I shall look to you for our

protection. I believe you are talking of going to Nauvoo; if you go, sir, I wish to go along. I refuse not to answer any law, but I do not consider myself safe here.

Gov.—I am in hopes that you will be acquitted; but if I go, I will certainly take you along. I do not, however, apprehend danger. I think you are perfectly safe, either here or anywhere else. I cannot, however, interfere with the law. I am placed in peculiar circumstances and seem to be blamed by all parties.

Joseph Smith—Governor Ford, I ask nothing but what is legal. I have a right to expect protection at least from you; for, independent of law, you have pledged your faith, and that of the state, for my protection, and I wish to go to Nauvoo.

Gov.—And you shall have protection, General Smith. I did not make this promise without consulting my officers, who all pledged their honor to its fulfillment. I do not know that I shall go tomorrow to Nauvoo, but if I do, I will take you along. (TPJS, 384)[143]

INTOLERANCE

I suppose I am not allowed to go into an investigation of anything that is not contained in the Bible. If I do, I think there are so many ever-wise men here, that they would cry, "treason" and put me to death. So I will go to the old Bible and turn commentator today. (TPJS, 348)[130]

INVESTMENTS

We . . . suggest . . . that there be no organization of large bodies upon common stock principles, in property, or of large companies of firms, until the Lord shall signify it in a proper manner, as it opens such a dreadful field for the avaricious, the indolent, and the corrupt hearted to prey upon the innocent and virtuous, and honest. (TPJS, 144)[47]

JEALOUSY

The Elders ... are combating the prejudices of a crooked and perverse generation, by having in their possession ... religious principles, which are misrepresented by almost all those whose crafts are in danger by the same. (TPJS, 83)[31]

JESUS CHRIST

I do not think there have been many good men on the earth since the days of Adam; but there was one good man and his name was Jesus. (TPJS, 303)[109]

◆◆◆

As the Father hath power in Himself, so hath the Son power in Himself, to lay down His life and take it again, so He has a body of His own. The Son doeth what He hath seen the Father do; then the Father hath some day laid down His life and taken it again; so He has a body of His own; each one will be in His own body. (TPJS, 312)[113]

◆◆◆

Jesus Christ is the heir of this Kingdom— the Only Begotten of the Father according to the flesh, and holds the keys over all this world. (TPJS, 323)[119]

◆◆◆

The Savior has the words of eternal life. Nothing else can profit us. (TPJS, 364)[132]

JEWS

So great a responsibility rested upon the generation in which our Savior lived, for,

says he, "That upon you may come all the righteous blood shed upon the earth, from the blood of righteous Abel unto the blood of Zacharias, son of Barachias, whom ye slew between the temple and the altar. Verily I say unto you, all these things shall come upon this generation" (Matthew 23:35, 36). Hence as they possessed greater privileges than any other generation, not only pertaining to themselves, but to their dead, their sin was greater, as they not only neglected their own salvation but that of their progenitors. (TPJS, 222)[74]

JOHN THE BAPTIST

How is it that John [the Baptist] was considered one of the greatest prophets? First. He was entrusted with a divine mission of preparing the way before the face of the Lord.

Second. He was entrusted with the important mission ... to baptize the Son of Man.

Thirdly. John ... was the only legal administrator in the affairs of the kingdom ... on the earth, and holding the keys of power. (TPJS, 275)[93]

JOSEPH

Trusting in that God who has said that these things are hid from the wise and prudent and revealed unto babes, I step forth into the field to tell you what the Lord is doing, and what you must do, to enjoy the smiles of your Savior in these last days. (TPJS, 14)[9]

◆◆◆

The eyes of my Maker are upon me, and ... to Him I am accountable for every word I say, wishing nothing worse to my fellow-men than their eternal salvation. (TPJS, 17)[9]

♦ ♦ ♦

Anxieties inexpressible crowd themselves continually upon my mind for the Saints, when I consider the many temptations to which we are subject, from the cunning and flattery of the great adversary of our souls. (TPJS, 29)[16]

♦ ♦ ♦

When I consider that soon the heavens are to be shaken, and the earth tremble and reel to and fro; and that the heavens are to be unfolded as a scroll when it is rolled up; and that every mountain and island are to flee away, I cry out in my heart, What manner of persons ought we to be in all holy conversation and godliness! (TPJS, 29)[16]

♦ ♦ ♦

Impressed with the truth . . . [about darkness covering the earth and minds of men] what can be the feelings of those who have been partakers of the heavenly gift and have tasted the good word of God, and the powers of the world to come? Who but those that can see the awful precipice upon which the world of mankind stands in this generation, can labor in the vineyard of the Lord without feeling a sense of the world's deplorable situation? Who but those who have duly considered the condescension of the Father of our spirits, in providing a sacrifice for His creatures, a plan of redemption, a power of atonement, a scheme of salvation, having as its great objects, the bringing of men back into the presence of the King of heaven, crowning them in the celestial glory, and making them heirs with the Son to that inheritance which is incorruptible, undefiled, and which fadeth not away—who but such can realize the importance of a perfect walk before all men, and a diligence in

calling upon all men to partake of these blessings? How indescribably glorious are these things to mankind! Of a truth they may be considered tidings of great joy to all people; and tidings, too, that ought to fill the earth and cheer the heart of everyone when sounded in his ears. The reflection that everyone is to receive according to his own diligence and perseverance while in the vineyard, ought to inspire everyone who is called to be a minister of these glad tidings, to so improve his talent that he may gain other talents, that when the Master sits down to take an account of the conduct of His servants, it may be said, Well done, good and faithful servant: thou hast been faithful over a few things; I will now make thee ruler over many things: enter thou into the joy of thy Lord. (TPJS, 47)[21]

♦ ♦ ♦

We remember your losses and sorrows [Bro. Peck]; our first ties are not broken; we participate with you in the evil as well as the good, in the sorrows as well as the joys; our union, we trust, is stronger than death, and shall never be severed. (TPJS, 79)[29]

♦ ♦ ♦

I feel for my fellow men; I do it in the name of the Lord, being moved upon by the Holy Spirit. Oh, that I could snatch them from the vortex of misery, into which I behold them plunging themselves, by their sins that I might be enabled by the warning voice, to be an instrument of bringing them to unfeigned repentance, that they might have faith to stand in the evil day! (TPJS, 87)[31]

♦ ♦ ♦

I am determined to do all that I can to uphold you, although I may do many things inadvertently that are not right in the sight of God. (TPJS, 90)[33]

❖❖❖

I have sometimes spoken too harshly from the impulse of the moment, and inasmuch as I have wounded your feelings, brethren, I ask your forgiveness, for I love you and will hold you up with all my heart in all righteousness, before the Lord, and before all men. (TPJS, 106)[37]

❖❖❖

Be assured, brethren, I am willing to stem the torrent of all opposition, in storms and in tempests, in thunders and in lightnings, by sea and by land, in the wilderness or among false brethren, or mobs, or wherever God in His providence may call us. (TPJS, 106)[37]

❖❖❖

"The ends of the earth shall enquire after thy name, and fools shall have thee in derision, and hell shall rage against thee, while the pure in heart, and the wise, and the noble, and the virtuous, shall seek thy counsel, and authority and blessings constantly from under thy hand, and thy people shall never be turned against thee by the testimony of traitors; and although their influence shall cast thee into trouble, and into bars and walls, thou shalt be had in honor, and but for a small moment and thy voice shall be more terrible in the midst of thine enemies, than the fierce lion, because of thy righteousness; and thy God shall stand by thee forever and ever." (TPJS, 143)[47]

❖❖❖

"If thou art called to pass through tribulations; if thou art in perils among false brethren; if thou art in perils among robbers; if thou art in perils by land or by sea; if thou art accused with all manner of false accusations; if thine enemies fall upon thee; if they tear thee from the society from thy father and mother and brethren and sisters; and if with a drawn sword thine enemies tear thee from the bosom of thy wife, and thine offspring, and thine elder son, although but six years of age, shall cling to thy garments, and shall say, My father, my father, why can't you stay with us? O my father, what are the men going to do with you? And if then he shall be thrust from thee by the sword, and thou be dragged to prison, and thine enemies prowl around thee like wolves for the blood of the lamb; and if thou shouldst be cast into the pit, or into the hands of murderers, and the sentence of death passed upon thee; if thou be cast into the deep, if the billowing surge conspire against thee; if fierce winds become thine enemy; if the heavens gather blackness, and all the elements combine to hedge up the way; and above all, if the very jaws of hell shall gape open the mouth wide after thee, know thou, my son, that all these things shall give thee experience, and shall be for thy good. The Son of Man hath descended below them all; art thou greater than he?" (TPJS, 143)[47]

❖❖❖

Therefore, hold on thy way, and the Priesthood shall remain with thee, for their [persecution] bounds are set, they cannot pass. Thy days are known, and thy years shall not be numbered less; therefore, fear not what man can do, for God shall be with you forever and ever. (TPJS, 143)[47]

❖❖❖

When the Twelve or any other witnesses stand before the congregation of the earth, and they preach in the power and demonstration of the Spirit of God, and the people are astonished and confounded at the doctrine, and say, "That man has preached a powerful discourse, a great sermon," then let that man or those men take care that they do not ascribe the glory unto themselves, but be careful that they are humble, and ascribe the praise and glory to God and the Lamb; for it is by the power of the Holy Priesthood and the Holy Ghost that they have power to speak. What art thou, O man, but dust? And from whom receivest thou thy power and blessings, but from God? (TPJS, 155)[49]

•••

Whatever you may hear about me or Kirtland, take no notice of it; for if it be a place of refuge, the devil will use his greatest efforts to trap the Saints. (TPJS, 161)[49]

•••

Inasmuch as long-suffering, patience, and mercy have ever characterized the dealings of our heavenly Father towards the humble and penitent, I feel disposed to copy the example, cherish the same principles, and by so doing being a savior of my fellow men. (TPJS, 165)[53]

•••

You must be aware in some measure of my feelings, when I contemplate the great work which is now rolling on, and the relation which I sustain to it, while it is extending to distant lands. . . . I realize in some measure my responsibility, and the need I have for support from above, that I may be able to teach this people. (TPJS, 178)[55]

•••

The reason we do not have the secrets of the Lord revealed unto us, is because we do not keep them but reveal them; we do not keep our own secrets, but reveal our difficulties to the world, even to our enemies, then how would we keep the secrets of the Lord? I can keep a secret till Doomsday. (TPJS, 195)[66]

•••

In the earlier ages of the world a righteous man, and a man of God and intelligence, had a better chance to do good, to be believed and received than at the present day; but in these days, such a man is much opposed and persecuted by most of the inhabitants of the earth, and he has much sorrow to pass through here. (TPJS, 196)[68]

•••

It has been hard for me to live on earth and see these young men upon whom we have leaned for support and comfort taken from us in the midst of their youth. . . . I have sometimes thought that I should have felt more reconciled to have been called away myself if it had been the will of God; yet I know we ought to be still and know it is of God, and be reconciled to His will. (TPJS, 215)[72]

•••

It will be but a short time before we shall all in like manner be called [home]. . . . Some have supposed that Brother Joseph could not die; but this is a mistake: it is true there have been times when I have had the promise of my life to accomplish such and such things, but, having now accomplished those things, I have not at present any lease of my life, I am as liable to die as other men. (TPJS, 216)[72]

•••

[Joseph said that] if God had appointed him, and chosen him as an instrument to lead the Church, why not let him lead it through? Why stand in the way when he is appointed to do a thing? Who knows the mind of God? Does He not reveal things differently than what we expect? He remarked that he was continually rising, although he had everything bearing him down, standing in his way, and opposing; notwithstanding all this opposition, he always comes out right in the end. (TPJS, 224)[75]

•••

[To the Relief Society, Joseph] spoke of delivering the keys of the Priesthood to the

Church . . . for according to his prayers, God had appointed him elsewhere. (TPJS, 225)[75]

♦♦♦

I am happy and thankful for the privilege of being present on this occasion. Great exertions have been made on the part of our enemies to carry me to Missouri and destroy my life; but the Lord has hedged up the way, and they have not, as yet, accomplished their purpose. God has enabled me to keep out of their hands. I have warred a good warfare, insomuch as I have outgeneraled or whipped all [their] corrupt host. (TPJS, 257)[84]

♦♦♦

My feelings at the present are that inasmuch as the Lord Almighty has preserved me until today, He will continue to preserve me, by the united faith and prayers of the Saints, until I have fully accomplished my mission in this life, and so firmly established the dispensation of the fullness of the Priesthood in these last days, that all the powers of earth and hell can never prevail against it. (TPJS, 258)[84]

♦♦♦

Although I do wrong, I do not the wrongs that I am charged with doing; the wrong that I do is through the frailty of human nature, like other men. No man lives without fault. (TPJS, 258)[84]

♦♦♦

All those that rise up against me will surely feel the weight of their iniquity upon their own heads. (TPJS, 258)[84]

♦♦♦

When I do the best I can—when I am accomplishing the greatest good, then the most evil and wicked surmisings are got up against me. (TPJS, 259)[84]

♦♦♦

If a man stands and opposes the world of sin, he may expect to have all wicked and corrupt spirits arrayed against him. (TPJS, 259)[84]

♦♦♦

He that will war the true Christian warfare against the corruptions of these last days will have wicked men and angels of devils, and all the infernal powers of darkness continually arrayed against him. (TPJS, 259)[84]

♦♦♦

Surely "facts are stubborn things." It will be as it ever has been, the world will prove Joseph Smith a true prophet by circumstantial evidence, in experiments, as they did Moses and Elijah. (TPJS, 267)[86]

♦♦♦

I told them I was but a man, and they must not expect me to be perfect; if they expected perfection from me, I should expect it from them; but if they would bear with my infirmities and the infirmities of the brethren, I would likewise bear with their infirmities. (TPJS, 268)[87]

♦♦♦

When my enemies take away my rights, I will bear it and keep out of the way; but if they take away your rights, I will fight for you. (TPJS, 268)[87]

♦♦♦

I know what I say; I understand my mission and business. God Almighty is my shield; and what can man do if God is my friend? I shall not be sacrificed until my time comes; then I shall be offered freely. (TPJS, 274)[91]

♦♦♦

I thank God for preserving me from my enemies; I have no enemies but for the truth's sake. I have no desire but to do all men good. I feel to pray for all men. (TPJS, 275)[91]

♦♦♦

What if all the world should embrace the Gospel? They would then see eye to eye, and the blessings of God would be poured out upon the people, which is the desire of my whole soul. Amen. (TPJS, 275)[91]

♦♦♦

I have, of late, had repeated solicitations to have something to do in relation to the political farce about dividing the country; but as my feelings revolt at the idea of having anything to do with politics, I have declined in every instance in having anything to do on the subject. I think it would be well for politicians to regulate their own affairs. I wish to be let alone, that I may attend strictly to the spiritual welfare of the church. (TPJS, 275)[92]

♦♦♦

This morning I . . . visited with a brother and sister from Michigan, who thought that "a prophet is always a prophet"; but I told them that a prophet was a prophet only when he was acting as such. (TPJS, 278)[94]

♦♦♦

I am a lawyer; I am a big lawyer and comprehend heaven, earth and hell, to bring forth knowledge that shall cover up all lawyers, doctors and other big bodies. (TPJS, 279)[95]

♦♦♦

Every honest man who has visited the city of Nauvoo since it existed, can bear record of better things, and place me in the front ranks of those who are known to do good for the sake of goodness, and show all liars, hypocrites and abominable creatures that, while vice sinks them down to darkness and woe, virtue exalts me and the Saints to light and immortality. (TPJS, 280)[96]

♦♦♦

If I had not actually got into this work and been called of God, I would back out. (TPJS, 286)[99]

♦♦♦

The world is full of technicalities and misrepresentation, which I calculate to overthrow, and speak of things as they actually exist. (TPJS, 292)[101]

♦♦♦

It is my meditation all the day, and more than my meat and drink, to know how I shall make the Saints of God comprehend the visions that roll like an overflowing surge before my mind. (TPJS, 296)[102]

♦♦♦

O that I had the language of the archangel to express my feelings once to my friends! But I never expect to in this life. When others rejoice, I rejoice; when they mourn, I mourn. (TPJS, 296)[102]

♦♦♦

Hosanna, hosanna, hosanna to Almighty God, that rays of light begin to burst forth upon us even now. I cannot find words in which to express myself. I am not learned, but I have as good feelings as any man. (TPJS, 296)[102]

♦♦♦

The way I know in whom to confide— God tells me in whom I may place confidence. (TPJS, 301)[105]

♦♦♦

Paul saw the third heavens, and I more. (TPJS, 301)[106]

♦♦♦

I do not want you to think that I am very righteous, for I am not. God judges men according to the use they make of the light which He gives them. (TPJS, 303)[109]

◆◆◆

Many persons think a prophet must be a great deal better than anybody else. Suppose I would condescend—yes, I will call it condescend, to be a great deal better than any of you, I would be raised up to the highest heaven; and who should I have to accompany me? (TPJS, 303)[109]

◆◆◆

I do not know when I shall have the privilege of speaking in a house large enough to convene the people. I find my lungs are failing with continual preaching in the open air to large assemblies. (TPJS, 303)[109]

◆◆◆

The opinions of men, so far as I am concerned, are to me as the crackling of thorns under the pot, or the whistling of the wind. I break the ground; I lead the way. (TPJS, 304)[109]

◆◆◆

I am like a huge, rough stone rolling down from a high mountain; and the only polishing I get is when some corner gets rubbed off by coming in contact with something else, striking with accelerating force against religious bigotry, priest-craft, lawyer-craft, doctor-craft, lying editors, suborned judges and jurors, and the authority of perjured executives, backed by mobs, blasphemers, licentious and corrupt men and women—all hell knocking off a corner here and a corner there. Thus I will become a smooth and polished shaft in the quiver of the Almighty, who will give me dominion over all and every one of them, when their refuge of lies shall fail, and their hiding place shall be destroyed, while these smooth-polished stones with which I come in contact become marred. (TPJS, 304)[109]

◆◆◆

I could explain a hundred fold more than I ever have of the glories of the kingdoms manifested to me in the vision, were I permitted, and were the people prepared to receive them. (TPJS, 305)[109]

◆◆◆

The Saints need not think because I am familiar with them and am playful and cheerful, that I am ignorant of what is going on. (TPJS, 307)[111]

◆◆◆

Iniquity of any kind cannot be sustained in the Church, and it will not fare well where I am; for I am determined while I do lead the Church, to lead it right. (TPJS, 307)[111]

◆◆◆

"I am a rough stone. The sound of the hammer and chisel was never heard on me until the Lord took me in hand. I desire the learning and wisdom of heaven alone. I have not the least idea, if Christ should come to the earth and preach such rough things as He preached to the Jews, but that this generation would reject Him for being so rough." (TPJS, 307)[113]

◆◆◆

Sectarian priests cry out concerning me, and ask, "Why is it this babbler gains so many followers, and retains them?" I answer, It is because I possess the principle of love. All I can offer the world is a good heart and a good hand. (TPJS, 313)[113]

◆◆◆

If a skillful mechanic . . . succeeds in welding together iron or steel more perfectly than any other mechanic, is he not deserving of praise? And if by the principles of truth I succeed in uniting men of all denominations in the bonds of love, shall I not have attained a good object? (TPJS, 313)[114]

◆◆◆

There is no greater love than this, that a man lay down his life for his friends. I discover hundreds and thousands of my brethren ready to sacrifice their lives for me. (TPJS, 315)[114]

◆◆◆

Although I was called of my heavenly Father to lay the foundation of this great work and kingdom in this dispensation, and testify of His revealed will to scattered Israel, I am subject to like passions as other men, like the prophets of olden times. (TPJS, 315)[114]

◆◆◆

The burdens which roll upon me are very great. My persecutors allow me no rest, and I find that in the midst of business and care the spirit is willing, but the flesh is weak. (TPJS, 315)[114]

◆◆◆

Men often come to me with their troubles, and seek my will, crying, Oh, Brother Joseph, help me! Help me! But when I am in trouble few of them sympathize with me or extend to me relief. (TPJS, 315)[114]

◆◆◆

I am not like other men. My mind is continually occupied with the business of the day, and I have to depend entirely upon the living God for everything I say on such [funeral] occasions as these. (TPJS, 320)[118]

◆◆◆

That which hath been hid from before the foundation of the world is revealed to babes and sucklings in the last days. (TPJS, 321)[118]

◆◆◆

I know a man that has been caught up to the third heavens, and can say, with Paul, that we have seen and heard things that are not lawful to utter. (TPJS, 323)[119]

◆◆◆

I prophecy they never will have power to kill me till my work is accomplished, and I am ready to die. (TPJS, 328)[122]

◆◆◆

I never stole the value of a pin's head, or a picayune in my life; and when you are hungry don't steal. Come to me and I will feed you. (TPJS, 329)[122]

◆◆◆

It is good economy to entertain strangers—to entertain sectarians. Come up to Nauvoo, ye sectarian priests of the everlasting Gospel, as they call it, and you shall have my pulpit all day. (TPJS, 329)[122]

◆◆◆

I have tried a number of years to get the minds of the Saints prepared to receive the things of God; but we frequently see some of them, after suffering all they have for the work of God, will fly to pieces like glass as soon as anything comes that is contrary to their traditions: they cannot stand the fire at all. How many will be able to abide a celestial law, and go through and receive their exaltation, I am unable to say, as many are called, but few are chosen. (TPJS, 331)[123]

◆◆◆

My only trouble at the present time is concerning ourselves, that the Saints *will be divided, broken up, and scattered,* before we get our salvation secure; for there are so many fools in the world for the devil to operate upon, it gives him the advantage oftentimes. (TPJS, 331)[123]

◆◆◆

I would not have suffered my name to have been used by my friends on anywise as President of the United States, or candidate for that office, if I and my friends could have had the privilege of enjoying our religious and civil rights as American citizens, even those rights which the Constitution guarantees unto all her citizens alike. But this as a people we have been denied from the beginning. (TPJS, 331)[124]

◆◆◆

If I lose my life in a good cause I am willing to be sacrificed on the altar of virtue, righteousness and truth, in maintaining the laws and Constitution of the United States, if need be, for the general good of man. (TPJS, 332)[124]

◆◆◆

The object with me is to obey and teach others to obey God in just what He tells us to do. (TPJS, 332)[125]

◆◆◆

It mattereth not whether the principle is popular or unpopular, I will always maintain a true principle, even if I stand alone in it. (TPJS, 332)[125]

◆◆◆

As to politics, I care but little about the presidential chair, I would not give half as much for the office of President of the United States as I would for the one I now hold as Lieutenant-General of the Nauvoo Legion. (TPJS, 333)[127]

◆◆◆

I know much that I do not tell. I have had bribes offered me, but I have rejected them. (TPJS, 334)[127]

◆◆◆

When I get hold of the Eastern papers, and see how popular I am, I am afraid myself that I shall be elected; but if I should be, I would not say, *"Your cause is just, but I can do nothing for you."* (TPJS, 334)[127]

◆◆◆

The government will not receive any advice or counsel from me; they are self-sufficient. But they must go to hell and work out their own salvation with fear and trembling. (TPJS, 334)[127]

◆◆◆

Now, what I am after is the knowledge of God, and I take my own course to obtain it. (TPJS, 337)[128]

◆◆◆

I will make every doctrine plain that I present, and it shall stand upon a firm basis, and I am at the defiance of the world, for I will take shelter under the broad cover of the wings of the work in which I am engaged. It matters not to me if all hell boils over; I regard it only as I would the crackling of the thorns under a pot. (TPJS, 339)[128]

◆◆◆

The Lord once told me that what I asked for I should have. I have been afraid to ask God to kill my enemies, lest some of them should peradventure, repent. (TPJS, 340)[128]

◆◆◆

In relation to the power over the minds of mankind which I hold, I would say, It is consequence of the power of truth in the doctrines which I have been an instrument in the hands of God of presenting unto them, and not because of any compulsion on my part. (TPJS, 341)[129]

◆◆◆

Did I ever exercise any compulsion over any man? Did I not give him the liberty of disbelieving any doctrine I have preached, if he saw fit? Why do not my enemies strike a blow at the doctrine? They cannot do it: it is truth, and I defy all men to upset it. I am the voice of one crying in the wilderness, "Repent ye of your sins and prepare the way for the coming of the Son of Man; for the kingdom of God has come unto you, and henceforth the axe is laid unto the root of the tree; and every tree that bringeth not forth good fruit, God Almighty . . . shall hew it down and cast it into the fire." (TPJS, 341)[129]

• • •

My first object is to find out the character of the only wise and true God, and what kind of being he is. (TPJS, 344)[130]

• • •

If I am so fortunate to be the man to comprehend God, and explain or convey the principles to your hearts, so that the Spirit seals them upon you, then let every man and woman henceforth sit in silence . . . and never lift their hands or voices . . . against the man of God or servants of God again. (TPJS, 344)[130]

• • •

If any man is authorized to take away my life because he thinks and says I am a false teacher, then, upon the same principle, we should be justified in taking away the life of every false teacher, and where would be the end of blood? And who would not be the sufferer? (TPJS, 344)[130]

• • •

I am going to enquire after God; for I want you all to know him, and to be familiar with him. . . . You will then know that I am his servant; for I speak as one having authority. (TPJS, 345)[130]

• • •

I suppose I am not allowed to go into an investigation of anything that is not contained in the Bible. If I do, I think there are so many ever-wise men here, that they would cry, "treason" and put me to death. So I will go to the old Bible and turn commentator today. (TPJS, 348)[130]

• • •

Now, I ask all who hear me, why the learned men who are preaching salvation, say that God created the heavens and the earth out of nothing? The reason is, that they are unlearned in the things of God, and have not the gift of the Holy Ghost; they account it blasphemy in any one to contradict their idea. If you tell them that God made the world out of something, they will call you a fool. But I am learned, and know more than all the world put together. The Holy ghost does, anyhow, and He is within me, and comprehends more than all the world; and I will associate myself with Him. (TPJS, 350)[130]

• • •

I know the Scriptures and understand them. (TPJS, 357)[130]

• • •

I love you all; but I hate some of your deeds. I am your best friend, and if persons miss their mark it is their own fault. If I reprove a man, and he hates me, he is a fool; for I love all men, especially these my brethren and sisters. (TPJS, 361)[130]

• • •

No man knows my history. I cannot tell it; I shall never undertake it. I don't blame any one for not believing my history. If I had not experienced what I have, I could not have believed it myself. I never did harm any man since I was born in the world. My voice is always for peace.
I cannot lie down until all my work is finished. (TPJS, 361)[130]

• • •

God made Aaron to be the mouthpiece for the children of Israel, and He will make me be god to you in His stead, and the Elders to be mouth for me. (TPJS, 363)[131]

• • •

The Savior said . . . the keys of knowledge, power and revelations should be revealed to a witness who should hold the testimony to the world. It has always been my province to dig up hidden mysteries—new things—for my hearers. (TPJS, 364)[132]

✦✦✦

All the testimony is that the Lord in the last days would commit the keys of the Priesthood to a witness over all people. Has the Gospel of the kingdom commenced in the last days? And will God take it from the man until He takes him Himself? (TPJS, 364)[132]

✦✦✦

He that arms himself with gun, sword, or pistol, except in the defense of truth, will sometime be sorry for it. I never carry any weapon with me bigger than my penknife. When I was dragged before the cannon and muskets in Missouri, I was unarmed. God will always protect me until my mission is fulfilled. (TPJS, 365)[132]

✦✦✦

I calculate to be one of the instruments of setting up the kingdom of Daniel by the word of the Lord. (TPJS, 366)[132]

✦✦✦

I intend to lay a foundation that will revolutionize the whole world. (TPJS, 366)[132]

✦✦✦

They that hurl all their hell and fiery billows upon me . . . will roll off me as fast as they come on. But I have an order of things to save the poor fellows at any rate, and get them saved; for I will send men to preach to them in prison and save them if I can. (TPJS, 366)[132]

✦✦✦

When did I ever teach anything wrong from this stand? When was I ever confounded? (TPJS, 368)[132]

✦✦✦

I never told you I was perfect; but there is no error in the revelations which I have taught. (TPJS, 368)[132]

✦✦✦

I am bold to declare I have taught all the strong doctrines publicly, and always teach stronger doctrines in public than in private. (TPJS, 370)[133]

✦✦✦

Did I build on any other man's foundation? I have got all the truth which the Christian world possessed, and an independent revelation in the bargain, and God will bear me off triumphant. (TPJS, 376)[133]

✦✦✦

I told Stephen Markham that if I and Hyrum were ever taken again we should be massacred, or I was not a prophet of God. (TPJS, 376)[134]

✦✦✦

If my life is of no value to my friends it is of none to myself. (TPJS, 377)[136]

✦✦✦

[On the way to Carthage, Joseph said to the company that was with him:] I am going like a lamb to the slaughter, but I am calm as a summer's morning. I have a conscience void of offence toward God and toward all men. If they take my life I shall die an innocent man, and my blood shall cry from the ground for vengeance, and it shall be said of me, "He was murdered in cold blood"! (TPJS, 379)[137]

✦✦✦

When [the small company started back to Carthage] Joseph said, "Boys, if I don't come back, take care of yourselves; I am going like a lamb to the slaughter." When they passed his farm he took a good look at it, and after they had passed it, he turned round several times to look again, at which some of the company made remarks, when Joseph said, "If some of you had got such a farm and knew you would not see it any more, you would want to take a good look at it for the last time." (TPJS, 380)[138]

•••

Several of the officers of the troops in Carthage, and other gentlemen, curious to see the prophet, visited Joseph in his room. General Smith asked them if there was anything in his appearance that indicated he was the desperate character his enemies represented him to be; and he asked them to give him their honest opinion on the subject. The reply was, "No, Sir. Your appearance would indicate the very contrary, General Smith; but we cannot see what is in your heart, neither can we tell what are your intentions." To which Joseph replied, "Very true, gentlemen, you cannot see what is in my heart, and you are therefore unable to judge me or my intentions; but I can see what is in your hearts, and will tell you what I see. I can see that you thirst for blood, and nothing but my blood will satisfy you. It is not for crime of any description that I and my brethren are thus continually persecuted and harassed by our enemies, but there are other motives, and some of them I have expressed, so far as relates to myself; and inasmuch as you and the people thirst for blood, I prophesy, in the name of the Lord, that you shall witness scenes of blood and sorrow to your entire satisfaction. Your souls shall be perfectly satiated with blood, and many of you who are now present shall have an opportunity to face the cannon's mouth from sources you think not of; and those people that desire this great evil upon me and my brethren, shall be filled with regret and sorrow because of the scenes of

desolation and distress that await them. They shall seek for peace, and shall not be able to find it. Gentlemen, you will find what I have told you to be true. (TPJS, 381)[139]

•••

I have had a good deal of anxiety about my safety since I left Nauvoo, which I never had before when I was under arrest. I could not help those feelings, and they have depressed me. (TPJS, 382)[140]

•••

Patriarch John Smith came from Macedonia to jail to see his nephews, Joseph and Hyrum. The road was thronged with mobbers. Three of them snapped their guns at him, and he was threatened by many others who recognized him. The guard at the jail refused him entrance.

Joseph saw him through the prison window, and said to the guard, "Let the old gentleman come in, he is my uncle." The guard replied they did not care who the hell he was uncle to, he should not go in.

Joseph replied, "You will not hinder so old and infirm a man as he is from coming in," and then said, "Come in, uncle," on which after searching him closely the guard let him pass into the jail, where he remained about an hour. (TPJS, 382)[141]

•••

[In the jail they] retired to rest late. Joseph and Hyrum occupied the only bedstead in the room, while their friends lay side by side on the mattresses on the floor. Dr. Richards sat up writing until his last candle left him in the dark. The report of a gun fired close by caused Joseph to rise, leave the bed, and lay himself on the floor, having Dan Jones on his left, and John S. Fullmer on his right, "Lay your head on my arm for a pillow, Brother John" [he said]; and when they were all quiet they conversed in a low tone about the prospects of their deliverance. Joseph gave expression to several presentiments that he had to die, and said, "I would like to see my family again," and "I would to God that I could preach to the Saints in Nauvoo once more." (TPJS, 383)[142]

♦♦♦

Dr. Richards retired to the bed which Joseph had left, and when all were apparently fast asleep, Joseph whispered to Dan Jones, "Are you afraid to die?" Dan said, "Has that time come, think you? Engaged in such a cause I do not think that death would have many terrors." Joseph replied, "You will yet see Wales, and fulfill the mission appointed to you before you die." (TPJS, 384)[142]

♦♦♦

Both Joseph and Hyrum bore a faithful testimony [in the Carthage Jail] to the Latter-day work, and the coming forth of the Gospel over all the earth, exhorting the brethren present to faithfulness and preserving diligence in proclaiming the Gospel, building up the Temple, and performing all the duties connected with our holy religion. (TPJS, 394)[145]

JOY

The law of heaven is presented to man, and as such guarantees to all who obey it a reward far beyond any earthly consideration. (TPJS, 50)[21]

♦♦♦

God has created man with a mind capable of instruction, and a faculty which may be enlarged in proportion to the heed and diligence given to the light communicated from heaven to the intellect; and that the nearer man approaches perfection, the clearer are his views, and the greater his enjoyments, till he has overcome the evils of his life and lost every desire for sin; and like the ancients, arrives at that point of faith where he is wrapped in the power and glory of his Maker and is caught up to dwell with Him. (TPJS, 51)[21]

♦♦♦

Live worthy of the blessings that shall follow, after much tribulation, to satiate the souls of them that hold out faithful to the end. (TPJS, 78)[29]

♦♦♦

Let us be faithful and silent, brethren, and if God gives you a manifestation, keep it to yourselves; be watchful and prayerful, and you shall have a prelude of those joys that God will pour out on that day. (TPJS, 91)[33]

♦♦♦

If a Priest understands his duty, his calling, and ministry, and preaches by the Holy Ghost, his enjoyment is as great as if he were one of the Presidency. (TPJS, 112)[41]

♦♦♦

If there is anything calculated to interest the mind of the Saints, to awaken in them the finest sensibilities, and arouse them to enterprise and exertion, surely it is the great and precious promises made by our heavenly Father to the children of Abraham; and those engaged in seeking the outcasts of Israel, and the dispersed of Judah, cannot fail to enjoy the spirit of the Lord and have the choicest blessings of heaven rest upon them in copious effusions. (TPJS, 163)[51]

♦♦♦

They that turn many to righteousness shall shine as the stars for ever and ever. (TPJS, 253)[81]

♦♦♦

In obedience there is joy and peace unspotted, unalloyed; and as God has designed our happiness—and the happiness of all His creatures, he never has—He never will institute an ordinance or give a commandment to His people that is not calculated in its nature to promote that happiness which he has designed, and which will not end in the greatest amount of good and glory to those who become the recipients of His law and ordinances. (TPJS, 256)[83]

♦ ♦ ♦

"No good thing will I withhold from them who walk uprightly before me, and do my will in all things—who will listen to my voice and to the voice of my servant, whom I have sent; for I delight in those who seek diligently to know my precepts, and abide by the law of my kingdom; for all things shall be made known unto them in mine own due time, and in the end they shall have joy." (TPJS, 257)[83]

♦ ♦ ♦

By seeing the blessings of the endowment rolling on, and the kingdom increasing and spreading from sea to sea, we shall rejoice that we were not overcome by these foolish [persecutors]. (TPJS, 259)[84]

♦ ♦ ♦

There is joy in the presence of the angels of God over one sinner that repenteth, more than over ninety-and-nine just persons that are so righteous, that they will be damned anyhow; you cannot save them. (TPJS, 277)[93]

♦ ♦ ♦

Those who have died in Jesus Christ may expect to enter into all that fruition of joy when they come forth, which they possessed or anticipated here. (TPJS, 295)[102]

♦ ♦ ♦

Hosanna, hosanna, hosanna to Almighty God, that rays of light begin to burst forth upon us even now. I cannot find words in which to express myself. I am not learned, but I have as good feelings as any man. (TPJS, 296)[102]

♦ ♦ ♦

When we depart, we shall hail our mothers, fathers, friends, and all whom we love, who have fallen asleep in Jesus. There will be no fear of mobs, persecutions, or malicious lawsuits and arrests; but it will be an eternity of felicity. (TPJS, 360)[130]

JUDGE NOT

No man is capable of judging a matter, in council, unless his own heart is pure; . . . we frequently are so filled with prejudice, or have a beam in our own eye, that we are not capable of passing right decisions. (TPJS, 69)[22]

♦ ♦ ♦

Our acts are recorded, and at a future day they will be laid before us, and if we should fail to judge right and injure our fellow-beings, they may there, perhaps, condemn us. (TPJS, 69)[22]

♦ ♦ ♦

I preached to the Saints, setting forth the evils that existed, and that would exist, by reason of hasty judgment, or decisions upon any subject given by any people, or in judging before they had heard both sides of a question. (TPJS, 118)[44]

♦ ♦ ♦

Outward appearance is not always a criterion by which to judge our fellow man. (TPJS, 137)[47]

♦ ♦ ♦

It is an unhallowed principle to say that such and such have transgressed because they have been preyed upon by disease or death, for all flesh is subject to death. (TPJS, 162)[50]

•••

What many people call sin is not sin. . . . If you do not accuse each other, God will not accuse you. . . . If you will not accuse me, I will not accuse you. If you will throw a cloak of charity over my sins, I will over yours—for charity covereth a multitude of sins. (TPJS, 193)[64]

•••

Don't be limited in your views with regard to your neighbor's virtue, but beware of self-righteousness, and be limited in the estimate of your own virtues, and not think yourself more righteous than others. (TPJS, 228)[75]

•••

Search yourselves—the tongue is an unruly member—hold your tongues about things of no moment—a little tale will set the world on fire. At [certain] time[s] the truth on the guilty should not be told openly. . . . We must use precaution in bringing sinners to justice, lest . . . we draw the indignation of a Gentile world upon us. . . . It is necessary to hold an influence in the world, and thus spare ourselves an extermination; and also accomplish our end in spreading the Gospel, or holiness, in the earth. . . . To the iniquitous show yourselves merciful. (TPJS, 239)[78]

•••

The Saints need not think because I am familiar with them and am playful and cheerful, that I am ignorant of what is going on. (TPJS, 307)[111]

•••

If any man is authorized to take away my life because he thinks and says I am a false teacher, then, upon the same principle, we should be justified in taking away the life of every false teacher, and where would be the end of blood? And who would not be the sufferer? (TPJS, 344)[130]

JUDGING

No person through the discerning of spirits can bring a charge against another, they must be proven guilty by positive evidence, or they stand clear. (TPJS, 214)[71]

•••

In all our councils, especially while on trial of any one, we should see and observe all things appertaining to the subject, and discern the spirit by which either party was governed. We should be in a situation to understand every spirit and judge righteous judgment and not be asleep. We should keep order and not let the council be imposed upon by unruly conduct. (TPJS, 307)[111]

JUDGMENT

There is to be a day when all will be judged of their works, and rewarded according to the same; . . . those who have kept the faith will be crowned with a crown of righteousness; be clothed in white raiment; be admitted to the marriage feast; be free from every affliction, and reign with Christ on the earth, where, according to the ancient promise, they will partake of the fruit of the vine new in the glorious kingdom with Him. (TPJS, 66)[21]

•••

All who have died without a knowledge of this Gospel, who would have received it if they had been permitted to tarry, shall be heirs of the celestial kingdom of God; also all that shall die henceforth without a knowledge of it, who would have received it with all their hearts, shall be heirs of that kingdom, "For I, the Lord, will judge all men according to their works, according to the desire of their hearts." And I also beheld that all children who die before they arrive at the years of accountability, are saved in the celestial kingdom of heaven. (TPJS, 106)[38]

•••

All those who have not had an opportunity of hearing the Gospel, and being administered unto by an inspired man in the flesh, must have it hereafter, before they can be finally judged. (TPJS, 121)[45]

•••

The lips betray the haughty and overbearing imaginations of the heart; by his words and his deeds let him be judged. (TPJS, 137)[47]

•••

The Doctrine of the Resurrection of the Dead and the Eternal Judgment are necessary to preach among the first principles of the Gospel of Jesus Christ. (TPJS, 149)[48]

•••

It is an unhallowed principle to say that such and such have transgressed because they have been preyed upon by disease or death, for all flesh is subject to death. (TPJS, 162)[50]

•••

let it prove as a warning to all to deal justly before God, and with all mankind, then we shall be clear in the day of judgment. (TPJS, 216)[72]

•••

[Jehovah] holds the reins of judgment in His hands; He is a wise Lawgiver, and will judge all men, not according to the narrow, contracted notions of men, but, "according to the deeds done in the body whether they be good or evil," or whether these deeds were done in England, America, Spain, Turkey, or India. He will judge them, "not according to what they have not, but according to what they have," those who have lived without law, will be judged without law, and those who have a law, will be judged by the law. We need not doubt the wisdom and intelligence of the Great Jehovah; He will award judgment or mercy to all nations according to their several deserts, their means of obtaining intelligence, the laws by which they are governed, the facilities afforded them of obtaining correct information, and His inscrutable designs in relation to the human family; and when the designs of God shall be made manifest, and the curtain of futurity be withdrawn, we shall all of us have to confess that the Judge of all the earth has done right. (TPJS, 218)[74]

•••

The world has had a fair trial for six thousand years; the Lord will try the seventh thousand Himself; "He whose right it is, will possess the kingdom, and reign until He has put all things under His feet"; iniquity will hide its hoary head, Satan will be bound, and the works of darkness destroyed; righteousness will be put to the line, and judgment to the plummet, and "he that fears the Lord will alone be exalted in that day." (TPJS, 252)[81]

•••

Our heavenly Father is more liberal in His views, and boundless in His mercies and blessings, than we are ready to believe or receive; and, at the same time, is more terrible to the workers of iniquity, more awful in the executions of His punishments, and more ready to detect every false way, than we are apt to suppose Him to be. (TPJS, 257)[83]

•••

And, in consequence of rejecting the Gospel of Jesus Christ and the Prophets whom God hath sent, the judgments of God have rested upon people, cities, and nations, in various ages of the world, which was the case with the cities of Sodom and Gomorrah, that were destroyed for rejecting the prophets. (TPJS, 271)[91]

•••

God judges men according to the use they make of the light which He gives them. (TPJS, 303)[109]

JUST REWARDS

God ere long, will call all his servants before Him, and there from His own hand they will receive a just recompense and a righteous reward for all their labors. (TPJS, 57)[21]

•••

The Lord says that every man is to receive according to his works. Reflect for a moment, . . . and enquire whether you would consider yourselves worthy a seat at the marriage seat with Paul and others like him, if you had been unfaithful? Had you not fought the good fight, and kept the faith, could you expect to receive? (TPJS, 64)[21]

•••

There is to be a day when all will be judged of their works, and rewarded according to the same; . . . those who have kept the faith will be crowned with a crown of righteousness; be clothed in white raiment; be admitted to the marriage feast; be free from every affliction, and reign with Christ on the earth, where, according to the ancient promise, they will partake of the fruit of the vine new in the glorious kingdom with Him. (TPJS, 66)[21]

•••

"As in Adam all die, even so in Christ shall all be made alive"; all shall be raised from the dead. . . . The Lamb of God hath brought to pass the resurrection, so that all shall rise from the dead.

Some dwell in higher glory than others. (TPJS, 367)[132]

JUSTICE

God has respect to the feelings of His Saints, and He will not suffer them to be tantalized with impunity. (TPJS, 19)[10]

•••

It is your privilege to use every lawful means in your power to seek redress for your grievances from your enemies, and prosecute them to the extent of the law. (TPJS, 32)[18]

•••

All regularly organized and well established governments have certain laws by which, more or less, the innocent are protected and the guilty punished. (TPJS, 49)[21]

•••

No person through the discerning of spirits can bring a charge against another, they must be proven guilty by positive evidence, or they stand clear. (TPJS, 214)[71]

•••

If human laws award to each man his deserts, and punish all delinquents according to their several crimes, surely the Lord will not be more cruel than man, for He is a wise legislator, and His laws are more equitable, His enactments more just, and His decisions more perfect than those of man; and as man judges his fellow man by law, and punishes him according to the penalty of the law, so does God of heaven judge "according to the deeds done in the body." . . . The hearer cannot believe without he hear a "sent" preacher, and cannot be condemned for what he has not heard, and being without law, will have to be judged without law. (TPJS, 221)[74]

♦♦♦

The Lord says that every man is to receive according to his works. Reflect for a moment, . . . and enquire whether you would consider yourselves worthy a seat at the marriage seat with Paul and others like him, if you had been unfaithful? Had you not fought the good fight, and kept the faith, could you expect to receive? (TPJS, 64)[21]

♦♦♦

A view of [salvation for the dead] . . . reconciles the Scriptures of truth, justifies the ways of God to man, places the human family upon equal footing, and harmonizes with every principle of righteousness, justice and truth. We will conclude with the words of Peter: "For the time past of our life may suffice us to have wrought the will of the Gentiles." "For, for this cause was the Gospel preached also to them that are dead, that they might be judged according to men in the flesh, but live according to God in the Spirit." (TPJS, 223)[74]

♦♦♦

"Fret not thyself because of evildoers." God will see to it. (TPJS, 239)[78]

♦♦♦

We must use precaution in bringing sinners to justice, lest in exposing these heinous sins we draw the indignation of a Gentile world upon us. (TPJS, 239)[78]

♦♦♦

How many have had to wander in sheep skins and goat skins, and live in caves and dens of the mountains, because the world was unworthy of their society! . . . But remember, brethren, he that offends one of the least of the Saints, would be better off with a millstone tied to his neck and he and the stone plunged into the depth of the sea! (TPJS, 261)[85]

♦♦♦

When my enemies take away my rights, I will bear it and keep out of the way; but if they take away your rights, I will fight for you. (TPJS, 268)[87]

♦♦♦

God judges men according to the use they make of the light which He gives them. (TPJS, 303)[109]

♦♦♦

When I get hold of the Eastern papers, and see how popular I am, I am afraid myself that I shall be elected; but if I should be, I would not say, "*Your cause is just, but I can do nothing for you.*" (TPJS, 334)[127]

KINDNESS

(*See also* COMPASSION; FORGIVENESS)

The kindness of a man should never be forgotten. (TPJS, 31)[17]

◆◆◆

How will the serpent ever lose its venom, while the servants of God possess the same disposition, and continue to make war upon it? Men must become harmless before the brute creation, and when men lose their viscous dispositions and cease to destroy the animal race, the lion and the lamb can dwell together and the sucking child can play with the serpent in safety. (TPJS, 71)[24]

◆◆◆

We received some letters last evening—one from Emma, one from Don C. Smith, and one from Bishop Partridge—all breathing a kind and consoling spirit. We were much gratified with their contents. We had been a long time without information; and when we read those letters they were to our souls as the gentle air is refreshing, but our joy was mingled with grief, because of the sufferings of the poor and much injured Saints. . . . The floodgates of our hearts were lifted and our eyes were a fountain of tears, but those who have not been enclosed in the walls of prison without cause of provocation, can have but little idea how sweet the voice of a friend is; one token of friendship from any source whatever awakens and calls into action every sympathetic feeling; it brings up in an instant everything that is passed; it seizes the present with the avidity of lightning; it grasps after the future with the fierceness of a tiger; it moves the mind backward and forward, from one thing to another, until finally all enmity, malice and hatred, and past differences, misunderstandings and mismanagements are slain victorious at the feet of hope; and when the heart is sufficiently contrite, then the voice of inspiration steals along and whispers. (TPJS, 134)[47]

◆◆◆

When a man is born down with trouble, when he is perplexed with care and difficulty, if he can meet a smile instead of an argument or a murmur . . . if he can meet with mildness, it will calm down his soul and soothe his feelings; when the mind is going to despair, it needs a solace of affection and kindness. (TPJS, 228)[75]

◆◆◆

When you go home, never give a cross or unkind word to your husbands, but let kindness, charity and love crown your works henceforward. (TPJS, 229)[75]

◆◆◆

Nothing is so much calculated to lead people to forsake sin as to take them by the hand, and watch over them with tenderness. When persons manifest the least kindness and love to me, O, what power it has over my mind, while the opposite course has a tendency to harrow up all the harsh feelings and depress the human mind. (TPJS, 240)[79]

◆◆◆

Remember that he that gives a cup of cold water in the name of a disciple to one of the Saints in prison, or secluded from friends by reason of vexatious law suits, intended for persecution, shall in no wise lose his reward. (TPJS, 261)[85]

♦♦♦

It is a time-honored adage that love begets love. Let us pour forth love—show forth our kindness unto all mankind, and the Lord will reward us with everlasting increase; cast our bread upon the waters and we shall receive it after many days, increased to an hundredfold. (TPJS, 316)[115]

♦♦♦

I never did harm any man since I was born in the world. My voice is always for peace. (TPJS, 361)[130]

KINGDOM OF GOD

The conditions of God's kingdom are such, that all who are made partakers of that glory, are under the necessity of learning something respecting it previous to their entering into it. But the foreigner can come to this country without knowing a syllable of its laws, or even subscribing to obey them after he arrives. (TPJS, 51)[21]

♦♦♦

The Melchizedek Priesthood . . . holds the highest authority which pertains to . . . the keys of the Kingdom of God in all ages of the world to the latest posterity on the earth; and is the channel through which all knowledge, doctrine, the Plan of Salvation and every important matter is revealed from heaven. (TPJS, 166)[54]

♦♦♦

The designs of God, [in contrast to the governments of man] have been to promote the universal good of the . . . world; to establish peace and good will among men; to promote the principles of eternal truth; to bring about a state of things that shall unite man to his fellow man;

cause the world to "beat their swords into plowshares, and their spears into pruning hooks," [and] make the nations of the earth dwell in peace. (TPJS, 248)[81]

♦♦♦

Some say the kingdom of God was not set up on the earth until the day of Pentecost, and that John did not preach baptism of repentance for the remission of sins. But I say, in the name of the Lord, that the kingdom of God was set up on the earth from the days of Adam to the present time, whenever there has been a righteous man on earth unto whom God revealed His word and gave power and authority to administer in His name. And where there is a priest of God—a minister who has power and authority from God to administer in the ordinances of the gospel and officiate in the priesthood of God—there is the kingdom of God. (TPJS, 271)[91]

♦♦♦

We will keep the laws of the land; we do not speak against them. . . . We speak of the kingdom of God on the earth, not the kingdom of men. (TPJS, 272)[91]

♦♦♦

Where there is no kingdom of God there is no salvation. What constitutes the kingdom of God? Where there is a prophet, priest, or a righteous man unto whom God gives His oracles, there is the kingdom of God; and where the oracles of God are not, there the kingdom of God is not. (TPJS, 272)[91]

♦♦♦

There is a difference between the kingdom of God and the fruits and blessings that flow from the kingdom; because there were more miracles, gifts, visions, healings, tongues, etc., in the days of Jesus Christ and His apostles, and on the day of Pentecost, than under John's administration, it does not prove by any means that John had not the kingdom of God, any more than it would that a woman had not a milkpan because she had not a pan of milk, for while the pan might be compared to the kingdom, the milk might be compared to the blessings of the kingdom. (TPJS, 273)[91]

♦♦♦

Whenever men can find out the will of God and find an administrator legally authorized from God, there is the kingdom of God. (TPJS, 274)[91]

♦♦♦

It is one thing to see the kingdom of God, and another thing to enter into it. We must have a change of heart to see the kingdom of God, and subscribe the articles of adoption to enter therein. (TPJS, 328)[122]

♦♦♦

To seal those who dwell on earth to those who dwell in heaven. This is the power of Elijah and the keys of the kingdom of Jehovah. (TPJS, 338)[128]

♦♦♦

In relation to the kingdom of God, the devil always sets up his kingdom at the very same time in opposition to God. (TPJS, 365)[132]

♦♦♦

I calculate to be one of the instruments of setting up the kingdom of Daniel by the word of the Lord, and I intend to lay a foundation that will revolutionize the whole world. (TPJS, 366)[132]

♦♦♦

KINGDOM OF HEAVEN

If . . . the grave has no victory, those who keep the sayings of Jesus and obey His teachings have not only a promise of a resurrection from the dead, but an assurance of being admitted into His glorious kingdom: for He Himself says, "Where I am, shall also my servants be." (TPJS, 62)[21]

♦♦♦

They shall be heirs of God and joint heirs with Jesus Christ. What is it? To inherit the same power, the same glory and the same exaltation, until you arrive at the station of a God, and ascend the throne of eternal power, the same as those who have gone before. What did Jesus do? Why, I do the things I saw my Father do when worlds came rolling into existence. My Father worked out his kingdom with fear and trembling, and I must do the same; and when I get my kingdom, I shall present it to my Father, so that he may obtain kingdom upon kingdom, and it will exalt Him in glory. He will then take a higher exaltation, and I will take his place, and thereby become exalted myself. So that Jesus treads in the tracks of his Father, and inherits what God did before; and God is thus glorified and exalted in the salvation and exaltation of all His children. (TPJS, 347)[130]

KNOWLEDGE

One of the most important points in the faith of the Church . . . is the gathering of Israel . . . that happy time . . . when He will turn to them a pure language, and the earth will be filled with sacred knowledge, as the waters cover the great deep. (TPJS, 92)[35]

♦♦♦

It was not until apostasy and rebellion against the things of God that the true knowledge of the universe as well as the knowledge of other truths, became lost among men. (TPJS, 119)[44]

◆◆◆

The things of God are of deep import; and time, and experience, and careful and ponderous and solemn thoughts can only find them out. Thy mind, O man! If thou will lead a soul unto salvation, must stretch as high as the utmost heavens, and search into and contemplate the darkest abyss and the broad expanse of eternity. (TPJS, 137)[47]

◆◆◆

Even the least Saint may know all things as fast as he is able to bear them. (TPJS, 149)[48]

◆◆◆

There are two Comforters spoken of. One is the Holy Ghost . . . that all Saints receive after faith, repentance, and baptism. This first Comforter or the Holy Ghost has no other effect than pure intelligence. It is more powerful in expanding the mind, enlightening the understanding and storing the intellect with present knowledge. (TPJS, 149)[48]

◆◆◆

The Melchizedek Priesthood . . . is the channel through which all knowledge, doctrine, the Plan of Salvation and every other important matter is revealed from heaven. (TPJS, 166)[54]

◆◆◆

It mattereth not whether we live long or short on the earth after we come to a knowledge of [gospel] principles and obey them unto the end. (TPJS, 199)[68]

◆◆◆

A man is saved no faster than he gets knowledge, for if he does not get knowledge, he will be brought into captivity by some evil power in the other world, as evil spirits will have more knowledge, and consequently more power than many men who are on the earth.

Hence it needs revelation to assist us, and give us knowledge of the things of God. (TPJS, 217)[73]

◆◆◆

It is a desirable honor that you should so walk before our heavenly Father as to save yourselves; we are all responsible to God for the manner we improve the light and wisdom given by our Lord to enable us to save ourselves. (TPJS, 227)[75]

◆◆◆

We cannot keep all the commandments without first knowing them, and we cannot expect to know all, or more than we now know unless we comply with or keep those we have already received. (TPJS, 256)[83]

◆◆◆

I am a lawyer; I am a big lawyer and comprehend heaven, earth and hell, to bring forth knowledge that shall cover up all lawyers, doctors and other big bodies. (TPJS, 279)[95]

◆◆◆

Knowledge does away with darkness, suspense and doubt; for these cannot exist where knowledge is. (TPJS, 287)[101]

◆◆◆

In knowledge there is power. God has more power than all other beings, because he has knowledge; and hence he knows how to subject all other beings to Him. He has power over all. (TPJS, 288)[101]

◆◆◆

It is not wisdom that we should have all knowledge at once presented before us; but that we should have a little at a time, then we can comprehend it. (TPJS, 297)[103]

◆◆◆

The principle of knowledge is the principle of salvation. . . . everyone that does not obtain knowledge to be saved will be condemned. The principle of salvation is given us through the knowledge of Jesus Christ. (TPJS, 297)[103]

♦♦♦

[Quoting Peter, Joseph said:] "And add to your faith virtue," knowledge, temperance, patience, godliness, brotherly kindness, charity; "for if these things be in you, and abound, they make you that ye shall neither be barren, nor unfruitful in the knowledge of our Lord Jesus Christ." . . . There could not anything be given, pertaining to life and godliness, without knowledge. (TPJS, 305)[109]

♦♦♦

Knowledge is the power of salvation. (TPJS, 306)[109]

♦♦♦

"I am a rough stone. The sound of the hammer and chisel was never heard on me until the Lord took me in hand. I desire the learning and wisdom of heaven alone. I have not the least idea, if Christ should come to the earth and preach such rough things as He preached to the Jews, but that this generation would reject Him for being so rough." (TPJS, 307)[113]

♦♦♦

A man never has half so much fuss to unlock a door, if he has a key, as though he had not, and had to cut it open with his jack-knife. (TPJS, 308)[113]

♦♦♦

One of the grand fundamental principles of "Mormonism" is to receive truth, let it come from whence it may. (TPJS, 313)[114]

♦♦♦

I do not grudge the world all the religion they have got; they are welcome to all the knowledge they possess. (TPJS, 320)[118]

♦♦♦

What would it profit us to come unto the spirits of the just men, but to learn and come up to the standard of their knowledge? (TPJS, 320)[118]

♦♦♦

Could you gaze into heaven five minutes you would know more than you would by reading all that ever was written on the subject. (TPJS, 324)[121]

♦♦♦

We have received a portion of knowledge from God by immediate revelation, and from the same source we can receive all knowledge. (TPJS, 329)[123]

♦♦♦

Now, what I am after is the knowledge of God, and I take my own course to obtain it. (TPJS, 337)[128]

♦♦♦

If men do not comprehend the character of God, they do not comprehend themselves. (TPJS, 343)[130]

♦♦♦

My first object is to find out the character of the only wise and true God, and what kind of being he is. (TPJS, 344)[130]

♦♦♦

I am going to enquire after God; for I want you all to know him, and to be familiar with him. . . . You will then know that I am his servant; for I speak as one having authority. (TPJS, 345)[130]

♦♦♦

Now, I ask all who hear me, why the learned men who are preaching salvation, say that God created the heavens and the earth out of nothing? The reason is, that they are unlearned in the things of God, and have not the gift of the Holy Ghost; they account it blasphemy in any one to contradict their idea. If you tell them that God made the world out of something, they will call you a fool. But I am learned, and know more than all the world put together. The Holy Ghost does, anyhow, and He is within me, and comprehends more than all the world; and I will associate myself with Him. (TPJS, 350)[130]

◆◆◆

[Learning of the council in heaven] . . . we begin to learn the only true God, and what kind of a being we have got to worship. Having a knowledge of God, we begin to know how to approach him, and how to ask so as to receive an answer. When we understand the character of God, and know how to come to him, he begins to unfold the heavens to us, and to tell us all about it. When we are ready to come to him, he is ready to come to us. (TPJS, 350)[130]

◆◆◆

Knowledge saves a man; and in the world of spirits no man can be exalted but by knowledge. . . . If a man has knowledge, he can be saved; although, if he has been guilty of great sins, he will be punished for them, But when he consents to obey the Gospel, whether here or in the world of spirits, he is saved. (TPJS, 357)[130]

◆◆◆

I know the Scriptures and understand them. (TPJS, 357)[130]

◆◆◆

In the world of spirits no man can be exalted but by knowledge. (TPJS, 357)[130]

◆◆◆

The Savior said . . . the keys of knowledge, power and revelations should be revealed to a witness who should hold the testimony to the world. It has always been my province to dig up hidden mysteries—new things—for my hearers. (TPJS, 364)[132]

◆◆◆

I advise all to go on to perfection, and search deeper and deeper into the mysteries of Godliness. (TPJS, 364)[132]

◆◆◆

No man can limit the bounds or the eternal existence of eternal time. Hath he beheld the eternal world, and is he authorized to say that there is only one God? He makes himself a fool if he thinks or says so, and there is an end of his career or progress in knowledge. He cannot obtain all knowledge, for he has sealed up the gate to it. (TPJS, 371)[133]

LANGUAGE

(See also CLARITY; WORDS)

I wish to mention here, that the title page of the Book of Mormon is a literal translation, taken from the very last leaf, on the left hand side of the collection or book of plates, which contained the record which has been translated, the language of the whole running the same as all Hebrew writing in general; and that said title page is not by any means a modern composition, either of mine or of any other man who has lived or does live in this generation. (TPJS, 7)[1]

♦♦♦

One of the most important points in the faith of the Church . . . is the gathering of Israel . . . that happy time . . . when [God] . . . will turn to them a pure language, and the earth will be filled with sacred knowledge, as the waters cover the great deep. (TPJS, 92)[35]

♦♦♦

Our light speeches, which may have escaped our lips from time to time . . . have nothing to do with the fixed purposes of our hearts; therefore it sufficeth us to say, that our souls were vexed from day to day. (TPJS, 124)[46]

♦♦♦

The lips betray the haughty and overbearing imaginations of the heart; by his words and his deeds let him be judged. (TPJS, 137)[47]

♦♦♦

How vain and trifling have been our spirits, our councils, our meetings, our private as well as public conversations—too low, too mean, too vulgar, too condescending for the dignified characters of the called and chosen of God. (TPJS, 137)[47]

♦♦♦

Be honest, open, and frank in all your intercourse with mankind. (TPJS, 156)[49]

♦♦♦

Let every word be seasoned with grace. (TPJS, 156)[49]

♦♦♦

[If Jesus] comes to a little child, He will adapt himself to the language and capacity of a little child. (TPJS, 162)[49]

♦♦♦

When you go home, never give a cross or unkind word to your husbands, but let kindness, charity and love crown your works henceforward. (TPJS, 229)[75]

♦♦♦

Search yourselves—the tongue is an unruly member—hold your tongues about things of no moment—a little tale will set the world on fire. At [certain] time[s] the truth on the guilty should not be told openly. . . . We must use precaution in bringing sinners to justice, lest . . . we draw the indignation of a Gentile world upon us. (TPJS, 239)[78]

♦♦♦

If you know anything calculated to disturb the peace or injure the feelings of your brother or sister, hold your tongues and the least harm will be done. (TPJS, 259)[84]

♦♦♦

O that I had the language of the archangel to express my feelings once to my friends! But I never expect to in this life. When others rejoice, I rejoice; when they mourn, I mourn. (TPJS, 296)[102]

♦♦♦

It is my meditation all the day, and more than my meat and drink, to know how I shall make the Saints of God comprehend the visions that roll like an overflowing surge before my mind. (TPJS, 296)[102]

♦♦♦

Hosanna, hosanna, hosanna to Almighty God, that rays of light begin to burst forth upon us even now. I cannot find words in which to express myself. I am not learned, but I have as good feelings as any man. (TPJS, 296)[102]

♦♦♦

[Moroni writes in the Book of Mormon] "none other people knoweth our [Reformed Egyptian] language," therefore the Lord, and not man, had to interpret, after the people were all dead. (TPJS, 300)[104]

♦♦♦

Peter penned the most sublime language of any of the apostles. (TPJS, 301)[106]

♦♦♦

The Lord deals with this people as a tender parent with a child, communicating light and intelligence and the knowledge of His ways as they can bear it. (TPJS, 305)[109]

♦♦♦

I will make every doctrine plain that I present, and it shall stand upon a firm basis, and I am at the defiance of the world, for I will take shelter under the broad cover of the wings of the work in which I am engaged. It matters not to me if all hell boils over; I regard it only as I would the crackling of the thorns under a pot. (TPJS, 339)[128]

♦♦♦

I do not intend to please your ears with superfluity of words or oratory, or with much learning; but I intend to edify you with the simple truths from heaven. (TPJS, 342)[130]

♦♦♦

Out of the abundance of the heart of man the mouth speaketh. (TPJS, 358)[130]

♦♦♦

A good man will speak good things and holy principles, and an evil man evil things. I feel, in the name of the Lord, to rebuke all such bad principles, liars, etc., and I warn all of you to look out whom you are going after. (TPJS, 367)[132]

♦♦♦

LAST DISPENSATION

(*See* DISPENSATION OF THE FULLNESS OF TIMES)

LAW

The law of heaven is presented to man, and as such guarantees to all who obey it a reward far beyond any earthly consideration; though it does not . . . exempt [one] from the afflictions and troubles arising from different sources in consequence of acts of wicked men on earth. Still in the midst of all this there is a promise predicated upon the fact that it is a law of heaven, which transcends the law of man, as far as eternal life [transcends] the temporal; and as the blessings which God is able to give, are greater than those which can be given by man. (TPJS, 50)[21]

♦♦♦

All well established and properly organized governments have certain fixed and prominent laws for the regulation and management of the same. If man has grown to wisdom and is capable of discerning the propriety of laws to govern nations, what less can be expected from the Ruler and Upholder of the universe? (TPJS, 55)[21]

•••

It is reasonable to suppose that man departed from the first teachings, or instructions which he received from heaven in the first age, and refused by his disobedience to be governed by them. Consequently, he formed such laws as best suited his own mind, or as he supposed, were best adapted to his situation. But that God has influenced man more or less since that time in the formation of law for His benefit we have no hesitancy in believing. (TPJS, 57)[21]

•••

LAW OF HEAVEN

(*See also* GOD'S LAW)

Certainly, if the law of man is binding upon man when acknowledged, how much more must the law of heaven be! (TPJS, 50)[21]

•••

The law of heaven is presented to man, and as such guarantees to all who obey it a reward far beyond any earthly consideration; though it does not . . . exempt [one] from the afflictions and troubles arising from different sources in consequence of acts of wicked men on earth. Still in the midst of all this there is a promise predicated upon the fact that it is a law of heaven, which transcends the law of man, as far as eternal life [transcends] the temporal; and as the blessings which God is able to give, are greater than those which can be given by man. (TPJS, 50)[21]

•••

If man has grown to wisdom and is capable of discerning the propriety of

laws to govern nations, what less can be expected from the Ruler and Upholder of the universe? (TPJS, 55)[21]

•••

Lucifer . . . sought for things which were unlawful. Hence he was sent down . . . and the greatness of his punishment is that he shall not have a tabernacle. (TPJS, 297)[103]

•••

We have no claim in our eternal compact, in relation to eternal things, unless our actions and contracts and all things tend to this. (TPJS, 306)[109]

•••

The organization of the spiritual and heavenly worlds, and of spiritual and heavenly beings, was agreeable to the most perfect order and harmony: their limits and bounds were fixed irrevocably, and voluntarily subscribed to in their heavenly estate by themselves, and were by our first parents subscribed to upon the earth. Hence the importance of embracing and subscribing to principles of eternal truth by all men upon the earth that expect eternal life. (TPJS, 325)[121]

•••

The law [of Moses] . . . was added [to the Gospel already being preached] because of transgression. (TPJS, 60)[21]

LAYING ON OF HANDS

(*See also* HEALING)

What is the sign of the healing of the sick? The laying on of hands is the sign or way marked out by James, and the custom of the ancient Saints as ordered by the Lord, and we cannot obtain the blessings by pursuing any other course except the way marked out by the Lord. (TPJS, 198)[68]

•••

If God gave His sanction by healing . . . there could be no more sin in any female laying hands on and praying for the sick, than in wetting the face with water; it is no sin for anybody to administer that has faith, or if the sick have faith to be healed by their administration. (TPJS, 225)[75]

LEADERSHIP

There should exist the greatest freedom and familiarity among the rulers in Zion. (TPJS, 24)[13]

•••

Pure and steadfast love for those who are his benefactors . . . should characterize a President of the Church of Christ. (TPJS, 30)[17]

•••

Selfishness and independence of mind . . . too often manifested [by a leader] destroy the confidence of those who would [otherwise] lay down their lives for him. (TPJS, 30)[17]

•••

I am well aware that you [the Twelve] have to sustain my character against the vile calumnies and reproaches of this ungodly generation, and that you delight in doing so. (TPJS, 89)[33]

•••

I am determined to do all that I can to uphold you, although I may do many things inadvertently that are not right in the sight of God. (TPJS, 90)[33]

•••

Be assured, brethren, I am willing to stem the torrent of all opposition, in storms and in tempests, in thunders and in lightnings, by sea and by land, in the wilderness or among false brethren, or mobs, or wherever God in His providence may call us. (TPJS, 106)[37]

•••

The things of God are of deep import; and time, and experience, and careful and ponderous and solemn thoughts can only find them out. Thy mind, O man! If thou will lead a soul unto salvation, must stretch as high as the utmost heavens, and search into and contemplate the darkest abyss and the broad expanse of eternity. (TPJS, 137)[47]

•••

None but fools will trifle with the souls of men. (TPJS, 137)[47]

•••

How vain and trifling have been our spirits, our councils, our meetings, our private as well as public conversations— too low, too mean, too vulgar, too condescending for the dignified characters of the called and chosen of God. (TPJS, 137)[47]

•••

We are called to hold the keys of the mysteries of those things that have been kept hid from the foundation of the world until now. (TPJS, 137)[47]

•••

No power or influence can or ought to be maintained by virtue of the Priesthood, only by persuasion, by long-suffering, by gentleness, and meekness, and by love unfeigned; by kindness, and pure knowledge, which shall greatly enlarge the soul without hypocrisy, and without guile, reproving betimes with sharpness, when moved upon by the Holy Ghost, and then showing forth afterwards an increase of love toward him whom thou hast reproved, lest he esteem thee to be his enemy; that he may know that thy faithfulness is stronger than the cords of death; let thy bowels also be full of charity towards all men, and to the household of faith, and let virtue garnish thy thoughts unceasingly, then shall thy confidence wax strong in the presence of God, and the doctrine of the Priesthood shall distill upon thy soul as the dews from heaven. The Holy ghost shall be thy constant companion, and thy sceptre an unchanging sceptre of righteousness and truth, and thy dominion shall be an everlasting dominion, and without compulsory means, it shall flow unto thee forever and ever. (TPJS, 142)[47]

♦♦♦

[Joseph said that] if God had appointed him, and chosen him as an instrument to lead the Church, why not let him lead it through? Why stand in the way when he is appointed to do a thing? Who knows the mind of God? Does He not reveal things differently than what we expect? He remarked that he was continually rising, although he had everything bearing him down, standing in his way, and opposing; notwithstanding all this opposition, he always comes out right in the end. (TPJS, 224)[75]

♦♦♦

The servants of the Lord are required to guard against those things that are calculated to do the most evil. The little foxes spoil the vines—little evils do the most injury to the Church. If you have evil feelings, and speak of them to one another, it has a tendency to do mischief. (TPJS, 258)[84]

♦♦♦

It is my meditation all the day, and more than my meat and drink, to know how I shall make the Saints of God comprehend the visions that roll like an overflowing surge before my mind. (TPJS, 296)[102]

♦♦♦

The way to get along in any important matter is to gather unto yourselves wise men, experienced and aged men, to assist in council in all times of trouble. (TPJS, 299)[103]

♦♦♦

The opinions of men, so far as I am concerned, are to me as the crackling of thorns under the pot, or the whistling of the wind. I break the ground; I lead the way. (TPJS, 304)[109]

♦♦♦

Iniquity of any kind cannot be sustained in the Church, and it will not fare well where I am; for I am determined while I do lead the Church, to lead it right. (TPJS, 307)[111]

♦♦♦

As to politics, I care but little about the presidential chair, I would not give half as much for the office of President of the United States as I would for the one I now hold as Lieutenant-General of the Nauvoo Legion. (TPJS, 333)[127]

♦♦♦

When I get hold of the Eastern papers, and see how popular I am, I am afraid myself that I shall be elected; but if I should be, I would not say, "*Your cause is just, but I can do nothing for you.*" (TPJS, 334)[127]

♦♦♦

In relation to the power over the minds of mankind which I hold, I would say, It is in consequence of the power of truth in the doctrines which I have been an instrument in the hands of God of presenting unto them, and not because of any compulsion on my part. (TPJS, 341)[129]

♦♦♦

If I am so fortunate to be the man to comprehend God, and explain or convey the principles to your hearts, so that the Spirit seals them upon you, then let every man and woman henceforth sit in silence . . . and never lift their hands or voices . . . against the man of God or servants of God again. (TPJS, 344)[130]

◆◆◆

I am going to enquire after God; for I want you all to know him, and to be familiar with him. . . . You will then know that I am his servant; for I speak as one having authority. (TPJS, 345)[130]

◆◆◆

God made Aaron to be the mouthpiece for the children of Israel, and He will make me be god to you in His stead, and the Elders to be mouth for me. (TPJS, 363)[131]

◆◆◆

The Savior said . . . the keys of knowledge, power and revelations should be revealed to a witness who should hold the testimony to the world. It has always been my province to dig up hidden mysteries—new things—for my hearers. (TPJS, 364)[132]

LEARNING

God has created man with a mind capable of instruction, and a faculty which may be enlarged in proportion to the heed and diligence given to the light communicated from heaven to the intellect; and that the nearer man approaches perfection, the clearer are his views, and the greater his enjoyments, till he has overcome the evils of his life and lost every desire for sin; and like the ancients, arrives at that point of faith where he is wrapped in the power and glory of his Maker and is caught up to dwell with Him. (TPJS, 51)[21]

◆◆◆

He that can mark the power of Omniscience, inscribed upon the heavens,

can also see God's own handwriting in the sacred volume; and he who reads it oftenest will like it best, and he who is acquainted with it, will know the hand wherever he can see it. (TPJS, 56)[21]

◆◆◆

The things of God are of deep import; and time, and experience, and careful and ponderous and solemn thoughts can only find them out. Thy mind, O man! If thou will lead a soul unto salvation, must stretch as high as the utmost heavens, and search into and contemplate the darkest abyss and the broad expanse of eternity. (TPJS, 137)[47]

◆◆◆

Why will not man learn wisdom by precept at this late age of the world, when we have such a cloud of witnesses and examples before us, and not be obliged to learn by sad experience everything we know. (TPJS, 155)[49]

◆◆◆

It is a desirable honor that you should so walk before our heavenly Father as to save yourselves; we are all responsible to God for the manner we improve the light and wisdom given by our Lord to enable us to save ourselves. (TPJS, 227)[75]

◆◆◆

As a Church and a people it behooves us to be wise, and to seek to know the will of God, and then be willing to do it; for "blessed is he that heareth the word of the Lord, and keepeth it," say the Scriptures. (TPJS, 253)[81]

◆◆◆

We cannot keep all the commandments without first knowing them, and we cannot expect to know all, or more than we now know unless we comply with or keep those we have already received. (TPJS, 256)[83]

❖❖❖

It is not wisdom that we should have all knowledge at once presented before us; but that we should have a little at a time, then we can comprehend it. (TPJS, 297)[103]

❖❖❖

I hope sober-thinking and sound-reasoning people will sooner listen to the voice of truth, than be led astray by the vain pretensions of the self-wise. (TPJS, 299)[104]

❖❖❖

I am a rough stone. The sound of the hammer and chisel was never heard on me until the Lord took me in hand. I desire the learning and wisdom of heaven alone. (TPJS, 307)[113]

❖❖❖

One of the grand fundamental principles of "Mormonism" is to receive truth, let it come from whence it may. (TPJS, 313)[114]

❖❖❖

We should gather all the good and true principles in the world and treasure them up, or we shall not come out true "Mormons." (TPJS, 316)[115]

❖❖❖

What would it profit us to come unto the spirits of the just men, but to learn and come up to the standard of their knowledge? (TPJS, 320)[118]

❖❖❖

Could you gaze into heaven five minutes, you would know more than you would by reading all that ever was written on the subject. (TPJS, 324)[121]

❖❖❖

All the minds and spirits that God ever sent into the world are susceptible of enlargement. (TPJS, 354)[130]

❖❖❖

I advise all to go on to perfection, and search deeper and deeper into the mysteries of Godliness. (TPJS, 364)[132]

❖❖❖

The Savior said . . . the keys of knowledge, power and revelations should be revealed to a witness who should hold the testimony to the world. It has always been my province to dig up hidden mysteries—new things—for my hearers. (TPJS, 364)[132]

LEGACY

We contemplate a people who have embraced a system of religion, unpopular, and the adherence to which has brought upon them repeated persecutions. A people who for their love of God, and attachment to His cause, have suffered hunger, nakedness, perils, and almost every privation. A people who, for the sake of their religion have had to mourn the premature death of parents, husbands, wives, and children. A people, who have preferred death to slavery and hypocrisy, and have honorably maintained their characters, and stood firm and immovable, in times that have tried men's souls. . . . Your names will be handed down to posterity as Saints of God and virtuous men. (TPJS, 185)[59]

❖❖❖

The blessings of the Most High will rest upon our tabernacles, and our name will be handed down to future ages; our children will rise up and call us blessed; and generations yet unborn will dwell with peculiar delight upon the scenes that we have passed through, the privations that we have endured; the untiring zeal that we have manifested; the all but insurmountable difficulties that we have overcome in laying the foundation of a work that brought about the glory and blessing which they will realize; a work that God and angels have contemplated with delight for generations past; that fired the souls of the ancient patriarchs and prophets; a work that is destined to bring about the destruction of the powers of darkness, the renovation of the earth, the glory of God, and the salvation of the human family. (TPJS, 232)[76]

LETTERS TO OFFICIALS

[In a letter to Governor Carlin of Illinois, Joseph wrote:] . . . I am perfectly satisfied . . . with your remarks. I shall consider myself and our citizens secure from harm under the broad canopy of the law under your administration. We look to you for protection in the event of any violence being used towards us, knowing that our innocence with regard to all the accusations in circulation will be duly evidenced before an enlightened public. (TPJS, 255)[82]

•••

[Letter to O. H. Browning, Defense Attorney]

Lawyer Browning:.

Sir.—Myself and brother Hyrum are in jail on charge of treason, to come up for examination on Saturday morning the 29th inst., and we request your professional services at that time, on our defense, without fail.

Most respectfully your servant,

JOSEPH SMITH

P. S.—There is no cause of action, for we have not been guilty of any crime, neither is there any just cause of suspicion against us; but certain circumstances make your attendance very necessary. (TPJS, 394)[146]

LEVITICAL PRIESTHOOD

The Levitical Priesthood is forever hereditary—fixed on the head of Aaron

and his sons forever, and was in active operation down to Zacharias the father of John. Zacharias would have had no child had not God given him a son. He sent his angel to declare unto Zacharias that his wife Elizabeth should bear him a son, whose name was to be called John.

The keys of the Aaronic Priesthood were committed unto him, and he was as the voice of one crying in the wilderness saying: "Prepare ye the way of the Lord and make his paths straight." (TPJS, 319)[117]

•••

The Levitical Priesthood, consist[s] of priests to administer in outward ordinances, made without an oath. (TPJS, 323)[119]

LIBERTY

Exalt the standard of Democracy! . . . That the blood of our fathers may not cry from the ground against us. Sacred is the memory of that blood which bought for us our liberty. (TPJS, 117)[42]

•••

It is a love of liberty which inspires my soul—civil and religious liberty to the whole of the human race. Love of liberty was diffused into my soul by my grandfathers while they dandled me on their knees; and shall I want friends? No. (TPJS, 313)[114]

LIFE

I know that Zion, in the due time of the Lord, will be redeemed; but how many will be the days of her purification, tribulation, and affliction, the Lord has kept hid from my eyes; and when I enquire concerning this subject, the voice of the Lord is: Be still, and know that I am God; all those who suffer for my name shall reign with me, and he that layeth down his life for my sake shall find it again. (TPJS, 34)[19]

It mattereth not whether we live long or short on the earth after we come to a knowledge of [gospel] principles and obey them unto the end. (TPJS, 199)[68]

•••

If my life is of no value to my friends it is of none to myself. (TPJS, 377)[136]

LONG-SUFFERING

Remember not to murmur at the dealings of God with His creatures. You are not as yet brought into as trying circumstances as were the ancient Prophets and Apostles . . . of whom the world was not worthy . . . amidst all their afflictions they rejoiced that they were counted worthy to receive persecution for Christ's sake. (TPJS, 32)[18]

•••

I know that Zion, in the due time of the Lord, will be redeemed; but how many will be the days of her purification, tribulation, and affliction, the Lord has kept hid from my eyes; and when I enquire concerning this subject, the voice of the Lord is: Be still, and know that I am God; all those who suffer for my name shall reign with me, and he that layeth down his life for my sake shall find it again. (TPJS, 34)[19]

•••

I pray . . . that you all may be kept in the faith unto the end: let your sufferings be what they may, it is better in the eyes of God that you should die, than that you should give up the land of Zion, the inheritances which you have purchased with your monies; for every man that giveth not up his inheritance, though he should die, yet, when the Lord shall come, he shall stand upon it, and with Job, in his flesh he shall see God. Therefore, this is my

counsel, that you retain your lands. (TPJS, 35)[19]

•••

Rumor with her ten thousand tongues is diffusing her uncertain sounds in almost every ear; but in these times of sore trial, let the Saints be patient and see the salvation of God. (TPJS, 42)[20]

•••

Those who cannot endure persecution, and stand in the day of affliction, cannot stand in the day when the Son of God shall burst the veil, and appear in all the glory of His Father, with all the holy angels. (TPJS, 42)[20]

•••

Live worthy of the blessings that shall follow, after much tribulation, to satiate the souls of them that hold out faithful to the end. (TPJS, 78)[29]

•••

Be assured, brethren, I am willing to stem the torrent of all opposition, in storms and in tempests, in thunders and in lightnings, by sea and by land, in the wilderness or among false brethren, or mobs, or wherever God in His providence may call us. (TPJS, 106)[37]

•••

After having suffered so great sacrifice and having passed through so great a season of sorrow, we trust that a ram may be caught in the thicket speedily, to relieve the sons and daughters of Abraham from their great anxiety, and to light up the lamp of salvation upon their countenances, that they may hold on now, after having gone so far unto everlasting life. (TPJS, 136)[47]

•••

Walls and irons, doors and creaking hinges, and half-scared-to-death guards and jailers, grinning like some damned spirits, lest an innocent man should make his escape to bring to light the damnable deeds of a murderous mob, are calculated in their very nature to make the soul of an honest man feel stronger than the powers of hell. (TPJS, 139)[47]

◆ ◆ ◆

In His Almighty name we are determined to endure tribulation as good soldiers unto the end. (TPJS, 139)[47]

◆ ◆ ◆

We ought at all times to be very careful that . . . high-mindedness shall never have place in our hearts; but condescend to men of low estate, and with all long-suffering bear the infirmities of the weak. (TPJS, 141)[47]

◆ ◆ ◆

Inasmuch as long-suffering, patience, and mercy have ever characterized the dealings of our heavenly Father towards the humble and penitent, I feel disposed to copy the example, cherish the same principles, and by so doing being a savior of my fellow men. (TPJS, 165)[53]

◆ ◆ ◆

As you increase in innocence and virtue, as you increase in goodness, let your heart expand, let them be enlarged toward others; be long-suffering, and bear with the faults and errors of mankind. (TPJS, 228)[75]

◆ ◆ ◆

Men or women [can] not be compelled into the kingdom of God, but must be dealt with in long-suffering, and at last we shall save them. (TPJS, 241)[78]

LOVE

Pure and steadfast love for those who are his benefactors . . . should characterize a President of the Church of Christ. (TPJS, 30)[17]

◆ ◆ ◆

Our love should never fail, but increase more and more. (TPJS, 31)[17]

◆ ◆ ◆

It is a duty which every Saint ought to render to his brethren freely—to always love them, and ever succor them. To be justified before God we must love one another; we must overcome evil; we must visit the fatherless and the widow in their affliction, and we must keep ourselves unspotted from the world; for such virtues flow from the great fountain of pure religion, strengthening our faith by adding every good quality that adorns the children of the blessed Jesus, we can pray in the season of prayer; we can love our neighbor as ourselves, and be faithful in tribulation, knowing that the reward of such is greater in the kingdom of heaven. What a consolation! What a joy! Let me live the life of the righteous, and let my reward be like his! (TPJS, 76)[29]

◆ ◆ ◆

We remember your losses and sorrows [Bro. Peck]; our first ties are not broken; we participate with you in the evil as well as the good, in the sorrows as well as the joys; our union, we trust, is stronger than death, and shall never be severed. (TPJS, 79)[29]

◆ ◆ ◆

I feel for my fellow men; I do it in the name of the Lord being moved upon by the Holy Spirit. Oh, that I could snatch them from the vortex of misery, into which I behold them plunging themselves, by their sins that I might be enabled by the warning voice, to be an instrument of bringing them to unfeigned repentance, that might have faith to stand in the evil day! (TPJS, 87)[31]

◆ ◆ ◆

Wives, submit yourselves unto your own husbands, as it is fit in the Lord. Husbands, love your wives, and be not bitter against them. (TPJS, 88)[31]

•••

I have sometimes spoken too harshly from the impulse of the moment, and inasmuch as I have wounded your feelings, brethren, I ask your forgiveness, for I love you and will hold you up with all my heart in all righteousness, before the Lord, and before all men. (TPJS, 106)[37]

•••

No power or influence can or ought to be maintained by virtue of the Priesthood, only by persuasion, by long-suffering, by gentleness, and meekness, and by love unfeigned; by kindness, and pure knowledge, which shall greatly enlarge the soul without hypocrisy, and without guile, reproving betimes with sharpness, when moved upon by the Holy Ghost, and then showing forth afterwards an increase of love toward him whom thou hast reproved, lest he esteem thee to be his enemy; that he may know that thy faithfulness is stronger than the cords of death; let thy bowels also be full of charity towards all men, and to the household of faith, and let virtue garnish thy thoughts unceasingly, then shall thy confidence wax strong in the presence of God, and the doctrine of the Priesthood shall distill upon thy soul as the dews from heaven. The Holy ghost shall be thy constant companion, and thy sceptre an unchanging sceptre of righteousness and truth, and thy dominion shall be an everlasting dominion, and without compulsory means, it shall flow unto thee forever and ever. (TPJS, 142)[47]

•••

There is a love from God that should be exercised toward those of our faith, who walk uprightly, which is peculiar to

itself; but it is without prejudice; it also gives scope to the mind, which enables us to conduct ourselves with greater liberality towards all that are not of our faith, than what they exercise towards one another. These principles approximate nearer to the mind of God, because it is like God, or Godlike. (TPJS, 147)[47]

•••

Love is one of the chief characteristics of Deity, and ought to be manifested by those who aspire to be the sons of God. (TPJS, 174)[54]

•••

A man filled with the love of God, is not content with blessing his family alone, but ranges through the whole world, anxious to bless the whole human race. (TPJS, 174)[54]

•••

Let every selfish feeling be not only buried, but annihilated; and let love to God and man predominate, and reign triumphant in every mind, that their hearts may become like unto Enoch's of old, and comprehend all things. (TPJS, 178)[55]

•••

Be on the alert to concentrate our energies. . . . The best feelings should exist in our midst; and then, by the help of the Almighty, we shall go on from victory to victory, and from conquest to conquest; our evil passions will be subdued, our prejudices depart; we shall find no room in our bosoms for hatred; vice will hide its deformed head, and we shall stand approved in the sight of Heaven, and be acknowledged the sons of God. (TPJS, 179)[55]

•••

Be faithful, let your love and moderation be known unto all men; be patient, be mindful to observe all the commandments of your heavenly Father, and the God of all grace shall bless you. Even so. Amen. (TPJS, 187)[59]

♦♦♦

"What greater love hath any man than that he lay down his life for his friend"; then why not fight for our friend until we die? (TPJS, 195)[66]

♦♦♦

Nothing is so much calculated to lead people to forsake sin as to take them by the hand, and watch over them with tenderness. When persons manifest the least kindness and love to me, O, what power it has over my mind, while the opposite course has a tendency to harrow up all the harsh feelings and depress the human mind. (TPJS, 240)[79]

♦♦♦

It is the object of this [Relief] Society to reform persons, not to take those that are corrupt and foster them in their wickedness; but if they repent, we are bound to take them, and by kindness sanctify and cleanse them from all unrighteousness by our influence in watching over them. Nothing will have such influence over people as the fear of being disfellowshipped by so goodly a society as this. (TPJS, 240)[79]

♦♦♦

God does not look on sin with allowance, but when men have sinned, there must be allowance made for them. (TPJS, 240)[79]

♦♦♦

The nearer we get to our heavenly Father, the more we are disposed to look with compassion on perishing souls; we feel that we want to take them upon our shoulders, and cast their sins behind our backs. . . . if you would have God have mercy on you, have mercy on one another. (TPJS, 241)[79]

♦♦♦

The best measure or principle to bring the poor to repentance is to administer to their wants. (TPJS, 241)[79]

♦♦♦

I have no enemies but for the truth's sake. I have no desire but to do all men good. I feel to pray for all men. (TPJS, 275)[91]

♦♦♦

It is my meditation all the day, and more than my meat and drink, to know how I shall make the Saints of God comprehend the visions that roll like an overflowing surge before my mind. (TPJS, 296)[102]

♦♦♦

If I have no expectation of seeing my father, mother, brothers, sisters and friends again, my heart would burst in a moment, and I should go down to my grave. (TPJS, 296)[102]

♦♦♦

Many persons think a prophet must be a great deal better than anybody else. Suppose I would condescend—yes, I will call it condescend, to be a great deal better than any of you, I would be raised up to the highest heaven; and who should I have to accompany me? (TPJS, 303)[109]

♦♦♦

Joseph remarked that all was well between him and the heavens; that he had no enmity against any one; and as the prayer of Jesus, or his pattern, so prayed Joseph—Father, forgive me my trespasses as I forgive those who trespass against me, for I freely forgive all men. If we would secure and cultivate the love of others, we must love others, even our enemies as well as friends. (TPJS, 312)[114]

♦♦♦

Sectarian priests cry out concerning me, and ask, "Why is it this babbler gains so many followers, and retains them?" I answer, It is because I possess the principle of love. All I can offer the world is a good heart and a good hand. (TPJS, 313)[114]

◆◆◆

There is no greater love than this, that a man lay down his life for his friends. I discover hundreds and thousands of my brethren ready to sacrifice their lives for me. (TPJS, 315)[114]

◆◆◆

Charity, which is love, covereth a multitude of sins, and I have often covered up all the faults among you; but the prettiest thing is to have no faults at all. We should cultivate a meek, quiet and peaceable spirit. (TPJS, 316)[115]

◆◆◆

It is a time-honored adage that love begets love. Let us pour forth love—show forth our kindness unto all mankind, and the Lord will reward us with everlasting increase; cast our bread upon the waters and we shall receive it after many days, increased to an hundredfold. (TPJS, 316)[115]

◆◆◆

The Lord once told me that what I asked for I should have. I have been afraid to ask God to kill my enemies, lest some of them should peradventure, repent. (TPJS, 340)[128]

◆◆◆

I have no enmity against any man. I love you all; but I hate some of your deeds. I am your best friend, and if persons miss their mark it is their own fault. If I reprove a man, and he hates me, he is a fool; for I love all men, especially these my brethren and sisters. (TPJS, 361)[130]

◆◆◆

They that hurl all their hell and fiery billows upon me . . . will roll off me as fast as they come on. But I have an order of things to save the poor fellows at any rate, and get them saved; for I will send men to preach to them in prison and save them if I can. (TPJS, 366)[132]

◆◆◆

If my life is of no value to my friends it is of none to myself. (TPJS, 377)[136]

◆◆◆

They retired to rest late. Joseph and Hyrum occupied the only bedstead in the [jail] room, while their friends lay side by side on the mattresses on the floor. Dr. Richards sat up writing until his last candle left him in the dark. The report of a gun fired close by caused Joseph to rise, leave the bed, and lay himself on the floor, having Dan Jones on his left, and John S. Fullmer on his right, "Lay your head on my arm for a pillow, Brother John"; and when they were all quiet they conversed in a low tone about the prospects of their deliverance. Joseph gave expression to several presentiments that he had to die, and said, "I would like to see my family again," and "I would to God that I could preach to the Saints in Nauvoo once more." (TPJS, 383)[142]

◆◆◆

[In a letter to Emma, he wrote] P. S.— Dear Emma, I am very much resigned to my lot, knowing I am justified, and have done the best that could be done. Give my love to the children and all my friends, Mr. Brewer, and all who enquire after me; and as for treason, I know I have not committed any, and they cannot prove anything of the kind, so you need not have any fears that anything can happen to us on that account. May God bless you all. Amen. (TPJS, 391)[144]

LOYALTY

In all your trials, troubles, temptations, afflictions, bonds, imprisonments and death, see to it that you do not betray heaven; that you do not betray Jesus Christ; that you do not betray the brethren; that you do not betray the revelations of God, whether in Bible, Book of Mormon, or Doctrine and Covenants, or any other . . . revealed unto man. . . . Yea, in all your kickings and flounderings, see to it that you do not this thing, lest innocent blood be found upon your skirts, and you go down to hell. All other sins are not to be compared to sinning against the Holy Ghost, and proving a traitor to the brethren. (TPJS, 156)[49]

LYING

(*See also* DECEPTION)

I have been drawn into this course of proceeding by persecution, that is brought upon us from false rumors and misrepresentations concerning my sentiments. (TPJS, 83)[31]

◆◆◆

Those who cry transgression do it because they are the servants of sin and are the children of disobedience themselves; and those who swear falsely against my servants, that they might bring them into bondage and death; wo unto them; because they have offended my little ones; they shall be severed from the ordinances of mine house. (TPJS, 135)[47]

◆◆◆

A frank and open rebuke provoketh a good man to emulation; and in the hour of trouble he will be your best friend. But on the other hand, it will draw out all the corruptions of corrupt hearts; and lying and the poison of asps is under their tongues; and they do cause the pure in heart to be cast into prison, because they want them out of their way. (TPJS, 137)[47]

◆◆◆

Lying spirits are going forth in the earth. There will be great manifestations of spirits, both false and true. (TPJS, 161)[49]

MAN

Every man lives for himself. . . . But except a man be born again, he cannot see the kingdom of God. . . . He may receive a glory like unto the moon [i.e. of which the light of the moon is typical]. Or a star, [i.e. of which the light of the stars is typical] but he can never come unto Mount Zion, and unto the city of the living God . . . unless he becomes as a little child, and is taught by the Spirit of God. (TPJS, 12)[8]

◆◆◆

All men are naturally disposed to walk in their own paths as they are pointed out by their own fingers, and are not willing to consider and walk in the path which is pointed out by another, saying, This is the way, walk ye in it, although he should be an unerring director, and the Lord his God sent him. (TPJS, 26)[15]

◆◆◆

I have learned in my travels that man is treacherous and selfish, but few excepted. (TPJS, 30)[17]

•••

It is reasonable to suppose that man departed from the first teachings, or instructions which he received from heaven in the first age, and refused by his disobedience to be governed by them. Consequently, he formed such laws as best suited his own mind, or as he supposed, were best adapted to his situation. But that God has influenced man more or less since that time in the formation of law for His benefit we have no hesitancy in believing. . . . Though man in his own supposed wisdom would not admit the influence of a power superior to his own. (TPJS, 57)[21]

•••

Does it remain for a people who never had faith enough to call down one scrap of revelation from heaven, and for all they have now are indebted to the faith of another people who lived hundreds and thousands of years before them, does it remain for them to say how much God has spoken and how much He has not spoken? (TPJS, 61)[21]

•••

Such is the darkness and ignorance of this generation, that they look upon it as incredible that a man should have any intercourse with his Maker. (TPJS, 89)[32]

•••

Men are in the habit, when the truth is exhibited by the servants of God, of saying, All is mystery; they have spoken in parables, and therefore, are not to be understood. It is true they have eyes to see, and see not, but none are so blind as those who will not see. (TPJS, 96)[34]

•••

Men who have no principle of righteousness in themselves, and whose hearts are full of iniquity, and have no desire for the principles of truth, do not understand the word of truth when they hear it. The devil taketh away the word of truth out of their hearts, because there is no desire of righteousness in them. (TPJS, 96)[34]

•••

If the Church knew all the commandments, one-half they would condemn through prejudice and ignorance. (TPJS, 112)[41]

•••

"Behold, there are many called, but few are chosen. And why are they not chosen? Because their hearts are so set upon the things of this world, and aspire to the honors of men, that they do not learn this one lesson—that the rights of the Priesthood are inseparably connected with the powers of heaven, and that the powers of heaven cannot be controlled nor handled only upon the principles of righteousness. That they may be conferred upon us, it is true; but when we undertake to cover our sins, or to gratify our pride, our vain ambition, or to exercise control, or dominion, or compulsion, upon the souls of the children of men in any degree of unrighteousness, behold, the heavens withdraw themselves, the Spirit of the Lord is grieved; and when it is withdrawn, Amen to the Priesthood, or the authority of that man. Behold! Ere he is aware, he is left to himself to kick against the pricks, to persecute the saints, and to fight against God.

"We have learned by sad experience that it is the nature and disposition of almost all men, as soon as they get a little authority, as they suppose, they will immediately begin to exercise unrighteous dominion. Hence, many are called, but few are chosen." (TPJS, 142)[47]

•••

"There are many yet on the earth among all sects, parties, denominations, who are blinded by the subtle craftiness of men, whereby they lie in wait to deceive, and who are only kept from the truth because they know not where to find it." (TPJS, 145)[47]

◆◆◆

The time is soon coming, when no man will have any peace, but in Zion and her stakes. (TPJS, 161)[49]

◆◆◆

[Some men,] . . . intelligent, learned, virtuous and lovely, walking in uprightness and in all good conscience, so far as they have been able . . . [are left to] discern duty from the muddy stream of tradition, or from the blotted page of the book of nature. (TPJS, 192)[63]

◆◆◆

In the earlier ages of the world a righteous man, and a man of God and intelligence, had a better chance to do good, to be believed and received than at the present day; but in these days, such a man is much opposed and persecuted by most of the inhabitants of the earth, and he has much sorrow to pass through here. (TPJS, 196)[68]

◆◆◆

Various and conflicting are the opinions of men concerning the Plan of Salvation, the requisitions of the Almighty, the necessary preparations for heaven, the state and condition of departed spirits, and the happiness or misery that is consequent upon the practice of righteousness or iniquity according to several notions of virtue and vice. [And one sect tends to condemn the other sect.] (TPJS, 217)[74]

◆◆◆

The great designs of God in relation to the salvation of the human family, are very little understood by the professedly wise and intelligent generation in which we live. (TPJS, 217)[74]

◆◆◆

Various and conflicting are the opinions of men in regard to the gift of the Holy Ghost. . . . It is not to be wondered at that men should be ignorant . . . of the nature . . . of the Holy Ghost, when we consider that the human family have been enveloped in gross darkness and ignorance for many centuries past, without revelation. (TPJS, 242)[80]

◆◆◆

We believe in [the gift of the Holy Ghost] in all its fullness, and power, and greatness, and glory; but whilst we do this, we believe in it rationally, consistently, and scripturally, and not according to the wild vagaries, foolish notions and traditions of men. (TPJS, 243)[80]

◆◆◆

The great and wise of ancient days have failed in all their attempts to promote eternal power, peace and happiness. Their nations have crumbled to pieces; their thrones have been cast down in their turn, and their cities, and their mightiest works of art have been annihilated; or their dilapidated towers, or time-worn monuments have left us but feeble traces of their former magnificence and ancient grandeur. They proclaim as with a voice of thunder, those imperishable truths—that man's strength is weakness, his wisdom is folly, his glory is his shame. (TPJS, 249)[81]

◆◆◆

The world itself presents one great theater of misery, woe, and "distress of nations and perplexity." All, all, speak with a voice of thunder, that man is not able to govern himself, to legislate for himself, to protect himself, to promote his own good, nor the good of the world. (TPJS, 250)[81]

◆◆◆

Although I do wrong, I do not the wrongs that I am charged with doing; the wrong that I do is through the frailty of human nature, like other men. No man lives without fault. (TPJS, 258)[84]

◆◆◆

Faith has been wanting, not only among the heathen, but in professed Christendom, also, so that . . . all the gifts and blessings have been wanting. (TPJS, 270)[90]

◆◆◆

Now, in this world, mankind are naturally selfish, ambitious and striving to excel one above another; yet some are willing to build up others as well as themselves. (TPJS, 297)[103]

◆◆◆

The inhabitants of the [American] continent anciently were so constituted, and were so determined and persevering, either in righteousness or wickedness, that God visited them, immediately either with great judgments or blessings. But the present generation, if they were going to battle, if they got any assistance from God, they would have to obtain it by faith. (TPJS, 299)[103]

◆◆◆

Paul said, "the world by wisdom know not God," so the world by speculation are destitute of revelation. (TPJS, 300)[104]

◆◆◆

I do not think there have been many good men on the earth since the days of Adam; but there was one good man and his name was Jesus. (TPJS, 303)[109]

◆◆◆

The inhabitants of the earth are asleep; they know not the day of their visitation. (TPJS, 305)[109]

◆◆◆

Many things are insoluble to the children of men in the last days; for instance, that God should raise the dead, and forgetting that things have been hid from before the foundation of the world, which are to be revealed to babes in the last days. (TPJS, 309)[113]

◆◆◆

There are a great many wise men and women too in our midst who are too wise to be taught; therefore they must die in their ignorance, and in the resurrection they will find their mistake. Many seal up the door of heaven by saying . . . God may reveal and I will believe. (TPJS, 309)[113]

◆◆◆

Men often come to me with their troubles, and seek my will, crying, Oh, Brother Joseph, help me! Help me! But when I am in trouble few of them sympathize with me or extend to me relief. (TPJS, 315)[114]

◆◆◆

I find that in the midst of business and care the spirit is willing, but the flesh is weak. (TPJS, 315)[114]

◆◆◆

It is the constitutional disposition of mankind to set up stakes and bounds to the works and ways of the Almighty. (TPJS, 320)[118]

◆◆◆

This generation is as corrupt as the generation of the Jews that crucified Christ; and if He were here today, and should preach the same doctrine He did then, they would put Him to death. (TPJS, 328)[122]

◆◆◆

There are but a very few beings in the world who understand rightly the character of God. The great majority of mankind do not comprehend anything, either that which is past, or that which is to come, as it respects their relationship to God . . . and consequently they know but little above the brute beast, or more than to eat, drink and sleep . . . unless it is given by the inspiration of the Almighty. (TPJS, 343)[130]

•••

If men do not comprehend the character of God, they do not comprehend themselves. (TPJS, 343)[130]

•••

Another subject . . . calculated to exalt man . . . I shall therefore just touch upon . . . is associated with the subject of the resurrection of the dead—namely, the soul—the mind of man—the immortal spirit. Where did it come from? All learned men and doctors of divinity say that God created it in the beginning; But it is not so. . . . Hear it, all ye ends of the world; for God has told me so. . . . I am going to tell of things more noble.

We say that God himself is a self-existent being. Who told you so? It is correct enough; but how did it get into your heads? Who told you that man did not exist in like manner upon the same principles? Man does exist upon the same principles. God made a tabernacle and put a spirit into it, and it became a living soul. . . . It does not say in the Hebrew [Bible] that God created the spirit of man. It says "God made man out of the earth and put into him Adam's spirit, and so became a living body." (TPJS, 352)[130]

•••

The best men bring forth the best works. The man who tells you words of life is the man who can save you. (TPJS, 358)[130]

•••

No man can limit the bounds or the eternal existence of eternal time. Hath he beheld the eternal world, and is he authorized to say that there is only one God? He makes himself a fool if he thinks or says so, and there is an end of his career or progress in knowledge. He cannot obtain all knowledge, for he has sealed up the gate to it. (TPJS, 371)[133]

MANNERS

(See also COURTESY)

It is an insult to a meeting for persons to leave just before its close. If they must go out, let them go half an hour before. No gentlemen will go out of a meeting just at closing. (TPJS, 287)[100]

•••

As president of this house, I forbid any man leaving just as we are going to close the meeting. He is no gentleman who will do it. I don't care who does it, even if it were the king of England. I forbid it. (TPJS, 296)[102]

MAN'S GOVERNMENT

All regularly organized and well established governments have certain laws by which, more or less, the innocent are protected and the guilty punished. (TPJS, 49)[21]

•••

It is reasonable to suppose that man departed from the first teachings, or instructions which he received from heaven in the first age, and refused by his disobedience to be governed by them. Consequently, he formed such laws as best suited his own mind, or as he supposed, were best adapted to his situation. But that God has influenced man more or less since that time in the formation of law for His benefit we have no hesitancy in believing. (TPJS, 57)[21]

◆◆◆

If there are any among you who aspire after their own aggrandizement, and seek their own opulence, while their brethren are groaning in poverty, and are under sore trials and temptations, they cannot be benefited by the intercession of the Holy Spirit. (TPJS, 141)[47]

◆◆◆

The government of the Almighty [whether religious or over nations] has always been very dissimilar to the government of men. . . . The government of God has always tended to promote peace, unity, harmony, strength, and happiness; while that of man has been productive of confusion, disorder, weakness, and misery. (TPJS, 248)[81]

◆◆◆

The greatest acts of the mighty men have been to depopulate nations and to overthrow kingdoms; and whilst they have exalted themselves and become glorious, it has been at the expense of the lives of the innocent, the blood of the oppressed, the moans of the widow, and the tears of the orphans. (TPJS, 248)[81]

◆◆◆

The great and wise of ancient days have failed in all their attempts to promote eternal power, peace and happiness. Their nations have crumbled to pieces; their thrones have been cast down in their turn, and their cities, and their mightiest works of art have been annihilated; or their dilapidated towers, or time-worn monuments have left us but feeble traces of their former magnificence and ancient grandeur. They proclaim as with a voice of thunder, those imperishable truths—that man's strength is weakness, his wisdom is folly, his glory is his shame. (TPJS, 249)[81]

◆◆◆

Monarchial, aristocratical, and republican governments of their various kinds and grades, have, in their turn, been raised to dignity, and prostrated in the dust. The plans of the greatest politicians, the wisest senators, and most profound statesmen have been exploded; and the proceedings of the greatest chieftains, the bravest generals, and the wisest kings have fallen to the ground. Nation has succeeded nation, and we have inherited nothing but their folly. History records their [childish] plans, their short-lived glory, their feeble intellect and their ignoble deeds. (TPJS, 249)[81]

◆◆◆

The world itself presents one great theater of misery, woe, and "distress of nations and perplexity." All, all, speak with a voice of thunder, that man is not able to govern himself, to legislate for himself, to protect himself, to promote his own good, nor the good of the world. (TPJS, 250)[81]

◆◆◆

The earth is groaning under corruption, oppression, tyranny and bloodshed; and God is coming out of His hiding place. (TPJS, 253)[81]

◆◆◆

The different states, and even Congress itself, have passed many laws diametrically contrary to the Constitution of the United States. (TPJS, 279)[95]

◆◆◆

Executive writs could be issued when they ought to be, and not be made instruments of cruelty to oppress the innocent, and persecute men whose religion is unpopular. (TPJS, 327)[122]

◆◆◆

The government will not receive any advice or counsel from me; they are self-sufficient. But they must go to hell and work out their own salvation with fear and trembling. (TPJS, 334)[127]

•••

If any man is authorized to take away my life because he thinks and says I am a false teacher, then, upon the same principle, we should be justified in taking away the life of every false teacher, and where would be the end of blood? And who would not be the sufferer? (TPJS, 344)[130]

•••

Meddle not with any man for his religion; and all governments ought to permit every man to enjoy his religion unmolested. No man is authorized to take away life in consequence of difference in religion, which all laws and governments ought to tolerate and protect, right or wrong. (TPJS, 344)[130]

MARRIAGE

Wives, submit yourselves unto your own husbands, as it is fit in the Lord. Husbands, love your wives, and be not bitter against them. (TPJS, 88)[31]

•••

[Mormons] believe that if their companion dies, they have a right to marry again. But we do disapprove of the custom . . . in marrying in five or six weeks, or even in two or three months, after the death of their companion. We believe that due respect ought to be had to the memory of the dead, and the feelings of both friends and children. (TPJS, 119)[45]

•••

When you go home, never give a cross or unkind word to your husbands, but let kindness, charity and love crown your works henceforward. (TPJS, 229)[75]

•••

Except a man and his wife enter into an everlasting covenant and be married for eternity, while in this probation, by the power and authority of the Holy Priesthood, they will cease to increase when they die; that is, they will not have any children after the resurrection. But those who are married by the power and authority of the priesthood in this life, and continue without committing the sin against the Holy Ghost, will continue to increase and have children in the celestial glory. (TPJS, 300)[105]

MARTYRS

Remember not to murmur at the dealings of God with His creatures. You are not as yet brought into as trying circumstances as were the ancient Prophets and Apostles . . . of whom the world was not worthy. . . . amidst all their afflictions they rejoiced that they were counted worthy to receive persecution for Christ's sake. (TPJS, 32)[18]

•••

I know that Zion, in the due time of the Lord, will be redeemed; but how many will be the days of her purification, tribulation, and affliction, the Lord has kept hid from my eyes; and when I enquire concerning this subject, the voice of the Lord is: Be still, and know that I am God; all those who suffer for my name shall reign with me, and he that layeth down his life for my sake shall find it again. (TPJS, 34)[19]

•••

There seems to be a whispering that the angels of heaven . . . have taken counsel together; and . . . have taken cognizance of the testimony of those who were murdered at Haun's Mills, and also those who were martyred . . . elsewhere, and have passed some decisions peradventure in favor of the saints, and those who were called to suffer without cause. (TPJS, 141)[47]

◆◆◆

I know what I say; I understand my mission and business. God Almighty is my shield; and what can man do if God is my friend? I shall not be sacrificed until my time comes; then I shall be offered freely. (TPJS, 274)[91]

◆◆◆

If it has been demonstrated that I have been willing to die for a "Mormon," I am bold to declare before Heaven that I am just as ready to die in defending the rights of a Presbyterian, a Baptist, or a good man of any other denomination; for the same principle which would trample upon the rights of the Latter-day Saints would trample upon the rights of the Roman Catholics, or of any other denomination who may be unpopular and too weak to defend themselves. (TPJS, 313)[113]

◆◆◆

If I lose my life in a good cause I am willing to be sacrificed on the altar of virtue, righteousness and truth, in maintaining the laws and Constitution of the United States, if need be, for the general good of man. (TPJS, 332)[124]

◆◆◆

Rejoice, O Israel! Your friends who have been murdered for the truth's sake in the persecutions shall triumph gloriously in the celestial world, while their murderers shall welter for ages in torment, even until they shall have paid the uttermost farthing. (TPJS, 359)[130]

◆◆◆

[On the way to Carthage, Joseph, Hyrum and others were met a] Captain Dunn with a company of about sixty militia on which seeing Joseph said, "Do

not be alarmed, brethren, for they cannot do more to you than the enemies of truth did to the ancient Saints—they can only kill the body." (TPJS, 379)[137]

◆◆◆

[On their way to Carthage, Joseph said to the company that was with him] I am going like a lamb to the slaughter, but I am calm as a summer's morning. I have a conscience void of offence toward God and toward all men. If they take my life I shall die an innocent man, and my blood shall cry from the ground for vengeance, and it shall be said of me, "He was murdered in cold blood"! (TPJS, 379)[137]

MATTER

(*See also* ELEMENTS)

The elements are eternal. That which has a beginning will surely have an end; take a ring, it is without beginning or end—cut it for a beginning place and at the same time you have an ending place. (TPJS, 181)[56]

◆◆◆

The spirit is a substance; . . . it is material, but . . . it is more pure, elastic and refined matter than the body; . . . it existed before the body, can exist in the body; and will exist separate from the body, when the body will be mouldering in the dust; and will in the resurrection, be again united with it. (TPJS, 207)[71]

◆◆◆

There is no such thing as immaterial matter. All spirit is matter, but is more fine or pure, and can only be discerned by purer eyes. We cannot see it, but when our bodies are purified, we shall see that it is all matter. (TPJS, 301)[107]

◆◆◆

You ask the learned doctors why they say the world was made out of nothing;

and they will answer, "Doesn't the Bible say He *created* the world?" And they infer, from the word create, that it must have been made out of nothing. Now, the word create came from the word *baurau* which does not mean to create out of nothing; it means to organize; the same as a man would organize materials and build a ship. Hence, we infer that God had materials to organize the world out of chaos— chaotic matter, which is element, and in which dwells all the glory. Elements had an existence from the time He had. The pure principles of element are principles which can never be destroyed; they may be organized and re-organized, but not destroyed. They had no beginning, and can have no end. (TPJS, 350)[130]

MEEKNESS

Some of the company thought I was not a very meek Prophet; so I told them: "I am meek and lowly of heart," and will personify Jesus for a moment, to illustrate the principle, and cried out with a loud voice, "Woe unto you, ye doctors, woe unto you, ye lawyers; woe unto you, ye scribes, Pharisees, and hypocrites!" But you cannot find the place where I ever went that I found fault with their food, their drink, their house, their lodgings; no, never; and this is what is meant by the meekness and lowliness of Jesus. (TPJS, 270)[90]

MELCHIZEDEK PRIESTHOOD

There are two Priesthoods spoken of in the Scriptures, vis., the Melchizedek and the Aaronic or Levitical. Although there are two Priesthoods, yet the Melchizedek Priesthood comprehends the Aaronic or Levitical Priesthood, and is the grand head, and holds the highest authority which pertains to the Priesthood, and the

keys of the Kingdom of God in all ages of the world to the latest posterity on the earth; and is the channel through which all knowledge, doctrine, the Plan of Salvation and every important matter is revealed from heaven. (TPJS, 166)[54]

•••

All the prophets had the Melchizedek Priesthood and were ordained by God himself. (TPJS, 181)[56]

•••

Those holding the fullness of the Melchizedek Priesthood are kings and priests of the Most High God, holding the keys of power and blessings. In fact, that Priesthood is a perfect law of theocracy, and stands as God to give law unto the people, administering endless lives to the sons and daughters of Adam. (TPJS, 322)[119]

•••

The Melchizedek Priesthood holds the right from the eternal God . . . and . . . is as eternal as God Himself, having neither beginning of days nor end of life . . . and is by an oath and covenant. (TPJS, 323)[119]

MERCY

(*See also* COMPASSION; FAIRNESS; FORGIVENESS)

To all, we say, be merciful and you shall find mercy. Seek to help save souls, not to destroy them; for verily you know, that "there is more joy in heaven over one sinner that repents than over ninety and nine just persons that [feel they] need no repentance." (TPJS, 77)[29]

•••

Ever keep in exercise the principle of mercy, and be ready to forgive our brother on the first intimation of repentance, and asking forgiveness; and should we ever forgive our brother, or even our enemy, before he repent or ask forgiveness, our heavenly Father would be equally as merciful unto us. (TPJS, 155)[49]

♦♦♦

Inasmuch as long-suffering, patience, and mercy have ever characterized the dealings of our heavenly Father towards the humble and penitent, I feel disposed to copy the example, cherish the same principles, and by so doing being a savior of my fellow men. (TPJS, 165)[53]

♦♦♦

There is never a time when the spirit is too old to approach God. All are within the reach of pardoning mercy, who have not committed the unpardonable sin, which hath no forgiveness. (TPJS, 191)[63]

♦♦♦

As females possess refined feelings and sensitiveness, they are also subject to overmuch zeal, which must ever prove dangerous, and cause them to be rigid in a religious capacity—[they] should be armed with mercy, notwithstanding the iniquity among us. (TPJS, 238)[78]

♦♦♦

To the iniquitous show yourselves merciful. (TPJS, 239)[78]

♦♦♦

I want the innocent to go free—rather spare ten iniquitous among you, than condemn one innocent one. . . , "Fret not thyself because of evildoers." God will see to it. (TPJS, 239)[78]

♦♦♦

God does not look on sin with allowance, but when men have sinned, there must be allowance made for them. (TPJS, 240)[79]

♦♦♦

Nothing is so much calculated to lead people to forsake sin as to take them by the hand, and watch over them with tenderness. When persons manifest the least kindness and love to me, O, what power it has over my mind, while the opposite course has a tendency to harrow up all the harsh feelings and depress the human mind. (TPJS, 240)[79]

♦♦♦

We must be merciful to one another, and overlook small things. (TPJS, 240)[79]

♦♦♦

The nearer we get to our heavenly Father, the more we are disposed to look with compassion on perishing souls; we feel that we want to take them upon our shoulders, and cast their sins behind our backs . . . if you would have God have mercy on you, have mercy on one another. (TPJS, 241)[79]

♦♦♦

There should be no license for sin, but mercy should go hand in hand with reproof. (TPJS, 241)[79]

♦♦♦

Our heavenly Father is more liberal in His views, and boundless in His mercies and blessings, than we are ready to believe or receive; and, at the same time, is more terrible to the workers of iniquity, more awful in the executions of His punishments, and more ready to detect every false way, than we are apt to suppose Him to be. (TPJS, 257)[83]

♦♦♦

I love that man better who swears a stream as long as my arm, yet deals justice to his neighbors and mercifully deals his substance to the poor, than the long, smooth-faced hypocrite. (TPJS, 303)[109]

•••

Never exact of a friend in adversity what you would require in prosperity. (TPJS, 317)[116]

MILLENNIUM

There are sins which may be forgiven in the world to come, although the sin of blasphemy [against the Holy Ghost] cannot be forgiven. (TPJS, 219)[74]

•••

The world has had a fair trial for six thousand years; the Lord will try the seventh thousand Himself; "He whose right it is, will possess the kingdom, and reign until He has put all things under His feet"; iniquity will hide its hoary head, Satan will be bound, and the works of darkness destroyed; righteousness will be put to the line, and judgment to the plummet, and "he that fears the Lord will alone be exalted in that day." (TPJS, 252)[81]

•••

Christ and the resurrected Saints will reign over the earth during the thousand years. They will not probably dwell upon the earth, but will visit it when they please, or when it is necessary to govern it. (TPJS, 268)[88]

•••

There will be wicked men on the earth during the thousand years. The heathen nations who will not come up to worship will be visited with the judgments of God, and must eventually be destroyed from the earth. (TPJS, 268)[88]

MISDIRECTION

We have reason to believe that many things were introduced among the Saints before God had signified the times; and notwithstanding the principles and plans may have been good, yet aspiring men, or in other words, men who had not the substance of godliness about them, perhaps undertook to handle edged tools. Children, you know, are fond of tools, while they are not yet able to use them. (TPJS, 144)[47]

•••

Nothing is a greater injury to the children of men than to be under the influence of a false spirit when they think they have the Spirit of God. Thousands have felt the influence of its terrible power and baneful effects. . . . Pain, misery and ruin have followed in their train; nations have been convulsed, kingdoms overthrown, provinces laid waste, and blood, carnage and desolation are habiliments in which it has been clothed. (TPJS, 205)[71]

•••

The world has always mistook false prophets for true ones, and those that were sent of God, they considered to be false prophets, and hence they killed, stoned, punished and imprisoned the true prophets . . . and though the most honorable men of the earth, they banished them from their society as vagabonds, whilst they cherished, honored and supported knaves, vagabonds, hypocrites, imposters, and the basest of men. (TPJS, 206)[71]

MISSION TO SPIRIT PRISON

We have an account of our Savior preaching to the spirits in prison, to spirits that had been imprisoned from the days of Noah; and what did He preach to them? That they were to stay there? Certainly not! Let His own declaration testify, "He hath sent me to heal the broken-hearted, to preach deliverance to the captives, and recovering of sight to the blind, to set at liberty them that are bruised." (Luke 4:18) Isaiah has it—"To bring out the prisoners from the prison, and them that sit in darkness from the prison house." (Isaiah 17:7.) It is very evident from this that He not only went to preach to them, but to deliver, or bring them out of the prison house. (TPJS, 219)[74]

MISSIONARY WORK

If they receive not your testimony in one place, flee to another, remembering to cast no reflections, nor throw out any bitter sayings. If you do your duty, it will be just as well with you, as though all men embraced the Gospel. (TPJS, 43)[20]

◆◆◆

Avoid contentions and vain disputes with men of corrupt minds, who do not desire to know the truth. (TPJS, 43)[20]

◆◆◆

Impressed with the [fact of darkness covering the earth and minds of men] what can be the feelings of those who have been partakers of the heavenly gift and have tasted the good word of God, and the powers of the world to come? Who but those that can see the awful precipice upon which the world of mankind stands in this generation, can labor in the vineyard of the Lord without feeling a sense of the world's deplorable situation? Who but those who have duly considered the condescension of the Father of our spirits, in providing a sacrifice for His creatures, a plan of redemption, a power of atonement, a scheme of salvation, having as its great objects, the bringing of men back into the presence of the King of heaven, crowning them in the celestial glory, and making them heirs with the Son to that inheritance which

is incorruptible, undefiled, and which fadeth not away—who but such can realize the importance of a perfect walk before all men, and a diligence in calling upon all men to partake of these blessings? How indescribably glorious are these things to mankind! Of a truth they may be considered tidings of great joy to all people; and tidings, too, that ought to fill the earth and cheer the heart of everyone when sounded in his ears. The reflection that everyone is to receive according to his own diligence and perseverance while in the vineyard, ought to inspire everyone who is called to be a minister of these glad tidings, to so improve his talent that he may gain other talents, that when the Master sits down to take an account of the conduct of His servants, it may be said, "Well done, good and faithful servant: thou hast been faithful over a few things; I will now make thee ruler over many things: enter thou into the joy of thy Lord." (TPJS, 47)[21]

◆◆◆

If . . . there is an importance in this respect [of obeying God's laws] is there not a responsibility of great weight resting upon those who are called to declare these truths to men? (TPJS, 57)[21]

◆◆◆

Souls are as precious in the sight of God as they ever were; and the Elders were never called to drive any down to hell, but to persuade and invite all men everywhere to repent, that they may become the heirs of salvation. (TPJS, 77)[29]

◆◆◆

I feel it my duty to drop a few hints, that perhaps the Elders traveling through the world, [may] warn the inhabitants of the earth to flee the wrath to come, and save themselves from this untoward generation. (TPJS, 79)[30]

•••

When . . . traveling through the world . . . [Elders] should commence their labor with parents, or guardians; and their teachings should be such as are calculated to turn the hearts of the fathers to the children, and the hearts of children to the fathers; and no influence should be used with children, contrary to the consent of their parents or guardians; but all such as can be persuaded in a lawful and righteous manner, and with common consent, we should feel it our duty to influence . . . [families] to gather with the people of God. But otherwise let the responsibility rest upon the heads of parents or guardians. (TPJS, 86)[31]

•••

And if children embrace the Gospel, and their parents or guardians are unbelievers, teach them to stay at home and be obedient to their parents or guardians, if they require it; but if they consent to let them gather with the people of God, let them do so, and there shall be no wrong; and let all things be done carefully and righteously, and God will extend to all such His guardian care. (TPJS, 87)[31]

•••

It is the duty of Elders, when they enter into any house, to let their labors and warning voice be unto the master of the house; and if he receive the Gospel, then he may extend his influence to his wife. . . . But if a man forbid his wife, or his children, before they are of age, to receive the Gospel, then it should be the duty of the Elder to go his way, and use no influence against him, and let the responsibility be upon his head. (TPJS, 87)[31]

•••

I feel for my fellow men; I do it in the name of the Lord being moved upon by the Holy Spirit. Oh, that I could snatch them from the vortex of misery, into which I behold them plunging themselves, by their sins that I might be enabled by the warning voice, to be an instrument of bringing them to unfeigned repentance, that they might have faith to stand in the evil day! (TPJS, 87)[31]

•••

The Elders . . . [are] to go in all meekness, in sobriety, and preach Jesus Christ and Him crucified; not to contend with others on account of their faith. . . . and all who observe it . . . shall always be filled with the Holy Ghost. (TPJS, 109)[40]

•••

All are to preach the Gospel, by the power and influence of the Holy Ghost; and no man can preach the Gospel without the Holy Ghost. (TPJS, 112)[41]

•••

After all that has been said, the greatest and most important duty is to preach the Gospel. (TPJS, 113)[41]

•••

The Saints ought to lay hold of every door that shall seem to be opened to them, to obtain foothold on the earth, and be making all the preparation that is within their power for the terrible storms that are now gathering in the heavens. (TPJS, 141)[47]

•••

There are many yet on the earth among all sects, parties, denominations, who are blinded by the subtle craftiness of men, whereby they lie in wait to deceive, and who are only kept from the truth because they know not where to find it. (TPJS, 145)[47]

•••

Faith comes by hearing the word of God; that testimony is always attended by the spirit of prophesy and revelation. (TPJS, 148)[48]

•••

Ye are not sent out to be taught, but to teach. (TPJS, 156)[49]

•••

It is a day of warning, and not of many words. (TPJS, 156)[49]

•••

We ought to have the building up of Zion as our greatest object. The last revelation says, Ye shall not have time to have gone over the earth, until these things come. It will come as did the cholera, wars, fire and earthquakes; one pestilence after another until the Ancient of Days comes, then judgment will be given to the Saints. (TPJS, 160)[49]

•••

No man can be a minister of Jesus Christ except he has a testimony of Jesus; and this is the spirit of prophecy. (TPJS, 160)[49]

•••

Those engaged in seeking the outcasts of Israel, and the dispersed of Judah, cannot fail to enjoy the spirit of the Lord and have the choicest blessings of heaven rest upon them in copious effusions. (TPJS, 163)[51]

•••

He who has scattered Israel has promised to gather them; therefore inasmuch as you are to be instrumental in this great work, He will endow you with power, might, wisdom and intelligence, and every qualification necessary; while your minds will expand wider and wider, until you can circumscribe the earth and the heavens, reach forth into eternity, and contemplate the mighty acts of Jehovah in all their variety and glory. (TPJS, 163)[51]

•••

[Some men,] . . . intelligent, learned, virtuous and lovely, walking in uprightness and in all good conscience, so far as they have been able . . . [are left to] discern duty from the muddy stream of tradition, or from the blotted page of the book of nature. (TPJS, 192)[63]

•••

The gift of tongues by the power of the Holy Ghost in the Church, is for the benefit of the servants of God to preach to unbelievers, as on the day of Pentecost. (TPJS, 195)[67]

•••

There is now a day of salvation to such as repent and reform;—and they who repent not should be cast out from this society; yet we should woo them to return to God, lest they escape not the damnation of hell! (TPJS, 238)[78]

•••

Men or women [can]not be compelled into the kingdom of God, but must be dealt with in long-suffering, and at last we shall save them. (TPJS, 241)[78]

•••

The best measure or principle to bring the poor to repentance is to administer to their wants. (TPJS, 241)[78]

•••

The Ladies' Relief Society is not only to relieve the poor, but to save souls. (TPJS, 242)[78]

•••

They that turn many to righteousness shall shine as the stars for ever and ever. (TPJS, 253)[81]

•••

We don't ask any people to throw away any good they have got; we only ask them to come and get more. (TPJS, 275)[91]

•••

Declare the first principles, and let the mysteries alone, lest ye be overthrown. (TPJS, 292)[101]

•••

If a skillful mechanic . . . succeeds in welding together iron or steel more perfectly than any other mechanic, is he not deserving of praise? And if by the principles of truth I succeed in uniting men of all denominations in the bonds of love, shall I not have attained a good object? (TPJS, 313)[114]

•••

Christians should cease wrangling and contending with each other, and cultivate the principles of union and friendship in their midst . . . before the millennium can be ushered in and Christ takes possession of His kingdom. (TPJS, 314)[114]

MODESTY

We believe that . . . the Saints . . . will from henceforth be always ready to obey the truth without having men's persons in admiration because of advantage. (TPJS, 146)[47]

•••

Let not any man publish his own righteousness, for others can see that for [themselves]; sooner let him confess his sins, and then he will be forgiven, and he will bring forth more fruit. (TPJS, 194)[66]

•••

Don't be limited in your views with regard to your neighbor's virtue, but beware of self-righteousness, and be limited in the estimate of your own virtues, and not think yourself more righteous than others. (TPJS, 228)[75]

•••

I do not want you to think that I am very righteous, for I am not. God judges men according to the use they make of the light which He gives them. (TPJS, 303)[109]

MORE SURE WORD OF PROPHECY

(See also CALLING & ELECTION MADE SURE)

After a person . . . receives the Holy Ghost . . . which is the first Comforter, then let him continue to humble himself before God, hungering and thirsting after righteousness, and living by every word of God, and the Lord will soon say unto him, Son, thou shalt be exalted. When the Lord has thoroughly proved him, and finds that the man is determined to serve Him at all hazards, then the man will find his calling and his election made sure, . . . then it will be his privilege to receive the other Comforter, which the Lord promised the Saints. . . . Now what is this other Comforter? It is no more nor less than the Lord Jesus Christ Himself; . . . when any man obtains this last Comforter, he will have the personage of Jesus Christ to attend him . . . from time to time, and even He will manifest the Father unto him, and they will take up their abode with him, and the Lord will teach him face to face, and he may have a perfect knowledge of the mysteries of the Kingdom of God. (TPJS, 149)[48]

•••

The more sure word of prophecy means a man's knowing that he is sealed up unto eternal life by revelation and the spirit of prophecy, through the power of the holy priesthood. (TPJS, 301)[106]

♦♦♦

We have a more sure word of prophecy, whereunto you do well to take heed, as unto a light that shineth in a dark place. We were eyewitnesses of his majesty and heard the voice of his excellent glory. (TPJS, 303)[109]

MORTALITY

(See also THIS LIFE)

The law of heaven is presented to man, and as such guarantees to all who obey it a reward far beyond any earthly consideration. . . . It is a law of heaven, which transcends the law of man, as far as eternal life [transcends] the temporal; and as the blessings which God is able to give, are greater than those which can be given by man. (TPJS, 50)[21]

♦♦♦

It is an unhallowed principle to say that such and such have transgressed because they have been preyed upon by disease or death, for all flesh is subject to death. (TPJS, 162)[50]

♦♦♦

We came to this earth that we might have a body and present it pure before God in the celestial kingdom. (TPJS, 181)[56]

♦♦♦

We have no claim in our eternal compact, in relation to eternal things, unless our actions and contracts and all things tend to this. (TPJS, 306)[109]

♦♦♦

Although I was called of my heavenly Father to lay the foundation of this great work and kingdom in this dispensation, and testify of His revealed will to scattered Israel, I am subject to like passions as other men, like the prophets of olden times. (TPJS, 315)[114]

♦♦♦

I find that in the midst of business and care the spirit is willing, but the flesh is weak. (TPJS, 315)[114]

♦♦♦

What is the object of our coming into existence, then dying and falling away, to be here no more? It is but reasonable to suppose that God would reveal something in reference to the matter, and it is a subject we ought to study more than any other . . . for the world is ignorant in reference to their true condition and relation. If we have any claim on our heavenly Father for anything, it is for knowledge on this important subject. . . . Knowledge of these things can only be obtained through experience through the ordinances of God set forth for that purpose. Could you gaze into heaven five minutes, you would know more than you would by reading all that ever was written on the subject. (TPJS, 324)[121]

♦♦♦

All the minds and spirits that God ever sent into the world are susceptible of enlargement. (TPJS, 354)[130]

♦♦♦

[On the way to Carthage, Joseph, Hyrum and others met a] Captain Dunn with a company of about sixty mounted militia on which seeing Joseph said, "Do not be alarmed, brethren, for they cannot do more to you than the enemies of truth did to the ancient Saints—they can only kill the body." (TPJS, 379)[137]

MOURNING

We believe that due respect ought to be had to the memory of the dead, and the feelings of both friends and children. (TPJS, 120)[45]

•••

The Lord takes many away even in infancy, that they may escape the envy of man, and the sorrows and evils of this present world; they were too pure, too lovely, to live on earth; therefore, if rightly considered, instead of mourning we have reason to rejoice as they are delivered from evil, and we shall soon have them again. (TPJS, 196)[68]

•••

All children are redeemed by the blood of Jesus Christ, and the moment that children leave this world, they are taken to the bosom of Abraham. The only difference between the old and young dying is, one lives longer in heaven and eternal light and glory than the other, and is freed a little sooner from this miserable wicked world. Notwithstanding all this glory, we for a moment lose sight of it, and mourn the loss, but we do not mourn as those without hope. (TPJS, 197)[68]

•••

When we lose a near and dear friend, upon whom we have set our hearts, it should be a caution unto us not to set our affections too firmly upon others, knowing that they may in like manner be taken from us. Our affections should be placed upon God and His work more intensely than upon our fellow beings. (TPJS, 216)[72]

•••

God has revealed His Son from the heavens and the doctrine of the resurrection also; and we have a knowledge that those we bury here God will bring up again, clothed upon and quickened by the Spirit of the great God. . . . Let these truths sink down in our hearts, that we may even here begin to enjoy that which shall be in full hereafter. (TPJS, 296)[102]

•••

How consoling to the mourners when they are called to part with a husband, wife, father, mother, child, or dear relative, to know that, although the earthly tabernacle is laid down and dissolved, they shall rise again to dwell in everlasting burnings in immortal glory, not to sorrow, suffer, or die any more; but they shall be heirs of God and joint heirs with Jesus Christ. (TPJS, 347)[130]

•••

When I talk to . . . mourners, what have they lost? Their relatives and friends are only separated from their bodies for a short season: their spirits which existed with God have left the tabernacle of clay only for a little moment, as it were; and they now exist in a place where they converse together the same as we do on the earth. (TPJS, 353)[130]

•••

We have reason to have the greatest hope and consolations for our dead of any people on the earth; for we have seen them walk worthily in our midst, and seen them sink asleep in the arms of Jesus; and those who have died in the faith are now in the celestial kingdom of God. And hence is the glory of the sun. (TPJS, 359)[130]

•••

Those who have died in the faith are now in the celestial kingdom of God. And hence is the glory of the sun . . . for at the resurrection . . . [they] will rise in perfect felicity and go to celestial glory, while many must wait myriads of years before they can receive the like blessings; and your expectations and hopes are far above what man can conceive; Don't mourn, don't weep. I know it by the testimony of the Holy Ghost that is within me; and you may wait for your friends to come forth to meet you in the morn of the celestial world. (TPJS, 359)[130]

•••

When we depart, we shall hail our mothers, fathers, friends, and all whom we love, who have fallen asleep in Jesus. There will be no fear of mobs, persecutions, or malicious lawsuits and arrests; but it will be an eternity of felicity. (TPJS, 360)[130]

MURDER

No murderer hath eternal life. Even David must wait for those times of refreshing, before he can come forth and his sins be blotted out . . . for such . . . cannot be forgiven, until they have paid the last farthing. (TPJS, 188)[60]

♦ ♦ ♦

The prayers of all the ministers in the world can never close the gates of hell against a murderer. (TPJS, 189)[60]

♦ ♦ ♦

Rejoice, O Israel! Your friends who have been murdered for the truth's sake in the persecutions shall triumph gloriously in the celestial world, while their murderers shall welter for ages in torment, even until they shall have paid the uttermost farthing. (TPJS, 359)[130]

MURMURING

Remember not to murmur at the dealings of God with His creatures. You are not as yet brought into as trying circumstances as were the ancient Prophets and Apostles . . . of whom the world was not worthy . . . amidst all their afflictions they rejoiced that they were counted worthy to receive persecution for Christ's sake. (TPJS, 32)[18]

♦ ♦ ♦

I am aware that I ought not to murmur, and do not murmur, only in this, that those who are innocent are compelled to suffer for the iniquities of the guilty. (TPJS, 34)[19]

MYSTERIES

We are called to hold the keys of the mysteries of those things that have been kept hid from the foundation of the world until now. (TPJS, 137)[47]

♦ ♦ ♦

Declare the first principles, and let the mysteries alone, lest ye be overthrown. (TPJS, 292)[101]

♦ ♦ ♦

I could explain a hundred fold more than I ever have of the glories of the kingdoms manifested to me in the vision, were I permitted, and were the people prepared to receive them. (TPJS, 305)[109]

♦ ♦ ♦

Many men will say, "I will never forsake you, but will stand by you all the times," But the moment you teach them some of the mysteries of the kingdom of God that are retained in the heavens and are to be revealed to the children of men when they are prepared for them they will be the first to stone you and put you to death. (TPJS, 309)[113]

♦ ♦ ♦

That which hath been hid from before the foundation of the world is revealed to babes and sucklings in the last days. (TPJS, 321)[118]

♦ ♦ ♦

It has always been my province to dig up hidden mysteries—new things—for my hearers. (TPJS, 364)[132]

♦ ♦ ♦

I advise all to go on to perfection, and search deeper and deeper into the mysteries of Godliness. (TPJS, 364)[132]

NATURE

"The firmament showeth His handiwork;" and a moment's reflection is sufficient to teach every man of common intelligence, that all these are not the mere productions of *chance,* nor could they be supported by any power less than an Almighty hand. (TPJS, 56)[21]

♦♦♦

The name of our city [Nauvoo] is of Hebrew origin, and signifies a beautiful situation, or place, carrying with it, also, the idea of rest; and truly descriptive of the most delightful location. It is situated on the east bank of the Mississippi River, at the head of the Des Moines Rapids, in Hancock County, bounded on the east by an extensive prairie of surpassing beauty, and on the north, west and south by the Mississippi. (TPJS, 182)[57]

♦♦♦

The proceedings of the legislature, in regard to the citizens of this place, have been marked with philanthropy and benevolence; and they have laid us under great and lasting obligations, in granting us the several liberal charters we now enjoy, and by which we hope to prosper until our city becomes the most splendid, our University the most learned, and our Legion the most effective of any in the Union. (TPJS, 186)[59]

♦♦♦

Every honest man who has visited the city of Nauvoo since it existed, can bear record of better things, and place me in the front ranks of those who are known to do good for the sake of goodness, and show all liars, hypocrites and abominable creatures that, while vice sinks them down to darkness and woe, virtue exalts me and the Saints to light and immortality. (TPJS, 280)[96]

♦♦♦

[On his fateful start for Carthage] Joseph paused when they got to the temple, and looked with admiration first on that, and then on the city, and remarked, "This is the loveliest place and the best people under the heavens; little do they know the trials that await them." (TPJS, 379)[137]

♦♦♦

When [the small company started back to Carthage] . . . Joseph said, "Boys, if I don't come back, take care of yourselves; I am going like a lamb to the slaughter." When they passed his farm he took a good look at it, and after they had passed it, he turned around several times to look again, at which some of the company made remarks, when Joseph said, "If some of you had got such a farm and knew you would not see it any more, you would want to take a good look at it for the last time." (TPJS, 380)[138]

NEIGHBORS

Don't be limited in your views with regard to your neighbor's virtue, but beware of self-righteousness, and be limited in the estimate of your own virtues, and not think yourself more righteous than others. (TPJS, 228)[75]

♦♦♦

NEW JERUSALEM

You will see, from Revelations 21:2, there was a New Jerusalem coming down from God out of heaven, adorned as a bride for her husband; . . . I shall say with brevity, that there is a New Jerusalem to be established on this continent, and also Jerusalem shall be rebuilt on the eastern continent. (TPJS, 86)[31]

NEXT LIFE

If . . . the grave has no victory, those who keep the sayings of Jesus and obey His teachings have not only a promise of a resurrection from the dead, but an assurance of being admitted into His glorious kingdom: for He Himself says, "Where I am, shall also my servants be." (TPJS, 62)[21]

◆◆◆

There are sins which may be forgiven in the world to come, although the sin of blasphemy [against the Holy Ghost] cannot be forgiven. (TPJS, 219)[74]

◆◆◆

All your losses will be made up to you in the resurrection, provided you continue faithful. By the vision of the Almighty I have seen it. (TPJS, 296)[102]

◆◆◆

If I have no expectation of seeing my father, mother, brothers, sisters and friends again, my heart would burst in a moment, and I should go down to my grave. (TPJS, 296)[102]

◆◆◆

The unpardonable sin is to shed innocent blood, or be accessory thereto. All other sins will be visited with judgment in the flesh, and the spirit being delivered to the buffetings of Satan until the day of the Lord Jesus.

Except a man and his wife enter into an everlasting covenant and be married for eternity, while in this probation, by the power and authority of the Holy Priesthood, they will cease to increase when they die; that is, they will not have any children after the resurrection. But those who are married by the power and authority of the priesthood in this life, and continue without committing the sin against the Holy Ghost, will continue to increase and have children in the celestial glory. (TPJS, 301)[105]

◆◆◆

Paul saw the third heavens, and I more. (TPJS, 301)[106]

◆◆◆

The spirits of just men are made ministering servants to those who are sealed unto life eternal, and it is through them that the sealing power comes down. (TPJS, 325)[121]

◆◆◆

When men are prepared, they are better off to go hence. The spirits of the just are exalted to a greater and more glorious work; hence they are blessed in their departure to the world of spirits. Enveloped in flaming fire, they are not far from us, and know and understand our thoughts, and emotions, and are often pained therewith. (TPJS, 326)[121]

◆◆◆

All sin, and all blasphemies, and every transgression, except one, that man can be guilty of, may be forgiven; and there is a salvation for all men, either in this world or the world to come, who have not committed the unpardonable sin, there being a provision either in this world or the world of spirits. (TPJS, 356)[130]

◆◆◆

When we depart, we shall hail our mothers, fathers, friends, and all whom we love, who have fallen asleep in Jesus. There will be no fear of mobs, persecutions, or malicious lawsuits and arrests; but it will be an eternity of felicity. (TPJS, 360)[130]

♦♦♦

There are mansions for those who obey a celestial law, and there are other mansions for those who come short of the law[—]every man in his own order. (TPJS, 366)[131]

♦♦♦

"As in Adam all die, even so in Christ shall all be made alive"; all shall be raised from the dead. The Lamb of God hath brought to pass the resurrection, so that all shall rise from the dead. . . . Some dwell in higher glory than others. (TPJS, 367)[132]

♦♦♦

Paul says, "There is one glory of the sun, and another glory of the moon, and another glory of the stars; for one star differeth from another star in glory. So also is the resurrection of the dead." They who obtain a glorious resurrection from the dead, are exalted far above principalities, powers, thrones, dominions and angels, and are expressly declared to be heirs of God and joint heirs with Jesus Christ, all having eternal power. (TPJS, 374)[133]

NURTURANCE

[Joseph said that] it was according to revelation that the sick should be nursed with herbs and mild food, and not by the hand of an enemy. Who are better qualified to administer than our faithful and zealous sisters, whose hearts are full of faith, tenderness, sympathy and compassion. No one. (TPJS, 229)[75]

OBEDIENCE

Live in strict obedience to the commandments of God, and walk humbly before Him, and He will exalt thee in His own due time. (TPJS, 27)[15]

♦♦♦

We know not what we shall be called to pass through before Zion is delivered and established; therefore, we have great need to live near to God, and always be in strict obedience to all His commandments, that we may have a conscience void of offense toward God and man. (TPJS, 32)[18]

♦♦♦

The law of heaven is presented to man, and as such guarantees to all who obey it a reward far beyond any earthly consideration. (TPJS, 50)[21]

♦♦♦

We take the sacred writings into our hands, and admit that they were given by direct inspiration for the good of man. We believe that God condescended to speak from the heavens and declare His will concerning the human family, to give them just and holy laws, to regulate their conduct and guide them in a direct way, that in due time He might take them to Himself, and make them joint heirs with His Son. But when this fact is admitted, that the immediate will of heaven is contained in the Scriptures, are we not bound as rational creatures to live in accordance to all its precepts? Will the mere admission that this is the will of heaven ever benefit us if we do not comply with all its teachings? Do we not offer violence to the Supreme Intelligence of heaven, when we admit the truth of its teachings, and do not obey them? Do we not descend below our own knowledge, and the better wisdom which heaven has endowed us with, by such a course of conduct? (TPJS, 53)[21]

♦ ♦ ♦

If . . . the grave has no victory, those who keep the sayings of Jesus and obey His teachings have not only a promise of a resurrection from the dead, but an assurance of being admitted into His glorious kingdom: for He Himself says, "Where I am, there shall also my servants be." (TPJS, 62)[21]

♦ ♦ ♦

"Children, obey your parents in all things, for this is well pleasing unto the Lord." (Colossians 3:20) (TPJS, 88)[31]

♦ ♦ ♦

We believe that . . . the Saints . . . will from henceforth be always ready to obey the truth without having men's persons in admiration because of advantage. (TPJS, 146)[47]

♦ ♦ ♦

Why will not man learn wisdom by precept at this late age of the world, when we have such a cloud of witnesses and examples before us, and not be obliged to learn by sad experience everything we know. (TPJS, 155)[49]

♦ ♦ ♦

"If we keep the commandments of God, we should bring forth fruit and be

the friends of God, and know what the Lord did." (TPJS, 194)[66]

♦ ♦ ♦

It mattereth not whether we live long or short on the earth after we come to a knowledge of [the gospel] principles and obey them unto the end. (TPJS, 199)[68]

♦ ♦ ♦

If you wish to go where God is, you must be like God, or possess the principles which God possesses; for if we are not drawing towards God in principle, we are going from Him and drawing towards the devil. (TPJS, 216)[73]

♦ ♦ ♦

[Joseph said that] it was the folly and nonsense of the human heart for a person to be aspiring to other stations than those to which they are appointed of God for them to occupy; that it was better for individuals to magnify their respective calling, and wait patiently till God shall say to them, "come up higher." (TPJS, 223)[75]

♦ ♦ ♦

Every person should stand, and act in the place appointed. (TPJS, 225)[75]

♦ ♦ ♦

As well might the devil seek to dethrone Jehovah, as overthrow an innocent soul that resists everything which is evil. (TPJS, 226)[75]

♦ ♦ ♦

It is a desirable honor that you should so walk before our heavenly Father as to save yourselves; we are all responsible to God for the manner we improve the light and wisdom given by our Lord to enable us to save ourselves. (TPJS, 227)[75]

♦ ♦ ♦

Wisdom to govern the house of Israel was given to Solomon, and the judges of Israel; and if he had always been their king, and they subject to his mandate, and obedient to his laws, they would still have been a great and mighty people—the rulers of the universe, and the wonder of the world. (TPJS, 251)[81]

•••

[Several ancient governments were set up by God.] If, then, God puts up one, and sets down another at His pleasure, and made instruments of kings, unknown to themselves, to fulfill His prophecies, how much more was He able, if man would have been subject to His mandate, to regulate the affairs of this world, and promote peace and happiness among the human family. (TPJS, 251)[81]

•••

We have been chastened by the hand of God heretofore for not obeying His commands, although we never violated any human law, . . . yet we have treated lightly His commands, and departed from His ordinances, and the Lord has chastened us sore, and we have felt His arm and kissed the rod; let us be wise in time to come and ever remember that "to obey is better than sacrifice, and to hearken than the fat of rams." (TPJS, 253)[81]

•••

As God governed Abraham, Isaac and Jacob as families, and the children of Israel as a nation; so we, as a Church, must be under His guidance if we are prospered, preserved and sustained. Our only confidence can be in God; our only wisdom obtained from Him; and He alone must be our protector and safeguard, spiritually and temporally, or we fall. (TPJS, 253)[81]

•••

As a Church and a people it behooves us to be wise, and to seek to know the will of God, and then be willing to do it; for

"blessed is he that heareth the word of the Lord, and keepeth it," say the Scriptures. (TPJS, 253)[81]

•••

We are trying here to gird up our loins, and purge from our midst the workers of iniquity; . . . that as God's people, under His direction, and obedient to His law, we may grow up in righteousness and truth; and when His purposes shall be accomplished, we may receive an inheritance among those that are sanctified. (TPJS, 254)[81]

•••

In obedience there is joy and peace unspotted, unalloyed; and as God has designed our happiness—and the happiness of all His creatures, he never has—He never will institute an ordinance or give a commandment to His people that is not calculated in its nature to promote that happiness which he has designed, and which will not end in the greatest amount of good and glory to those who become the recipients of His law and ordinances. (TPJS, 256)[83]

•••

If we seek first the kingdom of God, all good things will be added. (TPJS, 256)[83]

•••

We cannot keep all the commandments without first knowing them, and we cannot expect to know all, or more than we now know unless we comply with or keep those we have already received. (TPJS, 256)[83]

•••

That which is wrong under one circumstance, may be, and often is right under another. God said, "Thou shalt not kill;" at another time He said, "Thou shalt utterly destroy." This is the principle on which the government of heaven is conducted—by revelation adapted to the circumstances in which the children of the kingdom are placed. (TPJS, 256)[83]

◆◆◆

Whatever God requires is right, no matter what it is, although we may not see the reason thereof till long after the events transpire. So with Solomon: first he asked wisdom, and God gave it him, and with it every desire of his heart, even things which might be considered abominable to all who understand the order of heaven only in part, but which in reality were right because God gave and sanctioned by special revelation. (TPJS, 256)[83]

◆◆◆

Our heavenly Father is more liberal in His views, and boundless in His mercies and blessings, than we are ready to believe or receive; and, at the same time, is more terrible to the workers of iniquity, more awful in the executions of His punishments, and more ready to detect every false way, than we are apt to suppose Him to be. (TPJS, 257)[83]

◆◆◆

No good thing will I withhold from them who walk uprightly before me, and do my will in all things—who will listen to my voice and to the voice of my servant, whom I have sent; for I delight in those who seek diligently to know my precepts, and abide by the law of my kingdom; for all things shall be made known unto them in mine own due time, and in the end they shall have joy." (TPJS, 257)[83]

◆◆◆

We will keep the laws of the land; we do not speak against them. . . . We speak of the kingdom of God on the earth, not the kingdom of men. (TPJS, 272)[91]

◆◆◆

We have no claim in our eternal compact, in relation to eternal things,

unless our actions and contracts and all things tend to this. (TPJS, 306)[109]

◆◆◆

We have no new commandment to give, but admonish Elders and members to live by every word that proceedeth forth from the mouth of God, lest they come short of the glory that is reserved for the faithful. (TPJS, 306)[110]

◆◆◆

To become a joint heir of the heirship of the Son, one must put away all his false traditions. (TPJS, 321)[119]

◆◆◆

When God offers a blessing or knowledge to a man, and he refuses to receive it, he will be damned. (TPJS, 322)[119]

◆◆◆

The organization of the spiritual and heavenly worlds, and of spiritual and heavenly beings, was agreeable to the most perfect order and harmony: their limits and bounds were fixed irrevocably, and voluntarily subscribed to in their heavenly estate by themselves, and were by our first parents subscribed to upon the earth. Hence the importance of embracing and subscribing to principles of eternal truth by all men upon the earth that expect eternal life. (TPJS, 325)[121]

◆◆◆

Any person who is exalted to the highest mansion has to abide a celestial law, and the whole law too. (TPJS, 331)[123]

◆◆◆

It mattereth not whether the principle is popular or unpopular, I will always maintain a true principle, even if I stand alone in it. (TPJS, 332)[125]

◆◆◆

To get salvation we must not only do some things, but everything which God has commanded. (TPJS, 332)[125]

•••

The object with me is to obey and teach others to obey God in just what He tells us to do. (TPJS, 332)[125]

•••

If we start right, it is easy to go right all the time; but if we start wrong, we may go wrong, and it be a hard matter to get right. (TPJS, 343)[130]

•••

All spirits who have not obeyed the Gospel in the flesh must either obey it in the spirit or be damned. (TPJS, 355)[130]

•••

Knowledge, he can be saved; although, if he has been guilty of great sins, he will be punished for them. But when he consents to obey the Gospel, whether here or in the world of spirits, he is saved. . . . All will suffer until they obey Christ himself. (TPJS, 357)[130]

•••

I exhort you to give heed to all the virtue and the teachings which I have given you. (TPJS, 367)[132]

OBLIGATION

We take the sacred writings into our hands, and admit that they were given by direct inspiration for the good of man. We believe that God condescended to speak from the heavens and declare His will concerning the human family, to give them just and holy laws, to regulate their conduct and guide them in a direct way, that in due time He might take them to Himself, and make them joint heirs with His Son. But when this fact is admitted, that the immediate will of heaven is contained in the Scriptures, are we not bound as rational creatures to live in accordance to all its precepts? Will the mere admission that this is the will of heaven ever benefit us if we do not comply with all its teachings? Do we not offer violence to the Supreme Intelligence of heaven, when we admit the truth of its teachings, and do not obey them? Do we not descend below our own knowledge, and the better wisdom which heaven has endowed us with, by such a course of conduct? (TPJS, 53)[21]

•••

The Lord has told us to build the Temple and the Nauvoo House; and that command is as binding upon us as any other; and that man who engages not in these things is as much a transgressor as though he broke any other commandment; he is not a doer of God's will, not a fulfiller of His laws. (TPJS, 253)[81]

•••

When God offers a blessing or knowledge to a man, and he refuses to receive it, he will be damned. (TPJS, 322)[119]

•••

The organization of the spiritual and heavenly worlds, and of spiritual and heavenly beings, was agreeable to the most perfect order and harmony: their limits and bounds were fixed irrevocably, and voluntarily subscribed to in their heavenly estate by themselves, and were by our first parents subscribed to upon the earth. Hence the importance of embracing and subscribing to principles of eternal truth by all men upon the earth that expect eternal life. (TPJS, 325)[121]

•••

To get salvation we must not only do some things, but everything which God has commanded. (TPJS, 332)[125]

OLD AGE

There is never a time when the spirit is too old to approach God. All are within the reach of pardoning mercy, who have not committed the unpardonable sin, which hath no forgiveness. (TPJS, 191)[63]

♦♦♦

The way to get along in any important matter is to gather unto yourselves wise men, experienced and aged men, to assist in council in all times of trouble. (TPJS, 299)[103]

♦♦♦

In order to receive your children to yourselves you must have a promise— some ordinance; some blessing, in order to ascend above principalities, or else it may be an angel. They must rise just as they died; we can there hail our lovely infants with the same glory—the same loveliness in the celestial glory, where they all enjoy alike. They differ in stature, in size, the same glorious spirit gives them the likeness of glory in bloom and beauty. The old man with his silvery hairs will glory in bloom and beauty. No man can describe it to you—no man can write it. (TPJS, 368)[132]

OPEN-MINDEDNESS

(See also TRUTH-SEEKING)

The very principle upon which the disciples were accounted blessed, was because [in their willingness,] they were permitted to see [the Lord] with their eyes and hear with their ears . . . [in contrast to] the multitude that received not His saying. (TPJS, 95)[34]

♦♦♦

We have reason to be truly humble before the God of our fathers, that He hath left these things on record for us, so plain, that notwithstanding the exertions and

combined influence of the priests of Baal, they have not power to blind our eyes, and darken our understanding, if we will but open our eyes, and read with candor, for a moment. (TPJS, 96)[34]

♦♦♦

Men are in the habit, when the truth is exhibited by the servants of God, of saying, All is mystery; they have spoken in parables, and therefore, are not to be understood. It is true they have eyes to see, and see not, but none are so blind as those who will not see. (TPJS, 96)[34]

♦♦♦

The things of God are of deep import; and time, and experience, and careful and ponderous and solemn thoughts can only find them out. Thy mind, O man! If thou will lead a soul unto salvation, must stretch as high as the utmost heavens, and search into and contemplate the darkest abyss and the broad expanse of eternity. (TPJS, 137)[47]

♦♦♦

There are many yet on the earth among all sects, parties, denominations, who are blinded by the subtle craftiness of men, whereby they lie in wait to deceive, and who are only kept from the truth because they know not where to find it. (TPJS, 145)[47]

♦♦♦

"Mormonism" . . . is now taking a deep hold in the hearts and affections of all those, who are noble-minded enough to lay aside the prejudice of education, and investigate the subject with candor and honesty. (TPJS, 184)[59]

♦♦♦

We never can comprehend the things of God and of heaven, but by revelation. We may spiritualize and express opinions to all eternity; but that is no authority. (TPJS, 292)[101]

◆◆◆

I hope sober-thinking and sound-reasoning people will sooner listen to the voice of truth, than be led astray by the vain pretensions of the self-wise. (TPJS, 299)[104]

◆◆◆

I could explain a hundred fold more than I ever have of the glories of the kingdoms manifested to me in the vision, were I permitted, and were the people prepared to receive them. (TPJS, 305)[109]

◆◆◆

One of the grand fundamental principles of "Mormonism" is to receive truth, let it come from whence it may. (TPJS, 313)[114]

◆◆◆

What would it profit us to come unto the spirits of the just men, but to learn and come up to the standard of their knowledge? (TPJS, 320)[118]

◆◆◆

There has been a great difficulty in getting anything into the heads of this generation. . . . Even the Saints are slow to understand. (TPJS, 331)[123]

◆◆◆

I advise all to go on to perfection, and search deeper and deeper into the mysteries of Godliness. (TPJS, 364)[132]

OPINIONS

Various and conflicting are the opinions of men concerning the Plan of Salvation, the requisitions of the Almighty, the necessary preparations for heaven, the state and condition of departed spirits, and the happiness or misery that is consequent upon the practice of righteousness or iniquity according to several notions of virtue and vice. [And one sect tends to condemn the other sect.] (TPJS, 217)[74]

◆◆◆

We may spiritualize and express opinions to all eternity; but that is no authority. (TPJS, 292)[101]

◆◆◆

The opinions of men, so far as I am concerned, are to me as the crackling of thorns under the pot, or the whistling of the wind. I break the ground; I lead the way. (TPJS, 304)[109]

◆◆◆

One truth revealed from heaven is worth all the sectarian notions in existence. (TPJS, 338)[128]

OPPORTUNITY

Fellow sojourners upon the earth, it is your privilege to purify yourselves and come up to the same glory, and see for yourselves, and know for yourselves. (TPJS, 13)[8]

◆◆◆

The law of heaven is presented to man, and as such guarantees to all who obey it a reward far beyond any earthly consideration. (TPJS, 50)[21]

◆◆◆

Darkness prevails at this time as it did at the time Jesus Christ was about to be crucified. The powers of darkness strove to obscure the glorious Sun of righteousness, that began to dawn upon the world, and was soon to burst in great blessings upon the heads of the faithful. (TPJS, 90)[33]

◆◆◆

We want all honest men to have a chance to gather and build up a city of righteousness, when even upon the bells of the horses shall be written *"Holiness to the Lord."* (TPJS, 93)[35]

◆◆◆

All those who have not had an opportunity of hearing the Gospel, and being administered unto by an inspired man in the flesh, must have it hereafter, before they can be finally judged. (TPJS, 121)[45]

◆◆◆

The Saints ought to lay hold of every door that shall seem to be opened to them, to obtain foothold on the earth, and be making all the preparation that is within their power for the terrible storms that are now gathering in the heavens. (TPJS, 141)[47]

OPPOSITION

From apostates the faithful have received the severest persecutions. (TPJS, 67)[21]

◆◆◆

The Elders . . . are combating the prejudices of a crooked and perverse generation, by having in their possession . . . religious principles, which are misrepresented by almost all those whose crafts are in danger by the same. (TPJS, 83)[31]

◆◆◆

Darkness prevails at this time as it did at the time Jesus Christ was about to be crucified. The powers of darkness strove to obscure the glorious Sun of righteousness, that began to dawn upon the world, and was soon to burst in great blessings upon the heads of the faithful. (TPJS, 90)[33]

◆◆◆

The Church of the Latter-day Saints, like an impenetrable, immovable rock in the midst of the mighty deep, exposed to the storms and tempests of Satan, . . . has, thus far, remained steadfast, and is still braving the mountain waves of opposition . . . urged onward with redoubled fury by the enemy of righteousness, with his pitch fork of lies. (TPJS, 99)[3]

◆◆◆

We hope that this adversary of truth [*Mormonism Unveiled*] will continue to stir up the sink of iniquity, that the people may the more readily discern between the righteous and the wicked. (TPJS, 99)[34]

◆◆◆

Be assured, brethren, I am willing to stem the torrent of all opposition, in storms and in tempests, in thunders and in lightnings, by sea and by land, in the wilderness or among false brethren, or mobs, or wherever God in His providence may call us. (TPJS, 106)[37]

◆◆◆

Such inhumanity, and relentless cruelty and barbarity as were practiced against the Saints in Missouri can scarcely be found in the annals of history. (TPJS, 126)[46]

◆◆◆

Walls and irons, doors and creaking hinges, and half-scared-to-death guards and jailers, grinning like some damned spirits, lest an innocent man should make his escape to bring to light the damnable deeds of a murderous mob, are calculated in their very nature to make the soul of an honest man feel stronger than the powers of hell. (TPJS, 139)[47]

◆◆◆

Whatever you may hear about me or Kirtland, take no notice of it; for if it be a place of refuge, the devil will use his greatest efforts to trap the Saints. (TPJS, 161)[49]

•••

In the earlier ages of the world a righteous man, and a man of God and intelligence, had a better chance to do good, to be believed and received than at the present day; but in these days, such a man is much opposed and persecuted by most of the inhabitants of the earth, and he has much sorrow to pass through here. (TPJS, 196)[68]

•••

If any revelations are given of God, they are universally opposed by the priests and Christendom at large; for they reveal their wickedness and abominations. (TPJS, 217)[73]

•••

[Joseph said that] if God had appointed him, and chosen him as an instrument to lead the Church, why not let him lead it through? Why stand in the way when he is appointed to do a thing? Who knows the mind of God? Does He not reveal things differently than what we expect? He remarked that he was continually rising, although he had everything bearing him down, standing in his way, and opposing; notwithstanding all this opposition, he always comes out right in the end. (TPJS, 224)[75]

•••

When I do the best I can—when I am accomplishing the greatest good, then the most evil and wicked surmisings are got up against me. (TPJS, 259)[84]

•••

If a man stands and opposes the world of sin, he may expect to have all wicked and corrupt spirits arrayed against him. (TPJS, 259)[84]

•••

He that will war the true Christian warfare against the corruptions of these last days will have wicked men and angels of devils, and all the infernal powers of darkness continually arrayed against him. (TPJS, 259)[84]

•••

It will not be beyond the common use of terms, to say that good is among the most important [words] in use, and though known by various names in different languages, still its meaning is the same, and is ever in opposition to "bad." (TPJS, 300)[104]

•••

I am like a huge, rough stone rolling down from a high mountain; and the only polishing I get is when some corner gets rubbed off by coming in contact with something else, striking with accelerating force against religious bigotry, priest-craft, lawyer-craft, doctor-craft, lying editors, suborned judges and jurors, and the authority of perjured executives, backed by mobs, blasphemers, licentious and corrupt men and women—all hell knocking off a corner here and a corner there. Thus I will become a smooth and polished shaft in the quiver of the Almighty, who will give me dominion over all and every one of them, when their refuge of lies shall fail, and their hiding place shall be destroyed, while these smooth-polished stones with which I come in contact become marred. (TPJS, 304)[109]

•••

Whenever light shone, it stirred up darkness. Truth and error, good and evil cannot be reconciled. (TPJS, 325)[121]

•••

False prophets always arise to oppose the true prophets, and they will prophesy so very near the truth that they will deceive almost the very chosen ones. (TPJS, 365)[132]

In relation to the kingdom of God, the devil always sets up his kingdom at the very same time in opposition to God. (TPJS, 365)[132]

ORDER

In ancient days councils were conducted with such strict propriety, that no one was allowed to whisper, be weary, leave the room, or get uneasy in the least, until the voice of the Lord, by revelation, or the voice of the council by the Spirit, was obtained. (TPJS, 69)[22]

♦♦♦

And if children embrace the Gospel, and their parents or guardians are unbelievers, teach them to stay at home and be obedient to their parents or guardians, if they require it; but if they consent to let them gather with the people of God, let them do so, and there shall be no wrong; and let all things be done carefully and righteously, and God will extend to all such His guardian care. (TPJS, 87)[30]

♦♦♦

It is the duty of Elders, when they enter into any house, to let their labors and warning voice be unto the master of the house; and if he receive the Gospel, then he may extend his influence to his wife. . . . But if a man forbid his wife, or his children, before they are of age, to receive the Gospel, then it should be the duty of the Elder to go his way, and use no influence against him, and let the responsibility be upon his head. (TPJS, 87)[30]

♦♦♦

The order of the house of God has been, and ever will be, the same, even after Christ comes; and after the termination of the thousand years it will be the same; and we shall finally enter into the celestial kingdom of God, and enjoy it forever. (TPJS, 91)[33]

♦♦♦

Revelations of the mind and will of God to the Church, are to come through the presidency. This is the order of heaven, and the power and privilege of this priesthood. (TPJS, 111)[41]

♦♦♦

Adam received commandments and instructions from God: this was the order from the beginning. (TPJS, 168)[54]

♦♦♦

The Almighty is a lover of order and good government. (TPJS, 187)[59]

♦♦♦

God never had any prophets that acted in this way [strange fits, trembling, fainting, swooning or in trances]; there was nothing indecorous in the proceedings of the Lord's prophets in any age; neither had the apostles nor prophets in the apostles' day anything of this kind. . . . Paul says, "Let everything be done decently and in order," but here we find the greatest disorder and indecency in the conduct of both men and women. The same would apply to . . . many of our modern revivalists. (TPJS, 209)[71]

♦♦♦

It is an insult to a meeting for persons to leave just before its close. If they must go out, let them go half an hour before. No gentlemen will go out of a meeting just at closing. (TPJS, 287)[100]

♦♦♦

As president of this house, I forbid any man leaving just as we are going to close the meeting. He is no gentleman who will do it. I don't care who does it, even if it were the king of England. I forbid it. (TPJS, 296)[102]

♦♦♦

We should keep order and not let the council be imposed upon by unruly conduct. (TPJS, 307)[111]

ORDINANCES

The mere shedding of the blood of beasts or offering anything else in sacrifice, could not procure a remission of sins, except it were performed in faith of something to come; if it could, Cain's offering must have been as good as Abel's. And if Abel was taught of the coming of the Son of God, was he not taught also of His ordinances? (TPJS, 59)[21]

♦♦♦

The ordinance of washing of feet [of the twelve] . . . is necessary now, as much it was in the days of the Savior; and we must have a place prepared, that we may attend to this ordinance aside from the world. . . . It was never intended for any but official members. It is calculated to unite our hearts, that we may be one in feeling and sentiment, and that our faith may be strong, so that Satan cannot overthrow us, nor have any power over us here. (TPJS, 90)[33]

♦♦♦

Wherever the ordinances of the Gospel are administered, there is the Priesthood. (TPJS, 158)[49]

♦♦♦

Ordinances must be kept in the very way God has appointed; otherwise their Priesthood will prove a cursing instead of a blessing . . . [as with Cain, who was initially] authorized to offer sacrifice, but not offering it in righteousness, was cursed. (TPJS, 169)[54]

♦♦♦

[God] never will institute an ordinance or give a commandment to His people that is not calculated in its nature to promote that happiness which he has designed, and which will not end in the greatest amount of good and glory to those who become the recipients of His law and ordinances. (TPJS, 256)[83]

♦♦♦

All the ordinances, systems and administrations on the earth are of no use to the children of men, unless they are ordained and authorized of God, for nothing will save a man but a legal administrator; for none others will be acknowledged either by God or angels. (TPJS, 274)[91]

♦♦♦

The main object was to build unto the Lord a house whereby [God] . . . could reveal unto His people the ordinances of His house and the glories of His kingdom, and teach the people the way of salvation; for there are certain ordinances and principles that, when they are taught and practiced, must be done in a place or house built for that purpose. (TPJS, 308)[113]

♦♦♦

Ordinances instituted in the heavens before the foundation of the world, in the priesthood, for the salvation of men, are not to be altered or changed. All must be saved on the same principles. (TPJS, 308)[113]

♦♦♦

Where there is no change of priesthood, there is no change of ordinances, says Paul. (TPJS, 308)[113]

♦♦♦

All men who become heirs of God and joint heirs of Jesus Christ will have to receive the fullness of the ordinances of his kingdom; and those who will not receive all the ordinances will come short of the fullness of that glory, if they do not lose the whole. (TPJS, 309)[113]

◆◆◆

When a seal is put upon the father and mother, it secures their posterity, so that they cannot be lost, but will be saved by virtue of the covenant of their father and mother. (TPJS, 321)[118]

◆◆◆

Any person who is exalted to the highest mansion has to abide a celestial law, and the whole law too. (TPJS, 331)[123]

ORGANIZATION

"At the first organization in heaven we were all present, and saw the Savior chosen and appointed and the Plan of Salvation made, and we sanctioned it." (TPJS, 181)[56]

◆◆◆

Everlasting covenant was made between three personages before organization of this earth; these personages, according to Abraham's record, are called God the first, the Creator; God the second, the Redeemer; and God the third, the witness or Testator. (TPJS, 190)[61]

◆◆◆

You ask the learned doctors why they say the world was made out of nothing; and they will answer, "Doesn't the Bible say He *created* the world"? And they infer, from the word create, that it must have been made out of nothing. Now, the word create came from the word *baurau* which does not mean to create out of nothing; it means to organize; the same as a man would organize materials and build a ship. Hence, we infer that God had materials to organize the world out of chaos— chaotic matter, which is element, and in which dwells all the glory. Elements had an existence from the time he had. The pure principles of element are principles which can never be destroyed; they may be organized and re-organized, but not destroyed. They had no beginning, and can have no end. (TPJS, 351)[130]

◆◆◆

Another subject . . . calculated to exalt man. . . . I shall therefore just touch upon . . . is associated with the subject of the resurrection of the dead—namely, the soul—the mind of man—the immortal spirit. Where did it come from? All learned men and doctors of divinity say that God created it in the beginning; But it is not so: . . . . Hear it, all ye ends of the world; for God has told me so; . . . I am going to tell of things more noble.

We say that God himself is a self-existent being. Who told you so? It is correct enough; but how did it get into your heads? Who told you that man did not exist in like manner upon the same principles? Man does exist upon the same principles. God made a tabernacle and put a spirit into it, and it became a living soul. . . . It does not say in the Hebrew [Bible] that God created the spirit of man. It says "God made man out of the earth and put into him Adam's spirit, and so became a living body. (TPJS, 352)[130]

P

PARADISE

Blessed are the dead who die in the Lord, for they rest from their labors and their works do follow them. (TPJS, 200)[68]

PARENTING

Souls are as precious in the sight of God as they ever were. (TPJS, 77)[29]

◆ ◆ ◆

No power or influence can or ought to be maintained by virtue of the Priesthood, only by persuasion, by long-suffering, by gentleness, and meekness, and by love unfeigned; by kindness, and pure knowledge, which shall greatly enlarge the soul without hypocrisy, and without guile, reproving betimes with sharpness, when moved upon by the Holy Ghost, and then showing forth afterwards an increase of love toward him whom thou hast reproved, lest he esteem thee to be his enemy; that he may know that thy faithfulness is stronger than the cords of death; let thy bowels also be full of charity towards all men, and to the household of faith, and let virtue garnish thy thoughts unceasingly, then shall thy confidence wax strong in the presence of God, and the doctrine of the Priesthood shall distill upon thy soul as the dews from heaven. The Holy ghost shall be thy constant companion, and thy sceptre an unchanging sceptre of righteousness and truth, and thy dominion shall be an everlasting dominion, and without compulsory means, it shall flow unto thee forever and ever. (TPJS, 142)[47]

◆ ◆ ◆

There are many teachers, but, perhaps, not many fathers. (TPJS, 144)[47]

◆ ◆ ◆

The Great Parent of the universe looks upon the whole of the human family with a fatherly care and a paternal regard; He views them as his offspring, and without any of those contracted feelings that influence the children of men, causes "His sun to rise of the evil and on the good, and sendeth rain on the just and on the unjust." (TPJS, 218)[74]

◆ ◆ ◆

[God's children cannot] be compelled into the kingdom of God, but must be dealt with in long-suffering, and at last we shall save them. (TPJS, 241)[79]

◆ ◆ ◆

The Lord deals with this people as a tender parent with a child, communicating light and intelligence and the knowledge of His ways as they can bear it. (TPJS, 305)[109]

PARTING WORDS TO HIS FAMILY

[In a letter to Emma, Joseph wrote] P.S.—Dear Emma, I am very much resigned to my lot, knowing I am justified, and have done the best that could be done. Give my love to the children and all my friends, Mr. Brewer, and all who enquire after me; and as for treason, I know I have not committed any, and they cannot prove anything of the kind, so you need not have any fears that anything can happen to us on that account. May God bless you all. Amen. (TPJS, 391)[144]

PATIENCE

Rumor with her ten thousand tongues is diffusing her uncertain sounds in almost every ear; but in these times of sore trial, let the Saints be patient and see the salvation of God. (TPJS, 42)[20]

♦♦♦

Inasmuch as long-suffering, patience, and mercy have ever characterized the dealings of our heavenly Father towards the humble and penitent, I feel disposed to copy the example, cherish the same principles, and by so doing being a savior of my fellow men. (TPJS, 165)[53]

♦♦♦

As you increase in innocence and virtue, as you increase in goodness, let your heart expand, let them be enlarged toward others; be long-suffering, and bear with the faults and errors of mankind. (TPJS, 228)[75]

♦♦♦

When my enemies take away my rights, I will bear it and keep out of the way; but if they take away your rights, I will fight for you. (TPJS, 268)[87]

♦♦♦

I do not dwell upon your faults, and you shall not upon mine. (TPJS, 316)[115]

PEACE

How will the serpent ever lose its venom, while the servants of God possess the same disposition, and continue to make war upon it? Men must become harmless before the brute creation, and when men lose their viscous dispositions and cease to destroy the animal race, the lion and the lamb can dwell together and the sucking child can play with the serpent in safety. (TPJS, 71)[24]

♦♦♦

Let us be faithful and silent, brethren, and if God gives you a manifestation, keep it to yourselves; be watchful and prayerful, and you shall have a prelude of those joys that God will pour out on that day. (TPJS, 91)[33]

♦♦♦

There seems to be a whispering that the angels of heaven . . . have taken counsel together; and . . . have taken cognizance of the testimony of those who were murdered at Haun's Mills, and also those who were martyred . . . elsewhere, and have passed some decisions peradventure in favor of the saints, and those who were called to suffer without cause. (TPJS, 141)[47]

♦♦♦

Therefore . . . let us cheerfully do all things that lie in our power, and then may we stand still with the utmost assurance, to see the salvation of God, and for His arm to be revealed. (TPJS, 146)[47]

♦♦♦

The time is soon coming, when no man will have any peace, but in Zion and her stakes. (TPJS, 161)[49]

♦♦♦

The great and wise of ancient days have failed in all their attempts to promote eternal power, peace and happiness. Their nations have crumbled to pieces; their thrones have been cast down in their turn, and their cities, and their mightiest works of art have been annihilated; or their dilapidated towers, or time-worn monuments have left us but feeble traces of their former magnificence and ancient grandeur. They proclaim as with a voice of thunder, those imperishable truths—that man's strength is weakness, his wisdom is folly, his glory is his shame. (TPJS, 249)[81]

♦♦♦

In obedience there is joy and peace unspotted, unalloyed; and as God has designed our happiness—and the happiness of all His creatures, he never has—He never will institute an ordinance or give a commandment to His people that is not calculated in its nature to promote that happiness which he has designed, and which will not end in the greatest amount of good and glory to those who become the recipients of His law and ordinances. (TPJS, 256)[83]

•••

Joseph remarked that all was well between him and the heavens; that he had no enmity against any one; and as the prayer of Jesus, or his pattern, so prayed Joseph—Father, forgive me my trespasses as I forgive those who trespass against me, for I freely forgive all men. If we would secure and cultivate the love of others, we must love others, even our enemies as well as friends. (TPJS, 312)[114]

•••

Never afflict thy soul for what an enemy hath put it out of thy power to do, if thy desires are ever so just. (TPJS, 317)[116]

•••

When we depart, we shall hail our mothers, fathers, friends, and all whom we love, who have fallen asleep in Jesus. There will be no fear of mobs, persecutions, or malicious lawsuits and arrests; but it will be an eternity of felicity. (TPJS, 360)[130]

PERFECTION

(*See also* GODLINESS)

God has created man with a mind capable of instruction, and a faculty which may be enlarged in proportion to the heed and diligence given to the light communicated from heaven to the intellect; and that the nearer man approaches perfection, the clearer are his views, and the greater his enjoyments, till he has overcome the evils of his life and lost every desire for sin; and like the ancients, arrives at that point of faith where he is wrapped in the power and glory of his Maker and is caught up to dwell with Him. (TPJS, 51)[21]

•••

God has in reserve a time, or period appointed in His bosom, when He will bring all his subjects, who have obeyed his voice and kept His commandments, into His celestial rest. This rest is of such perfection and glory, that man has need of a preparation before he can, according to the laws of that kingdom, enter it and enjoy its blessings. This being the fact, God has given certain laws to the human family, which, if observed, are sufficient to prepare them to inherit this rest. This, then, we conclude, was the purpose of God in giving His laws to us. (TPJS, 54)[21]

•••

Let honesty, and sobriety, and candor, and solemnity, and virtue, and pureness, and meekness, and simplicity crown our heads in every place; and in fine, become as little children, without malice, guile or hypocrisy. (TPJS, 137)[47]

•••

By learning the Spirit of God and understanding it, you may grow into the principle of revelation, until you become perfect in Christ Jesus. (TPJS, 151)[48]

•••

The Kingdom of Heaven is like a grain of mustard seed. . . . small, but brings forth a large tree, and the fowls lodge in the branches. The fowls are the angels [which] come down, combine together [and] gather their children. . . . We cannot be made perfect without them, nor they without us. (TPJS, 159)[49]

♦♦♦

Females, if they are pure and innocent, can come in the presence of God; for what is more pleasing to God than innocence? . . . If we would come before God, we must keep ourselves pure, as He is pure. (TPJS, 227)[75]

♦♦♦

Jesus designs to save people out of their sins. Said Jesus, "Ye shall do the work, which ye see me do." These are the grand key-words for the society to act upon. (TPJS, 239)[78]

♦♦♦

Be virtuous and pure; be men of integrity and truth; keep the commandments of God; and then you will be able more perfectly to understand the difference between right and wrong—between the things of God and the things of men; and your path will be like that of the just, which shineth brighter and brighter unto the perfect day. (TPJS, 247)[80]

♦♦♦

Although I do wrong, I do not the wrongs that I am charged with doing; the wrong that I do is through the frailty of human nature, like other men. No man lives without fault. (TPJS, 258)[84]

♦♦♦

I am like a huge, rough stone rolling down from a high mountain; and the only polishing I get is when some corner gets rubbed off by coming in contact with something else, striking with accelerating force against religious bigotry, priest-craft, lawyer-craft, doctor-craft, lying editors, suborned judges and jurors, and the authority of perjured executives, backed by mobs, blasphemers, licentious and corrupt men and women—all hell knocking off a corner here and a corner there. Thus I will become a smooth and polished shaft in the quiver of the Almighty, who will give me dominion over all and every one of them, when their refuge of lies shall fail, and their hiding place shall be destroyed, while these smooth-polished stones with which I come in contact become marred. (TPJS, 304)[109]

♦♦♦

To get salvation we must not only do some things, but everything which God has commanded. (TPJS, 332)[125]

♦♦♦

I advise all to go on to perfection, and search deeper and deeper into the mysteries of Godliness. (TPJS, 364)[132]

♦♦♦

I never told you I was perfect; but there is no error in the revelations which I have taught. (TPJS, 368)[132]

PERSECUTION

We are informed . . . that those [persecutors] are very violent, and threaten immediate extermination upon all those who profess our doctrine. How far they will be suffered to execute their threats, we know not, but we trust in the Lord, and leave the event with Him to govern in His own wise providence. (TPJS, 28)[16]

♦♦♦

Remember not to murmur at the dealings of God with His creatures. You are not as yet brought into as trying circumstances as were the ancient Prophets and Apostles . . . of whom the world was not worthy . . . amidst all their afflictions they rejoiced that they were counted worthy to receive persecution for Christ's sake. (TPJS, 32)[18]

♦♦♦

I know that Zion, in the due time of the Lord, will be redeemed; but how many will be the days of her purification, tribulation, and affliction, the Lord has kept hid from my eyes; and when I enquire concerning this subject, the voice of the Lord is: Be still, and know that I am God; all those who suffer for my name shall reign with me, and he that layeth down his life for my sake shall find it again. (TPJS, 34)[19]

♦♦♦

Those who cannot endure persecution, and stand in the day of affliction, cannot stand in the day when the Son of God shall burst the veil, and appear in all the glory of His Father, with all the holy angels. (TPJS, 42)[20]

♦♦♦

The law of heaven is presented to man, and as such guarantees to all who obey it a reward far beyond any earthly consideration; though it does not . . . exempt [one] from the afflictions and troubles arising from different sources in consequence of acts of wicked men on earth. Still in the midst of all this there is a promise predicated upon the fact that it is a law of heaven, which transcends the law of man, as far as eternal life [transcends] the temporal; and as the blessings which God is able to give, are greater than those which can be given by man. (TPJS, 50)[21]

♦♦♦

From apostates the faithful have received the severest persecutions. (TPJS, 67)[21]

♦♦♦

The Elders . . . are combating the prejudices of a crooked and perverse generation, by having in their possession . . . religious principles, which are misrepresented by almost all those whose crafts are in danger by the same. (TPJS, 83)[31]

♦♦♦

I have been drawn into this course of proceeding by persecution, that is brought upon us from false rumors and misrepresentations concerning my sentiments. (TPJS, 83)[31]

♦♦♦

I am well aware that you [the Twelve] have to sustain my character against the vile calumnies and reproaches of this ungodly generation, and that you delight in doing so. (TPJS, 89)[33]

♦♦♦

I say unto you, that those who have thus vilely treated us . . . shall be hanged upon their own gallows; or, in other words, shall fall into their own gin, and snare, and ditch, and trap, which they have prepared for us, and shall go backwards and stumble and fall, and their name shall be blotted out, and God shall reward them according to all their abominations. (TPJS, 123)[46]

♦♦♦

We have reproved in the gate, and men have laid snares for us. We have spoken words, and men have made us offenders. And notwithstanding all this, our minds are not yet darkened, but feel strong in the Lord. (TPJS, 124)[46]

♦♦♦

Now, dear brethren, if any men ever had reason to claim this promise "great is your reward in heaven, for so persecuted they the Prophets which were before you.," we are the men; for we know that the world not only hate us, but they speak all manner of evil of us falsely, for no other reason than that we have been endeavoring to teach the fullness of the Gospel of Jesus Christ. (TPJS, 124)[46]

♦♦♦

Such inhumanity, and relentless cruelty and barbarity as were practiced against the

Saints in Missouri can scarcely be found in the annals of history. (TPJS, 126)[46]

◆ ◆ ◆

We think . . . that every species of wickedness and cruelty practiced upon us will only tend to bind our hearts together and seal them together in love. . . . We are driven from our homes and smitten without cause. . . . We are compelled to hear nothing but blasphemous oaths, and witness a scene of blasphemy, and drunkenness and hypocrisy, and debaucheries of every description. (TPJS, 130)[47]

◆ ◆ ◆

Inasmuch as God hath said that He would have a tried people, that He would purge them as gold, now we think that this time He has chosen His own crucible, wherein we have been tried. (TPJS, 135)[47]

◆ ◆ ◆

In the earlier ages of the world a righteous man, and a man of God and intelligence, had a better chance to do good, to be believed and received than at the present day; but in these days, such a man is much opposed and persecuted by most of the inhabitants of the earth, and he has much sorrow to pass through here. (TPJS, 196)[68]

◆ ◆ ◆

If a man stands and opposes the world of sin, he may expect to have all wicked and corrupt spirits arrayed against him. (TPJS, 259)[84]

◆ ◆ ◆

By seeing the blessings of the endowment rolling on, and the kingdom increasing and spreading from sea to sea, we shall rejoice that we were not overcome by these foolish [persecutors]. (TPJS, 259)[84]

◆ ◆ ◆

He that will war the true Christian warfare against the corruptions of these last days will have wicked men and angels of devils, and all the infernal powers of darkness continually arrayed against him. (TPJS, 259)[84]

◆ ◆ ◆

How many have had to wander in sheep skins and goat skins, and live in caves and dens of the mountains, because the world was unworthy of their society! . . . But remember, brethren, he that offends one of the least of the Saints, would be better off with a millstone tied to his neck and he and the stone plunged into the depth of the sea! (TPJS, 261)[85]

◆ ◆ ◆

Mr. Stollars stated that James Mullone, of Springfield, told him as follows: . . . "I have been to Nauvoo, and seen Joe Smith, the Prophet: he had a gray horse, and I asked him where he got it"; and Joe said, "You see that white cloud." "Yes." "Well, as it came along, I got the horse from that cloud." This is a fair specimen of the ten thousand foolish lies circulated by this generation to bring the truth and its advocates into disrepute. (TPJS, 270)[90]

◆ ◆ ◆

I am like a huge, rough stone rolling down from a high mountain; and the only polishing I get is when some corner gets rubbed off by coming in contact with something else, striking with accelerating force against religious bigotry, priest-craft, lawyer-craft, doctor-craft, lying editors, suborned judges and jurors, and the authority of perjured executives, backed by mobs, blasphemers, licentious and corrupt men and women—all hell knocking off a corner here and a corner there. Thus I will become a smooth and polished shaft in the quiver of the Almighty, who will give me dominion over all and every one of them, when their refuge of lies shall fail, and their hiding place shall be destroyed, while these smooth-polished stones with which I come in contact become marred. (TPJS, 304)[109]

◆ ◆ ◆

Many men will say, "I will never forsake you, but will stand by you all the times." But the moment you teach them some of the mysteries of the kingdom of God that are retained in the heavens and are to be revealed to the children of men when they are prepared for them they will be the first to stone you and put you to death. (TPJS, 309)[113]

◆ ◆ ◆

It always has been when a man was sent of God with the priesthood and he began to preach the fullness of the gospel, that he was thrust out by his friends, who are already to butcher him if he teaches things which they imagine to be wrong; and Jesus was crucified upon this principle. (TPJS, 310)[113]

◆ ◆ ◆

My persecutors allow me no rest, and I find that in the midst of business and care the spirit is willing, but the flesh is weak. (TPJS, 315)[114]

◆ ◆ ◆

Executive writs could be issued when they ought to be, and not be made instruments of cruelty to oppress the innocent, and persecute men whose religion is unpopular. (TPJS, 327)[122]

◆ ◆ ◆

This generation is as corrupt as the generation of the Jews that crucified Christ; and if He were here today, and should preach the same doctrine He did then, they would put Him to death. (TPJS, 328)[122]

◆ ◆ ◆

I would not have suffered my name to have been used by my friends on anywise as President of the United States, or candidate for that office, if I and my friends could have had the privilege of enjoying our religious and civil rights as American citizens, even those rights which the Constitution guarantees unto all her citizens alike. But this as a people we have been denied from the beginning. (TPJS, 331)[124]

◆ ◆ ◆

If any man is authorized to take away my life because he thinks and says I am a false teacher, then, upon the same principle, we should be justified in taking away the life of every false teacher, and where would be the end of blood? And who would not be the sufferer? (TPJS, 344)[130]

◆ ◆ ◆

Rejoice, O Israel! Your friends who have been murdered for the truth's sake in the persecutions shall triumph gloriously in the celestial world, while their murderers shall welter for ages in torment, even until they shall have paid the uttermost farthing. (TPJS, 359)[130]

◆ ◆ ◆

The character of the old churches [has] always been slandered by all apostates since the world began. (TPJS, 375)[133]

◆ ◆ ◆

[On the way to Carthage, Joseph said to the company that was with him] I am going like a lamb to the slaughter, but I am calm as a summer's morning. I have a conscience void of offence toward God and toward all men. If they take my life I shall die an innocent man, and my blood shall cry from the ground for vengeance, and it shall be said of me, "He was murdered in cold blood"! (TPJS, 379)[137]

PERSECUTORS

We are informed . . . that those [persecutors] are very violent, and threaten immediate extermination upon all those who profess our doctrine. How far they will be suffered to execute their threats, we know not, but we trust in the Lord, and leave the event with Him to govern in His own wise providence. (TPJS, 28)[16]

♦♦♦

There is a superior intelligence bestowed upon such as obey the Gospel with full purpose of heart, which, if sinned against, the apostate is left naked and destitute of the Spirit of God, and he is, in truth, nigh unto cursing, and his end is to be burned. When once that light which was in them is taken from them, they become as much darkened as they were previously enlightened, and then, no marvel, if all their power should be enlisted against the truth . . . they, like Judas, seek the destruction of those who were their greatest benefactors. (TPJS, 67)[21]

♦♦♦

Those who cry transgression do it because they are the servants of sin and are the children of disobedience themselves; and those who swear falsely against my servants, that they might bring them into bondage and death; wo unto them; because they have offended my little ones; they shall be severed from the ordinances of mine house. (TPJS, 135)[47]

♦♦♦

A frank and open rebuke provoketh a good man to emulation; and in the hour of trouble he will be your best friend. But on the other hand, it will draw out all the corruptions of corrupt hearts; and lying and the poison of asps is under their tongues; and they do cause the pure in heart to be cast into prison, because they want them out of their way. (TPJS, 137)[47]

♦♦♦

[Joseph said that] . . . God had called him to lead the Church, and he would lead it right; those that undertake to interfere will be ashamed when their own folly is made manifest. (TPJS, 225)[75]

♦♦♦

I prophesied that the saints would continue to suffer much affliction and would be driven to the Rocky Mountains, many would apostatize, others would be put to death by our persecutors or lose their lives in consequence of exposure or disease, and some of you will live to go and assist in making settlements and build cities and see the Saints become a mighty people in the midst of the Rocky Mountains. (TPJS, 255)[82]

♦♦♦

All those that rise up against me will surely feel the weight of their iniquity upon their own heads. (TPJS, 258)[84]

♦♦♦

I thank God for preserving me from my enemies; I have no enemies but for the truth's sake. I have no desire but to do all men good. I feel to pray for all men. (TPJS, 275)[91]

♦♦♦

The burdens which roll upon me are very great. My persecutors allow me no rest, and I find that in the midst of business and care the spirit is willing, but the flesh is weak. (TPJS, 315)[114]

♦♦♦

I prophecy they never will have power

to kill me till my work is accomplished, and I am ready to die. (TPJS, 328)[122]

• • •

Beware, O earth, how you fight against the saints of God and shed innocent blood; for in the days of Elijah, his enemies came upon him, and fire was called down from heaven and destroyed them. (TPJS, 340)[128]

• • •

Woe, woe be to that man or set of men who lift up their hands against God and His witness in these last days: for they shall deceive almost the very chosen ones! (TPJS, 365)[132]

• • •

False prophets always arise to oppose the true prophets and they will prophesy so very near the truth that they will deceive almost the very chosen ones. (TPJS, 365)[132]

• • •

They that hurl all their hell and fiery billows upon me . . . will roll off me as fast as they come on. But I have an order of things to save the poor fellows at any rate, and get them saved; for I will send men to preach to them in prison and save them if I can. (TPJS, 366)[132]

PERSEVERANCE

I pray . . . that you all may be kept in the faith unto the end: let your sufferings be what they may. (TPJS, 35)[19]

• • •

Those who cannot endure persecution, and stand in the day of affliction, cannot stand in the day when the Son of God shall burst the veil, and appear in all the glory of His Father, with all the holy angels. (TPJS, 42)[20]

• • •

The Lord says that every man is to receive according to his works. Reflect for a moment, . . . and enquire whether you would consider yourselves worthy a seat at the marriage seat with Paul and others like him, if you had been unfaithful? Had you not fought the good fight, and kept the faith, could you expect to receive? (TPJS, 64)[21]

• • •

The great Plan of Salvation is a theme which ought to occupy our strict attention, and be regarded as one of heaven's best gifts to mankind. No consideration whatever ought to deter us from showing ourselves approved in the sight of God. (TPJS, 68)[21]

• • •

I am determined to do all that I can to uphold you, although I may do many things inadvertently that are not right in the sight of God. (TPJS, 90)[33]

• • •

"My son, peace be unto thy soul; thine adversity and thine affliction shall be but a small moment; and then if thou endure it well, God shall exalt thee on high." (TPJS, 134)[47]

• • •

After having suffered so great sacrifice and having passed through so great a season of sorrow, we trust that a ram may be caught in the thicket speedily, to relieve the sons and daughters of Abraham from their great anxiety, and to light up the lamp of salvation upon their countenances, that they may hold on now, after having gone so far unto everlasting life. (TPJS, 136)[47]

• • •

In His Almighty name we are determined to endure tribulation as good soldiers unto the end. (TPJS, 139)[47]

♦♦♦

A man can bear a heavy burthen by practice and continuing to increase it. (TPJS, 299)[103]

♦♦♦

I have tried a number of years to get the minds of the Saints prepared to receive the things of God; but we frequently see some of them, after suffering all they have for the work of God, will fly to pieces like glass as soon as anything comes that is contrary to their traditions: they cannot stand the fire at all. How many will be able to abide a celestial law, and go through and receive their exaltation, I am unable to say, as many are called, but few are chosen. (TPJS, 331)[123]

♦♦♦

I cannot lie down until all my work is finished. (TPJS, 361)[130]

PERSUASION

(See also ENCOURAGEMENT)

The Saints ought to lay hold of every door that shall seem to be opened to them, to obtain foothold on the earth, and be making all the preparation that is within their power for the terrible storms that are now gathering in the heavens. (TPJS, 141)[47]

♦♦♦

Nothing is so much calculated to lead people to forsake sin as to take them by the hand, and watch over them with tenderness. When persons manifest the least kindness and love to me, O, what power it has over my mind, while the opposite course has a tendency to harrow up all the harsh feelings and depress the human mind. (TPJS, 240)[79]

♦♦♦

Men or women [can]not be compelled into the kingdom of God, but must be dealt with in long-suffering, and at last we shall save them. (TPJS, 241)[79]

PETTINESS

Avoid contentions and vain disputes with men of corrupt minds, who do not desire to know the truth. (TPJS, 43)[20]

♦♦♦

As females possess refined feelings and sensitiveness, they are also subject to overmuch zeal, which must ever prove dangerous, and cause them to be rigid in a religious capacity—[they] should be armed with mercy, notwithstanding the iniquity among us. (TPJS, 238)[78]

♦♦♦

We must be merciful to one another, and overlook small things. (TPJS, 240)[79]

PHYSICAL BODIES

We came to this earth that we might have a body and present it pure before God in the celestial kingdom. (TPJS, 181)[56]

♦♦♦

The great principle of happiness consists in having a body. (TPJS, 181)[56]

♦♦♦

All beings who have bodies have power over those who have not. The devil has no power over us only as we permit him. The moment we revolt at anything which comes from God, the devil takes power. (TPJS, 181)[56]

♦♦♦

No person can have . . . salvation except through a tabernacle. (TPJS, 297)[103]

♦♦♦

The devil steals a tabernacle because he has not one of his own; but if he steals one, he is always liable to be turned out of doors. (TPJS, 298)[103]

◆◆◆

God made a tabernacle and put a spirit into it, and it became a living soul. . . . It does not say in the Hebrew [Bible] that God created the spirit of man. It says "God made man out of the earth and put into him Adam's spirit, and so became a living body. (TPJS, 352)[130]

PLAN OF SALVATION

Impressed with the . . . [fact of darkness covering the earth and minds of men,] what can be the feelings of those who have been partakers of the heavenly gift and have tasted the good word of God, and the powers of the world to come? Who but those that can see the awful precipice upon which the world of mankind stands in this generation, can labor in the vineyard of the Lord without feeling a sense of the world's deplorable situation? Who but those who have duly considered the condescension of the Father of our spirits, in providing a sacrifice for His creatures, a plan of redemption, a power of atonement, a scheme of salvation, having as its great objects, the bringing of men back into the presence of the King of heaven, crowning them in the celestial glory, and making them heirs with the Son to that inheritance which is incorruptible, undefiled, and which fadeth not away—who but such can realize the importance of a perfect walk before all men, and a diligence in calling upon all men to partake of these blessings? How indescribably glorious are these things to mankind! Of a truth they may be considered tidings of great joy to all people; and tidings, too, that ought to fill the earth and cheer the heart of everyone when sounded in his ears. The reflection that everyone is to receive according to his own diligence and perseverance while in the vineyard, ought to inspire everyone who is called to be a minister of these glad tidings, to so improve his talent that he may gain other talents, that when the Master sits down to take an account of the conduct of His servants, it may be said, "Well done, good and faithful servant: thou hast been faithful over a few things; I will now make thee ruler over many things: enter thou into the joy of thy Lord." (TPJS, 47)[21]

◆◆◆

Notwithstanding the transgression, by which man had cut himself off from an immediate intercourse with his Maker without a Mediator, it appears that the great and glorious plan of His redemption was previously provided: the sacrifice prepared; the atonement wrought out in the mind and purpose of God, even in the person of the Son, through whom man was now to look for acceptance and through whose merits he was now taught that he alone could find redemption, since the word had been pronounced, Unto dust thou shalt return. (TPJS, 57)[21]

◆◆◆

The great Plan of Salvation is a theme which ought to occupy our strict attention, and be regarded as one of heaven's best gifts to mankind. No consideration whatever ought to deter us from showing ourselves approved in the sight of God. (TPJS, 68)[21]

◆◆◆

The Melchizedek Priesthood . . . is the channel through which all knowledge, doctrine, the Plan of Salvation and every important matter is revealed from heaven. (TPJS, 166)[54]

◆◆◆

"At the first organization in heaven we were all present, and saw the Savior chosen and appointed and the Plan of Salvation made, and we sanctioned it." (TPJS, 181)[56]

◆ ◆ ◆

Various and conflicting are the opinions of men concerning the Plan of Salvation. (TPJS, 217)[74]

◆ ◆ ◆

The great designs of God in relation to the salvation of the human family, are very little understood by the professedly wise and intelligent generation in which we live. (TPJS, 218)[74]

◆ ◆ ◆

The Great Jehovah contemplated the whole of the events connected with the earth, pertaining to the Plan of Salvation, before it rolled into existence, or ever, "the morning stars sang together" for joy; the past, the present, and the future were and are, with Him, one eternal "now." (TPJS, 220)[74]

◆ ◆ ◆

[The Lord] knew of the fall of Adam, the iniquities of the Antediluvians, of the depth of iniquity that would be connected with the human family, their weakness and strength, their power and glory, apostasies, their crimes, their righteousness and iniquity; He comprehended the fall of man, and his redemption; He knew the Plan of Salvation and pointed it out; He was acquainted with the situation of all nations and with their destiny; He ordered all things according to the council of His will. (TPJS, 220)[74]

◆ ◆ ◆

[The Lord] knows the situation of both the living and the dead, and has made ample provision for their redemption, according to their several circumstances, and the laws of the kingdom of God, whether in this world, or in the world to come. (TPJS, 220)[74]

PLEAS TO GOD

Oh God! Where art Thou? And where is the pavilion that covereth Thy hiding place? How long shall Thy hand be stayed, and Thine eye, yea Thy pure eye, behold from the eternal heavens, the wrongs of Thy people, and of Thy servants, and Thy ear be penetrated with their cries? Yea, O Lord, how long shall they suffer these wrongs and unlawful oppressions, before Thine heart shall be softened towards them? (TPJS, 131)[47]

◆ ◆ ◆

O Lord God Almighty, Maker of Heaven, Earth and Seas, and of all things that in them are, and who controlest and subjectest the devil, and the dark and benighted dominion of Sheol! Stretch forth Thy hand, let Thine eye pierce; let Thy pavilion be taken up; let Thy hiding place no longer be covered; let Thine ear be inclined; let Thine heart be softened, and Thy bowels moved with compassion towards us; let Thine anger be kindled against our enemies; and in the fury of Thine heart, with Thy sword avenge us of our wrongs; remember Thy suffering Saints, O our God! And Thy servants will rejoice in Thy name forever. (TPJS, 132)[47]

PLURAL MARRIAGE

In obedience there is joy and peace unspotted, unalloyed; and as God has designed our happiness—and the happiness of all His creatures, he never has—He never will institute an ordinance or give a commandment to His people that is not calculated in its nature to promote that happiness which he has designed, and which will not end in the greatest amount of good and glory to those who become the recipients of His law and ordinances. (TPJS, 256)[83]

♦♦♦

Everything that God gives us is lawful and right; and it is proper that we should enjoy His gifts and blessings whenever and wherever He is disposed to bestow; but if we should seize upon those same blessings and enjoyments without law, without revelation, without commandment, those blessings and enjoyments would prove cursings and vexations in the end, and we should have to lie down in sorrow and wailings of everlasting regret. (TPJS, 256)[83]

♦♦♦

Whatever God requires is right, no matter what it is, although we may not see the reason thereof till long after the events transpire. So with Solomon: first he asked wisdom, and God gave it him, and with it every desire of his heart, even things which might be considered abominable to all who understand the order of heaven only in part, but which in reality were right because God gave and sanctioned by special revelation. (TPJS, 256)[83]

♦♦♦

According to the law, I hold the keys of this power [the doctrine of plurality of wives] in the last days; for there is never but one on earth at a time on whom the power and its keys are conferred; *and I have constantly said no man shall have but one wife at a time, unless the Lord directs otherwise.* (TPJS, 324)[120]

PLURALITY OF GODS

Everlasting covenant was made between three personages before the organization of this earth; these personages, according to Abraham's record, are called God the

first, the Creator; God the second, the Redeemer; and God the third, the witness or Testator. (TPJS, 190)[61]

♦♦♦

Jesus designs to save people out of their sins. Said Jesus, "Ye shall do the work, which ye see me do." These are the grand key-words for the society to act upon. (TPJS, 239)[78]

♦♦♦

There is much said about God and the godhead. The scriptures say there are Gods many and Lords many, but to us there is but one living and true God, and the heaven of heavens could not contain him; for he took the liberty to go into other heavens. (TPJS, 311)[113]

♦♦♦

Gods have an ascendancy over the angels, who are ministering servants. In the resurrection, some [people] are raised to be angels, others are raised to become Gods. (TPJS, 312)[113]

♦♦♦

Here, then, is eternal life—to know the only wise and true God; and you have got to learn how to be Gods yourselves, and to be kings and priests to God, the same as all Gods have done before you, namely, by going from one small degree to another, and from a small capacity to a great one; from grace to grace, from exaltation to exaltation, until you attain to the resurrection of the dead, and are able to dwell in everlasting burnings, and to sit in glory, as do those who sit enthroned in everlasting power. And I want you to know that God, in the last days, while certain individuals are proclaiming his name, is not trifling with you or me. [Elder B. H. Roberts writes in a footnote, "The argument here made by the Prophet is very much strengthened by the following passage: "The Son can do nothing of himself, but what he seeth the Father do; for what things soever he doeth, these also doeth the Son likewise" (St. John 5:19). Elder Roberts further wrote, "Whatever happened to (Christ) . . . whether within our individual reach or not, is assuredly within reach of humanity. That is what (Christ) . . . urged again and again, "Be born again." "Be ye perfect." "Ye are the sons of God." "My Father and your Father, my God and your God."] (TPJS, 346)[130]

♦♦♦

But they shall be heirs of God and joint heirs with Jesus Christ. What is it? To inherit the same power, the same glory and the same exaltation, until you arrive at the station of a God, and ascend the throne of eternal power, the same as those who have gone before. What did Jesus do? Why, I do the things I saw my Father do when worlds came rolling into existence. My Father worked out his kingdom with fear and trembling, and I must do the same; and when I get my kingdom, I shall present it to my Father, so that he may obtain kingdom upon kingdom, and it will exalt him in glory. He will then take a higher exaltation, and I will take his place, and thereby become exalted myself. So that Jesus treads in the tracks of his Father, and inherits what God did before; and God is thus glorified and exalted in the salvation and exaltation of all his children. (TPJS, 347)[130]

♦♦♦

I have always declared God to be a distinct personage, Jesus Christ a separate and distinct personage from God the Father, and that the Holy Ghost was a distinct personage and a Spirit; and these three constitute three distinct personages and three Gods. If this is in accordance with the New Testament, lo and behold! We have three Gods anyhow, and they are plural; and who can contradict it? . . .

The doctrine of a plurality of Gods is as prominent in the Bible as any other doctrine. It is all over the face of the Bible. It stands beyond the power of controversy. A wayfaring man, though a fool, need not err therein. (TPJS, 370)[133]

♦♦♦

Paul says there are Gods many and Lords many. I want to set it forth in a plain and simple manner; but to us there is but one God—that is pertaining to us; and he is in all and through all. But if Joseph Smith says there are Gods many and Lords many, they cry, "Away with him! Crucify him! Crucify him!" (TPJS, 370)[133] . . . From the Hebrew Bible . . . the first word shows a plurality of Gods. . . . *Berosheit baurau Eloheim ait aushamayeen vehau auraits.* . . . It read first, "In the beginning the head of the Gods brought forth the Gods." (TPJS, 371)[133]

♦♦♦

I once asked a learned Jew, "If the Hebrew language compels us to render all words ending in heim in the plural, why not render the first *Eloheim* plural?" He replied, "That is the rule with few exceptions; but in this case it would ruin the Bible."

The heads of the Gods appointed one God for us; and when you take [that] view of the subject, it sets one free to see all the beauty, holiness and perfection of the Gods. All I want is to get the simple, naked truth, and the whole truth. (TPJS, 372)[133]

♦♦♦

Every man who reigns in celestial glory is a God to his dominions. (TPJS, 374)[133]

♦♦♦

Oh, Thou God who art King of kings and Lord of lords, the sectarian world, by their actions, declare, "We cannot believe Thee." (TPJS, 375)[133]

POLITICS

I have, of late, had repeated solicitations to have something to do in relation to the political farce about dividing the country; but as my feelings revolt at the idea of having anything to do with politics, I have declined in every instance in having anything to do on the subject. I think it would be well for politicians to regulate their own affairs. I wish to be let alone, that I may attend strictly to the spiritual welfare of the church. (TPJS, 275)[92]

♦♦♦

I would not have suffered my name to have been used by my friends on anywise as President of the United States, or candidate for that office, if I and my friends could have had the privilege of enjoying our religious and civil rights as American citizens, even those rights which the Constitution guarantees unto all her citizens alike. But this as a people we have been denied from the beginning. (TPJS, 331)[124]

♦♦♦

If I lose my life in a good cause I am willing to be sacrificed on the altar of virtue, righteousness and truth, in maintaining the laws and Constitution of the United States, if need be, for the general good of man. (TPJS, 332)[124]

♦♦♦

As to politics, I care but little about the presidential chair, I would not give half as much for the office of President of the United States as I would for the one I now hold as Lieutenant-General of the Nauvoo Legion. (TPJS, 333)[127]

♦♦♦

When I get hold of the Eastern papers, and see how popular I am, I am afraid myself that I shall be elected; but if I should be, I would not say, "*Your cause is just, but I*

can do nothing for you." (TPJS, 334)[127]

♦♦♦

The government will not receive any advice or counsel from me; they are self-sufficient. But they must go to hell and work out their own salvation with fear and trembling. (TPJS, 334)[127]

PONDERING

The things of God are of deep import; and time, and experience, and careful and ponderous and solemn thoughts can only find them out. Thy mind, O man! If thou will lead a soul unto salvation, must stretch as high as the utmost heavens, and search into and contemplate the darkest abyss and the broad expanse of eternity. (TPJS, 137)[47]

♦♦♦

I exhort you to give heed to all the virtue and the teachings which I have given you. (TPJS, 367)[132]

POPULARITY

It mattereth not whether the principle is popular or unpopular, I will always maintain a true principle, even if I stand alone in it. (TPJS, 332)[125]

♦♦♦

When I get hold of the Eastern papers, and see how popular I am, I am afraid myself that I shall be elected; but if I should be, I would not say, "*Your cause is just, but I can do nothing for you.*" (TPJS, 334)[127]

POTENTIAL

Every man lives for himself.. . . . But except a man be born again, he cannot see the kingdom of God. . . . He may receive a glory like unto the moon, [i.e. of which the light of the moon is typical] or a star, [i.e. of which the light of the stars is typical] but he can never come unto Mount Zion, and unto the city of the living God . . . unless he becomes as a little child, and is taught by the Spirit of God. (TPJS, 12)[8]

•••

God has created man with a mind capable of instruction, and a faculty which may be enlarged in proportion to the heed and diligence given to the light communicated from heaven to the intellect; and that the nearer man approaches perfection, the clearer are his views, and the greater his enjoyments, till he has overcome the evils of his life and lost every desire for sin; and like the ancients, arrives at that point of faith where he is wrapped in the power and glory of his Maker and is caught up to dwell with Him. (TPJS, 51)[21]

•••

If you live up to your privileges, the angels cannot be restrained from being your associates. (TPJS, 226)[75]

•••

They shall be heirs of God and joint heirs with Jesus Christ. What is it? To inherit the same power, the same glory and the same exaltation, until you arrive at the station of a God, and ascend the throne of eternal power, the same as those who have gone before. What did Jesus do? Why, I do the things I saw my Father do when worlds came rolling into existence. My Father worked out his kingdom with fear and trembling, and I must do the same; and when I get my kingdom, I shall present it to my Father, so that he may obtain kingdom upon kingdom, and it will exalt him in glory. He will then take a higher exaltation, and I will take his place, and thereby become exalted myself. So that Jesus treads in the tracks of his Father, and inherits what God did before; and God is

thus glorified and exalted in the salvation and exaltation of all his children. (TPJS, 347)[130]

•••

All the minds and spirits that God ever sent into the world are susceptible of enlargement. (TPJS, 354)[130]

POWER

"Behold, there are many called, but few are chosen. And why are they not chosen? Because their hearts are so set upon the things of this world, and aspire to the honors of men, that they do not learn this one lesson—that the rights of the Priesthood are inseparably connected with the powers of heaven, and that the powers of heaven cannot be controlled nor handled only upon the principles of righteousness. That they may be conferred upon us, it is true; but when we undertake to cover our sins, or to gratify our pride, our vain ambition, or to exercise control, or dominion, or compulsion, upon the souls of the children of men in any degree of unrighteousness, behold, the heavens withdraw themselves, the Spirit of the Lord is grieved; and when it is withdrawn, Amen to the Priesthood, or the authority of that man. Behold! Ere he is aware, he is left to himself to kick against the pricks, to persecute the saints, and to fight against God.

"We have learned by sad experience that it is the nature and disposition of almost all men, as soon as they get a little authority, as they suppose, they will immediately begin to exercise unrighteous dominion. Hence, many are called, but few are chosen." (TPJS, 142)[47]

•••

Inasmuch as you are to be instrumental in this great work, . . . [God] will endow you with power, might, wisdom and intelligence, and every qualification necessary; while your minds will expand wider and wider, until you can circumscribe the earth and the heavens, reach forth into eternity, and contemplate the mighty acts of Jehovah in all their variety and glory. (TPJS, 163)[51]

•••

All beings who have bodies have power over those who have not. The devil has no power over us only as we permit him. The moment we revolt at anything which comes from God, the devil takes power. (TPJS, 181)[56]

•••

All men have power to resist the devil. (TPJS, 189)[61]

•••

It would seem also, that wicked spirits have their bounds, limits and laws by which they are governed or controlled, and know their future destiny; . . . they possess a power that none but those who have the Priesthood can control. (TPJS, 208)[71]

•••

As well might the devil seek to dethrone Jehovah, as overthrow an innocent soul that resists everything which is evil. (TPJS, 226)[75]

•••

We have overcome in laying the foundation of a work . . . that God and angels have contemplated with delight for generations past; that fired the souls of the ancient patriarchs and prophets; a work that is destined to bring about the destruction of the powers of darkness, the renovation of the earth, the glory of God, and the salvation of the human family. (TPJS, 232)[76]

•••

My feelings at the present are that inasmuch as the Lord Almighty has preserved me until today, He will continue to preserve me, by the united faith and prayers of the Saints, until I have fully accomplished my mission in this life, and so firmly established the dispensation of the fullness of the Priesthood in these last days, that all the powers of earth and hell can never prevail against it. (TPJS, 258)[84]

•••

In knowledge there is power. God has more power than all other beings, because he has knowledge; and hence he knows how to subject all other beings to Him. He has power over all. (TPJS, 288)[101]

•••

Salvation is nothing more nor less than to triumph over all our enemies and put them under our feet. And when we have power to put all enemies under our feet in the world, and a knowledge to triumph over all evil spirits in the world to come, then we are saved. (TPJS, 297)[103]

•••

Salvation means a man's being placed beyond the power of all his enemies. (TPJS, 301)[106]

•••

A man never has half so much fuss to unlock a door, if he has a key, as though he had not, and had to cut it open with his jack-knife. (TPJS, 308)[113]

•••

Truth will cut its own way. (TPJS, 313)[114]

•••

The Lord once told me that what I asked for I should have. I have been afraid to ask God to kill my enemies, lest some of them should peradventure, repent. (TPJS, 340)[128]

•••

In relation to the power over the minds of mankind which I hold, I would say, It is in consequence of the power of truth in the doctrines which I have been an instrument in the hands of God of presenting unto them, and not because of any compulsion on my part. (TPJS, 341)[129]

•••

The effectual prayers of the righteous avail much. (TPJS, 342)[130]

•••

But they shall be heirs of God and joint heirs with Jesus Christ. What is it? To inherit the same power, the same glory and the same exaltation, until you arrive at the station of a God, and ascend the throne of eternal power, the same as those who have gone before. What did Jesus do? Why, I do the things I saw my Father do when worlds came rolling into existence. My Father worked out his kingdom with fear and trembling, and I must do the same; and when I get my kingdom, I shall present it to my Father, so that he may obtain kingdom upon kingdom, and it will exalt him in glory. He will then take a higher exaltation, and I will take his place, and thereby become exalted myself. So that Jesus treads in the tracks of his Father, and inherits what God did before; and God is thus glorified and exalted in the salvation and exaltation of all his children. (TPJS, 347)[130]

•••

It will not be by sword or gun that this kingdom will roll on: the power of truth is such that all nations will be under the necessity of obeying the Gospel. (TPJS, 366)[132]

PRAISE

Be careful of one another's feelings, and walk in love, honoring one another more than themselves, as is required by the Lord. (TPJS, 25)[13]

•••

The man who willeth to do well, we should extol his virtues, and speak not of his faults behind his back. (TPJS, 31)[17]

•••

When the Twelve or any other witnesses stand before the congregation of the earth, and they preach in the power and demonstration of the Spirit of God, and the people are astonished and confounded at the doctrine, and say, "That man has preached a powerful discourse, a great sermon," then let that man or those men take care that they do not ascribe the glory unto themselves, but be careful that they are humble, and ascribe the praise and glory to God and the Lamb; for it is by the power of the Holy Priesthood and the Holy Ghost that they have power to speak. What art thou, O man, but dust? And from whom receivest thou thy power and blessings, but from God? (TPJS, 155)[49]

•••

Let the Twelve and all Saints be willing to . . . act for each other's good, and pray for one another, and honor our brother or make honorable mention of his name, and not backbite and devour our brother. (TPJS, 155)[49]

•••

Don't be limited in your views with regard to your neighbor's virtue. (TPJS, 228)[75]

•••

Now, in this world, mankind are naturally selfish, ambitious and striving to excel one above another; yet some are willing to build up others as well as themselves. (TPJS, 297)[103]

♦♦♦

If a skillful mechanic . . . succeeds in welding together iron or steel more perfectly than any other mechanic, is he not deserving of praise? And if by the principles of truth I succeed in uniting men of all denominations in the bonds of love, shall I not have attained a good object? (TPJS, 313)[114]

PRAYER

You cannot watch [Satan] too closely, nor pray too much. (TPJS, 25)[14]

♦♦♦

There is never a time when the spirit is too old to approach God. All are within the reach of pardoning mercy, who have not committed the unpardonable sin, which hath no forgiveness. (TPJS, 191)[63]

♦♦♦

[Joseph] . . . made a promise in the name of the Lord, saying that that soul who has righteousness enough to ask God in the secret place for life, every day of their lives, shall live to three score years and ten. (TPJS, 241)[79]

♦♦♦

Seek to know God in your closets, call upon Him in the fields. Follow the directions of the Book of Mormon, and pray over, and for your families, your cattle, your flocks, your herds, your corn, and all things that you possess; ask the blessings of God upon all your labors, and everything that you engage in. (TPJS, 247)[80]

♦♦♦

The effectual prayers of the righteous avail much. (TPJS, 342)[130]

♦♦♦

[In learning of the council in heaven] . . . we begin to learn the only true God, and what kind of a being we have got to worship. Having a knowledge of God, we begin to know how to approach him, and how to ask so as to receive an answer. When we understand the character of God, and know how to come to him, he begins to unfold the heavens to us, and to tell us all about it. (TPJS, 350)[130]

♦♦♦

When we are ready to come to [God], . . . he is ready to come to us. (TPJS, 350)[130]

PRECAUTION

(See also CAUTION; PRUDENCE)

You cannot watch [Satan] too closely, nor pray too much. (TPJS, 25)[14]

♦♦♦

We must use precaution in bringing sinners to justice, lest . . . we draw the indignation of a Gentile world upon us. . . . To the iniquitous show yourselves merciful. (TPJS, 239)[78]

PRECEPT

Why will not man learn wisdom by precept at this late age of the world, when we have such a cloud of witnesses and examples before us, and not be obliged to learn by sad experience everything we know? (TPJS, 155)[49]

PREJUDICE

We frequently are so filled with prejudice, or have a beam in our own eye, that we are not capable of passing right decisions. (TPJS, 69)[22]

♦♦♦

The Elders . . . are combating the prejudices of a crooked and perverse generation, by having in their possession . . . religious principles, which are misrepresented by almost all those whose crafts are in danger by the same. (TPJS, 83)[31]

♦♦♦

It is true they have eyes to see, and see not, but none are so blind as those who will not see. (TPJS, 96)[34]

♦♦♦

If the Church knew all the commandments, one-half they would condemn through prejudice and ignorance. (TPJS, 112)[41]

♦♦♦

Be aware of those prejudices which sometimes so strangely present themselves, and are so congenial to human nature, against our friend, neighbors, and brethren of the world, who choose to differ from us in opinion and in matters of faith. Our religion is between us and our God. Their religion is between them and their God. (TPJS, 146)[47]

♦♦♦

Prejudice, with its attendant train of evil, is giving way before the force of truth whose benign rays are penetrating the nations afar off. (TPJS, 184)[59]

♦♦♦

"Mormonism" . . . is now taking a deep hold in the hearts and affections of all those, who are noble-minded enough to lay aside the prejudice of education, and investigate the subject with candor and honesty. (TPJS, 184)[59]

PREPARATION

The conditions of God's kingdom are such, that all who are made partakers of that glory, are under the necessity of learning something respecting it previous to their entering into it. But the foreigner can come to this country without knowing a syllable of its laws, or even subscribing to obey them after he arrives. (TPJS, 51)[21]

♦♦♦

God has in reserve a time, or period appointed in His bosom, when He will bring all his subjects, who have obeyed his voice and kept His commandments, into His celestial rest. This rest is of such perfection and glory, that man has need of a preparation before he can, according to the laws of that kingdom, enter it and enjoy its blessings. This being the fact, God has given certain laws to the human family, which, if observed, are sufficient to prepare them to inherit this rest. This, then, we conclude, was the purpose of God in giving His laws to us. (TPJS, 54)[21]

♦♦♦

The great Plan of Salvation is a theme which ought to occupy our strict attention, and be regarded as one of heaven's best gifts to mankind. No consideration whatever ought to deter us from showing ourselves approved in the sight of God. (TPJS, 68)[21]

♦♦♦

Strive to be prepared in your hearts, be faithful in all things. . . . We must be clean every whit. (TPJS, 91)[33]

♦♦♦

The Saints ought to lay hold of every door that shall seem to be opened to them, to obtain foothold on the earth, and be making all the preparation that is within their power for the terrible storms that are now gathering in the heavens. (TPJS, 141)[47]

♦♦♦

Even the least Saint may know all things as fast as he is able to bear them. (TPJS, 149)[48]

♦♦♦

We ought to have the building up of Zion as our greatest object. The last revelation says, Ye shall not have time to have gone over the earth, until these things come. It will come as did the cholera, wars, fire and earthquakes; one pestilence after another until the Ancient of Days comes, then judgment will be given to the Saints. (TPJS, 160)[49]

•••

It mattereth not whether we live long or short on the earth after we come to a knowledge of [gospel] principles and obey them unto the end. (TPJS, 199)[68]

•••

Let it prove as a warning to all to deal justly before God, and with all mankind, then we shall be clear in the day of judgment. (TPJS, 216)[72]

•••

The Lord cannot always be known by the thunder of His voice, by the display of His glory or by the manifestation of His power, and those that are the most anxious to see these things, are the least prepared to meet them. (TPJS, 247)[80]

•••

This [passing of Brother Barnes] has been a warning voice to us all to be sober and diligent and lay aside mirth, vanity and folly, and to be prepared to die tomorrow. (TPJS, 296)[102]

•••

I could explain a hundred fold more than I ever have of the glories of the kingdoms manifested to me in the vision, were I permitted, and were the people prepared to receive them. (TPJS, 305)[109]

•••

We have no claim in our eternal compact, in relation to eternal things, unless our actions and contracts and all things tend to this. (TPJS, 306)[109]

•••

We have no new commandment to give, but admonish Elders and members to live by every word that proceedeth forth from the mouth of God, lest they come short of the glory that is reserved for the faithful. (TPJS, 306)[110]

•••

The keys of the Aaronic Priesthood were committed unto . . . [John] and he was as the voice of one crying in the wilderness saying: "Prepare ye the way of the Lord and make his paths straight." (TPJS, 319)[117]

•••

When men are prepared, they are better off to go hence [in death] to a more important work. (TPJS, 326)[121]

•••

I have tried a number of years to get the minds of the Saints prepared to receive the things of God; but we frequently see some of them, after suffering all they have for the work of God, will fly to pieces like glass as soon as anything comes that is contrary to their traditions: they cannot stand the fire at all. How many will be able to abide a celestial law, and go through and receive their exaltation, I am unable to say, as many are called, but few are chosen. (TPJS, 331)[123]

•••

I am the voice of one crying in the wilderness, "Repent ye of your sins and prepare the way for the coming of the Son of Man; for the kingdom of God has come unto you, and henceforth the axe is laid unto the root of the tree; and every tree that bringeth not forth good fruit, God Almighty . . . shall hew it down and cast it into the fire." (TPJS, 341)[129]

[In learning of the council in heaven] . . . we begin to learn the only true God, and what kind of a being we have got to worship. Having a knowledge of God, we begin to know how to approach him, and how to ask so as to receive an answer. When we understand the character of God, and know how to come to him, he begins to unfold the heavens to us, and to tell us all about it. When we are ready to come to him, he is ready to come to us. (TPJS, 350)[130]

PRIDE

Have not the pride, high-mindedness, and unbelief of the Gentiles, provoked the Holy One of Israel to withdraw His Holy Spirit from them, and send forth His judgments to scourge them for their wickedness? This is certainly the case. (TPJS, 15)[9]

♦♦♦

All men are naturally disposed to walk in their own paths as they are pointed out by their own fingers, and we are not willing to consider and walk in the path which is pointed out by another, saying, This is the way, walk ye in it, although he should be an unerring director, and the Lord his God sent him. (TPJS, 26)[15]

♦♦♦

Anxieties inexpressible crowd themselves continually upon my mind for the Saints, when I consider the many temptations to which we are subject, from the cunning and flattery of the great adversary of our souls. (TPJS, 29)[16]

♦♦♦

Let not any man publish his own righteousness, for others can see that for him; sooner let him confess his sins, and then he will be forgiven, and he will bring forth more fruit. (TPJS, 194)[66]

♦♦♦

All the religious world is boasting of righteousness; it is the doctrine of the devil to retard the human mind, and hinder our progress, by filling us with self-righteousness. (TPJS, 241)[79]

♦♦♦

If we get puffed up by thinking that we have much knowledge, we are apt to get a contentious spirit, and correct knowledge is necessary to cast out that spirit. (TPJS, 287)[101]

♦♦♦

The evil of being puffed up with correct [though useless] knowledge is not so great as the evil of contention. (TPJS, 287)[101]

PRIESTHOOD

[The] Priesthood . . . may be illustrated by the figure of the human body, which has different members, which have different offices to perform; all are necessary in their place, and the body is not complete without all the members. (TPJS, 112)[41]

♦♦♦

In viewing the Church as a whole, we may strictly denominate it one Priesthood. (TPJS, 112)[41]

♦♦♦

We are called to hold the keys of the mysteries of those things that have been kept hid from the foundation of the world until now. (TPJS, 137)[47]

♦♦♦

"No power or influence can or ought to be maintained by virtue of the Priesthood, only by persuasion, by long-suffering, by gentleness, and meekness, and by love unfeigned; by kindness, and pure knowledge, which shall greatly enlarge the soul without hypocrisy, and without guile, reproving betimes with sharpness, when moved upon by the Holy Ghost, and then showing forth afterwards an increase of love toward him whom thou hast reproved, lest he esteem thee to be his enemy; that he may know that thy faithfulness is stronger than the cords of death; let thy bowels also be full of charity towards all men, and to the household of faith, and let virtue garnish thy thoughts unceasingly, then shall thy confidence wax strong in the presence of God, and the doctrine of the Priesthood shall distill upon thy soul as the dews from heaven. The Holy ghost shall be thy constant companion, and thy sceptre an unchanging sceptre of righteousness and truth, and thy dominion shall be an everlasting dominion, and without compulsory means, it shall flow unto thee forever and ever." (TPJS, 142)[47]

◆◆◆

The Priesthood is an everlasting principle, and existed with God from eternity, and will to eternity, without beginning of days or end of years. The keys have to be brought from heaven whenever the Gospel is sent. When they are revealed, it is by Adam's authority. (TPJS, 157)[49]

◆◆◆

The Priesthood was first given to Adam. . . . He obtained it in the Creation, before the world was formed. . . . He had dominion given him over every living creature. He is Michael the Archangel. . . . Then [the Priesthood was given] to Noah, who is Gabriel: he stands next in authority to Adam in the Priesthood; he was called of God to this office, and was the father of all living in this day, and to him was given the dominion. These men held keys first on earth, and in heaven. (TPJS, 157)[49]

◆◆◆

Wherever the ordinances of the Gospel are administered, there is the Priesthood. (TPJS, 158)[49]

◆◆◆

There are two Priesthoods spoken of in the Scriptures, vis., the Melchizedek and the Aaronic or Levitical. Although there are two Priesthoods, yet the Melchizedek Priesthood comprehends the Aaronic or Levitical Priesthood, and is the grand head, and holds the highest authority which pertains to the Priesthood, and the keys of the Kingdom of God in all ages of the world to the latest posterity on the earth; and is the channel through which all knowledge, doctrine, the Plan of Salvation and every important matter is revealed from heaven. (TPJS, 166)[54]

◆◆◆

[The] institution [of the Priesthood] was prior to "the foundation of this earth, or [when] the morning stars sang together, or the Sons of God shouted for joy." And is the highest and holiest Priesthood, and is after the order of the Son of God, and all other Priesthoods are only parts, ramifications, powers and blessings belonging to the same, and are held, controlled and directed by it. It is the channel through which the Almighty commenced revealing His glory at the beginning of the creation of this earth, and through which He has continued to reveal himself to the children of men to the present time, and through which He will make known His purposes to the end of time. (TPJS, 167)[54]

◆◆◆

There are many things which belong to the powers of the Priesthood and the keys thereof, that have been kept hid from before the foundation of the world; they are hid from the wise and prudent to be revealed in the last times. (TPJS, 170)⁵⁴

♦♦♦

Elijah was the last prophet that held the keys of the Priesthood, and who will, before the last dispensation, restore the authority and deliver the keys of the Priesthood, in order that all the ordinances may be attended to in righteousness. (TPJS, 172)⁵⁴

♦♦♦

A woman has no right to found or organize a church—God never sent them to do it. (TPJS, 212)⁷¹

♦♦♦

[Joseph] spoke [to the Relief Society] of delivering the keys of the Priesthood to the Church . . . for according to his prayers, God had appointed him elsewhere. (TPJS, 226)⁷⁵

♦♦♦

Where there is no kingdom of God there is no salvation. What constitutes the kingdom of God? Where there is a prophet, priest, or a righteous man unto whom God gives His oracles, there is the kingdom of God; and where the oracles of God are not, there the kingdom of God is not. (TPJS, 272)⁹¹

♦♦♦

All the ordinances, systems and administrations on the earth are of no use to the children of men, unless they are ordained and authorized of God, for nothing will save a man but a legal administrator; for none others will be acknowledged either by God or angels. (TPJS, 274)⁹¹

♦♦♦

Salvation is for a man to be saved from all his enemies; for until a man can triumph over death, he is not saved. A knowledge of

the priesthood alone will do this. (TPJS, 305)¹⁰⁹

♦♦♦

If a man gets a fullness of the priesthood, there is no change of ordinances, says Paul. If God has not changed the ordinances and the priesthood, howl, ye sectarians! If he has, when and where has he revealed it? Have ye turned revelators? Then why deny revelation? (TPJS, 308)¹¹³

♦♦♦

Ordinances instituted in the heavens before the foundation of the world, in the priesthood, for the salvation of men, are not to be altered or changed. All must be saved on the same principles. (TPJS, 308)¹¹³

♦♦♦

Where there is no change of priesthood, there is no change of ordinances, says Paul. (TPJS, 308)¹¹³

♦♦♦

There is no salvation between the two lids of the Bible without a legal administrator. Jesus was then the legal administrator, and ordained His Apostles. (TPJS, 319)¹¹⁷

♦♦♦

All the testimony is that the Lord in the last days would commit the keys of the Priesthood to a witness over all people. Has the Gospel of the kingdom commenced in the last days? And will God take it from the man until He takes him Himself? (TPJS, 364)¹³²

PRINCIPLES

Men who have no principle of righteousness in themselves, and whose hearts are full of iniquity, and have no desire for the principles of truth, do not understand the word of truth when they hear it. The devil taketh away the word of truth out of their hearts, because there is no desire of righteousness in them. (TPJS, 96)[34]

♦♦♦

The fundamental principles of our religion are the testimonies of the Apostles and Prophets, concerning Jesus Christ, that He died, was buried, and rose again the third day, and ascended into heaven; and all other things which pertain to our religion are only appendages to it. But in connection with these, we believe in the gift of the Holy Ghost, the power of faith, the enjoyment of the spiritual gifts according to the will of God, the restoration of the house of Israel, and the final triumph of truth. (TPJS, 121)[45]

♦♦♦

Every principle proceeding from God is eternal and any principle which is not eternal is of the devil. (TPJS, 181)[56]

♦♦♦

We should gather all the good and true principles in the world and treasure them up, or we shall not come out true "Mormons." (TPJS, 316)[115]

♦♦♦

If we seek first the kingdom of God, all good things will be added. (TPJS, 256)[83]

PRIORITIES

My first object is to find out the character of the only wise and true God, and what kind of being he is. (TPJS, 344)[130]

PROCRASTINATION

Let this [early death] . . . prove as a warning to all not to procrastinate repentance, or wait till a death-bed, for it is the will of God that man should repent and serve Him in health, and blessing and

power of his mind, in order to secure his blessing, and not wait until he is called to die. (TPJS, 197)[68]

♦♦♦

We should take warning and not wait for death-bed to repent, as we see the infant taken away by death, so may the youth and middle-aged . . . be suddenly called into eternity. (TPJS, 197)[68]

PROGRESS

If you wish to go where God is, you must be like God, or possess the principles which God possesses; for if we are not drawing towards God in principle, we are going from Him and drawing towards the devil. (TPJS, 216)[73]

♦♦♦

[Quoting Peter, Joseph said,] "And add to your faith virtue," knowledge, temperance, patience, godliness, brotherly kindness, charity; "for if these things be in you, and abound, they make you that ye shall neither be barren, nor unfruitful in the knowledge of our Lord Jesus Christ." . . . There could not anything be given, pertaining to life and godliness, without knowledge. (TPJS, 305)[109]

♦♦♦

What would it profit us to come unto the spirits of the just men, but to learn and come up to the standard of their knowledge? (TPJS, 320)[118]

♦♦♦

Here, then, is eternal life—to know the only wise and true God; and you have got to learn how to be Gods yourselves, and to be kings and priests to God, the same as all Gods have done before you, namely, by going from one small degree to another, and from a small capacity to a great one; from grace to grace, from exaltation to exaltation, until you attain to the resurrection of the dead, and are able to dwell in everlasting burnings, and to sit in glory, as do those who sit enthroned in everlasting power. And I want you to know that God, in the last days, while certain individuals are proclaiming his name, is not trifling with you or me. [Elder B.H. Roberts writes in a footnote, "The argument here made by the Prophet is very much strengthened by the following passage: "The Son can do nothing of himself, but what he seeth the Father do; for what things soever he doeth, these also doeth the Son likewise" (St. John 5:19). Elder Roberts further wrote, "Whatever happened to him (Christ) . . . whether within our individual reach or not, is assuredly within reach of humanity. That is what he (Christ) urged again and again, "Be born again." "Be ye perfect." "Ye are the sons of God." "My Father and your Father, my God and your God".] (TPJS, 346)[130]

♦♦♦

PROMISE OF LONG LIFE

[Joseph] made a promise in the name of the Lord, saying that that soul who has righteousness enough to ask God in the secret place for life, every day of [his life] . . . shall live to three score years and ten. (TPJS, 241)[79]

PROMISE FOR THE RIGHTEOUS

There is to be a day when all will be judged of their works, and rewarded according to the same; . . . those who have kept the faith will be crowned with a crown of righteousness; be clothed in white raiment; be admitted to the marriage feast; be free from every affliction, and reign with Christ on the earth, where, according to the ancient promise, they will partake

of the fruit of the vine new in the glorious kingdom with Him. (TPJS, 66)[21]

PROPHECIES

And now I am prepared to say by the authority of Jesus Christ, that not many years shall pass away before the United States shall present such a scene of *bloodshed* as has not a parallel in the history of our nation. (TPJS, 17)[9]

♦♦♦

I say unto you, that those who have thus vilely treated us . . . shall be hanged upon their own gallows; or, in other words, shall fall into their own gin, and snare, and ditch, and trap, which they have prepared for us, and shall go backwards and stumble and fall, and their name shall be blotted out, and God shall reward them according to all their abominations. (TPJS, 123)[46]

♦♦♦

[Joseph said that] . . . God had called him to lead the Church, and he would lead it right; those that undertake to interfere will be ashamed when their own folly is made manifest. (TPJS, 225)[75]

♦♦♦

I prophesied that the saints would continue to suffer much affliction and would be driven to the Rocky Mountains, many would apostatize, others would be put to death by our persecutors or lose their lives in consequence of exposure or disease, and some of you will live to go and assist in making settlements and build cities and see the Saints become a mighty people in the midst of the Rocky Mountains. (TPJS, 255)[82]

♦♦♦

All those that rise up against me will surely feel the weight of their iniquity upon their own heads. (TPJS, 258)[84]

•••

I know what I say; I understand my mission and business. God Almighty is my shield; and what can man do if God is my friend? I shall not be sacrificed until my time comes; then I shall be offered freely. (TPJS, 274)[91]

•••

I prophesied, in the name of the Lord Jesus Christ, that Orrin Porter Rockwell would get away honorably from the Missourians. (TPJS, 285)[98]

•••

Judge [Stephen A. Douglas] you will aspire to the presidency of the United States; and if ever you turn your hand against me or the Latter-day Saints, you will feel the weight of the hand of the Almighty upon you; for the conversation of this day will stick to you through life. (TPJS, 303)[108]

•••

I prophesy they never will have power to kill me till my work is accomplished, and I am ready to die. (TPJS, 328)[122]

•••

I . . . prophesied that within five years we would be out of the power of our old enemies, whether they were apostates or of the world; and told the brethren to record it that when it comes to pass they need not say they had forgotten the saying. (TPJS, 333)[126]

•••

The prediction is that army will be against army; it may be that the Saints will have to beat their ploughs into swords, for it will not do for men to sit down patiently and see their children destroyed. (TPJS, 366)[132]

•••

I calculate to be one of the instruments of setting up the kingdom of Daniel by the word of the Lord, and I intend to lay a foundation that will revolutionize the whole world. . . . It will not be by sword or gun that this kingdom will roll on: the power of truth is such that all nations will be under the necessity of obeying the Gospel. (TPJS, 366)[132]

•••

I told Stephen Markham that if I and Hyrum were ever taken again we should be massacred, or I was not a prophet of God. (TPJS, 376)[134]

•••

Hyrum said, "Let us go back and give ourselves up, and see the thing out." After studying a few moments, Joseph said, "If you go back I will go with you, but we shall be butchered." (TPJS, 377)[136]

•••

[On his fateful start for Carthage] Joseph paused when they got to the temple, and looked with admiration first on that, and then on the city, and remarked, "This is the loveliest place and the best people under the heavens; little do they know the trials that await them." (TPJS, 379)[137]

•••

Several of the officers of the troops in Carthage, and other gentlemen, curious to see the prophet, visited Joseph in his room. General Smith asked them if there was anything in his appearance that indicated he was the desperate character his enemies represented him to be; and he asked them to give him their honest opinion on the subject. The reply was, "No, Sir. Your appearance would indicate the very contrary, General Smith; but we cannot see what is in your heart, neither can we tell what are your intentions." To which Joseph replied, "Very true, gentlemen, you cannot see what is in my heart, and you are therefore unable to judge me or my intentions; but I can see what is in your hearts, and will tell you what I see. I can see that you thirst for blood, and nothing but my blood will satisfy you. It is not for crime of any description that I and my brethren are thus continually persecuted and harassed by our enemies, but there are other motives, and some of them I have expressed, so far as relates to myself; and inasmuch as you and the people thirst for blood, I prophesy, in the name of the Lord, that you shall witness scenes of blood and sorrow to your entire satisfaction. Your souls shall be perfectly satiated with blood, and many of you who are now present shall have an opportunity to face the cannon's mouth from sources you think not of; and those people that desire this great evil upon me and my brethren, shall be filled with regret and sorrow because of the scenes of desolation and distress that await them. They shall seek for peace, and shall not be able to find it. Gentlemen, you will find what I have told you to be true. (TPJS, 381)[139]

♦♦♦

Dr. Richards retired to the bed which Joseph had left, and when all were apparently fast asleep, Joseph whispered to Dan Jones, "Are you afraid to die?" Dan said, "Has that time come, think you? Engaged in such a cause I do not think that death would have many terrors." Joseph replied, "You will yet see Wales, and fulfill the mission appointed to you before you die." (TPJS, 384)[142]

♦♦♦

PROPHECY

Seers and Prophets . . . are they who saw the mysteries of godliness; they saw the flood before it came. (TPJS, 12)[8]

♦♦♦

No man can be a minister of Jesus Christ except he has a testimony of Jesus; and this is the spirit of prophecy. (TPJS, 160)[49]

♦♦♦

Ye are the witnesses—having the testimony of Jesus which is the spirit of prophecy. (TPJS, 265)[85]

♦♦♦

Any man who says he is a teacher or a preacher of righteousness, and denies the spirit of prophecy, is a liar, and the truth is not in him; and by this key false teachers and imposters may be detected. (TPJS, 269)[89]

♦♦♦

We have a more sure word of prophecy, whereunto you do well to take heed, as unto a light that shineth in a dark place. We were eyewitnesses of his majesty and heard the voice of his excellent glory. (TPJS, 303)[109]

PROPHETS

There should exist the greatest freedom and familiarity among the rulers in Zion. (TPJS, 24)[13]

♦♦♦

All men are naturally disposed to walk in their own paths as they are pointed out by their own fingers, and we are not willing to consider and walk in the path which is pointed out by another, saying, This is the way, walk ye in it, although he should be an unerring director, and the Lord his God sent him. (TPJS, 26)[15]

♦♦♦

Pure and steadfast love for those who are his benefactors . . . should characterize a President of the Church of Christ. (TPJS, 30)[17]

♦♦♦

Seers and Prophets . . . are they who saw the mysteries of godliness; they saw the flood before it came. (TPJS, 12)[8]

•••

If . . . there is an importance in this respect [of obeying God's laws] is there not a responsibility of great weight resting upon those who are called to declare these truths to men? (TPJS, 57)[21]

•••

Be assured, brethren, I am willing to stem the torrent of all opposition, in storms and in tempests, in thunders and in lightnings, by sea and by land, in the wilderness or among false brethren, or mobs, or wherever God in His providence may call us. (TPJS, 106)[37]

•••

Revelations of the mind and will of God to the Church, are to come through the presidency. This is the order of heaven, and the power and privilege of this priesthood. (TPJS, 111)[41]

•••

All the prophets had the Melchizedek Priesthood and were ordained by God himself. (TPJS, 181)[56]

•••

The world has always mistook false prophets for true ones, and those that were sent of God, they considered to be false prophets, and hence they killed, stoned, punished and imprisoned the true prophets . . . and though the most honorable men of the earth, they banished them from their society as vagabonds, whilst they cherished, honored and supported knaves, vagabonds, hypocrites, imposters, and the basest of men. (TPJS, 206)[71]

•••

God never had any prophets that acted in

this way [strange fits, trembling, fainting, swooning or in trances]; there was nothing indecorous in the proceedings of the Lord's prophets in any age; neither had the apostles nor prophets in the apostles' day anything of this kind. . . . Paul says, "Let everything be done decently and in order," but here we find the greatest disorder and indecency in the conduct of both men and women. The same would apply to . . . many of our modern revivalists. (TPJS, 209)[71]

•••

The spirit of the prophets is subject to the prophets. (TPJS, 212)[71]

•••

[Joseph said that] if God had appointed him, and chosen him as an instrument to lead the Church, why not let him lead it through? Why stand in the way when he is appointed to do a thing? Who knows the mind of God? Does He not reveal things differently than what we expect? He remarked that he was continually rising, although he had everything bearing him down, standing in his way, and opposing; notwithstanding all this opposition, he always comes out right in the end. (TPJS, 224)[75]

•••

[Joseph said that] . . . God had called him to lead the Church, and he would lead it right. (TPJS, 225)[75]

•••

This morning I . . . visited with a brother and sister from Michigan, who thought that "a prophet is always a prophet"; but I told them that a prophet was a prophet only when he was acting as such. (TPJS, 278)[94]

•••

It is my meditation all the day, and more than my meat and drink, to know how I shall make the Saints of God comprehend the visions that roll like an overflowing surge before my mind. (TPJS, 296)[102]

◆ ◆ ◆

The way I know in whom to confide— God tells me in whom I may place confidence. (TPJS, 301)[105]

◆ ◆ ◆

Many persons think a prophet must be a great deal better than anybody else. Suppose I would condescend—yes, I will call it condescend, to be a great deal better than any of you, I would be raised up to the highest heaven; and who should I have to accompany me? (TPJS, 303)[109]

◆ ◆ ◆

We have a more sure word of prophecy, whereunto you do well to take heed, as unto a light that shineth in a dark place. We were eyewitnesses of his majesty and heard the voice of his excellent glory. (TPJS, 303)[109]

◆ ◆ ◆

The opinions of men, so far as I am concerned, are to me as the crackling of thorns under the pot, or the whistling of the wind. I break the ground; I lead the way. (TPJS, 304)[109]

◆ ◆ ◆

A man of God should be endowed with wisdom, knowledge, and understanding, in order to teach and lead the people of God. The sectarian priests are blind, and they lead the blind, and they will all fall into the ditch together. They build with hay, wood, and stubble, on the old revelations. (TPJS, 311)[113]

◆ ◆ ◆

Although I was called of my heavenly Father to lay the foundation of this great work and kingdom in this dispensation, and testify of His revealed will to scattered Israel, I am subject to like passions as other men, like the prophets of olden times. (TPJS, 315)[114]

◆ ◆ ◆

The object with me is to obey and teach others to obey God in just what He tells us to do. (TPJS, 332)[125]

◆ ◆ ◆

In relation to the power over the minds of mankind which I hold, I would say, It is in consequence of the power of truth in the doctrines which I have been an instrument in the hands of God of presenting unto them, and not because of any compulsion on my part. (TPJS, 341)[129]

◆ ◆ ◆

If I am so fortunate to be the man to comprehend God, and explain or convey the principles to your hearts, so that the Spirit seals them upon you, then let every man and woman henceforth sit in silence . . . and never lift their hands or voices . . . against the man of God or servants of God again. (TPJS, 344)[130]

◆ ◆ ◆

I am going to enquire after God; for I want you all to know him, and to be familiar with him. . . . You will then know that I am his servant; for I speak as one having authority. (TPJS, 345)[130]

◆ ◆ ◆

I cannot lie down until all my work is finished. (TPJS, 361)[130]

◆ ◆ ◆

The Savior said . . . the keys of knowledge, power and revelations should be revealed to a witness who should hold the testimony to the world. It has always been my province to dig up hidden mysteries—new things—for my hearers. (TPJS, 364)[132]

♦♦♦

I calculate to be one of the instruments of setting up the kingdom of Daniel by the word of the Lord, and I intend to lay a foundation that will revolutionize the whole world. (TPJS, 366)[132]

♦♦♦

When did I ever teach anything wrong from this stand? When was I ever confounded? (TPJS, 368)[132]

PROTECTION

(See also SAFETY)

If we will but cleanse ourselves and covenant before God, to serve Him, it is our privilege to have an assurance that God will protect us at all times. (TPJS, 9)[3]

♦♦♦

Thus shall the Lord watch over his generation, that they may be saved. (TPJS, 31)[17]

♦♦♦

All regularly organized and well established governments have certain laws by which, more or less, the innocent are protected and the guilty punished. (TPJS, 49)[21]

♦♦♦

The ordinance of washing of feet [of the Twelve] . . . is necessary now, as much it was in the days of the Savior; and we must have a place prepared, that we may attend to this ordinance aside from the world. . . . It was never intended for any but official members. It is calculated to unite our hearts, that we may be one in feeling and sentiment, and that our faith may be strong, so that Satan cannot overthrow us, nor have any power over us here. (TPJS, 90)[33]

♦♦♦

We . . . have an assurance of a better hope than that of our persecutors. Therefore God hath made broad our shoulders for the burden. We glory in our tribulation, because we know that God is with us, that He is our friend, and that He will save our souls. (TPJS, 123)[46]

♦♦♦

There seems to be a whispering that the angels of heaven . . . have taken counsel together; and . . . have taken cognizance of the testimony of those who were murdered at Haun's Mills, and also those who were martyred . . . elsewhere, and have passed some decisions peradventure in favor of the Saints, and those who were called to suffer without cause. (TPJS, 141)[47]

♦♦♦

I do not want to cloak iniquity—all things contrary to the will of God, should be cast from us, but don't do more hurt than good. . . . I want the innocent to go free—rather spare ten iniquitous among you, than condemn one innocent one. . . . "Fret not thyself because of evildoers." God will see to it. (TPJS, 239)[78]

♦♦♦

As God governed Abraham, Isaac and Jacob as families, and the children of Israel as a nation; so we, as a Church, must be under His guidance if we are prospered, preserved and sustained. Our only confidence can be in God; our only wisdom obtained from Him; and He alone must be our protector and safeguard, spiritually and temporally, or we fall. (TPJS, 253)[81]

♦♦♦

I am happy and thankful for the privilege of being present on this occasion. Great exertions have been made on the part of our enemies to carry me to Missouri and destroy my life; but the Lord has hedged up the way, and they have not, as yet, accomplished their purpose. God has enabled me to keep out of their hands. I have warred a good warfare, insomuch as I have outgeneraled or whipped all [their] corrupt host. (TPJS, 257)[84]

• • •

My feelings at the present are that, inasmuch as the Lord Almighty has preserved me until today, He will continue to preserve me, by the united faith and prayers of the Saints, until I have fully accomplished my mission in this life, and so firmly established the dispensation of the fullness of the Priesthood in these last days, that all the powers of earth and hell can never prevail against it. (TPJS, 258)[84]

• • •

Never, while the spirit of liberty . . . hold[s] communion in the flesh, let us hear of those who profess to be governed by the law of God, and make their garments clean in the blood of the Lamb, shrinking from the assistance of those who bear the ark of the Lord—in the hour of danger! (TPJS, 261)[85]

• • •

I know what I say; I understand my mission and business. God Almighty is my shield; and what can man do if God is my friend? I shall not be sacrificed until my time comes; then I shall be offered freely. (TPJS, 274)[91]

• • •

I thank God for preserving me from my enemies; I have no enemies but for the truth's sake. I have no desire but to do all men good. I feel to pray for all men. (TPJS, 275)[91]

• • •

The inhabitants of the [American] continent anciently were so constituted, and were so determined and persevering, either in righteousness or wickedness, that God visited them, immediately either with great judgments or blessings. But the present generation, if they were going to battle, if they got any assistance from God, they would have to obtain it by faith. (TPJS, 299)[103]

• • •

Meddle not with any man for his religion; and all governments ought to permit every man to enjoy his religion unmolested. No man is authorized to take away life in consequence of difference in religion, which all laws and governments ought to tolerate and protect, right or wrong. (TPJS, 344)[130]

• • •

I cannot lie down until all my work is finished. (TPJS, 361)[130]

• • •

He that arms himself with gun, sword, or pistol, except in the defense of truth, will sometime be sorry for it. I never carry any weapon with me bigger than my penknife. When I was dragged before the cannon and muskets in Missouri, I was unarmed. God will always protect me until my mission is fulfilled. (TPJS, 365)[132]

• • •

The prediction is that army will be against army; it may be that the Saints will have to beat their ploughs into swords, for it will not do for men to sit down patiently and see their children destroyed. (TPJS, 366)[132]

• • •

It will not be by sword or gun that this kingdom will roll on: the power of truth is such that all nations will be under the necessity of obeying the Gospel. (TPJS, 366)[132]

• • •

[On the way to Carthage, Joseph, Hyrum and others met a] Captain Dunn and a company of about sixty mounted militia, on seeing which Joseph said, "Do not be alarmed, brethren, for they cannot do more to you than the enemies of truth did to the ancient Saints—they can only kill the body." (TPJS, 379)[137]

• • •

It is the duty of all men to protect their lives and the lives of the household, whenever necessity requires, and no power has a right to forbid it, should the last extreme arrive . . . caution is the parent of safety. (TPJS, 391)[144]

PROVOCATION

When a man designedly provokes a serpent to bite him, the principle is the same as when a man drinks deadly poison knowing it to be such. In that case no man has any claim on the promises of God to be healed. (TPJS, 72)[25]

PRUDENCE

(*See also* CAUTION)

We must be wise as serpents and harmless as doves. (TPJS, 36)[19]

• • •

I preached to the Saints, setting forth the evils that existed, and that would exist, by reason of hasty judgment, or decisions upon any subject given by any people, or in judging before they had heard both sides of a question. (TPJS, 118)[44]

• • •

I do not want to cloak iniquity—all things contrary to the will of God, should be cast from us, but don't do more hurt than good. . . . I want the innocent to go free—rather spare ten iniquitous among you, than condemn one innocent one. . . .

"Fret not thyself because of evildoers." God will see to it. (TPJS, 239)[78]

• • •

We must use precaution in bringing sinners to justice, lest in exposing these heinous sins we draw the indignation of a Gentile world upon us. (TPJS, 239)[78]

• • •

At [certain] time[s] the truth on the guilty should not be told openly. . . . We must use precaution in bringing sinners to justice, lest . . . we draw the indignation of a Gentile world upon us. . . . It is necessary to hold an influence in the world, and thus . . . accomplish our end in spreading the Gospel, or holiness, in the earth. . . . To the iniquitous show yourselves merciful. (TPJS, 239)[78]

• • •

Declare the first principles, and let the mysteries alone, lest ye be overthrown. (TPJS, 292)[101]

• • •

I suppose I am not allowed to go into an investigation of anything that is not contained in the Bible. If I do, I think there are so many ever-wise men here, that they would cry, "treason" and put me to death. So I will go to the old Bible and turn commentator today. (TPJS, 348)[130]

• • •

Our lives have already been jeopardized by revealing the wicked and bloodthirsty purposes of our enemies; and for the future we must cease to do so. All we have said about them is truth, but it is not always wise to relate all the truth. (TPJS, 392)[145]

PUNISHMENT

I say unto you, that those who have thus vilely treated us . . . shall be hanged upon their own gallows; or, in other words, shall fall into their own gin, and snare, and ditch, and trap, which they have prepared for us, and shall go backwards and stumble and fall, and their name shall be blotted out, and God shall reward them according to all their abominations. (TPJS, 123)[46]

◆◆◆

It must needs be that offences come, but woe unto them by whom they come. (TPJS, 131)[47]

◆◆◆

All those that rise up against me will surely feel the weight of their iniquity upon their own heads. (TPJS, 258)[84]

◆◆◆

The unpardonable sin is to shed innocent blood, or be accessory thereto. All other sins will be visited with judgment in the flesh, and the spirit being delivered to the buffetings of Satan until the day of the Lord Jesus. (TPJS, 301)[105]

◆◆◆

A man is his own tormenter and his own condemner. . . . The torment of disappointment in the mind of man is as exquisite as a lake burning with fire and brimstone. (TPJS, 357)[130]

◆◆◆

If a man has knowledge, he can be saved; although, if he has been guilty of great sins, he will be punished for them. But when he consents to obey the Gospel, whether here or in the world of spirits, he is saved. . . . All will suffer until they obey Christ himself. (TPJS, 357)[130]

◆◆◆

The salvation of Jesus Christ was wrought out for all men, in order to triumph over the devil; for if it did not catch him in one place, it would in another; for he stood up as a Savior. All will suffer [however] until they obey Christ himself. (TPJS, 357)[130]

◆◆◆

Rejoice, O Israel! Your friends who have been murdered for the truth's sake in the persecutions shall triumph gloriously in the celestial world, while their murderers shall welter for ages in torment, even until they shall have paid the uttermost farthing. (TPJS, 359)[130]

PURE RELIGION

It is a duty which every Saint ought to render to his brethren freely—to always love them, and ever succor them. To be justified before God we must love one another; we must overcome evil; we must visit the fatherless and the widow in their affliction, and we must keep ourselves unspotted from the world; for such virtues flow from the great fountain of pure religion, strengthening our faith by adding every good quality that adorns the children of the blessed Jesus, we can pray in the season of prayer; we can love our neighbor as ourselves, and be faithful in tribulation, knowing that the reward of such is greater in the kingdom of heaven. What a consolation! What a joy! Let me live the life of the righteous, and let my reward be like his! (TPJS, 76)[29]

PURGED PEOPLE

(See also REFINEMENT)

The time has at last arrived when the God of Abraham, of Isaac, and of Jacob, has set his hand again the second time to recover the remnants of his people. . . . Their unbelief has not rendered the promise of God of none effect for there was another day limited . . . which was the day of His power; and then His people, Israel, should be a willing people;—and He would write His law in their hearts, and print it in their thoughts; their sins and their iniquities He would remember no more. (TPJS, 14)[9]

•••

The Messiah's kingdom on earth is of that kind of government, that there has always been numerous apostates, for the reason that it admits of no sins unrepented of without excluding the individual from its fellowship. (TPJS, 66)[21]

•••

Strive to be prepared in your hearts, be faithful in all things. . . . We must be clean every whit. (TPJS, 91)[33]

•••

Inasmuch as God hath said that He would have a tried people, that He would purge them as gold, now we think that this time He has chosen His own crucible, wherein we have been tried. (TPJS, 135)[47]

•••

How vain and trifling have been our spirits, our councils, our meetings, our private as well as public conversations—too low, too mean, too vulgar, too condescending for the dignified characters of the called and chosen of God. (TPJS, 137)[47]

•••

Ignorance, superstition and bigotry . . . is oftentimes in the way of the prosperity of this Church; like the torrent rain in the mountains, that floods the most pure and crystal stream with mire, and dirt, and filthiness, and obscures everything that was clear before, and all rushes along in one general deluge; but time weathers tide; and notwithstanding we are rolled in the mire of the flood for the time being, the next surge peradventure, as time rolls on, may bring to us the fountain as clear as crystal, and as pure as snow; while the filthiness, flood-wood and rubbish is left and purged out by the way. (TPJS, 138)[47]

•••

"How long can rolling waters remain impure? What power shall stay the heavens? As well might man stretch forth his puny arm to stop the Missouri River in its decreed course, or to turn it up stream, as to hinder the Almighty from pouring down knowledge from heaven, upon the heads of the Latter-day Saints." (TPJS, 139)[47]

•••

Your humble servant or servants, intend from henceforth to [morally disapprove] everything that is not in accordance with the fullness of the Gospel of Jesus Christ, and is not of a bold, and frank, and upright nature. (TPJS, 146)[47]

•••

President Joseph Smith arose. Spoke of the organization of the Female Relief Society; said he was deeply interested, that it might be built up to the Most High in an acceptable manner; that its rules must be observed; that none should be received into it but those who were worthy; proposed a close examination of every candidate. . . . Thus have a select society of the virtuous, and those who would walk circumspectly [and said] One object of the institution was to purge out iniquity. (TPJS, 201)[70]

•••

I do not want to cloak iniquity—all things contrary to the will of God, should be cast from us, but don't do more hurt than good. (TPJS, 239)[78]

•••

It is the object of this [Relief] Society to reform persons, not to take those that are corrupt and foster them in their wickedness; but if they repent, we are bound to take them, and by kindness sanctify and cleanse them from all unrighteousness by our influence in watching over them. Nothing will have such influence over people as the fear of being disfellowshipped by so goodly a society as this. (TPJS, 240)[79]

• • •

We are trying here to gird up our loins, and purge from our midst the workers of iniquity; . . . that as God's people, under His direction, and obedient to His law, we may grow up in righteousness and truth; and when His purposes shall be accomplished, we may receive an inheritance among those that are sanctified. (TPJS, 254)[80]

• • •

Iniquity of any kind cannot be sustained in the Church, and it will not fare well where I am; for I am determined while I do lead the Church, to lead it right. (TPJS, 307)[111]

• • •

Woe to ye rich men, who refuse to give to the poor, and then come and ask me for bread. Away with all your meanness, and be liberal. We need purging, purifying and cleansing. (TPJS, 329)[122]

PURITY

If we will but cleanse ourselves and covenant before God, to serve Him, it is our privilege to have an assurance that God will protect us at all times. (TPJS, 9)[3]

• • •

Fellow sojourners upon the earth, it is your privilege to purify yourselves and come up to the same glory, and see for yourselves, and know for yourselves. (TPJS, 13)[8]

• • •

The Lord will have a place whence His word will go forth, in these last days, in purity; for if Zion will not purify herself, so as to be approved of in all things, in His sight, He will seek another people;

for . . . [God's] work will go on until Israel is gathered, and they who will not hear His voice, must expect to feel His wrath. Let me say unto you, seek to purify yourselves . . . lest the Lord's anger be kindled to fierceness. (TPJS, 18)[10]

• • •

We know not what we shall be called to pass through before Zion is delivered and established; therefore, we have great need to live near to God, and always be in strict obedience to all His commandments, that we may have a conscience void of offense toward God and man. (TPJS, 32)[18]

• • •

Let honesty, and sobriety, and candor, and solemnity, and virtue, and pureness, and meekness, and simplicity crown our heads in every place; and in fine, become as little children, without malice, guile or hypocrisy. (TPJS, 137)[47]

• • •

Let . . . all Saints be willing to confess all their sins and not keep back a part; and let the Twelve be humble and not be exalted, and beware of pride, and not seek to excel one above another, but act for each other's good, and pray for one another, and honor our brother or make honorable mention of his name, and not backbite and devour our brother. (TPJS, 155)[49]

• • •

We came to this earth that we might have a body and present it pure before God in the celestial kingdom. (TPJS, 181)[56]

• • •

If [you] have done anything . . . that [you] are sorry for, or that [you] would not like to meet and answer for at the bar of God . . . let it prove as a warning to all to deal justly before God, and with all mankind, then we shall be clear in the day of judgment. (TPJS, 216)[72]

•••

As well might the devil seek to dethrone Jehovah, as overthrow an innocent soul that resists everything which is evil. (TPJS, 226)[75]

•••

The sympathies of the heads of the Church have induced . . . [members] to bear a long time with those who were corrupt until they were obliged to cut them off, lest all become contaminated. (TPJS, 226)[75]

•••

If you live up to your privileges, the angels cannot be restrained from being your associates. (TPJS, 226)[75]

•••

Females, if they are pure and innocent, can come in the presence of God; for what is more pleasing to God than innocence. (TPJS, 227)[75]

•••

If we would come before God, we must keep ourselves pure, as He is pure. (TPJS, 227)[75]

•••

Be virtuous and pure; be men of integrity and truth; keep the commandments of God; and then you will be able more perfectly to understand the difference between right and wrong—between the things of God and the things of men; and your path will be like that of the just,

which shineth brighter and brighter unto the perfect day. (TPJS, 247)[80]

•••

Charity, which is love, covereth a multitude of sins, and I have often covered up all the faults among you; but the prettiest thing is to have no faults at all. We should cultivate a meek, quiet and peaceable spirit. (TPJS, 316)[115]

PURPOSE OF LIFE

(*See also* MORTALITY; THIS LIFE)

We are inclined to think that man is unable, without assistance beyond what has been given to those before, of expressing in words the greatness of this important subject [of the Gospel Plan]. (TPJS, 57)[21]

•••

Happiness is the object and design of our existence; and will be the end thereof, if we pursue the path that leads to it; and this path is virtue, uprightness, faithfulness, holiness, and keeping all the commandments of God. (TPJS, 255)[83]

•••

All men know that they must die. And it is important that we should understand the reasons and causes of our exposure to the vicissitudes of life and of death, and the designs and purposes of God in our coming into the world, our sufferings here, and our departure hence. (TPJS, 324)[121]

RATIONALIZATION

Mankind will persist in self-justification until all their iniquity is exposed, and their character past being redeemed, and that which is treasured up in their hearts be exposed to the gaze of mankind. (TPJS, 18)[10]

♦♦♦

Men are in the habit, when the truth is exhibited by the servants of God, of saying, All is mystery; they have spoken in parables, and therefore, are not to be understood. It is true they have eyes to see, and see not, but none are so blind as those who will not see. (TPJS, 96)[34]

REALITY

Water, fire, truth and God are all realities. (TPJS, 139)[47]

♦♦♦

The world is full of technicalities and misrepresentation, which I calculate to overthrow, and speak of things as they actually exist. (TPJS, 292)[101]

REASON

We believe in [the gift of the Holy Ghost] in all its fullness, and power, and greatness, and glory; but whilst we do this, we believe in it rationally, consistently, and scripturally, and not according to the wild vagaries, foolish notions and traditions of men. (TPJS, 243)[80]

♦♦♦

If I esteem mankind to be in error, shall I bear them down? No. I will lift them up, and in their own way too, if I cannot persuade them my way is better; and I will not seek to compel any man to believe as I do, only by the force of reasoning, for truth will cut its own way. (TPJS, 313)[113]

REBELLION

It was not until apostasy and rebellion against the things of God that the true knowledge of the universe as well as the knowledge of other truths, became lost among men. (TPJS, 119)[44]

♦♦♦

A frank and open rebuke provoketh a good man to emulation. . . . But on the other hand, it will draw out all the corruptions of corrupt hearts; and lying and the poison of asps is under their tongues; and they do cause the pure in heart to be cast into prison, because they want them out of their way. (TPJS, 137)[47]

♦♦♦

All beings who have bodies have power over those who have not. The devil has no power over us only as we permit him. The moment we revolt at anything which comes from God, the devil takes power. (TPJS, 181)[56]

♦♦♦

There will be wicked men on the earth during the thousand years. The heathen nations who will not come up to worship will be visited with the judgments of God, and must eventually be destroyed from the earth. (TPJS, 268)[88]

♦♦♦

So long as a man will not give heed to the commandments, he must abide without salvation. (TPJS, 357)[130]

RECORD KEEPING

(*See also* DOCUMENTATION)

Our acts are recorded, and at a future day they will be laid before us, and if we should fail to judge right and injure our fellow-beings, they may there, perhaps, condemn us. (TPJS, 69)[22]

♦♦♦

An item . . . may appear, at the time, of little or no worth, but should it be published, and one of you lay hands on it after, you will find it of infinite worth, not only to your brethren, but it will be a feast to your own souls. (TPJS, 73)[26]

♦♦♦

Were you to be brought before the authorities, and be accused of any crime or misdemeanor, and be as innocent as the angels of God, unless you can prove yourselves to have been somewhere else, your enemies will prevail against you. (TPJS, 73)[26]

♦♦♦

The general affairs of the Church . . . should be transacted by a general conference of the most faithful and the most respectable of the authorities of the Church, and a minute of those transactions may be kept and forwarded from time to time, to your humble servant. (TPJS, 136)[47]

REDEMPTION

Is not the Gospel the news of the redemption? (TPJS, 59)[21]

♦♦♦

[The Lord] knows the situation of both the living and the dead, and has made ample provision for their redemption, according to their several circumstances, and the laws of the kingdom of God, whether in this world, or in the world to come. (TPJS, 220)[74]

REFINEMENT

(*See also* PURGED PEOPLE)

We know not what we shall be called to pass through before Zion is delivered and established; therefore, we have great need to live near to God, and always be in strict obedience to all His commandments, that we may have a conscience void of offense toward God and man. (TPJS, 32)[18]

♦♦♦

Our circumstances are calculated to awaken our spirits to a sacred remembrance of everything. (TPJS, 130)[47]

♦♦♦

"My son, peace be unto thy soul; thine adversity and thine affliction shall be but a small moment; and then if thou endure it well, God shall exalt thee on high." (TPJS, 134)[47]

♦♦♦

Inasmuch as God hath said that He would have a tried people, that He would purge them as gold, now we think that this time He has chosen His own crucible, wherein we have been tried. (TPJS, 135)[47]

♦♦♦

Walls and irons, doors and creaking hinges, and half-scared-to-death guards and jailers, grinning like some damned spirits, lest an innocent man should make his escape to bring to light the damnable deeds of a murderous mob, are calculated in their very nature to make the soul of an honest man feel stronger than the powers of hell. (TPJS, 139)[47]

"If thou art called to pass through tribulations; if thou art in perils among false brethren; if thou art in perils among robbers; if thou art in perils by land or by sea; if thou art accused with all manner of false accusations; if thine enemies fall upon thee; if they tear thee from the society from thy father and mother and brethren and sisters; and if with a drawn sword thine enemies tear thee from the bosom from thy wife, and thine offspring, and thine elder son, although but six years of age, shall cling to thy garments, and shall say, My father, my father, why can't you stay with us? O my father, what are the men going to do with you? And if then he shall be thrust from thee by the sword, and thou be dragged to prison, and thine enemies prowl around thee like wolves for the blood of the lamb; and if thou shouldst be cast into the pit, or into the hands of murderers, and the sentence of death passed upon thee; if thou be cast into the deep, if the billowing surge conspire against thee; if fierce winds become thine enemy; if the heavens gather blackness, and all the elements combine to hedge up the way; and above all, if the very jaws of hell shall gape open the mouth wide after thee, know thou, my son, that all these things shall give thee experience, and shall be for thy good. The Son of Man hath descended below them all; art thou greater than he?" (TPJS, 143)[47]

♦♦♦

[We must] be on the alert to concentrate our energies. . . . The best feelings should exist in our midst; and then, by the help of the Almighty, we shall go on from victory to victory, and from conquest to conquest; our evil passions will be subdued, our prejudices depart; we shall find no room in our bosoms for hatred; vice will hide its deformed head, and we shall stand approved in the sight of Heaven, and be

acknowledged the sons of God. (TPJS, 179)[54]

♦♦♦

If you live up to your privileges, the angels cannot be restrained from being your associates. (TPJS, 226)[75]

♦♦♦

I am like a huge, rough stone rolling down from a high mountain; and the only polishing I get is when some corner gets rubbed off by coming in contact with something else, striking with accelerating force against religious bigotry, priest-craft, lawyer-craft, doctor-craft, lying editors, suborned judges and jurors, and the authority of perjured executives, backed by mobs, blasphemers, licentious and corrupt men and women—all hell knocking off a corner here and a corner there. Thus I will become a smooth and polished shaft in the quiver of the Almighty, who will give me dominion over all and every one of them, when their refuge of lies shall fail, and their hiding place shall be destroyed, while these smooth-polished stones with which I come in contact become marred. (TPJS, 304)[109]

♦♦♦

"I am a rough stone. The sound of the hammer and chisel was never heard on me until the Lord took me in hand. I desire the learning and wisdom of heaven alone. I have not the least idea, if Christ should come to the earth and preach such rough things as He preached to the Jews, but that this generation would reject Him for being so rough." (TPJS, 307)[113]

♦♦♦

Men have to suffer that they may come upon Mount Zion and be exalted above the heavens. (TPJS, 323)[119]

♦♦♦

I have tried a number of years to get the minds of the Saints prepared to receive the things of God; but we frequently see some of them, after suffering all they have for the work of God, will fly to pieces like glass as soon as anything comes that is contrary to their traditions: they cannot stand the fire at all. How many will be able to abide a celestial law, and go through and receive their exaltation, I am unable to say, as many are called, but few are chosen. (TPJS, 331)[123]

• • •

"The firmament showeth His handiwork;" and a moment's reflection is sufficient to teach every man of common intelligence, that all these are not the mere productions of *chance,* nor could they be supported by any power less than an Almighty hand. (TPJS, 56)[21]

• • •

The Lord says that every man is to receive according to his works. Reflect for a moment, . . . and enquire whether you would consider yourselves worthy a seat at the marriage seat with Paul and others like him, if you had been unfaithful? Had you not fought the good fight, and kept the faith, could you expect to receive? (TPJS, 64)[21]

• • •

I exhort you to give heed to all the virtue and the teachings which I have given you. (TPJS, 367)[132]

• • •

When [the small company started back to Carthage] Joseph said, "Boys, if I don't come back, take care of yourselves; I am going like a lamb to the slaughter." When they passed his farm he took a good look at it, and after they had passed it, he turned round several times to look again, at which some of the company made remarks, when

Joseph said, "If some of you had got such a farm and knew you would not see it any more, you would want to take a good look at it for the last time." (TPJS, 380)[138]

RELIEF SOCIETY

President Joseph Smith arose. Spoke of the organization of the Female Relief Society; said he was deeply interested, that it might be built up to the Most High in an acceptable manner; that its rules must be observed; that none should be received into it but those who were worthy; proposed a close examination of every candidate . . . thus have a select society of the virtuous, and those who would walk circumspectly; commended them for their zeal [as long as it was] according to knowledge. [He said,] One object of the institution was to purge out iniquity. (TPJS, 201)[70]

• • •

This is a charitable [Relief] Society, and according to your natures; it is natural for females to have feelings of charity and benevolence. You are now placed in a situation in which you can act according to those sympathies which God has planted in your bosoms. (TPJS, 226)[75]

• • •

"You [sisters of the Relief Society] will receive instructions through the order of the Priesthood which God had established, through the medium of those appointed to lead, guide and direct the affairs of the Church in this last dispensation; and I now turn the key in your behalf in the name of the Lord, and this Society shall rejoice, and knowledge and intelligence shall flow down from this time henceforth; this is the beginning of better days to the poor and needy, who shall be made to rejoice and pour forth blessings on your heads. (TPJS, 228)[75]

❖❖❖

Let [the Relief] Society teach women how to behave towards their husbands, to treat them with mildness and affection. (TPJS, 228)[75]

❖❖❖

It is the object of this society to reform persons, not to take those that are corrupt and foster them in their wickedness; but if they repent, we are bound to take them, and by kindness sanctify and cleanse them from all unrighteousness by our influence in watching over them. Nothing will have such influence over people as the fear of being disfellowshipped by so goodly a society as this. (TPJS, 240)[79]

❖❖❖

The Ladies' Relief Society is not only to relieve the poor, but to save souls. (TPJS, 242)[79]

REMISSION OF SINS

In order to be benefited by the doctrine of repentance, we must believe in obtaining a remission of sins. And in order to obtain the remission of sins, we must believe in the doctrine of baptism in the name of the Lord Jesus Christ. (TPJS, 82)[30]

REPENTANCE

Souls are as precious in the sight of God as they ever were; and the Elders were never called to drive any down to hell, but to persuade and invite all men everywhere to repent, that they may become heirs of salvation. (TPJS, 77)[29]

❖❖❖

I feel for my fellow men; I do it in the name of the Lord being moved upon by the Holy Spirit. Oh, that I could snatch them from the vortex of misery, into which I behold them plunging themselves, by their sins that I might be enabled by the warning voice, to be an instrument of bringing them to unfeigned repentance, that they might have faith to stand in the evil day! (TPJS, 87)[31]

❖❖❖

I have sometimes spoken too harshly from the impulse of the moment, and inasmuch as I have wounded your feelings, brethren, I ask your forgiveness, for I love you and will hold you up with all my heart in all righteousness, before the Lord, and before all men. (TPJS, 106)[37]

❖❖❖

Repentance is a thing that cannot be trifled with every day. Daily transgression and daily repentance is not that which is pleasing in the sight of God. (TPJS, 148)[48]

❖❖❖

There is never a time when the spirit is too old to approach God. All are within the reach of pardoning mercy, who have not committed the unpardonable sin, which hath no forgiveness. (TPJS, 191)[63]

❖❖❖

Let this [early death] then, prove as a warning to all not to procrastinate repentance, or wait till a death-bed, for it is the will of God that man should repent and serve Him in health, and blessing and power of his mind, in order to secure his blessing, and not wait until he is called to die. (TPJS, 197)[68]

❖❖❖

We should take warning and not wait for death-bed to repent, as we see the infant taken away by death, so may the youth and middle-aged . . . be suddenly called into eternity. (TPJS, 197)[68]

❖❖❖

If [you] have done anything . . . that [you] are sorry for, or that [you] would not like to meet and answer for at the bar of God . . . let it prove as a warning to all to deal justly before God, and with all mankind, then we shall be clear in the day of judgment. (TPJS, 216)[72]

•••

Search your hearts, and see if you are like God. I have searched mine, and feel to repent of all my sins. (TPJS, 216)[73]

•••

There is now a day of salvation to such as repent and reform;—and they who repent not should be cast out from this society; yet we should woo them to return to God, lest they escape not the damnation of hell! (TPJS, 238)[78]

•••

I do not want to cloak iniquity—all things contrary to the will of God, should be cast from us, but don't do more hurt than good. . . . I want the innocent to go free—rather spare ten iniquitous among you, than condemn one innocent one. . . , "Fret not thyself because of evildoers." God will see to it. (TPJS, 239)[78]

•••

The best measure or principle to bring the poor to repentance is to administer to their wants. (TPJS, 241)[79]

•••

If there was sin among men, repentance was as necessary at one time or age of the world as another. (TPJS, 265)[85]

•••

There is joy in the presence of the angels of God over one sinner that repenteth, more than over ninety-and-nine just persons that are so righteous; they will be damned anyhow; you cannot save them. (TPJS, 277)[93]

•••

Knowledge saves a man; and in the world of spirits no man can be exalted but by knowledge. . . . If a man has knowledge, he can be saved; although, if he has been guilty of great sins, he will be punished for them. But when he consents to obey the Gospel, whether here or in the world of spirits, he is saved. (TPJS, 357)[130]

•••

God hath made a provision that every spirit in the eternal world can be ferreted out and saved unless he has committed that unpardonable sin. (TPJS, 357)[130]

•••

Hear it, all ye ends of the earth—all ye priests, all ye sinners, and all men. Repent! Repent! Obey the gospel. Turn to God; for your religion won't save you, and you will be damned. I do not say how long. (TPJS, 361)[130]

REQUIREMENTS OF THE LORD

[To the] first principles of the Gospel of Christ: . . . Add to your faith, virtue; and to virtue, knowledge; and to knowledge, temperance; and to temperance, patience; and to patience, godliness; and to godliness, brotherly kindness; and to brotherly kindness, charity [or love]; for if these things be in you, and abound, they make you that ye shall neither be barren nor unfruitful, in the knowledge of our Lord Jesus Christ. (TPJS, 16)[9]

RESILIENCE

(*See also* COPING; STRENGTH)

The Kingdom of Heaven is like unto a mustard seed. Behold, then is not this the Kingdom of Heaven that is raising its head in the last days in the majesty of its God, even the Church of the Latter-day Saints, like an impenetrable, immovable rock in the midst

R

of the mighty deep, exposed to the storms and tempests of Satan, but has, thus far, remained steadfast, and is still braving the mountain waves of opposition . . . urged onward with redoubled fury by the enemy of righteousness, with his pitch fork of lies. (TPJS, 98)[34]

♦♦♦

We have reproved in the gate, and men have laid snares for us. We have spoken words, and men have made us offenders. And notwithstanding all this, our minds are not yet darkened, but feel strong in the Lord. (TPJS, 124)[46]

♦♦♦

We think . . . that every species of wickedness and cruelty practiced upon us will only tend to bind our hearts together and seal them together in love. (TPJS, 130)[47]

♦♦♦

The truth, like the sturdy oak, has stood unhurt amid the contending elements, which have beat upon it with tremendous force. The floods have rolled, wave after wave, in quick succession, and have not swallowed it up. . . , "the floods have lifted up their voice; but the Lord of Hosts is mightier than the mighty waves of the sea": nor have the flames of persecution, with all the influence of mobs, been able to destroy it; but like Moses' bush, it has stood unconsumed. (TPJS, 184)[59]

♦♦♦

As well might the devil seek to dethrone Jehovah, as overthrow an innocent soul that resists everything which is evil. (TPJS, 226)[75]

♦♦♦

If you live up to your privileges, the angels cannot be restrained from being your associates. (TPJS, 226)[75]

♦♦♦

A man can bear a heavy burthen by practice and continuing to increase it. (TPJS, 299)[103]

♦♦♦

I am like a huge, rough stone rolling down from a high mountain; and the only polishing I get is when some corner gets rubbed off by coming in contact with something else, striking with accelerating force against religious bigotry, priest-craft, lawyer-craft, doctor-craft, lying editors, suborned judges and jurors, and the authority of perjured executives, backed by mobs, blasphemers, licentious and corrupt men and women—all hell knocking off a corner here and a corner there. Thus I will become a smooth and polished shaft in the quiver of the Almighty, who will give me dominion over all and every one of them, when their refuge of lies shall fail, and their hiding place shall be destroyed, while these smooth-polished stones with which I come in contact become marred. (TPJS, 304)[109]

♦♦♦

They that hurl all their hell and fiery billows upon me . . . will roll off me as fast as they come on. (TPJS, 366)[132]

RESISTING TEMPTATION

The devil could not compel mankind to do evil; all was voluntary. Those who resisted the Spirit of God, would be liable to be led into temptation, and then the association of heaven would be withdrawn from those who refused to be made partakers of such great glory. God would not exert any compulsory means, and the devil could not. (TPJS, 187)[60]

♦♦♦

All men have power to resist the devil. They who have tabernacles, have power over those who have not. (TPJS, 189)[61]

RESPECT

Our brethren [are to] be careful of one another's feelings, and walk in love, honoring one another more than themselves, as is required by the Lord. (TPJS, 24)[13]

•••

In ancient days councils were conducted with such strict propriety, that no one was allowed to whisper, be weary, leave the room, or get uneasy in the least, until the voice of the Lord, by revelation, or the voice of the council by the Spirit, was obtained. (TPJS, 69)[22]

•••

When . . . traveling through the world . . . [Elders] should commence their labor with parents, or guardians; and their teachings should be such as are calculated to turn the hearts of the fathers to the children, and the hearts of children to the fathers; and no influence should be used with children, contrary to the consent of their parents or guardians; but all such as can be persuaded in a lawful and righteous manner, and with common consent, we should feel it our duty to influence them to gather with the people of God. But otherwise let the responsibility rest upon the heads of parents or guardians. (TPJS, 86)[31]

•••

Let us be faithful and silent, brethren, and if God gives you a manifestation, keep it to yourselves; be watchful and prayerful, and you shall have a prelude of those joys that God will pour out on that day. (TPJS, 91)[33]

•••

[May not] the blood of our fathers . . . cry from the ground against us. Sacred is the memory of that blood which bought for us our liberty. (TPJS, 117)[42]

•••

[Mormons] believe that if their companion dies, they have a right to marry again. But we do disapprove of the custom . . . in marrying in five or six weeks, or even in two or three months, after the death of their companion. We believe that due respect ought to be had to the memory of the dead, and the feelings of both friends and children. (TPJS, 119)[45]

•••

None but fools will trifle with the souls of men. (TPJS, 137)[47]

•••

How much more dignified and noble are the thoughts of God, than the vain imaginations of the human heart! None but fools will trifle with the souls of men. (TPJS, 137)[47]

•••

We send our respects to fathers, mothers, wives and children, brothers and sisters; we hold them in the most sacred remembrance. (TPJS, 139)[47]

•••

He that offends one of the least of the Saints, would be better off with a millstone tied to his neck and he and the stone plunged into the depth of the sea! (TPJS, 261)[85]

•••

It is an insult to a meeting for persons to leave just before its close. If they must go out, let them go half an hour before. No gentlemen will go out of a meeting just at closing. (TPJS, 287)[100]

•••

As president of this house, I forbid any man leaving just as we are going to close the meeting. He is no gentleman who will do it. I don't care who does it, even if it were the king of England. I forbid it. (TPJS, 296)[102]

♦♦♦

Meddle not with any man for his religion; and all governments ought to permit every man to enjoy his religion unmolested. No man is authorized to take away life in consequence of difference in religion, which all laws and governments ought to tolerate and protect, right or wrong. (TPJS, 344)[130]

♦♦♦

After having suffered so great sacrifice and having passed through so great a season of sorrow, we trust that a ram may be caught in the thicket speedily, to relieve the sons and daughters of Abraham from their great anxiety, and to light up the lamp of salvation upon their countenances, that they may hold on now, after having gone so far unto everlasting life. (TPJS, 136)[47]

RESPONSIBILITY

We take the sacred writings into our hands, and admit that they were given by direct inspiration for the good of man. We believe that God condescended to speak from the heavens and declare His will concerning the human family, to give them just and holy laws, to regulate their conduct and guide them in a direct way, that in due time He might take them to Himself, and make them joint heirs with His Son. But when this fact is admitted, that the immediate will of heaven is contained in the Scriptures, are we not bound as rational creatures to live in accordance to all its precepts? Will the mere admission that this is the will of heaven ever benefit us if we do not comply with all its teachings? Do we not offer violence to the Supreme Intelligence of heaven, when we admit the truth of its teachings, and do not obey

them? Do we not descend below our own knowledge, and the better wisdom which heaven has endowed us with, by such a course of conduct? (TPJS, 53)[21]

♦♦♦

Righteousness must be the aim of the Saints in all things, and . . . great things must be expected of them. (TPJS, 77)[29]

♦♦♦

After all that has been said, the greatest and most important duty is to preach the Gospel. (TPJS, 113)[41]

♦♦♦

It is a desirable honor that you should so walk before our heavenly Father as to save yourselves; we are all responsible to God for the manner we improve the light and wisdom given by our Lord to enable us to save ourselves. (TPJS, 227)[75]

♦♦♦

The greatest responsibility in this world that God has laid upon us is to seek after our dead. (TPJS, 356)[130]

RESURRECTION

If . . . the grave has no victory, those who keep the sayings of Jesus and obey His teachings have not only a promise of a resurrection from the dead, but an assurance of being admitted into His glorious kingdom: for He Himself says, "Where I am, shall also my servants be." (TPJS, 62)[21]

♦♦♦

The Doctrines of the Resurrection of the Dead and the Eternal Judgment are necessary to preach among the first principles of the Gospel of Jesus Christ. (TPJS, 149)[48]

♦♦♦

[The] distinction is made between the doctrine of the actual resurrection and translation: translation obtains deliverance from the tortures and sufferings of the body, but their existence will prolong as to the labors and toils of the ministry, before they can enter into so great a rest and glory [as the resurrection]. (TPJS, 171)[54]

◆◆◆

All men will come from the grave as they lie down, whether old or young; there will not be "added unto their stature one cubit," neither taken from it; all will be raised by the power of God, having spirit in their bodies, and not blood. Children will be enthroned in the presence of God and the Lamb with bodies of the same stature that they had on earth, having been redeemed by the blood of the Lamb; they will there enjoy the fullness of that light, glory and intelligence, which is prepared in the celestial kingdom. (TPJS, 199)[68]

◆◆◆

Christ and the resurrected Saints will reign over the earth during the thousand years. They will not probably dwell upon the earth, but will visit it when they please, or when it is necessary to govern it. (TPJS, 268)[88]

◆◆◆

I suppose John saw being there of a thousand forms, that had been saved from ten thousand time ten thousand earths like this,—strange beasts of which we have no conception: all might be seen in heaven. The grand secret was to show John what there was in heaven. John learned that God glorified Himself by saving all that His hands had made, whether beasts, fowls, fishes or men; and He will glorify Himself with them. (TPJS, 291)[101]

◆◆◆

I will tell you what I want. If tomorrow I shall be called to lie in yonder tomb, in the morning of the resurrection let me strike hands with my father, and cry, "My father," and he will say, "My son, my son," as soon as the rock rends and before we come out of the graves.

And may we contemplate these things so? Yes, if we learn how to live and how to die. When we lie down we contemplate how we may rise in the morning; and it is pleasing for friends to lie down together, locked in the arms of love, to sleep and wake in each other's embrace and renew their conversation. (TPJS, 295)[102]

◆◆◆

So plain was the vision, that I actually saw men, before they had ascended from the tomb, as though they were getting up slowly. They took each other by the hand and said to each other, "My father, my son, my mother, my daughter, my brother, my sister." And when the voice calls for the dead to arise, suppose I am laid by the side of my father, what would be the first joy of my heart? To meet my father, my mother, my brother, my sister; and when they are by my side, I embrace them and they me. (TPJS, 295)[102]

◆◆◆

If I have no expectation of seeing my father, mother, brothers, sisters and friends again, my heart would burst in a moment, and I should go down to my grave. (TPJS, 296)[102]

◆◆◆

The expectation of seeing my friends in the morning of the resurrection cheers my soul and makes me bear up against the evils of life. It is like taking a long journey, and on their return we meet them with increased joy. (TPJS, 296)[102]

◆◆◆

God has revealed His Son from the heavens and the doctrine of the resurrection also; and we have a knowledge that those we bury here God will bring up again, clothed upon and quickened by the Spirit of the great God. . . . Let these truths sink down in our hearts, that we may even here begin to enjoy that which shall be in full hereafter. (TPJS, 296)[102]

◆◆◆

Gods have an ascendancy over the angels, who are ministering servants. In the resurrection, some [people] are raised to be angels, others are raised to become Gods. (TPJS, 312)[113]

◆◆◆

If men would acquire salvation, they have got to be subject, before they leave this world, to certain rules and principles, which were fixed by an unalterable decree before the world was.

The disappointment of hopes and expectations at the resurrection would be indescribably dreadful. (TPJS, 324)[121]

◆◆◆

How consoling to the mourners when they are called to part with a husband, wife, father, mother, child, or dear relative, to know that, although the earthly tabernacle is laid down and dissolved, they shall rise again to dwell in everlasting burnings in immortal glory, not to sorrow, suffer, or die any more. But they shall be heirs of God and joint heirs with Jesus Christ. (TPJS, 347)[130]

◆◆◆

When I talk to . . . mourners, what have they lost? Their relatives and friends are only separated from their bodies for a short season: their spirits which existed with God have left the tabernacle of clay only for a little moment, as it were; and they now exist in a place where they converse together the same as we do on the earth. (TPJS, 353)[130]

◆◆◆

Those who have died in the faith are now in the celestial kingdom of God. And hence is the glory of the sun. . . . for at the resurrection . . . [they] will rise in perfect felicity and go to celestial glory, while many must wait myriads of years before they can receive the like blessings; and your expectations and hopes are far above what man can conceive;

Don't mourn, don't weep. I know it by the testimony of the Holy Ghost that is within me; and you may wait for your friends to come forth to meet you in the morn of the celestial world. (TPJS, 359)[130]

◆◆◆

"As in Adam all die, even so in Christ shall all be made alive"; all shall be raised from the dead. . . . The Lamb of God hath brought to pass the resurrection, so that all shall rise from the dead. . . .

Some dwell in higher glory than others. (TPJS, 367)[132]

◆◆◆

In order to receive your children to yourselves you must have a promise— some ordinance; some blessing, in order to ascend above principalities, or else it may be an angel. They must rise just as they died; we can there hail our lovely infants with the same glory—the same loveliness in the celestial glory, where they all enjoy alike. They differ in stature, in size, the same glorious spirit gives them the likeness of glory in bloom and beauty. The old man with his silvery hairs will glory in bloom and beauty. No man can describe it to you—no man can write it. (TPJS, 368)[132]

◆◆◆

Paul says, "There is one glory of the sun, and another glory of the moon, and another glory of the stars; for one star differeth from another star in glory. So also is the resurrection of the dead." They who obtain a glorious resurrection from the dead, are exalted far above principalities, powers, thrones, dominions and angels, and are expressly declared to be heirs of God and joint heirs with Jesus Christ, all having eternal power. (TPJS, 374)[133]

REVELATION

God had often sealed up the heavens because of covetousness in the Church. (TPJS, 9)[4]

•••

The light of the latter-day glory begins to break forth through the dark atmosphere of sectarian wickedness, and their iniquity begins to roll up into view, and the nations of the Gentiles are like the waves of the sea, casting up mire and dirt, or all in commotion, and they are hastily preparing to act the part allotted them, when the Lord rebukes the nations, when He shall rule them with a rod of iron, and break them in pieces like a potter's vessel. (TPJS, 16)[9]

•••

It is reasonable to suppose that man departed from the first teachings, or instructions which he received from heaven in the first age, and refused by his disobedience to be governed by them. Consequently, he formed such laws as best suited his own mind, or as he supposed, were best adapted to his situation. But that God has influenced man more or less since that time in the formation of law for His benefit we have no hesitancy in believing . . . though man in his own supposed wisdom would not admit the influence of a power superior to his own. (TPJS, 57)[21]

•••

We ask, does it remain for a people . . . [to be] indebted to the faith [solely] of another people who lived hundreds and thousands of years before them, does it remain for them to say how much God has spoken and how much He has not spoken? . . . To say that God never said anything more to man than is recorded, would be saying . . . that He would not, after giving what is there contained, speak again. (TPJS, 61)[21]

•••

Take away the Book of Mormon and the revelations, and where is our religion? We have none; for without Zion, and a place of deliverance, we must fall. (TPJS, 71)[23]

•••

Such is the darkness and ignorance of this generation, that they look upon it as incredible that a man should have any intercourse with his Maker. (TPJS, 89)[32]

•••

The word of the Lord is precious. (TPJS, 93)[35]

•••

Revelations of the mind and will of God to the Church, are to come through the presidency. This is the order of heaven, and the power and privilege of this priesthood. It is also the privilege of any officer in this Church to obtain revelations, so far as relates to his particular calling and duty in the Church. (TPJS, 111)[41]

•••

We are called to hold the keys of the mysteries of those things that have been kept hid from the foundation of the world until now. (TPJS, 137)[47]

•••

And now, brethren, after your tribulations, if you do these things

" . . . let honesty, and sobriety, and candor, and solemnity, and virtue, and pureness, and meekness, and simplicity crown our heads in every place; and in fine, become as little children, without malice, guile or hypocrisy, and exercise fervent prayer and faith in the sight of God always, He shall give unto you knowledge by His Holy Spirit, yea by the unspeakable gift of the Holy Ghost, that has not been revealed since the world was until now; which our forefathers have waited with anxious expectation to be revealed in the last times, which their minds were pointed to by the angels, as held in reserve for the fullness of their glory; a time to come in the which nothing shall be withheld, whether there be one God or many Gods, they shall be manifest; all thrones and dominions, principalities and powers, shall be revealed and set forth upon all who have endured valiantly for the Gospel of Jesus Christ." (TPJS, 138)[47]

•••

"How long can rolling waters remain impure? What power shall stay the heavens? As well might man stretch forth his puny arm to stop the Missouri River in its decreed course, or to turn it up stream, as to hinder the Almighty from pouring down knowledge from heaven, upon the heads of the Latter-day Saints." (TPJS, 139)[47]

•••

By learning the Spirit of God and understanding it, you may grow into the principle of revelation, until you become perfect in Christ Jesus. (TPJS, 151)[48]

•••

Salvation cannot come without revelation; it is in vain for anyone to minister without it. . . . Whenever salvation has been administered, it has been by testimony. (TPJS, 160)[49]

•••

An open vision will manifest that which is more important. (TPJS, 161)[49]

•••

There are two Priesthoods spoken of in the Scriptures, vis., the Melchizedek and the Aaronic or Levitical. Although there are two Priesthoods, yet the Melchizedek Priesthood comprehends the Aaronic or Levitical Priesthood, and is the grand head, and holds the highest authority which pertains to the Priesthood, and the keys of the Kingdom of God in all ages of the world to the latest posterity on the earth; and is the channel through which all knowledge, doctrine, the plan of salvation and every important matter is revealed from heaven. (TPJS, 166)[54]

•••

Adam received commandments and instructions from God: this was the order from the beginning. (TPJS, 168)[54]

•••

No man knows the things of God, but by the Spirit of God, so no man knows the spirit of the devil, and his power and influence, but by possessing intelligence which is more than human. (TPJS, 205)[71]

•••

Unless some person or persons have a communication, or revelation from God, unfolding to them the operation of the spirit, they must eternally remain ignorant of these principles; for if one man cannot understand these things but by the Spirit of God, ten thousand men cannot; it is alike out of the reach of the wisdom of the learned, the tongue of the eloquent, [or] the power of the mighty. And we shall at last have to come to this conclusion, whatever we may think of revelation, that without it, we can neither know nor understand anything of God, or of the devil; and however unwilling the world may be to acknowledge this principle, it is evident from the multifarious creeds . . . that they understand nothing of this principle, and it is as equally as plain that without a divine communication they must remain in ignorance. (TPJS, 205)[71]

• • •

A man is saved no faster than he gets knowledge, for if he does not get knowledge, he will be brought into captivity by some evil power in the other world, as evil spirits will have more knowledge, and consequently more power than many men who are on the earth. Hence it needs revelation to assist us, and give us knowledge of the things of God. (TPJS, 217)[73]

• • •

If any revelations are given of God, they are universally opposed by the priests and Christendom at large; for they reveal their wickedness and abominations. (TPJS, 217)[73]

• • •

As God governed Abraham, Isaac and Jacob as families, and the children of Israel as a nation; so we, as a Church, must be under His guidance if we are prospered, preserved and sustained. Our only confidence can be in God; our only wisdom obtained from Him; and He alone must be our protector and safeguard, spiritually and temporally, or we fall. (TPJS, 253)[81]

• • •

The plea of many in this day is, that we have no right to receive revelations; but if we do not get revelations, we do not have the oracles of God; and if they have not the oracles of God, they are not the people of God. But say you, What will become of the world, or the various professors of religion who do not believe in revelation and the oracles of God as continued to his Church in all ages of the world, when He has a people

on earth? I tell you, in the name of Jesus Christ, they will be damned [or held back]; and when you get into the eternal world, you will find it will be so, they cannot escape the damnation of hell. (TPJS, 272)[91]

• • •

Whenever God gives a vision of an image, or beast, or figure of any kind, He always holds Himself responsible to give a revelation or interpretation of the meaning thereof, otherwise we are not responsible or accountable for our belief in it. Don't be afraid of being damned for not knowing the meaning of a vision or figure, if God has not given a revelation or interpretation of the subject. (TPJS, 291)[101]

• • •

We never can comprehend the things of God and of heaven, but by revelation. We may spiritualize and express opinions to all eternity; but that is no authority. (TPJS, 292)[101]

• • •

It is my meditation all the day, and more than my meat and drink, to know how I shall make the Saints of God comprehend the visions that roll like an overflowing surge before my mind. (TPJS, 296)[102]

• • •

Hosanna, hosanna, hosanna to Almighty God, that rays of light begin to burst forth upon us even now. I cannot find words in which to express myself. I am not learned, but I have as good feelings as any man. (TPJS, 296)[102]

• • •

With all their boasted religion, piety and sacredness [Christian religions] at the same time . . . are crying out against prophets, apostles, angels, revelations, prophesying and visions, etc. Why, they are just ripening for the damnation of hell. . . . For they reject the most glorious principle of the Gospel of Jesus Christ and treat with disdain and trample under foot the key that unlocks the heavens and puts in our possession the glories of the celestial world. (TPJS, 298)[103]

♦♦♦

Paul said, "the world by wisdom know not God," so the world by speculation are [all the more] destitute of revelation. (TPJS, 300)[104]

♦♦♦

Paul saw the third heavens, and I more. (TPJS, 301)[106]

♦♦♦

The Lord deals with this people as a tender parent with a child, communicating light and intelligence and the knowledge of His ways as they can bear it. (TPJS, 305)[109]

♦♦♦

I could explain a hundred fold more than I ever have of the glories of the kingdoms manifested to me in the vision, were I permitted, and were the people prepared to receive them. (TPJS, 305)[109]

♦♦♦

It is the constitutional disposition of mankind to set up stakes and bounds to the works and ways of the Almighty. (TPJS, 320)[118]

♦♦♦

That which hath been hid from before the foundation of the world is revealed to babes and sucklings in the last days. (TPJS, 321)[118]

♦♦♦

I know a man that has been caught up to the third heavens and can say, with Paul, that we have seen and heard things that are not lawful to utter. (TPJS, 323)[119]

♦♦♦

Could you gaze into heaven five minutes, you would know more than you would by reading all that ever was written on the subject. (TPJS, 324)[121]

♦♦♦

No man can receive the Holy Ghost without receiving revelation. The Holy Ghost is a revelator. (TPJS, 328)[122]

♦♦♦

We have received a portion of knowledge from God by immediate revelation, and from the same source. We can receive all knowledge. (TPJS, p 329)[123]

♦♦♦

One truth revealed from heaven is worth all the sectarian notions in existence. (TPJS, 338)[128]

♦♦♦

All things whatsoever God in his infinite wisdom has seen fit and proper to reveal to us, while we are dwelling in mortality, in regard to our mortal bodies . . . are revealed to our spirits precisely as though we had no bodies at all; and those revelations which will save our spirits will save our bodies. God reveals them to us in view of no eternal dissolution of the body, or tabernacle. (TPJS, 355)[130]

♦♦♦

I calculate to be one of the instruments of setting up the kingdom of Daniel by the word of the Lord, and I intend to lay a foundation that will revolutionize the whole world. (TPJS, 366)[132]

♦♦♦

I never told you I was perfect; but there is no error in the revelations which I have taught. (TPJS, 368)[132]

♦♦♦

When did I ever teach anything wrong from this stand? When was I ever confounded? (TPJS, 368)[132]

•••

All men are liars who say they are of the true Church without the revelations of Jesus Christ and the Priesthood of Melchizedek, which is after the order of the Son of God. (TPJS, 375)[133]

•••

Did I build on any other man's foundation? I have got all the truth which the Christian world possessed, and an independent revelation in the bargain, and God will bear me off triumphant. (TPJS, 376)[133]

REVERENCE

In ancient days councils were conducted with such strict propriety, that no one was allowed to whisper, be weary, leave the room, or get uneasy in the least, until the voice of the Lord, by revelation, or the voice of the council by the Spirit, was obtained. (TPJS, 69)[22]

•••

It is an insult to a meeting for persons to leave just before its close. If they must go out, let them go half an hour before. No gentlemen will go out of a meeting just at closing. (TPJS, 287)[100]

•••

As president of this house, I forbid any man leaving just as we are going to close the meeting. He is no gentleman who will do it. I don't care who does it, even if it were the king of England. I forbid it. (TPJS, 296)[102]

RIDICULE

Mr. Stollars stated that James Mullone, of Springfield, told him as follows: . . . "I have been to Nauvoo, and seen Joe Smith, the Prophet: he had a gray horse, and I asked him where he got it"; and Joe said,

"You see that white cloud." "Yes." "Well, as it came along, I got the horse from that cloud." This is a fair specimen of the ten thousand foolish lies circulated by this generation to bring the truth and its advocates into disrepute. (TPJS, 270)[90]

RIGHTEOUS CROWN

If the Saints are not to reign, for what purpose are they crowned? . . . By His servant John He [the Lord] said, "Behold, I come quickly: hold that fast which thou hast, that no man take thy crown." And again, "To him that overcometh will I grant to sit with Me in My throne, even as I also overcame, and am set down with My Father in His throne. (TPJS, 64)[21]

RIGHTEOUSNESS

In the 22nd chapter of Matthew's account of the Messiah, we find the Kingdom of Heaven likened unto a king who made a marriage for his son. . . . This son was the Messiah . . . The Saints, or those who are found faithful to the Lord, are the individuals who will be found worthy to inherit a seat at the marriage supper. . . . Let us be glad and rejoice, and give honor to Him; for the marriage of the Lamb is come, and His wife hath made herself ready. And to her was granted that she should be arrayed in fine linen, clean and white: For the fine linen is the righteousness of Saints. (TPJS, 63)[21]

•••

It is a duty which every Saint ought to render to his brethren freely—to always love them, and ever succor them. To be justified before God we must love one another; we must overcome evil; we must visit the fatherless and the widow in their affliction, and we must keep ourselves unspotted from the world; for such virtues flow from the great fountain of pure religion, strengthening our faith by adding every good quality that adorns the children of the blessed Jesus, we can pray in the season of prayer; we can love our neighbor as ourselves, and be faithful in tribulation, knowing that the reward of such is greater in the kingdom of heaven. What a consolation! What a joy! Let me live the life of the righteous, and let my reward be like his! (TPJS, 76)[29]

♦♦♦

Righteousness must be the aim of the Saints in all things, and . . . great things must be expected of them. (TPJS, 77)[29]

♦♦♦

Zion . . . is a place of righteousness, and all who build thereon are to worship the true and living God, and all believe in one doctrine, even the doctrine of our Lord and Savior Jesus Christ. (TPJS, 80)[30]

♦♦♦

Let the Twelve and all Saints be willing to confess all their sins and not keep back a part; and let the Twelve be humble and not be exalted, and beware of pride, and not seek to excel one above another, but act for each other's good, and pray for one another, and honor our brother or make honorable mention of his name, and not backbite and devour our brother. (TPJS, 155)[49]

♦♦♦

Is not God good? Then you be good; if He is faithful, then you be faithful. Add to your faith virtue, to virtue knowledge, and seek for every good thing. (TPJS, 217)[73]

♦♦♦

As well might the devil seek to dethrone Jehovah, as overthrow an innocent soul that resists everything which is evil. (TPJS, 226)[75]

♦♦♦

How glorious are the principles of righteousness! We are full of selfishness; The devil flatters us that we are very righteous, when [in fact] we are feeding on the faults of others. (TPJS, 241)[79]

♦♦♦

It is for us to be righteous, that we may be wise and understand; for none of the wicked shall understand; but the wise shall understand. (TPJS, 253)[81]

♦♦♦

Salvation is nothing more nor less than to triumph over all our enemies and put them under our feet. And when we have power to put all enemies under our feet in the world, and a knowledge to triumph over all evil spirits in the world to come, then we are saved. (TPJS, 297)[103]

♦♦♦

I do not want you to think that I am very righteous, for I am not. God judges men according to the use they make of the light which He gives them. (TPJS, 303)[109]

♦♦♦

There is no salvation between the two lids of the Bible without a legal administrator. Jesus was then the legal administrator, and ordained His Apostles. (TPJS, 319)[117]

♦♦♦

Hasten the work in the Temple, renew your exertions to forward all the work of the last days, and walk before the Lord in soberness and righteousness. (TPJS, 326)[121]

RIGHTFULNESS

Everything that God gives us is lawful and right; and it is proper that we should enjoy His gifts and blessings whenever and wherever He is disposed to bestow; But if we should seize upon those same blessings and enjoyments without law, without revelation, without commandment, those blessings and enjoyments would prove cursings and vexations in the end, and we should have to lie down in sorrow and wailings of everlasting regret. But in obedience there is joy and peace unspotted, unalloyed; and as God has designed our happiness—and the happiness of all His creatures, he never has—He never will institute an ordinance or give a commandment to His people that is not calculated in its nature to promote that happiness which he has designed, and which will not end in the greatest amount of good and glory to those who become the recipients of His law and ordinances. (TPJS, 256)[83]

RIGHTS

When my enemies take away my rights, I will bear it and keep out of the way; but if they take away your rights, I will fight for you. (TPJS, 268)[87]

♦♦♦

If it has been demonstrated that I have been willing to die for a "Mormon," I am bold to declare before Heaven that I am just as ready to die in defending the rights of a Presbyterian, a Baptist, or a good man of any other denomination; for the same principle which would trample upon the rights of the Latter-day Saints would trample upon the rights of the Roman Catholics, or of any other denomination who may be unpopular and too weak to defend themselves. (TPJS, 313)[113]

♦♦♦

I would not have suffered my name to have been used by my friends on anywise as President of the United States, or candidate for that office, if I and my friends could have had the privilege of enjoying our religious and civil rights as American citizens, even those rights which the Constitution guarantees unto all her citizens alike. But this as a people we have been denied from the beginning. (TPJS, 331)[124]

♦♦♦

Meddle not with any man for his religion; and all governments ought to permit every man to enjoy his religion unmolested. No man is authorized to take away life in consequence of difference in religion, which all laws and governments ought to tolerate and protect, right or wrong. (TPJS, 344)[130]

♦♦♦

It is the duty of all men to protect their lives and the lives of the household, whenever necessity requires, and no power has a right to forbid it. (TPJS, 391)[144]

S

SACREDNESS

Let us be faithful and silent, brethren, and if God gives you a manifestation, keep it to yourselves; be watchful and prayerful, and you shall have a prelude of those joys that God will pour out on that day. (TPJS, 91)[33]

♦♦♦

How much more dignified and noble are the thoughts of God, than the vain imaginations of the human heart! None but fools will trifle with the souls of men. (TPJS, 137)[47]

♦♦♦

Ordinances must be kept in the very way God has appointed; otherwise their Priesthood will prove a cursing instead of a blessing . . . [as with Cain, who was initially] authorized to offer sacrifice, but not offering it in righteousness, was cursed. (TPJS, 169)[54]

♦♦♦

There are many things which belong to the powers of the Priesthood and the keys thereof, that have been kept hid from before the foundation of the world; they are hid from the wise and prudent to be revealed in the last times. (TPJS, 170)[54]

♦♦♦

I could explain a hundred fold more than I ever have of the glories of the kingdoms manifested to me in the vision, were I permitted, and were the people prepared to receive them. (TPJS, 305)[109]

♦♦♦

I know a man that has been caught up to the third heavens, and can say, with Paul, that we have seen and heard things that are not lawful to utter. (TPJS, 323)[119]

SACRIFICE

I know that Zion, in the due time of the Lord, will be redeemed; but how many will be the days of her purification, tribulation, and affliction, the Lord has kept hid from my eyes; and when I enquire concerning this subject, the voice of the Lord is: Be still, and know that I am God; all those who suffer for my name shall reign with me, and he that layeth down his life for my sake shall find it again. (TPJS, 34)[19]

♦♦♦

[In the days of Adam,] sacrifice was instituted for a type, by which man was to discern the great Sacrifice which God had prepared; . . . Abel offered an acceptable sacrifice. . . . Certainly, the shedding of the blood of a beast could be beneficial to no man, except it was done in imitation, or as a type, or explanation of what was to be offered through the gift of God Himself . . . for a remission of sins. (TPJS, 58)[21]

♦♦♦

The mere shedding of the blood of beasts or offering anything else in sacrifice, could not procure a remission of sins, except it were performed in faith of something to come; if it could, Cain's offering must have been as good as Abel's. And if Abel was taught of the coming of the Son of God, was he not taught also of His ordinances? (TPJS, 59)[21]

♦♦♦

Whenever the Lord revealed Himself to men in ancient days, and commanded them to offer sacrifices to Him. . . . It was done that they might look forward in faith to the time of His coming, and rely upon the power of that atonement for a remission of their sins. (TPJS, 60)[21]

•••

Exalt the standard of Democracy! Down with that of priestcraft, and let all the people say Amen! That the blood of our fathers may not cry from the ground against us. Sacred is the memory of that blood which bought for us our liberty. (TPJS, 117)[42]

•••

After having suffered so great sacrifice and having passed through so great a season of sorrow, we trust that a ram may be caught in the thicket speedily, to relieve the sons and daughters of Abraham from their great anxiety, and to light up the lamp of salvation upon their countenances, that they may hold on now, after having gone so far unto everlasting life. (TPJS, 136)[47]

•••

"What greater love hath any man than that he lay down his life for his friend"; then why not fight for our friend until we die? (TPJS, 195)[66]

•••

I know what I say; I understand my mission and business. God Almighty is my shield; and what can man do if God is my friend? I shall not be sacrificed until my time comes; then I shall be offered freely. (TPJS, 274)[91]

•••

There is no greater love than this, that a man lay down his life for his friends. I discover hundreds and thousands of my brethren ready to sacrifice their lives for me. (TPJS, 315)[114]

•••

Men have to suffer that they may come upon Mount Zion and be exalted above the heavens. (TPJS, 323)[119]

•••

I am willing to be sacrificed on the altar of virtue, righteous and truth, in maintaining the laws and Constitution of the United States, if need be, for the general good of man. (TPJS, 332)[124]

•••

If my life is of no value to my friends it is of none to myself. (TPJS, 377)[136]

SAFETY

(*See also* PRECAUTION; PRUDENCE)

You cannot watch [Satan] too closely, nor pray too much. (TPJS, 25)[14]

•••

Thus shall the Lord watch over his generation, that they may be saved. (TPJS, 31)[17]

•••

As a Church and a people it behooves us to be wise, and to seek to know the will of God, and then be willing to do it; . . . If Enoch, Abraham, Moses, and the children of Israel, and all God's people were saved by keeping the commandments of God, we, if saved at all, shall be saved upon the same principle. (TPJS, 253)[81]

•••

We have been chastened by the hand of God heretofore for not obeying His commands, although we never violated any human law, . . . yet we have treated lightly His commands, and departed from His ordinances, and the Lord has chastened us sore, and we have felt His arm and kissed the rod; let us be wise in time to come and ever remember that "to obey is better than sacrifice, and to hearken than the fat of rams." (TPJS, 253)[81]

SALVATION

The things of God are of deep import; and time, and experience, and careful and ponderous and solemn thoughts can only find them out. Thy mind, O man! If thou will lead a soul unto salvation, must stretch as high as the utmost heavens, and search into and contemplate the darkest abyss and the broad expanse of eternity. (TPJS, 137)[47]

♦♦♦

Salvation cannot come without revelation; it is in vain for anyone to minister without it. . . . Whenever salvation has been administered, it has been by testimony. (TPJS, 160)[49]

♦♦♦

The first step in salvation of man is the laws of eternal and self-existent principles. Spirits are eternal. At the organization in heaven we were all present, and saw the Savior chosen and appointed and the Plan of Salvation made, and we sanctioned it. (TPJS, 181)[56]

♦♦♦

A man is saved no faster than he gets knowledge, for if he does not get knowledge, he will be brought into captivity by some evil power in the other world, as evil spirits will have more knowledge, and consequently more power than many men who are on the earth. Hence it needs revelation to assist us, and give us knowledge of the things of God. (TPJS, 217)[73]

♦♦♦

[The Lord] knows the situation of both the living and the dead, and has made

ample provision for their redemption, according to their several circumstances, and the laws of the kingdom of God, whether in this world, or in the world to come. (TPJS, 220)[74]

♦♦♦

There is now a day of salvation to such as repent and reform;—and they who repent not should be cast out from this society; yet we should woo them to return to God, lest they escape not the damnation of hell! (TPJS, 238)[78]

♦♦♦

Jesus designs to save people out of their sins. Said Jesus, "Ye shall do the work, which ye see me do." These are the grand key-words for the society to act upon. (TPJS, 239)[78]

♦♦♦

Men or women [can] not be compelled into the kingdom of God, but must be dealt with in long-suffering, and at last we shall save them. (TPJS, 241)[78]

♦♦♦

Where there is no kingdom of God there is no salvation. What constitutes the kingdom of God? Where there is a prophet, priest, or a righteous man unto whom God gives His oracles, there is the kingdom of God; and where the oracles of God are not, there the kingdom of God is not. (TPJS, 272)[91]

♦♦♦

All the ordinances, systems and administrations on the earth are of no use to the children of men, unless they are ordained and authorized of God, for nothing will save a man but a legal administrator; for none others will be acknowledged either by God or angels. (TPJS, 274)[91]

♦♦♦

The principle of knowledge is the principle of salvation. . . . Everyone that does not obtain knowledge to be saved will be condemned. The principle of salvation is given us through the knowledge of Jesus Christ. (TPJS, 297)[103]

•••

Salvation is nothing more nor less than to triumph over all our enemies and put them under our feet. And when we have power to put all enemies under our feet in the world, and a knowledge to triumph over all evil spirits in the world to come, then we are saved. (TPJS, 297)[103]

•••

No person can have . . . salvation except through a tabernacle. (TPJS, 297)[103]

•••

It is impossible for a man to be saved in ignorance. (TPJS, 301)[106]

•••

Salvation means a man's being placed beyond the power of all his enemies. (TPJS, 301)[106]

•••

Salvation is for a man to be saved from all his enemies; for until a man can triumph over death, he is not saved. A knowledge of the priesthood alone will do this. (TPJS, 305)[109]

•••

Knowledge is the power of salvation. (TPJS, 306)[109]

•••

Ordinances instituted in the heavens before the foundation of the world, in the priesthood, for the salvation of men, are not to be altered or changed. All must be saved on the same principles. (TPJS, 308)[113]

•••

There is no salvation between the two lids of the Bible without a legal administrator. Jesus was then the legal administrator, and ordained His Apostles. (TPJS, 319)[117]

•••

To get salvation we must not only do some things, but everything which God has commanded. (TPJS, 332)[125]

•••

All sin, and all blasphemies, and every transgression, except one, that man can be guilty of, may be forgiven; and there is a salvation for all men, either in this world or the world to come, who have not committed the unpardonable sin, there being a provision either in this world or the world of spirits. (TPJS, 356)[130]

•••

Knowledge saves a man; and in the world of spirits no man can be exalted but by knowledge. . . . If a man has knowledge, he can be saved; although, if he has been guilty of great sins, he will be punished for them, But when he consents to obey the Gospel, whether here or in the world of spirits, he is saved. (TPJS, 357)[130]

•••

So long as a man will not give heed to the commandments, he must abide without salvation. (TPJS, 357)[130]

•••

God hath made a provision that every spirit in the eternal world can be ferreted out and saved unless he has committed that unpardonable sin. (TPJS, 357)[130]

•••

The salvation of Jesus Christ was wrought out for all men, in order to triumph over the devil; for if it did not catch him in one place, it would in another; for he stood up as a Savior. All will suffer [however] until they obey Christ himself. (TPJS, 357)[130]

♦♦♦

If a man has knowledge, he can be saved; although, if he has been guilty of great sins, he will be punished for them. But when he consents to obey the Gospel, whether here or in the world of spirits, he is saved. (TPJS, 357)[130]

♦♦♦

Knowledge saves a man; and in the world of spirits no man can be exalted but by knowledge. . . . If a man has knowledge, he can be saved; although, if he has been guilty of great sins, he will be punished for them, But when he consents to obey the Gospel, whether here or in the world of spirits, he is saved. (TPJS, 357)[130]

♦♦♦

Hear it, all ye ends of the earth—all ye priests, all ye sinners, and all men. Repent! Repent! Obey the gospel. Turn to God; for your religion won't save you, and you will be damned. I do not say how long. (TPJS, 361)[130]

SALVATION FOR THE DEAD

All those who have not had an opportunity of hearing the Gospel, and being administered unto by an inspired man in the flesh, must have it hereafter, before they can be finally judged. (TPJS, 121)[45]

♦♦♦

The Kingdom of Heaven is like a grain of mustard seed . . . small, but brings forth a large tree, and the fowls lodge in the branches. The fowls are the angels [which] come down, combine together to gather their children, and gather them. We cannot be made perfect without them, nor they without us. (TPJS, 159)[49]

♦♦♦

Men, by actively engaging in rites of salvation substitutionally became instrumental in bringing multitudes of their kindred into the kingdom of God. (TPJS, 191)[63]

♦♦♦

It is no more incredible that God should *save* the dead, than that he should *raise* the dead. (TPJS, 191)[63]

♦♦♦

Jesus Christ became a ministering spirit [while His body was lying in the sepulcher] to the spirits in prison, to fulfill an important part of His mission, without which He could not have perfected His work, or entered into His rest. After His resurrection He appeared as an angel to His disciples. (TPJS, 191)[63]

♦♦♦

There is a way to release the spirits of the dead; that is by the power and authority of the Priesthood—by binding and loosing on earth. This doctrine appears glorious, inasmuch as it exhibits the greatness of divine compassion and benevolence in the extent of the plan of human salvation. (TPJS, 192)[63]

♦♦♦

Those Saints who neglect [temple work] in behalf of their deceased relatives, do it at the peril of their own salvation. (TPJS, 193)[63]

♦♦♦

We have an account of our Savior preaching to the spirits in prison, to spirits that had been imprisoned from the days of Noah; and what did He preach to them? That they were to stay there? Certainly not! Let His own declaration testify, "He hath sent me to heal the broken-hearted, to preach deliverance to the captives, and recovering of sight to the blind, to set at liberty them that are bruised." (Luke 4:18) Isaiah has it—"To bring out the prisoners from the prison, and them that sit in darkness from the prison house." (Isaiah 17:7) It is very evident from this that He not only went to preach to them, but to deliver, or bring them out of the prison house. (TPJS, 219)[74]

•••

What has become of our fathers? Will they all be damned for not obeying the Gospel when they never heard it? Certainly not. But they will possess the same privilege that we here enjoy, through the medium of the everlasting Priesthood, which not only administer on earth but also in heaven, and [in] the wise dispensations of the great Jehovah; hence [they] will be visited by the Priesthood, and come out of their prison upon the same principle as those who were disobedient in the days of Noah were visited by our Savior . . . and had the Gospel preached to them by Him in prison; and in order that they might fulfill all the requisitions of God, living friends were baptized for their dead friends, and thus fulfilled the requirement of God which says, "Except a man be born of the water and of the Spirit, he cannot enter into the kingdom of God," they were baptized of course, not for themselves, but for their dead. . . . Paul, in speaking of the doctrine, says, "Else what shall they do which are baptized for the dead if the dead rise not at all? Why are they then baptized for the dead?" (1 Cor. 15:29) (TPJS, 222)[74]

•••

A view of these things [salvation for the dead] reconciles the Scriptures of truth, justifies the ways of God to man, places the human family upon equal footing, and harmonizes with every principle of righteousness, justice and truth. We will conclude with the words of Peter: "For the time past of our life may suffice us to have

wrought the will of the Gentiles" "For, for this cause was the Gospel preached also to them that are dead, that they might be judged according to men in the flesh, but live according to God in the Spirit." (TPJS, 223)[74]

•••

[From the Greek translation, Jesus states] "This day thou shalt be with me in the world of spirits." (TPJS, 309)[113]

•••

The Saints have not too much time to save and redress their dead, and gather together their living relatives, that they may be saved also, before the earth will be smitten, and the consumption decreed falls upon the world. (TPJS, 330)[122]

•••

If the whole Church should go to with all their might to save their dead, seal their posterity, and gather their living friends, and spend none of their time in behalf of the world, they would hardly get through before night would come, when no man can work. (TPJS, 330)[123]

•••

To seal those who dwell on earth to those who dwell in heaven. This is the power of Elijah and the keys of the kingdom of Jehovah. (TPJS, 338)[128]

•••

The greatest responsibility in this world that God has laid upon us is to seek after our dead. (TPJS, 356)[130]

•••

Every man who has a friend in the eternal world can save him, unless he has committed the unpardonable sin. And so you can see how far you can be a savior. (TPJS, 357)[130]

•••

They that hurl all their hell and fiery billows upon me . . . will roll off me as fast as they come on. But I have an order of things to save the poor fellows at any rate, and get them saved; for I will send men to preach to them in prison and save them if I can. (TPJS, 366)[132]

SATAN

You cannot watch [Satan] too closely, nor pray too much. (TPJS, 25)[14]

◆◆◆

Anxieties inexpressible crowd themselves continually upon my mind for the Saints, when I consider the many temptations to which we are subject, from the cunning and flattery of the great adversary of our souls. (TPJS, 29)[16]

◆◆◆

Darkness prevails at this time as it did at the time Jesus Christ was about to be crucified. The powers of darkness strove to obscure the glorious Sun of righteousness, that began to dawn upon the world, and was soon to burst in great blessings upon the heads of the faithful. (TPJS, 90)[33]

◆◆◆

Satan will rage, and the spirit of the devil is now enraged. I know not how soon these [horrible] things will take place; but with a view of them, shall I cry peace? No; I will lift up my voice and testify of them. (TPJS, 161)[49]

◆◆◆

Whatever you may hear about me or Kirtland, take no notice of it; for if it be a place of refuge, the devil will use his greatest efforts to trap the Saints. (TPJS, 161)[49]

◆◆◆

Not every spirit, or vision, or singing, is of God. The devil is an orator; he is powerful;

he took our Savior on to a pinnacle of the Temple, and kept Him in the wilderness for forty days. (TPJS, 162)[49]

◆◆◆

The devil can speak in tongues; the adversary will come with his work; he can tempt all classes; can speak in English or Dutch. (TPJS, 162)[49]

◆◆◆

The great principle of happiness consists in having a body. The devil has no body, and therein is his punishment. He is pleased when he can [temporarily] obtain the tabernacle of man, and [for example] when cast out by the Savior he asked to go into the herd of swine, showing that he would prefer a swine's body to having none. (TPJS, 181)[56]

◆◆◆

All beings who have bodies have power over those who have not. The devil has no power over us only as we permit him. The moment we revolt at anything which comes from God, the devil takes power. (TPJS, 181)[56]

◆◆◆

Satan was generally blamed for the evils which we did, but if he was the cause of all our wickedness, men could not be condemned. The devil could not compel mankind to do evil; all was voluntary. Those who resisted the Spirit of God, would be liable to be led into temptation, and then the association of heaven would be withdrawn from those who refused to be made partakers of such great glory. God would not exert any compulsory means, and the devil could not. (TPJS, 187)[60]

◆◆◆

All men have power to resist the devil. They who have tabernacles, have power over those who have not. (TPJS, 189)[61]

◆◆◆

If Satan could not speak in tongues, he could not tempt a Dutchman, or any other nation, but the English, for he can tempt the Englishman, for he has tempted me, and I am an Englishman. (TPJS, 195)[67]

♦♦♦

No man knows the things of God, but by the Spirit of God, so no man knows the spirit of the devil, and his power and influence, but by possessing intelligence which is more than human. (TPJS, 205)[71]

♦♦♦

The devil cannot come in the sign of a dove. (TPJS, 276)[93]

♦♦♦

Lucifer . . . sought for things which were unlawful. Hence he was sent down . . . and the greatness of his punishment is that he shall not have a tabernacle. . . . So the devil, thinking to thwart the decree of God, by going up and down in the earth, seeking whom he may destroy—any person . . . that will yield to him, he will bind him, and take possession of the body and reign there, glorying in it mightily, not caring that he had got merely a stolen body; and by and by someone having authority will come along and cast him out and restore the tabernacle to its rightful owner. (TPJS, 297)[103]

♦♦♦

The devil steals a tabernacle because he has not one of his own; but if he steals one, he is always liable to be turned out of doors. (TPJS, 298)[103]

♦♦♦

The devil's retaliation is, he comes into this world, bind's up men's bodies, and occupies them himself. When the authorities come along, they eject him from a stolen habitation. (TPJS, 306)[109]

♦♦♦

My only trouble at the present time is concerning ourselves, that the Saints *will be divided, broken up, and scattered,* before we get our salvation secure; for there are so many fools in the world for the devil to operate upon, it gives him the advantage oftentimes. (TPJS, 331)[123]

♦♦♦

In relation to the kingdom of God, the devil always sets up his kingdom at the very same time in opposition to God. (TPJS, 365)[132]

♦♦♦

Inasmuch as long-suffering, patience, and mercy have ever characterized the dealings of our heavenly Father towards the humble and penitent, I feel disposed to copy the example, cherish the same principles, and by so doing being a savior of my fellow men. (TPJS, 165)[53]

SCRIPTURAL GAPS AND ERRORS

(*See also* INTERPRETATION OF SCRIPTURE)

From sundry revelations which had been received, it was apparent that many important points touching the salvation of men, had been taken from the Bible, or lost before it was compiled. (TPJS, 9)[5]

♦♦♦

Does it remain for [man] to say how much God has spoken and how much He has not spoken? (TPJS, 61)[21]

♦♦♦

Much instruction has been given to man since the beginning which we do not possess now. . . . Some . . . are bold to say that we have everything written in the Bible which God ever spoke to man since the world began, and that if He had ever said anything more we should certainly have received it. (TPJS, 61)[21]

◆ ◆ ◆

Does it remain for a people who never had faith enough to call down one scrap of revelation from heaven, and for all they have now are indebted to the faith of another people who lived hundreds and thousands of years before them, does it remain for them to say how much God has spoken and how much He has not spoken? (TPJS, 61)[21]

◆ ◆ ◆

President Smith arose and [said] . . . that the passage in the third verse [of I Corinthians, 12] . . . should be translated "no man can know [not *say*] that Jesus is the Lord, but by the Holy Ghost." (TPJS, 223)[75]

◆ ◆ ◆

I am now going to take exceptions to the present translation of the Bible in relation to [certain] matters. Our latitude and longitude can be determined in the original Hebrew with far greater accuracy than in the English version. (TPJS, 290)[101]

◆ ◆ ◆

It is the constitutional disposition of mankind to set up stakes and bounds to the works and ways of the Almighty. (TPJS, 320)[118]

◆ ◆ ◆

I believe the Bible as it read when it came from the pen of the original writers. Ignorant translators, careless transcribers, or designing and corrupt priests have committed many errors. (TPJS, 327)[122]

SCRIPTURE

(*See also* INTERPRETATION OF SCRIPTURE)

Brother Joseph Smith, Jr. said . . . that the promise of God was that the greatest blessings which God had to bestow should be given to those who contributed to the support of his family while he was translating the fullness of the Scriptures. (TPJS, 9)[4]

◆ ◆ ◆

Search the scriptures—search the revelations which we publish, and ask your heavenly Father, in the name of His Son Jesus Christ, to manifest the truth unto you, and if you will do it with an eye single to His glory nothing doubting, He will answer you by the power of His Holy Spirit. You will then know for yourselves and not for another. You will not then be dependent of man for the knowledge of God; nor will there be any room for speculation. No; for when men receive their instruction from Him that made them, they know. (TPJS, 11)[7]

◆ ◆ ◆

We take the sacred writings into our hands, and admit that they were given by direct inspiration for the good of man. We believe that God condescended to speak from the heavens and declare His will concerning the human family, to give them just and holy laws, to regulate their conduct and guide them in a direct way, that in due time He might take them to Himself, and make them joint heirs with His Son. But when this fact is admitted, that the immediate will of heaven is contained in the Scriptures, are we not bound as rational creatures to live in accordance to all its precepts? Will the mere admission that this is the will of heaven ever benefit us if we do not comply with all its teachings? Do we not offer violence to the Supreme Intelligence of heaven, when we admit the truth of its teachings, and do not obey them? Do we not descend below our own knowledge, and the better wisdom which heaven has endowed us with, by such a course of conduct? (TPJS, 53)[21]

• • •

He that can mark the power of Omniscience, inscribed upon the heavens, can also see God's own handwriting in the sacred volume; and he who reads it oftenest will like it best, and he who is acquainted with it, will know the hand wherever he can see it. (TPJS, 56)[21]

• • •

Does it remain for [man] to say how much God has spoken and how much He has not spoken? (TPJS, 61)[21]

• • •

Much instruction has been given to man since the beginning which we do not possess now. . . . Some . . . are bold to say that we have everything written in the Bible which God ever spoke to man since the world began, and that if He had ever said anything more we should certainly have received it. (TPJS, 61)[21]

• • •

Does it remain for a people who never had faith enough to call down one scrap of revelation from heaven, and for all they have now are indebted to the faith of another people who lived hundreds and thousands of years before them, does it remain for them to say how much God has spoken and how much He has not spoken? (TPJS, 61)[21]

• • •

The word of the Lord is precious. (TPJS, 93)[35]

• • •

We have reason to be truly humble before the God of our fathers, that He hath left these things on record for us, so plain, that notwithstanding the exertions and combined influence of the priests of Baal, they have not power to blind our eyes, and darken our understanding, if we will but open our eyes, and read with candor, for a moment. (TPJS, 96)[34]

• • •

I have a key by which I understand the scriptures. . . . To ascertain meaning, we must dig up the root and ascertain what it was that drew the saying out of Jesus. (TPJS, 276)[93]

• • •

There is no salvation between the two lids of the Bible without a legal administrator. Jesus was then the legal administrator, and ordained His Apostles. (TPJS, 319)[117]

• • •

It is the constitutional disposition of mankind to set up stakes and bounds to the works and ways of the Almighty. (TPJS, 320)[118]

• • •

I know the Scriptures and understand them. (TPJS, 357)[130]

• • •

The Savior has the words of eternal life. Nothing else can profit us. (TPJS, 364)[132]

SEALING POWER

There is a way to release the spirits of the dead; that is by the power and authority of the Priesthood—by binding and loosing on earth. This doctrine appears glorious, inasmuch as it exhibits the greatness of divine compassion and benevolence in the extent of the plan of human salvation. (TPJS, 192)[63]

• • •

When a seal is put upon the father and mother, it secures their posterity, so that they cannot be lost, but will be saved by virtue of the covenant of their father and mother. (TPJS, 321)[118]

♦♦♦

The spirits of just men are made ministering servants to those who are sealed unto life eternal, and it is through them that the sealing power comes down. (TPJS, 325)[121]

♦♦♦

To seal those who dwell on earth to those who dwell in heaven. This is the power of Elijah and the keys of the kingdom of Jehovah. (TPJS, 338)[128]

SEARCHING

(*See* TRUTH SEEKING, AND OPEN-MINDEDNESS)

SECOND COMFORTER

(*See also* MORE SURE WORD OF PROPHECY)

After a person . . . receives the Holy Ghost . . . which is the first Comforter, then let him continue to humble himself before God, hungering and thirsting after righteousness, and living by every word of God, and the Lord will soon say unto him, Son, thou shalt be exalted. When the Lord has thoroughly proved him, and finds that the man is determined to serve Him at all hazards, then the man will find his calling and his election made sure, . . . then it will be his privilege to receive the other Comforter, which the Lord promised the Saints. . . . Now what is this other Comforter? It is no more nor less than the Lord Jesus Christ Himself; . . . when any man obtains this last Comforter, he will have the personage of Jesus Christ to attend him . . . from time to time, and even He will manifest the Father unto him, and they will take up their abode with him, and the Lord will teach him face to face, and he may have a perfect knowledge of the mysteries of the Kingdom of God. (TPJS, 149)[48]

SECOND COMING

The signs of the coming of the Son of Man are already commenced. (TPJS, 160)[49]

♦♦♦

The Lord cannot always be known by the thunder of His voice, by the display of His glory or by the manifestation of His power, and those that are the most anxious to see these things, are the least prepared to meet them. (TPJS, 247)[80]

♦♦♦

The Lord will not come to reign over the righteous, in this world, in 1843, nor until everything for the Bridegroom is ready. (TPJS, 280)[96]

♦♦♦

The coming of the Son of Man never will be—never can be till the judgments spoken of for this hour are poured out: which judgments are commenced. Paul says, "Ye are children [so much] of the light, and not of the darkness, that that day should overtake you as a thief in the night." It is not the design of the Almighty to come upon the earth and crush it and grind it to powder, but He will reveal it to his servants the prophets. (TPJS, 286)[99]

♦♦♦

Jesus Christ never did reveal to any man the precise time that He would come. . . and all that say so are false teachers. (TPJS, 341)[128]

SECTARIAN WORLD

The light of the latter-day glory begins to break forth through the dark atmosphere of sectarian wickedness, and their iniquity begins to roll up into view, and the nations of the Gentiles are like the waves of the sea, casting up mire and dirt, or all in commotion, and they are hastily preparing to act the part allotted them, when the Lord rebukes the nations, when He shall rule them with a rod of iron, and break them in pieces like a potter's vessel. (TPJS, 16)[9]

•••

It is very difficult for us to communicate to the churches all that God has revealed to us, in consequence of tradition; for we are differently situated from any other people that ever existed upon this earth. (TPJS, 70)[23]

•••

The Elders . . . are combating the prejudices of a crooked and perverse generation, by having in their possession . . . religious principles, which are misrepresented by almost all those whose crafts are in danger by the same. (TPJS, 83)[31]

•••

Such is the darkness and ignorance of this generation, that they look upon it as incredible that a man should have any intercourse with his Maker. (TPJS, 89)[32]

•••

Men are in the habit, when the truth is exhibited by the servants of God, of saying, All is mystery; they have spoken in parables, and therefore, are not to be understood. It is true they have eyes to see, and see not, but none are so blind as those who will not see. (TPJS, 96)[34]

•••

There are many yet on the earth among all sects, parties, denominations, who are blinded by the subtle craftiness of men,

whereby they lie in wait to deceive, and who are only kept from the truth because they know not where to find it. (TPJS, 145)[47]

•••

Be aware of those prejudices which sometimes so strangely present themselves, and are so congenial to human nature, against our friend, neighbors, and brethren of the world, who choose to differ from us in opinion and in matters of faith. Our religion is between us and our God. Their religion is between them and their God. (TPJS, 146)[47]

•••

There is a love from God that should be exercised toward those of our faith, who walk uprightly, which is peculiar to itself; but it is without prejudice; it also gives scope to the mind, which enables us to conduct ourselves with greater liberality towards all that are not of our faith, than what they exercise towards one another. These principles approximate nearer to the mind of God, because it is like God, or Godlike. (TPJS, 147)[47]

•••

Men of the present time testify of heaven and hell, and have never seen either; and I will say that no man knows these things without this [testimony]. (TPJS, 160)[49]

•••

Unless some person or persons have a communication, or revelation from God, unfolding to them the operation of the spirit, they must eternally remain ignorant of these principles; for if one man cannot understand these things but by the Spirit of God, ten thousand men cannot; it is alike out of the reach of the wisdom of the learned, the tongue of the eloquent, [or] the power of the mighty. And we shall at last have to come to this conclusion, whatever we may think of revelation, that without it, we can neither know nor understand anything of God, or of the devil; and however unwilling the world may be to acknowledge this principle, it is evident from the multifarious creeds . . . that they understand nothing of this principle, and it is as equally as plain that without a divine communication they must remain in ignorance. (TPJS, 205)[71]

◆ ◆ ◆

The world has always mistook false prophets for true ones, and those that were sent of God, they considered to be false prophets, and hence they killed, stoned, punished and imprisoned the true prophets . . . and though the most honorable men of the earth, they banished them from their society as vagabonds, whilst they cherished, honored and supported knaves, vagabonds, hypocrites, imposters, and the basest of men. (TPJS, 206)[71]

◆ ◆ ◆

God never had any prophets that acted in this way [strange fits, trembling, fainting, swooning or in trances]; there was nothing indecorous in the proceedings of the Lord's prophets in any age; neither had the apostles nor prophets in the apostles' day anything of this kind. . . . Paul says, "Let everything be done decently and in order," but here we find the greatest disorder and indecency in the conduct of both men and women. The same would apply to . . . many of our modern revivalists. (TPJS, 209)[71]

◆ ◆ ◆

If any revelations are given of God, they are universally opposed by the priests and Christendom at large; for they reveal their wickedness and abominations. (TPJS, 217)[73]

◆ ◆ ◆

The great designs of God in relation to the salvation of the human family, are very little understood by the professedly wise and intelligent generation in which we live. (TPJS, 217)[74]

◆ ◆ ◆

Various and conflicting are the opinions of men concerning the Plan of Salvation, the requisitions of the Almighty, the necessary preparations for heaven, the state and condition of departed spirits, and the happiness or misery that is consequent upon the practice of righteousness or iniquity according to several notions of virtue and vice. [And one sect tends to condemn the other sect.] (TPJS, 217)[74]

◆ ◆ ◆

All the religious world is boasting of righteousness; it is the doctrine of the devil to retard the human mind, and hinder our progress, by filling us with self-righteousness. (TPJS, 241)[79]

◆ ◆ ◆

Various and conflicting are the opinions of men in regard to the gift of the Holy Ghost. . . . It is not to be wondered at that men should be ignorant . . . of the nature . . . of the Holy Ghost, when we consider that the human family have been enveloped in gross darkness and ignorance for many centuries past, without revelation. (TPJS, 242)[80]

◆ ◆ ◆

We believe in [the gift of the Holy Ghost] in all its fullness, and power, and greatness, and glory; but whilst we do this, we believe in it rationally, consistently, and scripturally, and not according to the wild vagaries, foolish notions and traditions of men. (TPJS, 243)[80]

◆ ◆ ◆

Any man who says he is a teacher or a preacher of righteousness, and denies the spirit of prophecy, is a liar, and the truth is not in him; and by this key false teachers and imposters may be detected. (TPJS, 269)[89]

•••

Faith has been wanting, not only among the heathen, but in professed Christendom, also, so that . . . all the gifts and blessings have been wanting. (TPJS, 270)[90]

•••

The plea of many in this day is, that we have no right to receive revelations; but if we do not get revelations, we do not have the oracles of God; and if they have not the oracles of God, they are not the people of God. But say you, What will become of the world, or the various professors of religion who do not believe in revelation and the oracles of God as continued to his Church in all ages of the world, when He has a people on earth? I tell you, in the name of Jesus Christ, they will be damned [or held back]; and when you get into the eternal world, you will find it will be so, they cannot escape the damnation of hell. (TPJS, 272)[91]

•••

We don't ask any people to throw away any good they have got; we only ask them to come and get more. (TPJS, 275)[91]

•••

With all their boasted religion, piety and sacredness [Christian religions] at the same time . . . are crying out against prophets, apostles, angels, revelations, prophesying and visions, etc. Why, they are just ripening for the damnation of hell. . . . For they reject the most glorious principle of the Gospel of Jesus Christ and treat with disdain and trample under foot the key that unlocks the heavens and puts in our possession the glories of the celestial world. (TPJS, 298)[103]

•••

I hope sober-thinking and sound-reasoning people will sooner listen to the voice of truth, than be led astray by the vain pretensions of the self-wise. (TPJS, 299)[104]

•••

Paul said, "the world by wisdom know not God," so the world by speculation are destitute of revelation. (TPJS, 300)[104]

•••

If a man gets a fullness of the priesthood, there is no change of ordinances, says Paul. If God has not changed the ordinances and the priesthood, howl, ye sectarians! If he has, when and where has he revealed it? Have ye turned revelators? Then why deny revelation? (TPJS, 308)[113]

•••

Many things are insoluble to the children of men in the last days; for instance, that God should raise the dead, and forgetting that things have been hid from before the foundation of the world, which are to be revealed to babes in the last days. (TPJS, 309)[113]

•••

A man of God should be endowed with wisdom, knowledge, and understanding, in order to teach and lead the people of God. The sectarian priests are blind, and they lead the blind, and they will all fall into the ditch together. They build with hay, wood, and stubble, on the old revelations. (TPJS, 311)[113]

•••

If a skillful mechanic . . . succeeds in welding together iron or steel more perfectly than any other mechanic, is he not deserving of praise? And if by the principles of truth I succeed in uniting men of all denominations in the bonds of love, shall I not have attained a good object? (TPJS, 313)[114]

♦♦♦

Sectarian priests cry out concerning me, and ask, "Why is it this babbler gains so many followers, and retains them?" I answer, It is because I possess the principle of love. All I can offer the world is a good heart and a good hand. (TPJS, 313)[114]

♦♦♦

Christians should cease wrangling and contending with each other, and cultivate the principles of union and friendship in their midst . . . before the millennium can be ushered in and Christ takes possession of His kingdom. (TPJS, 314)[114]

♦♦♦

[There are] nonsensical teachings of hireling priests, whose object and aim were to keep the people in ignorance for the sake of filthy lucre; or as the prophet says, to feed themselves, not the flock. (TPJS, 315)[114]

♦♦♦

I do not grudge the world all the religion they have got; they are welcome to all the knowledge they possess. (TPJS, 320)[118]

♦♦♦

It is the constitutional disposition of mankind to set up stakes and bounds to the works and ways of the Almighty. (TPJS, 320)[118]

♦♦♦

I cannot believe in any of the creeds of the different denominations, because they all have some things in them I cannot subscribe to, though all of them have some truth. I want to come up into the presence of God and learn all things; but the creeds set up stakes, and say, "Hitherto shalt thou come, and no further"; which I cannot subscribe to. (TPJS, 327)[122]

♦♦♦

It is good economy to entertain strangers—to entertain sectarians. Come up to Nauvoo, ye sectarian priests of the everlasting Gospel, as they call it, and you shall have my pulpit all day. (TPJS, 329)[122]

♦♦♦

One truth revealed from heaven is worth all the sectarian notions in existence. (TPJS, 338)[128]

♦♦♦

There are but a very few beings in the world who understand rightly the character of God. The great majority of mankind do not comprehend anything, either that which is past, or that which is to come, as it respects their relationship to God . . . and consequently they know but little above the brute beast, or more than to eat, drink and sleep . . . unless it is given by the inspiration of the Almighty. (TPJS, 343)[130]

♦♦♦

Meddle not with any man for his religion; and all governments ought to permit every man to enjoy his religion unmolested. No man is authorized to take away life in consequence of difference in religion, which all laws and governments ought to tolerate and protect, right or wrong. (TPJS, 344)[130]

♦♦♦

I suppose I am not allowed to go into an investigation of anything that is not contained in the Bible. If I do, I think there are so many ever-wise men here, that they would cry, "treason" and put me to death. So I will go to the old Bible and turn commentator today. (TPJS, 348)[130]

♦♦♦

Now, I ask all who hear me, why the learned men who are preaching salvation, say that God created the heavens and the earth out of nothing? The reason is, that they are unlearned in the things of God, and have not the gift of the Holy Ghost; they account it blasphemy in any one to contradict their idea. If you tell them that God made the world out of something, they will call you a fool. But I am learned, and know more than all the world put together. The Holy Ghost does, anyhow, and He is within me, and comprehends more than all the world; and I will associate myself with Him. (TPJS, 350)[130]

◆◆◆

Hear it, all ye ends of the earth—all ye priests, all ye sinners, and all men. Repent! Repent! Obey the Gospel. Turn to God; for your religion won't save you, and you will be damned. I do not say how long. (TPJS, 361)[130]

◆◆◆

It is in the order of heavenly things that God should always send a new dispensation into the world when men have apostatized from the truth and lost the priesthood, but when men come out and build upon other men's foundations, they do it on their own responsibility, without authority from God; and when the floods come and the winds blow, their foundations will be found to be sand, and their whole fabric will crumble to dust. (TPJS, 375)[133]

◆◆◆

The character of the old churches have always been slandered by all apostates since the world began. (TPJS, 375)[133]

◆◆◆

Oh, Thou God who art King of kings and Lord of lords, the sectarian world, by their actions, declare, "We cannot believe Thee." (TPJS, 375)[133]

◆◆◆

All men are liars who say they are of the true Church without the revelations of Jesus Christ and the Priesthood of Melchizedek, which is after the order of the Son of God. (TPJS, 375)[133]

◆◆◆

Did I build on any other man's foundation? I have got all the truth which the Christian world possessed, and an independent revelation in the bargain, and God will bear me off triumphant. (TPJS, 376)[133]

SELF-CENTEREDNESS

(See also ARROGANCE; PRIDE)

All men are naturally disposed to walk in their own paths as they are pointed out by their own fingers, and we are not willing to consider and walk in the path which is pointed out by another, saying, This is the way, walk ye in it, although he should be an unerring director, and the Lord his God sent him. (TPJS, 26)[15]

◆◆◆

Now, in this world, mankind are naturally selfish, ambitious and striving to excel one above another; yet some are willing to build up others as well as themselves. (TPJS, 297)[103]

◆◆◆

Woe to ye rich men, who refuse to give to the poor, and then come and ask me for bread. Away with all your meanness, and be liberal. We need purging, purifying and cleansing. (TPJS, 329)[122]

SELF-DECEPTION

Be aware of those prejudices which sometimes so strangely present themselves, and are so congenial to human nature, against our friend, neighbors, and brethren of the world, who choose to differ from us in opinion and in matters of faith. Our religion is between us and our God. Their religion is between them and their God. (TPJS, 146)[47]

SELF-EXAMINATION

The Lord says that every man is to receive according to his works. Reflect for a moment, . . . and enquire whether you would consider yourselves worthy a seat at the marriage seat with Paul and others like him, if you had been unfaithful? Had you not fought the good fight, and kept the faith, could you expect to receive? (TPJS, 64)[21]

◆◆◆

Search your hearts, and see if you are like God. I have searched mine, and feel to repent of all my sins. (TPJS, 216)[73]

SELF-JUSTIFICATION

Mankind will persist in self-justification until all their iniquity is exposed, and their character past being redeemed, and that which is treasured up in their hearts be exposed to the gaze of mankind. (TPJS, 18)[10]

SELF-RIGHTEOUSNESS

Let not any man publish his own righteousness, for others can see that for him; sooner let him confess his sins, and then he will be forgiven, and he will bring forth more fruit. (TPJS, 194)[66]

◆◆◆

The great designs of God in relation to the salvation of the human family, are very little understood by the professedly wise and intelligent generation in which we live. (TPJS, 217)[74]

◆◆◆

Beware of self-righteousness, and be limited in the estimate of your own virtues, and not think yourself more righteous than others. (TPJS, 228)[75]

◆◆◆

Sisters of the society, shall there be strife among you? I will not have it. You must repent, and get the love of God. Away with self-righteousness! (TPJS, 241)[79]

◆◆◆

All the religious world is boasting of righteousness; it is the doctrine of the devil to retard the human mind, and hinder our progress, by filling us with self-righteousness. (TPJS, 241)[79]

◆◆◆

We are full of selfishness; the devil flatters us that we are very righteous, when [in fact] we are feeding on the faults of others. (TPJS, 241)[79]

◆◆◆

If we get puffed up by thinking that we have much knowledge, we are apt to get a contentious spirit, and correct knowledge is necessary to cast out that spirit. (TPJS, 287)[101]

◆◆◆

The evil of being puffed up with correct [though useless] knowledge is not so great as the evil of contention. (TPJS, 287)[101]

◆◆◆

Paul said, "the world by wisdom know not God," so the world by speculation are destitute of revelation. (TPJS, 300)[104]

SELFISHNESS

Selfishness and independence of mind . . . too often manifested [in a leader] destroy the confidence of those who would [otherwise] lay down their lives for him. (TPJS, 30)[17]

• • •

I have learned in my travels that man is treacherous and selfish, but few excepted. (TPJS, 30)[17]

• • •

If there are any among you who aspire after their own aggrandizement, and seek their own opulence, while their brethren are groaning in poverty, and are under sore trials and temptations, they cannot be benefited by the intercession of the Holy Spirit. (TPJS, 141)[47]

• • •

Let every selfish feeling be not only buried, but annihilated; and let love to God and man predominate, and reign triumphant in every mind, that their hearts may become like unto Enoch's of old, and comprehend all things. (TPJS, 178)[55]

• • •

We are full of selfishness; the devil flatters us that we are very righteous, when [in fact] we are feeding on the faults of others. (TPJS, 241)[79]

• • •

It is an insult to a meeting for persons to leave just before its close. If they must go out, let them go half an hour before. No gentlemen will go out of a meeting just at closing. (TPJS, 287)[100]

• • •

As president of this house, I forbid any man leaving just as we are going to close the meeting. He is no gentleman who will do it. I don't care who does it, even if it were the king of England. I forbid it. (TPJS, 296)[102]

• • •

Now, in this world, mankind are naturally selfish, ambitious and striving to excel one above another; yet some

are willing to build up others as well as themselves. (TPJS, 297)[103]

• • •

Men often come to me with their troubles, and seek my will, crying, Oh, Brother Joseph, help me! Help me! But when I am in trouble few of them sympathize with me or extend to me relief. (TPJS, 315)[115]

• • •

Woe to ye rich men, who refuse to give to the poor, and then come and ask me for bread. Away with all your meanness, and be liberal. We need purging, purifying and cleansing. (TPJS, 329)[122]

SELFLESSNESS

Be careful of one another's feelings, and walk in love, honoring one another more than themselves, as is required by the Lord. (TPJS, 25)[13]

• • •

A man filled with the love of God, is not content with blessing his family alone, but ranges through the whole world, anxious to bless the whole human race. This has been your feeling, and caused you to forego the pleasures of home, that you might be a blessing to others, who are candidates for immortality, but strangers to truth; and for so doing, I pray that heaven's choicest blessings may rest upon you. (TPJS, 174)[55]

• • •

Let every selfish feeling be not only buried, but annihilated; and let love to God and man predominate, and reign triumphant in every mind, that their hearts may become like unto Enoch's of old, and comprehend all things. (TPJS, 178)[55]

• • •

Let us realize that we are not to live to ourselves, but to God; by so doing the greatest blessings will rest upon us both in time and in eternity. (TPJS, 179)[55]

◆◆◆

Let not any man publish his own righteousness, for others can see that for [themselves]; sooner let him confess his sins, and then he will be forgiven, and he will bring forth more fruit. (TPJS, 194)[66]

SENIORS

(See also OLD AGE)

The way to get along in any important matter is to gather unto yourselves wise men, experienced and aged men, to assist in council in all times of trouble. (TPJS, 299)[103]

SENSITIVITY

(See also TENDERNESS;
THOUGHTFULNESS)

Be careful of one another's feelings, and walk in love, honoring one another more than themselves, as is required by the Lord. (TPJS, 25)[13]

◆◆◆

Let the Elders be exceedingly careful about unnecessarily disturbing and harrowing up the feelings of the people. (TPJS, 43)[20]

◆◆◆

[Mormons] believe that if their companion dies, they have a right to marry again. But we do disapprove of the custom . . . in marrying in five or six weeks, or even in two or three months, after the death of their companion. We believe that due respect ought to be had to the memory of the dead, and the feelings of both friends and children. (TPJS, 119)[45]

◆◆◆

Our circumstances are calculated to awaken our spirits to a sacred remembrance of everything. (TPJS, 130)[47]

◆◆◆

Let [the Relief] Society teach women how to behave towards their husbands, to treat them with mildness and affection. (TPJS, 228)[75]

◆◆◆

As females possess refined feelings and sensitiveness, they are also subject to overmuch zeal, which must ever prove dangerous, and cause them to be rigid in a religious capacity—[they] should be armed with mercy, notwithstanding the iniquity among us. (TPJS, 238)[78]

◆◆◆

Search yourselves—the tongue is an unruly member—hold your tongues about things of no moment—a little tale will set the world on fire. At [certain] time[s] the truth on the guilty should not be told openly. . . . We must use precaution in bringing sinners to justice, lest . . . we draw the indignation of a Gentile world upon us. (TPJS, 239)[78]

◆◆◆

The Lord deals with this people as a tender parent with a child, communicating light and intelligence and the knowledge of His ways as they can bear it. (TPJS, 305)[109]

◆◆◆

Never exact of a friend in adversity what you would require in prosperity. (TPJS, 317)[116]

◆◆◆

I love you all; but I hate some of your deeds. I am your best friend, and if persons miss their mark it is their own fault. If I reprove a man, and he hates me, he is a fool; for I love all men, especially these my brethren and sisters. (TPJS, 361)[130]

SERVICE

Now for a man to consecrate his property, wife and children, to the Lord, is nothing more nor less than to feed the hungry, clothe the naked, visit the widow and fatherless, the sick and afflicted, and do all he can to administer to their relief in their afflictions, and for him and his house to serve the Lord. In order to do this, he and all his house must be virtuous, and must shun the very appearance of evil. (TPJS, 127)[46]

• • •

A man filled with the love of God, is not content with blessing his family alone, but ranges through the whole world, anxious to bless the whole human race. (TPJS, 174)[55]

• • •

It is the will of God that man should repent and serve Him in health, and blessing and power of his mind, in order to secure his blessing, and not wait until he is called to die. (TPJS, 197)[68]

• • •

The best measure or principle to bring the poor to repentance is to administer to their wants. (TPJS, 241)[79]

• • •

Now, in this world, mankind are naturally selfish, ambitious and striving to excel one above another; yet some are willing to build up others as well as themselves. (TPJS, 297)[103]

• • •

The best men bring forth the best works. The man who tells you words of life is the man who can save you. (TPJS, 358)[130]

• • •

If my life is of no value to my friends it is of none to myself. (TPJS, 377)[136]

• • •

SEVENTIES

The Twelve and the Seventy have particularly to depend upon their ministry for their support, and that of their families; and they have a right by virtue of their offices, to call upon the churches to assist them. (TPJS, 75)[28]

• • •

The duties of the Seventies are more particularly to preach the gospel, and build up churches, rather than regulate them, that a High Priest may take charge of them. (TPJS, 164)[51]

SIGN SEEKING

When a man designedly provokes a serpent to bite him, the principle is the same as when a man drinks deadly poison knowing it to be such. In that case no man has any claim on the promises of God to be healed. (TPJS, 72)[25]

• • •

Whenever you see a man seeking after a sign, you may set it down that he is an adulterous man. (TPJS, 157)[49]

SIGNS

The signs of the coming of the Son of Man are already commenced. (TPJS, 160)[49]

• • •

No matter who believeth, these signs, such as healing the sick, casting out devils, etc., should follow all that believe, whether male or female. (TPJS, 224)[75]

•••

The Lord cannot always be known by the thunder of His voice, by the display of His glory, or by the manifestation of His power, and those that are the most anxious to see these things, are the least prepared to meet them. (TPJS, 247)[80]

•••

The devil cannot come in the sign of a dove. (TPJS, 276)[93]

SIMPLICITY

(*See also* CLARITY)

We have reason to be truly humble before the God of our fathers, that He hath left these things on record for us, so plain . . . if we will but open our eyes, and read with candor, for a moment. (TPJS, 96)[34]

•••

It will be well to study plainness and simplicity in whatever you publish, "for my soul delighteth in plainness." (TPJS, 164)[51]

•••

Declare the first principles, and let the mysteries alone, lest ye be overthrown. (TPJS, 292)[101]

•••

The world is full of technicalities and misrepresentation, which I calculate to overthrow, and speak of things as they actually exist. (TPJS, 292)[101]

•••

I will make every doctrine plain that I present, and it shall stand upon a firm basis, and I am at the defiance of the world, for I will take shelter under the broad cover

of the wings of the work in which I am engaged. (TPJS, 339)[128]

•••

I do not intend to please your ears with superfluity of words or oratory, or with much learning; but I intend to edify you with the simple truths from heaven. (TPJS, 342)[130]

SIN

All other sins are not to be compared to sinning against the Holy Ghost, and proving a traitor to the brethren. (TPJS, 156)[49]

•••

All beings who have bodies have power over those who have not. The devil has no power over us only as we permit him. The moment we revolt at anything which comes from God, the devil takes power. (TPJS, 181)[56]

•••

[God] passes over no man's sins, but visits them with correction, and if His children will not repent of their sins He will discard them. (TPJS, 189)[60]

•••

What many people call sin is not sin. (TPJS, 193)[64]

•••

God does not look on sin with allowance, but when men have sinned, there must be allowance made for them. (TPJS, 240)[79]

•••

If there was sin among men, repentance was as necessary at one time or age of the world as another. (TPJS, 265)[85]

•••

The unpardonable sin is to shed innocent blood, or be accessory thereto. All other sins will be visited with judgment in the flesh, and the spirit being delivered to the buffetings of Satan until the day of the Lord Jesus. (TPJS, 301)[105]

• • •

If a man has knowledge, he can be saved; although, if he has been guilty of great sins, he will be punished for them. But when he consents to obey the Gospel, whether here or in the world of spirits, he is saved. . . . All will suffer until they obey Christ himself. (TPJS, 357)[130]

SINCERITY

None but fools will trifle with the souls of men. (TPJS, 137)[47]

• • •

Your humble servant or servants, intend from henceforth to [morally disapprove] everything that is not in accordance with the fullness of the Gospel of Jesus Christ, and is not of a bold, and frank, and upright nature. (TPJS, 146)[47]

• • •

Repentance is a thing that cannot be trifled with every day. Daily transgression and daily repentance is not that which is pleasing in the sight of God. (TPJS, 148)[48]

• • •

Be honest, open, and frank in all your intercourse with mankind. (TPJS, 156)[49]

• • •

I hope sober-thinking and sound-reasoning people will sooner listen to the voice of truth, than be led astray by the vain pretensions of the self-wise. (TPJS, 299)[104]

SLANDER

Mr. Stollars stated that James Mullone, of Springfield, told him as follows: . . . "I

have been to Nauvoo, and seen Joe Smith, the Prophet: he had a gray horse, and I asked him where he got it"; and Joe said, "You see that white cloud." "Yes." "Well, as it came along, I got the horse from that cloud." This is a fair specimen of the ten thousand foolish lies circulated by this generation to bring the truth and its advocates into disrepute. (TPJS, 270)[90]

• • •

The character of the old churches have always been slandered by all apostates since the world began. (TPJS, 375)[133]

SOLEMNITY

(See also PONDERING)

The things of God are of deep import; and time, and experience, and careful and ponderous and solemn thoughts can only find them out. Thy mind, O man! If thou will lead a soul unto salvation, must stretch as high as the utmost heavens, and search into and contemplate the darkest abyss and the broad expanse of eternity. (TPJS, 137)[47]

SONS OF PERDITION

(See also UNPARDONABLE SIN)

If men have received the good word of God, and tasted of the powers of the world to come, if they shall fall away, it is impossible to renew them again, seeing they have crucified the Son of God afresh, and put Him to an open shame. (TPJS, 339)[128]

• • •

When a man begins to be an enemy to this work, he hunts me, he seeks to kill me, and never ceases to thirst for my blood. He gets the spirit of the devil—the same spirit that they had who crucified the Lord of Life—the same spirit that sins against the

Holy Ghost. You cannot save such persons; you cannot bring them to repentance; they make open war, like the devil, and awful is the consequence. (TPJS, 358)[130]

SOULS

Souls are as precious in the sight of God as they ever were; and the Elders were never called to drive any down to hell, but to persuade and invite all men everywhere to repent, that they may become the heirs of salvation. (TPJS, 77)[29]

•••

None but fools will trifle with the souls of men. (TPJS, 137)[47]

•••

The elements are eternal. That which has a beginning will surely have an end. . . . If the soul of man had a beginning it will surely have an end . . . the word created should be formed, or organized. . . , "The first step in salvation of man is the laws of eternal and self-existent principles. Spirits are eternal. At the first organization in heaven we were all present, and saw the Savior chosen and appointed and the Plan of Salvation made, and we sanctioned it." (TPJS, 181)[56]

•••

Without attempting to describe this mysterious connection, and the laws that govern the body and the spirit of man, their relationship to each other, and the design of God in relation to the human body and spirit, I would just remark, that the spirits of men are eternal, that they are governed by the same Priesthood that Abraham, Melchizedek, and the Apostles were: that they are organized according to that Priesthood which is everlasting, "without beginning of days or end of years,"—that they all move in their respective spheres, and are governed by the law of God; that when they appear upon the earth they are in a probationary state, and are preparing, if righteous, for a future and greater glory. (TPJS, 208)[71]

•••

The Ladies' Relief Society is not only to relieve the poor, but to save souls. (TPJS, 242)[78]

•••

Another subject . . . calculated to exalt man. . . . I shall therefore just touch upon . . . is associated with the subject of the resurrection of the dead . . . namely, the soul—the mind of man—the immortal spirit. Where did it come from? All learned men and doctors of divinity say that God created it in the beginning; But it is not so: . . . . Hear it, all ye ends of the world; for God has told me so; . . . I am going to tell of things more noble.

We say that God himself is a self-existent being. Who told you so? It is correct enough; but how did it get into your heads? Who told you that man did not exist in like manner upon the same principles? Man does exist upon the same principles. God made a tabernacle and put a spirit into it, and it became a living soul. . . . It does not say in the Hebrew [Bible] that God created the spirit of man. It says "God made man out of the earth and put into him Adam's spirit, and so became a living body." (TPJS, 352)[130]

SPEAKING IN TONGUES

(*See also* GIFT OF TONGUES)

Any man that has the Holy Ghost, can speak of the things of God in his own tongue as well as to speak in another. (TPJS, 149)[48]

•••

Let no one speak in tongues unless he interpret, except by the consent of the one who is placed to preside. (TPJS, 162)[49]

❖❖❖

The devil can speak in tongues; the adversary will come with his work; he can tempt all classes; can speak in English or Dutch. (TPJS, 162)[49]

❖❖❖

It may be asked, how it was that [certain persons] could speak in tongues if they were of the devil. We would answer that they could be made to speak in another tongue, as well as their own, as they were under the control of that [particular] spirit, and the devil can tempt . . . the Turk, the Jew, or any other nation; and if these men were under the influence of his spirit, they of course could speak Hebrew, Latin, Greek, Italian, Dutch, or any other language that the devil knew. (TPJS, 212)[71]

SPIRIT

The spirit of man is not a created being; it existed from eternity and will exist to eternity. Anything created cannot be eternal; and earth, water, etc., had their existence in an elementary state, from eternity. . . . The Father called all spirits before Him at the creation of man, and organized them. (TPJS, 158)[49]

❖❖❖

There is no such thing as immaterial matter. All spirit is matter, but is more fine or pure, and can only be discerned by purer eyes. We cannot see it, but when our bodies are purified, we shall see that it is all matter. (TPJS, 301)[107]

SPIRIT OF GOD

By learning the Spirit of God and understanding it, you may grow into the principle of revelation, until you become perfect in Christ Jesus. (TPJS, 151)[48]

❖❖❖

Unless some person or persons have a communication, or revelation from God, unfolding to them the operation of the spirit, they must eternally remain ignorant of these principles; for if one man cannot understand these things but by the Spirit of God, ten thousand men cannot; it is alike out of the reach of the wisdom of the learned, the tongue of the eloquent, [or] the power of the mighty. And we shall at last have to come to this conclusion, whatever we may think of revelation, that without it, we can neither know nor understand anything of God, or of the devil; and however unwilling the world may be to acknowledge this principle, it is evident from the multifarious creeds . . . that they understand nothing of this principle, and it is as equally as plain that without a divine communication they must remain in ignorance. (TPJS, 205)[71]

❖❖❖

No man knows the things of God, but by the Spirit of God, so no man knows the spirit of the devil, and his power and influence, but by possessing intelligence which is more than human. (TPJS, 205)[71]

SPIRIT WORLD

Blessed are the dead who die in the Lord, for they rest from their labors and their works do follow them. (TPJS, 200)[68]

❖❖❖

[From the Greek translation, Jesus states] "This day thou shalt be with me in the world of spirits." (TPJS, 309)[113]

❖❖❖

The righteous and the wicked all go to the same world of spirits until the resurrection. The great misery of departed spirits in the world of spirits, where they go after death, is to know that they come short of the glory that others enjoy and that they might have enjoyed themselves, and they are their own accusers. (TPJS, 310)[113]

◆◆◆

When men are prepared, they are better off to go hence. The spirits of the just are exalted to a greater and more glorious work; hence they are blessed in their departure to the world of spirits. Enveloped in flaming fire, they are not far from us, and know and understand our thoughts, and emotions, and are often pained therewith. (TPJS, 326)[121]

◆◆◆

The mind or the intelligence which man possesses is co-[eternal] with God himself. . . . When I talk to . . . mourners, what have they lost? Their relatives and friends are only separated from their bodies for a short season: their spirits which existed with God have left the tabernacle of clay only for a little moment, as it were; and they now exist in a place where they converse together the same as we do on the earth. (TPJS, 353)[130]

◆◆◆

All spirits who have not obeyed the Gospel in the flesh must either obey it in the spirit or be damned. (TPJS, 355)[130]

◆◆◆

When we depart, we shall hail our mothers, fathers, friends, and all whom we love, who have fallen asleep in Jesus. There will be no fear of mobs, persecutions, or malicious lawsuits and arrests; but it will be an eternity of felicity. (TPJS, 360)[130]

SPIRITS

(*See also* CO-ETERNAL BEINGS)

The spirit of man is not a created being; it existed from eternity and will exist to eternity. Anything created cannot be eternal; and earth, water, etc., had their existence in an elementary state, from

eternity. . . . The Father called all spirits before Him at the creation of man, and organized them. (TPJS, 158)[49]

◆◆◆

The elements are eternal. That which has a beginning will surely have an end. . . . If the soul of man had a beginning it will surely have an end . . . the word created should be formed, or organized. . . , "The first step in salvation of man is the laws of eternal and self-existent principles. Spirits are eternal. At the first organization in heaven we were all present, and saw the Savior chosen and appointed and the plan of Salvation made, and we sanctioned it." (TPJS, 181)[56]

◆◆◆

Jesus Christ became a ministering spirit [while His body was lying in the sepulcher] to the spirits in prison, to fulfill an important part of His mission, without which He could not have perfected His work, or entered into His rest. After His resurrection He appeared as an angel to His disciples. (TPJS, 191)[63]

◆◆◆

The spirit is a substance; . . . it is material, but . . . it is more pure, elastic and refined matter than the body; . . . it existed before the body, can exist in the body; and will exist separate from the body, when the body will be mouldering in the dust; and will in the resurrection, be again united with it. (TPJS, 207)[71]

◆◆◆

Without attempting to describe this mysterious connection, and the laws that govern the body and the spirit of man, their relationship to each other, and the design of God in relation to the human body and spirit, I would just remark, that the spirits of men are eternal, that they are governed by the same Priesthood that Abraham,

Melchizedek, and the Apostles were: that they are organized according to that Priesthood which is everlasting, "without beginning of days or end of years,"—that they all move in their respective spheres, and are governed by the law of God; that when they appear upon the earth they are in a probationary state, and are preparing, if righteous, for a future and greater glory. (TPJS, 208)[71]

◆◆◆

Spirits can only be revealed in flaming fire and glory. Angels have advanced further, their light and glory being tabernacled; and hence they appear in bodily shape. (TPJS, 325)[121]

◆◆◆

The spirits of just men are made ministering servants to those who are sealed unto life eternal, and it is through them that the sealing power comes down. (TPJS, 325)[121]

◆◆◆

When men are prepared, they are better off to go hence. . . . The spirits of the just are exalted to a greater and more glorious work; hence they are blessed in their departure to the world of spirits. Enveloped in flaming fire, they are not far from us, and know and understand our thoughts, and emotions, and are often pained therewith. (TPJS, 326)[121]

◆◆◆

Another subject . . . calculated to exalt man. . . . I shall therefore just touch upon . . . is associated with the subject of the resurrection of the dead—namely, the soul—the mind of man—the immortal spirit. Where did it come from? All learned men and doctors of divinity say that God created it in the beginning; But it is not so: . . . . Hear it, all ye ends of the world; for God has told me so; . . . I am going to tell

of things more noble.

We say that God himself is a self-existent being. Who told you so? It is correct enough; but how did it get into your heads? Who told you that man did not exist in like manner upon the same principles? Man does exist upon the same principles. God made a tabernacle and put a spirit into it, and it became a living soul. . . . It does not say in the Hebrew [Bible] that God created the spirit of man. It says "God made man out of the earth and put into him Adam's spirit, and so became a living body. (TPJS, 352)[130]

◆◆◆

The intelligence of spirits had no beginning, neither will it have an end. . . . That which has a beginning may have an end. There never was a time when there were not spirits; for they are co-[eternal] with our Father in heaven. (TPJS, 353)[130]

◆◆◆

The mind or the intelligence which man possesses is co-[eternal] with God himself. . . . When I talk to . . . mourners, what have they lost? Their relatives and friends are only separated from their bodies for a short season: their spirits which existed with God have left the tabernacle of clay only for a little moment, as it were; and they now exist in a place where they converse together the same as we do on the earth. (TPJS, 353)[130]

◆◆◆

God never had the power to create the spirit of man at all. God himself could not create himself.

Intelligence is eternal and exists upon a self-existent principle. It is a spirit from age to age, and there is no creation about it. All the minds and spirits that God ever sent into the world are susceptible of enlargement. (TPJS, 354)[130]

◆◆◆

All things whatsoever God . . . has seen fit and proper to reveal to us, while we are dwelling in mortality, in regard to our mortal bodies . . . are revealed to our spirits precisely as though we had no bodies at all; and those revelations which will save our spirits will save our bodies. God reveals them to us in view of no eternal dissolution of the body, or tabernacle. (TPJS, 355)[130]

SPIRITUALITY

As well might the devil seek to dethrone Jehovah, as overthrow an innocent soul that resists everything which is evil. (TPJS, 226)[75]

◆◆◆

If you live up to your privileges, the angels cannot be restrained from being your associates. (TPJS, 226)[75]

◆◆◆

[Most] gifts of the Spirit are not visible to the natural vision, or understanding of men; indeed very few of them are. (TPJS, 244)[80]

◆◆◆

Be virtuous and pure; be men of integrity and truth; keep the commandments of God; and then you will be able more perfectly to understand the difference between right and wrong—between the things of God and the things of men; and your path will be like that of the just, which shineth brighter and brighter unto the perfect day. (TPJS, 247)[80]

◆◆◆

[Considering the council in heaven] . . . we begin to learn the only true God, and what kind of a being we have got to worship. Having a knowledge of God, we begin to know how to approach him, and how to ask so as to receive an answer.

When we understand the character of God, and know how to come to him, he begins to unfold the heavens to us, and to tell us all about it. When we are ready to come to him, he is ready to come to us. (TPJS, 350)[130]

STAKES

I have received instructions from the Lord that from henceforth wherever Elders of Israel shall build up churches and branches unto the Lord throughout the states, there shall be a stake of Zion. (TPJS, 363)[131]

STRENGTH

The Kingdom of Heaven is like unto a mustard seed. Behold, then is not this the Kingdom of Heaven that is raising its head in the last days in the majesty of its God, even the Church of the Latter-day Saints, like an impenetrable, immovable rock in the midst of the mighty deep, exposed to the storms and tempests of Satan, but has, thus far, remained steadfast, and is still braving the mountain waves of opposition . . . urged onward with redoubled fury by the enemy of righteousness, with his pitch fork of lies. (TPJS, 98)[34]

◆◆◆

We . . . have an assurance of a better hope than that of our persecutors. Therefore God hath made broad our shoulders for the burden. We glory in our tribulation, because we know that God is with us, that He is our friend, and that He will save our souls. (TPJS, 123)[46]

◆◆◆

We have reproved in the gate, and men have laid snares for us. We have spoken words, and men have made us offenders. And notwithstanding all this, our minds are not yet darkened, but feel strong in the Lord. (TPJS, 124)[46]

• • •

Walls and irons, doors and creaking hinges, and half-scared-to-death guards and jailers, grinning like some damned spirits, lest an innocent man should make his escape to bring to light the damnable deeds of a murderous mob, are calculated in their very nature to make the soul of an honest man feel stronger than the powers of hell. (TPJS, 139)[47]

• • •

"The ends of the earth shall enquire after thy name, and fools shall have thee in derision, and hell shall rage against thee, while the pure in heart, and the wise, and the noble, and the virtuous, shall seek thy counsel, and authority and blessings constantly from under thy hand, and thy people shall never be turned against thee by the testimony of traitors; and although their influence shall cast thee into trouble, and into bars and walls, thou shalt be had in honor, and but for a small moment and thy voice shall be more terrible in the midst of thine enemies, than the fierce lion, because of thy righteousness; and thy God shall stand by thee forever and ever." (TPJS, 143)[47]

• • •

Be on the alert to concentrate our energies. . . . The best feelings should exist in our midst; and then, by the help of the Almighty, we shall go on from victory to victory, and from conquest to conquest; our evil passions will be subdued, our prejudices depart; we shall find no room in our bosoms for hatred; vice will hide its deformed head, and we shall stand approved in the sight of Heaven, and be acknowledged the sons of God. (TPJS, 179)[54]

• • •

All men have power to resist the devil. (TPJS, 189)[61]

• • •

As well might the devil seek to dethrone Jehovah, as overthrow an innocent soul that resists everything which is evil. (TPJS, 226)[75]

• • •

You need not be teasing your husbands because of their deeds, but let the weight of your innocence, kindness and affection be felt, which is more mighty than a millstone hung about the neck; not war, not jangle, not contradiction or dispute, but meekness, love, purity—these are the things that should magnify you in the eyes of all good men. (TPJS, 227)[75]

• • •

Man's strength is weakness, his wisdom is folly, his glory is his shame. (TPJS, 249)[81]

• • •

A man can bear a heavy burthen by practice and continuing to increase it. (TPJS, 299)[103]

STRUGGLE

The burdens which roll upon me are very great. My persecutors allow me no rest, and I find that in the midst of business and care the spirit is willing, but the flesh is weak. (TPJS, 315)[115]

SUCCESS

If they receive not your testimony in one place, flee to another, remembering to cast no reflections, nor throw out any bitter sayings. If you do your duty, it will be just as well with you, as though all men embraced the Gospel. (TPJS, 43)[20]

SUFFERING

When I enquire . . . , the voice of the Lord is: Be still, and know that I am God; all those who suffer for my name shall reign with me, and he that layeth down his life for my sake shall find it again. (TPJS, 34)[19]

•••

I am aware that I ought not to murmur, and do not murmur, only in this, that those who are innocent are compelled to suffer for the iniquities of the guilty. (TPJS, 34)[19]

•••

The law of heaven is presented to man, and as such guarantees to all who obey it a reward far beyond any earthly consideration; though it does not . . . exempt [one] from the afflictions and troubles arising from different sources in consequence of acts of wicked men on earth. Still in the midst of all this there is a promise predicated upon the fact that it is a law of heaven, which transcends the law of man, as far as eternal life [transcends] the temporal; and as the blessings which God is able to give, are greater than those which can be given by man. (TPJS, 50)[21]

•••

Inasmuch as God hath said that He would have a tried people, that He would purge them as gold, now we think that this time He has chosen His own crucible, wherein we have been tried. (TPJS, 135)[47]

•••

After having suffered so great sacrifice and having passed through so great a season of sorrow, we trust that a ram may be caught in the thicket speedily, to relieve the sons and daughters of Abraham from their great anxiety, and to light up the lamp of salvation upon their countenances, that they may hold on now,

after having gone so far unto everlasting life. (TPJS, 136)[47]

•••

"If thou art called to pass through tribulations; if thou art in perils among false brethren; if thou art in perils among robbers; if thou art in perils by land or by sea; if thou art accused with all manner of false accusations; if thine enemies fall upon thee; if they tear thee from the society from thy father and mother and brethren and sisters; and if with a drawn sword thine enemies tear thee from the bosom from thy wife, and thine offspring, and thine elder son, although but six years of age, shall cling to thy garments, and shall say, My father, my father, why can't you stay with us? O my father, what are the men going to do with you? And if then he shall be thrust from thee by the sword, and thou be dragged to prison, and thine enemies prowl around thee like wolves for the blood of the lamb; and if thou shouldst be cast into the pit, or into the hands of murderers, and the sentence of death passed upon thee; if thou be cast into the deep, if the billowing surge conspire against thee; if fierce winds become thine enemy; if the heavens gather blackness, and all the elements combine to hedge up the way; and above all, if the very jaws of hell shall gape open the mouth wide after thee, know thou, my son, that all these things shall give thee experience, and shall be for thy good. The Son of Man hath descended below them all; art thou greater than he?" (TPJS, 143)[47]

•••

It is a false idea that the Saints will escape all the judgments, whilst the wicked suffer; for all flesh is subject to suffer. . . . It is an unhallowed principle to say that such and such have transgressed because they have been preyed upon by disease or death, for all flesh is subject to death. (TPJS, 162)[50]

•••

We contemplate a people who have embraced a system of religion, unpopular, and the adherence to which has brought upon them repeated persecutions. A people who for their love of God, and attachment to His cause, have suffered hunger, nakedness, perils, and almost every privation. A people who, for the sake of their religion have had to mourn the premature death of parents, husbands, wives, and children. A people, who have preferred death to slavery and hypocrisy, and have honorably maintained their characters, and stood firm and immovable, in times that have tried men's souls. . . . Your names will be handed down to posterity as Saints of God and virtuous men. (TPJS, 185)[59]

•••

Men have to suffer that they may come upon Mount Zion and be exalted above the heavens. (TPJS, 323)[119]

•••

All will suffer [however] until they obey Christ himself. (TPJS, 357)[130]

SUPPORT

Brother Joseph Smith, Jr. said . . . that the promise of God was that the greatest blessings which God had to bestow should be given to those who contributed to the support of his family while he was translating the fullness of the Scriptures. (TPJS, 9)[1]

•••

God has respect to the feelings of His Saints, and He will not suffer them to be tantalized with impunity. (TPJS, 19)[10]

•••

The Twelve and the Seventy have particularly to depend upon their ministry for their support, and that of their families; and they have a right by virtue of their offices, to call upon the churches to assist them. (TPJS, 75)[28]

•••

I am well aware that you [the Twelve] have to sustain my character against the vile calumnies and reproaches of this ungodly generation, and that you delight in so doing. (TPJS, 89)[33]

•••

[To the Twelve Joseph said:] I am determined that neither heights nor depths, principalities nor powers, things present or things to come, or any other creature, shall separate me from you. And I will now covenant with you before God, that I will not listen to or credit any derogatory report against any of you, nor condemn you upon any testimony beneath the heavens . . . until I can see you face to face and know of a surety; and I will place unremitted confidence in your word, for I believe you to be men of truth. And I ask the same of you, when I tell you anything, that you place equal confidence in my word, for I will not tell you I know anything that I do not know. (TPJS, 106)[37]

•••

I then called upon the quorums and congregation of Saints to acknowledge the Twelve Apostles, who were present, as Prophets, Seers, Revelators, and special witnesses to all the nations of the earth, holding the keys of the kingdom, to unlock it, or cause it to be done, among them, and uphold them by their prayers, which they assented to by rising. (TPJS, 109)[39]

•••

Can I rely on your prayers to our heavenly Father on my behalf, and on all the prayers of all my brethren and sisters in England, [whom having not seen, yet I love] that I may be enabled to escape every stratagem of Satan, surmount every difficulty, and bring this people to the enjoyment of those blessings which are reserved for the righteous? I ask this at your hands in the name of the Lord Jesus Christ. (TPJS, 178)[55]

◆◆◆

[Joseph said that] if God had appointed him, and chosen him as an instrument to lead the Church, why not let him lead it through? Why stand in the way when he is appointed to do a thing? Who knows the mind of God? Does He not reveal things differently than what we expect? He remarked that he was continually rising, although he had everything bearing him down, standing in his way, and opposing; notwithstanding all this opposition, he always comes out right in the end. (TPJS, 224)[75]

◆◆◆

[Joseph said that] . . . God had called him to lead the Church, and he would lead it right; those that undertake to interfere will be ashamed when their own folly is made manifest: (TPJS, 225)[75]

◆◆◆

[Joseph] exhorted the sisters always to concentrate their faith and prayers for, and place confidence in their husbands, whom God has appointed for them to honor, and in those faithful men whom God has placed at the head of the Church to lead His people. (TPJS, 226)[75]

◆◆◆

If you live up to your privileges, the angels cannot be restrained from being your associates. (TPJS, 226)[75]

◆◆◆

When a man is born down with trouble, when he is perplexed with care and difficulty, if he can meet a smile instead of an argument or a murmur—if he can meet with mildness, it will calm down his soul and soothe his feelings; when the mind is going to despair, it needs a solace of affection and kindness. (TPJS, 228)[75]

◆◆◆

Never . . . let us hear of those who profess to be governed by the law of God, . . . shrinking from the assistance of those who bear the ark of the Lord—in the hour of danger! (TPJS, 261)[85]

◆◆◆

I would esteem it one of the greatest blessings, if I am to be afflicted in this world, to have my lot cast where I can find brothers and friends all around me. (TPJS, 294)[102]

◆◆◆

If there is a place on earth where men should cultivate the spirit and pour in the oil and wine in the bosoms of the afflicted, it is . . . [at a funeral] . . . and although a stranger and afflicted when he arrives, he finds a brother and a friend ready to administer to his necessities. (TPJS, 294)[102]

◆◆◆

If I esteem mankind to be in error, shall I bear them down? No. I will lift them up, and in their own way too. (TPJS, 313)[113]

◆◆◆

If I am so fortunate to be the man to comprehend God, and explain or convey the principles to your hearts, so that the Spirit seals them upon you, then let every man and woman henceforth sit in silence . . . and never lift their hands or voices . . . against the man of God or servants of God again. (TPJS, 344)[130]

SUSTAINING LEADERS

I then called upon the quorums and congregation of Saints to acknowledge the Twelve Apostles, who were present, as Prophets, Seers, Revelators, and special witnesses to all the nations of the earth, holding the keys of the kingdom, to unlock it, or cause it to be done, among them, and uphold them by their prayers, which they assented to by rising. (TPJS, 109)[39]

SYMPATHY

Brethren, when we learn your sufferings, it awakens every sympathy of our hearts; it weighs us down; we cannot refrain from tears. (TPJS, 35)[19]

TACT

(See also DIPLOMACY)

There should be no license for sin, but mercy should go hand in hand with reproof. (TPJS, 241)[79]

TEACHING

If . . . there is an importance in this respect [of obeying God's laws] is there not a responsibility of great weight resting upon those who are called to declare these truths to men? (TPJS, 57)[21]

♦ ♦ ♦

Ye are not sent out to be taught, but to teach. (TPJS, 156)[49]

♦ ♦ ♦

You must be aware in some measure of my feelings, when I contemplate the great work which is now rolling on, and . . . I realize in some measure my responsibility, and the need I have for support from above, that I may be able to teach this people. (TPJS, 178)[55]

♦ ♦ ♦

It is my meditation all the day, and more than my meat and drink, to know how I

shall make the Saints of God comprehend the visions that roll like an overflowing surge before my mind. (TPJS, 296)[102]

♦ ♦ ♦

The Lord deals with this people as a tender parent with a child, communicating light and intelligence and the knowledge of His ways as they can bear it. (TPJS, 305)[109]

♦ ♦ ♦

If I esteem mankind to be in error, shall I bear them down? No. I will lift them up, and in their own way too, if I cannot persuade them my way is better; and I will not seek to compel any man to believe as I do, only by the force of reasoning, for truth will cut its own way. (TPJS, 313)[113]

♦ ♦ ♦

There has been a great difficulty in getting anything into the heads of this generation. . . . Even the Saints are slow to understand. (TPJS, 331)[123]

♦ ♦ ♦

The object with me is to obey and teach others to obey God in just what He tells us to do. (TPJS, 332)[125]

♦ ♦ ♦

I do not intend to please your ears with superfluity of words or oratory, or with much learning; but I intend to edify you with the simple truths from heaven. (TPJS, 342)[130]

TEARFUL FAMILY PARTING

Hyrum came out of the Mansion and gave his hands to Reynold Cahoon, at the same time saying, "A company of men are seeking to kill my brother Joseph, and the Lord has warned him to flee to the Rocky Mountains to save his life. Good-by, Brother Cahoon, we shall see you again." In a few minutes afterwards Joseph came from his family. His tears were flowing fast. He held a handkerchief to his face, and followed after Brother Hyrum without uttering a word. (TPJS, 377)[135]

TEMPLE WORK

The temple of the Lord . . . will be so constructed as to enable all the functions of the Priesthood to be duly exercised and where instructions from the Most High will be received, and from this place go forth to distant lands. Let us then concentrate all our powers, . . . and strive to emulate the action of the ancient covenant fathers, and patriarchs, in those things which are of such vast importance to this and every succeeding generation. (TPJS, 182)[57]

♦♦♦

Men, by actively engaging in rites of salvation substitutionally became instrumental in bringing multitudes of their kindred into the kingdom of God. (TPJS, 191)[63]

♦♦♦

It is no more incredible that God should *save* the dead, than that he should *raise* the dead. (TPJS, 191)[63]

♦♦♦

There is a way to release the spirits of the dead; that is by the power and authority of the Priesthood—by binding and loosing on earth. This doctrine appears glorious, inasmuch as it exhibits the greatness of divine compassion and benevolence in the extent of the plan of human salvation. (TPJS, 192)[63]

♦♦♦

Those Saints who neglect [temple work] in behalf of their deceased relatives, do it at the peril of their own salvation. (TPJS, 193)[63]

♦♦♦

I spent the day in the upper part of the store, that is in my private office . . . in council with General James Adams, of Springfield, Patriarch Hyrum Smith, Bishops Newel K. Whitney and George Miller, and President Brigham Young and Elders Heber C. Kimball and Willard Richards, instructing them in the principles and order of the Priesthood, attending to washings, anointings, endowments and the communication of keys pertaining to the Aaronic Priesthood, and so on to the highest order of the Melchizedek Priesthood, setting forth the order pertaining to the Ancient of Days, and all those plans and principles by which anyone is enabled to secure the fullness of those blessings which have been prepared for the Church of the Firstborn and come up and abide in the presence of the Eloheim in the eternal worlds. In this council was instituted the ancient order of things for the first time in these last days. And the communications I made to this council were of things spiritual, and to be received only by the spiritual minded: and there was nothing made known to these men but what will be made known to all the Saints of the last days, so soon as thy are prepared to receive . . . them, even to the weakest of the Saints. (TPJS, 237)[77]

◆ ◆ ◆

Hasten the work in the Temple, renew your exertions to forward all the work of the last days, and walk before the Lord in soberness and righteousness. (TPJS, 326)[121]

◆ ◆ ◆

The Saints have not too much time to save and redress their dead, and gather together their living relatives, that they may be saved also, before the earth will be smitten, and the consumption decreed falls upon the world. (TPJS, 330)[123]

◆ ◆ ◆

If the whole Church should go to with all their might to save their dead, seal their posterity, and gather their living friends, and spend none of their time in behalf of the world, they would hardly get through before night would come, when no man can work. (TPJS, 330)[123]

◆ ◆ ◆

The greatest responsibility in this world that God has laid upon us is to seek after our dead. (TPJS, 356)[130]

TEMPLES

The order of the house of God has been, and ever will be, the same, even after Christ comes; and after the termination of the thousand years it will be the same; and we shall finally enter into the celestial kingdom of God, and enjoy it forever. (TPJS, 91)[33]

◆ ◆ ◆

The temple of the Lord . . . will be so constructed as to enable all the functions of the Priesthood to be duly exercised and where instructions from the Most High will be received, and from this place go forth to distant lands. Let us then concentrate all our powers, . . . and strive to emulate the action of the ancient covenant fathers, and patriarchs, in those things which are of such vast importance to this and every succeeding generation. (TPJS, 182)[57]

◆ ◆ ◆

From the interest which is generally manifested by the Saints at large, we hope to accomplish much by a combination of effort, and a concentration of action, and erect the Temple and other buildings. (TPJS, 186)[59]

◆ ◆ ◆

The Lord has told us to build the Temple and the Nauvoo House; and that command is as binding upon us as any other; and that man who engages not in these things is as much a transgressor as though he broke any other commandment; he is not a doer of God's will, not a fulfiller of His laws. (TPJS, 253)[81]

◆ ◆ ◆

The main object was to build unto the Lord a house whereby He could reveal unto His people the ordinances of His house and the glories of His kingdom, and teach the people the way of salvation; for there are certain ordinances and principles that, when they are taught and practiced, must be done in a place or house built for that purpose. (TPJS, 308)[113]

◆ ◆ ◆

Some say it is better to give to the poor than build the Temple. The building of the Temple has sustained the poor who were driven from Missouri, and kept them from starving; and it has been the best means for this object which could be devised. (TPJS, 329)[122]

TEMPTATION

Anxieties inexpressible crowd themselves continually upon my mind for the Saints, when I consider the many temptations to which we are subject, from the cunning and flattery of the great adversary of our souls. (TPJS, 29)[16]

♦♦♦

The devil can speak in tongues; the adversary will come with his work; he can tempt all classes; can speak in English or Dutch. (TPJS, 162)[49]

♦♦♦

Satan was generally blamed for the evils which we did, but if he was the cause of all our wickedness, men could not be condemned. The devil could not compel mankind to do evil; all was voluntary. Those who resisted the Spirit of God, would be liable to be led into temptation, and then the association of heaven would be withdrawn from those who refused to be made partakers of such great glory. God would not exert any compulsory means, and the devil could not. (TPJS, 187)[60]

♦♦♦

All men have power to resist the devil. They who have tabernacles, have power over those who have not. (TPJS, 189)[61]

♦♦♦

If Satan could not speak in tongues, he could not tempt a Dutchman, or any other nation, but the English, for he can tempt the Englishman, for he has tempted me, and I am an Englishman. (TPJS, 195)[67]

♦♦♦

The devil, think[s] . . . to thwart the decree of God, by going up and down in the earth, seeking whom he may destroy— any person . . . that will yield to him, he will bind him, and take possession of the body and reign there, glorying in it mightily, not caring that he had got merely a stolen body; and by and by someone having authority will come along and cast him out and restore the tabernacle to its rightful owner. (TPJS, 297)[103]

♦♦♦

My only trouble at the present time is concerning ourselves, that the Saints *will be divided, broken up, and scattered,* before we get our salvation secure; for there are so many fools in the world for the devil to operate upon, it gives him the advantage oftentimes. (TPJS, 331)[123]

TENDERNESS
(*See also* SENSITIVITY)

When a man is born down with trouble, when he is perplexed with care and difficulty, if he can meet a smile instead of an argument or a murmur—if he can meet with mildness, it will calm down his soul and soothe his feelings; when the mind is going to despair, it needs a solace of affection and kindness. (TPJS, 228)[75]

♦♦♦

Nothing is so much calculated to lead people to forsake sin as to take them by the hand, and watch over them with tenderness. When persons manifest the least kindness and love to me, O, what power it has over my mind, while the opposite course has a tendency to harrow up all the harsh feelings and depress the human mind. (TPJS, 240)[79]

♦♦♦

The Lord deals with this people as a tender parent with a child, communicating light and intelligence and the knowledge of His ways as they can bear it. (TPJS, 305)[109]

TESTIMONY

Search the scriptures—search the revelations which we publish, and ask your heavenly Father, in the name of His Son Jesus Christ, to manifest the truth unto you, and if you will do it with an eye single to His glory nothing doubting, He will answer you by the power of His Holy Spirit. You will then know for yourselves and not for another. You will not then be dependent of man for the knowledge of God; nor will there be any room for speculation. No; for when men receive their instruction from Him that made them, they know. (TPJS, 11)[7]

◆ ◆ ◆

There is a superior intelligence bestowed upon such as obey the Gospel with full purpose of heart. (TPJS, 67)[21]

◆ ◆ ◆

The fundamental principles of our religion are the testimonies of the Apostles and Prophets, concerning Jesus Christ, that He died, was buried, and rose again the third day, and ascended into heaven; and all other things which pertain to our religion are only appendages to it. But in connection with these, we believe in the gift of the Holy Ghost, the power of faith, the enjoyment of the spiritual gifts according to the will of God, the restoration of the house of Israel, and the final triumph of truth. (TPJS, 121)[45]

◆ ◆ ◆

Faith comes by hearing the word of God; that testimony is always attended by the spirit of prophesy and revelation. (TPJS, 148)[48]

◆ ◆ ◆

No man can be a minister of Jesus Christ except he has a testimony of Jesus; and this is the spirit of prophecy. (TPJS, 160)[49]

◆ ◆ ◆

Men of the present time testify of heaven and hell, and have never seen either; and I will say that no man knows these things without . . . [a testimony]. (TPJS, 160)[49]

◆ ◆ ◆

It mattereth not whether we live long or short on the earth after we come to a knowledge of [gospel] principles and obey them unto the end. (TPJS, 199)[68]

◆ ◆ ◆

President Smith arose and. . . [s]aid that the passage in the third verse [of I Corinthians, Chapter twelve] . . . should be translated "no man can know [not *say*] that Jesus is the Lord, but by the Holy Ghost." (TPJS, 223)[75]

◆ ◆ ◆

Ye are the witnesses—having the testimony of Jesus which is the spirit of prophecy. (TPJS, 265)[85]

◆ ◆ ◆

We have a more sure word of prophecy, whereunto you do well to take heed, as unto a light that shineth in a dark place. We were eyewitnesses of his majesty and heard the voice of his excellent glory. (TPJS, 303)[109]

◆ ◆ ◆

Both Joseph and Hyrum bore a faithful testimony [in the Carthage Jail] to the Latter-day work, and the coming forth of the Gospel over all the earth, exhorting the brethren present to faithfulness and preserving diligence in proclaiming the Gospel, building up the Temple, and performing all the duties connected with our holy religion. (TPJS, 394)[145]

THIS LIFE

(*See also* MORTALITY;
PURPOSE OF LIFE)

Let this [early death] then, prove as a warning to all not to procrastinate repentance, or wait till a death-bed, for it is the will of God that man should repent and serve Him in health, and blessing and power of his mind, in order to secure his blessing, and not wait until he is called to die. (TPJS, 197)[68]

♦♦♦

It mattereth not whether we live long or short on the earth after we come to a knowledge of [gospel] principles and obey them unto the end. (TPJS, 199)[68]

♦♦♦

The world is full of technicalities and misrepresentation, which I calculate to overthrow, and speak of things as they actually exist. (TPJS, 292)[101]

♦♦♦

All men know that they must die. And it is important that we should understand the reasons and causes of our exposure to the vicissitudes of life and of death, and the designs and purposes of God in our coming into the world, our sufferings here, and our departure hence. (TPJS, 324)[121]

THOUGHTFULNESS

(See also CONSIDERATION)

Let the Elders be exceedingly careful about unnecessarily disturbing and harrowing up the feelings of the people. (TPJS, 43)[20]

♦♦♦

Let every word be seasoned with grace. (TPJS, 156)[49]

THOUGHTS

The things of God are of deep import; and time, and experience, and careful and ponderous and solemn thoughts can only find them out. (TPJS, 137)[47]

♦♦♦

Thy mind, O man! If thou will lead a soul unto salvation, must stretch as high as the utmost heavens, and search into and contemplate the darkest abyss and the broad expanse of eternity. (TPJS, 137)[47]

♦♦♦

How much more dignified and noble are the thoughts of God, than the vain imaginations of the human heart! None but fools will trifle with the souls of men. (TPJS, 137)[47]

♦♦♦

Out of the abundance of the heart of man the mouth speaketh. (TPJS, 358)[130]

TIME

Time and chance happen to all men. (TPJS, 148)[47]

TIMELINESS

Live in strict obedience to the commandments of God, and walk humbly before Him, and He will exalt thee in His own due time. (TPJS, 27)[15]

♦♦♦

We have reason to believe that many things were introduced among the Saints before God had signified the times; and notwithstanding the principles and plans may have been good, yet aspiring men, or in other words, men who had not the substance of godliness about them, perhaps undertook to handle edged tools. Children, you know, are fond of tools, while they are not yet able to use them. (TPJS, 144)[47]

♦♦♦

This principle [of timeliness] will justly apply to all of God's dealings with His children. Everything that God gives us is lawful and right; and it is proper that we should enjoy His gifts and blessings whenever and wherever He is disposed to bestow; but if we should seize upon those same blessings and enjoyments without law, without revelation, without commandment, those blessings and enjoyments would prove cursings and vexations in the end, and we should have to lie down in sorrow and wailings of everlasting regret. (TPJS, 256)[83]

• • •

Many men will say, "I will never forsake you, but will stand by you all the times," but the moment you teach them some of the mysteries of the kingdom of God that are retained in the heavens and are to be revealed to the children of men when they are prepared for them they will be the first to stone you and put you to death. (TPJS, 309)[113]

TOLERANCE

Bear and forbear one with another, for so the Lord does with us. Pray for your enemies in the Church and curse not your foes without: for vengeance is mine, saith the Lord, and I will repay. (TPJS, 77)[29]

• • •

Bear with those who do not feel themselves more worthy than yourselves. (TPJS, 137)[47]

• • •

Be aware of those prejudices which sometimes so strangely present themselves, and are so congenial to human nature, against our friend, neighbors, and brethren of the world, who choose to differ from us in opinion and in matters of faith. Our religion is between us and our God. Their religion is between them and their God. (TPJS, 146)[47]

• • •

There is a love from God that should be exercised toward those of our faith, who walk uprightly, which is peculiar to itself; but it is without prejudice; it also gives scope to the mind, which enables us to conduct ourselves with greater liberality towards all that are not of our faith, than what they exercise towards one another. These principles approximate nearer to the mind of God, because it is like God, or Godlike. (TPJS, 147)[47]

• • •

If you will throw a cloak of charity over my sins, I will over yours—for charity covereth a multitude of sins. . . . [Then] if you will follow the revelations and instructions which God gives you through me, I will take you into heaven as my back load. (TPJS, 193)[64]

• • •

As you increase in innocence and virtue, as you increase in goodness, let your hearts expand, let them be enlarged toward others; you must be long-suffering, and bear with the faults and errors of mankind. (TPJS, 228)[75]

• • •

We must be merciful to one another, and overlook small things. (TPJS, 240)[79]

• • •

I told them I was but a man, and they must not expect me to be perfect; if they expected perfection from me, I should expect it from them; but if they would bear with my infirmities and the infirmities of the brethren, I would likewise bear with their infirmities. (TPJS, 268)[87]

• • •

When my enemies take away my rights, I will bear it and keep out of the way; but if they take away your rights, I will fight for you. (TPJS, 268)[87]

✦✦✦

I do not dwell upon your faults, and you shall not upon mine. (TPJS, 316)[115]

✦✦✦

I do not grudge the world all the religion they have got; they are welcome to all the knowledge they possess. (TPJS, 320)[118]

✦✦✦

Meddle not with any man for his religion; and all governments ought to permit every man to enjoy his religion unmolested. No man is authorized to take away life in consequence of difference in religion, which all laws and governments ought to tolerate and protect, right or wrong. (TPJS, 344)[130]

✦✦✦

If any man is authorized to take away my life because he thinks and says I am a false teacher, then, upon the same principle, we should be justified in taking away the life of every false teacher, and where would be the end of blood? And who would not be the sufferer? (TPJS, 344)[130]

TRADITION

All men are naturally disposed to walk in their own paths as they are pointed out by their own fingers, and we are not willing to consider and walk in the path which is pointed out by another, saying, This is the way, walk ye in it, although he should be an unerring director, and the Lord his God sent him. (TPJS, 26)[15]

✦✦✦

It is very difficult for us to communicate to the churches all that God has revealed to us, in consequence of tradition; for we are differently situated from any other people that ever existed upon this earth. (TPJS, 70)[23]

✦✦✦

Men are in the habit, when the truth is exhibited by the servants of God, of saying, All is mystery; they have spoken in parables, and therefore, are not to be understood. It is true they have eyes to see, and see not, but none are so blind as those who will not see. (TPJS, 96)[34]

✦✦✦

[Some men,] . . . intelligent, learned, virtuous and lovely, walking in uprightness and in all good conscience, so far as they have been able . . . [are left to] discern duty from the muddy stream of tradition, or from the blotted page of the book of nature. (TPJS, 192)[63]

✦✦✦

It is often the case that . . . [new] members of this Church for want of better information, carry along with them their old notions of things, and sometimes fall into egregious errors. (TPJS, 242)[80]

✦✦✦

Many men will say, "I will never forsake you, but will stand by you all the times," but the moment you teach them some of the mysteries of the kingdom of God that are retained in the heavens and are to be revealed to the children of men when they are prepared for them they will be the first to stone you and put you to death. (TPJS, 309)[113]

✦✦✦

It always has been when a man was sent of God with the priesthood and he began to preach the fullness of the gospel, that he was thrust out by his friends, who are already to butcher him if he teaches things which they imagine to be wrong; and Jesus was crucified upon this principle. (TPJS, 310)[113]

✦✦✦

To become a joint heir of the heirship of the Son, one must put away all his false traditions. (TPJS, 321)[119]

♦♦♦

I have tried a number of years to get the minds of the Saints prepared to receive the things of God; but we frequently see some of them, after suffering all they have for the work of God, will fly to pieces like glass as soon as anything comes that is contrary to their traditions: they cannot stand the fire at all. How many will be able to abide a celestial law, and go through and receive their exaltation, I am unable to say, as many are called, but few are chosen. (TPJS, 331)[123]

♦♦♦

There has been a great difficulty in getting anything into the heads of this generation. . . . Even the Saints are slow to understand. (TPJS, 331)[123]

♦♦♦

If we start right, it is easy to go right all the time; but if we start wrong, we may go wrong, and it be a hard matter to get right. (TPJS, 343)[130]

TRAITORS AND BETRAYAL

I have learned in my travels that man is treacherous and selfish, but few excepted. (TPJS, 30)[17]

♦♦♦

A man who willfully turneth away from his friend without a cause, is not easily forgiven. (TPJS, 31)[17]

♦♦♦

We have reproved in the gate, and men have laid snares for us. We have spoken words, and men have made us offenders. (TPJS, 124)[46]

♦♦♦

Renegade "Mormon" dissenters are running through the world and spreading various foul and libelous reports against us, thinking thereby to gain the friendship of the world, because they know that we are not of the world, and that the world hates us; therefore they [the world] make a tool of these . . . [dissenters]; and by them try to do all the injury they can, and after that[,] they hate them worse than they do us, because they find them to be base traitors and sycophants. (TPJS, 126)[46]

♦♦♦

If men sin willfully after they have received the knowledge of the truth, there remaineth no more sacrifice for sin, but a certain fearful looking for of judgment and fiery indignation to come, which shall devour these adversaries. . . . Of how much more severe punishment suppose ye, shall he be thought worthy, who hath sold his brother, and denied the new and everlasting covenant by which he was sanctified, calling it an unholy thing, and doing despite to the Spirit of grace. (TPJS, 128)[46]

♦♦♦

In all your trials, troubles, temptations, afflictions, bonds, imprisonments and death, see to it that you do not betray heaven; that you do not betray Jesus Christ; that you do not betray the brethren; that you do not betray the revelations of God, whether in Bible, Book of Mormon, or Doctrine and Covenants, or any other . . . revealed unto man. . . . Yea, in all your kickings and flounderings, see to it that you do not this thing, lest innocent blood be found upon your skirts, and you go down to hell. All other sins are not to be compared to sinning against the Holy Ghost, and proving a traitor to the brethren. (TPJS, 156)[49]

♦♦♦

Many men will say, "I will never forsake you, but will stand by you all the times," But the moment you teach them some of the mysteries of the kingdom of God that are retained in the heavens and are to be revealed to the children of men when they are prepared for them they will be the first to stone you and put you to death. (TPJS, 309)[113]

•••

It always has been when a man was sent of God with the priesthood and he began to preach the fullness of the gospel, that he was thrust out by his friends, who are already to butcher him if he teaches things which they imagine to be wrong; and Jesus was crucified upon this principle. (TPJS, 310)[113]

•••

Notwithstanding my weaknesses, I am under the necessity of bearing the infirmities of others, who, when they get into difficulty, hang on to me tenaciously to get them out, and wish me to cover their faults. On the other hand, the same characters, when they discover a weakness in Brother Joseph, endeavor to blast his reputation, and publish it to all the world, and thereby aid my enemies in destroying the Saints. (TPJS, 315)[115]

•••

Men often come to me with their troubles, and seek my will, crying, Oh, Brother Joseph, help me! Help me! But when I am in trouble few of them sympathize with me or extend to me relief. (TPJS, 315)[115]

•••

This generation is as corrupt as the generation of the Jews that crucified Christ; and if He were here today, and should preach the same doctrine He did then, they would put Him to death. (TPJS, 328)[122]

•••

I testify again, as the Lord lives, God never will acknowledge any traitors or apostates. (TPJS, 375)[133]

TRANSLATED BEINGS

Distinction is made between the doctrine of the actual resurrection and translation: translation obtains deliverance from the tortures and sufferings of the body, but their existence will prolong as to the labors and toils of the ministry, before they can enter into so great a rest and glory [as the resurrection]. (TPJS, 171)[54]

•••

Translated bodies cannot enter into rest until they have undergone a change equivalent to death. Translated bodies are designed for future missions. (TPJS, 191)[63]

TRIBULATION

I have always expected that Zion would suffer some affliction, from what I could learn from the commandments which have been given. But I would remind you of a certain clause in one which says, that after much tribulation cometh the blessing. By this, and also others, and also one received of late, I know that Zion in due time of the Lord, will be redeemed; but how many will be the days of her purification, tribulation, and affliction, the Lord has kept hid from my eyes; and when I enquire concerning this subject, the voice of the Lord is: Be still and know that I am God. (TPJS, 34)[19]

•••

Those who cannot endure persecution, and stand in the day of affliction, cannot stand in the day when the Son of God shall burst the veil, and appear in all the glory of His Father, with all the holy angels. (TPJS, 42)[20]

•••

Live worthy of the blessings that shall follow, after much tribulation, to satiate the souls of them that hold out faithful to the end. (TPJS, 78)[29]

•••

"My son, peace be unto thy soul; thine adversity and thine affliction shall be but a small moment; and then if thou endure it well, God shall exalt thee on high." (TPJS, 134)[47]

•••

I have tried a number of years to get the minds of the Saints prepared to receive the things of God; but we frequently see some of them, after suffering all they have for the work of God, will fly to pieces like glass as soon as anything comes that is contrary to their traditions: they cannot stand the fire at all. How many will be able to abide a celestial law, and go through and receive their exaltation, I am unable to say, as many are called, but few are chosen. (TPJS, 331)[123]

TRUST

We are informed . . . that those [persecutors] are very violent, and threaten immediate extermination upon all those who profess our doctrine. How far they will be suffered to execute their threats, we know not, but we trust in the Lord, and leave the event with Him to govern in His own wise providence. (TPJS, 28)[16]

•••

That person who never forsaketh his trust should ever have the highest place of regard in our hearts. (TPJS, 31)[17]

•••

I know that Zion, in the due time of the Lord, will be redeemed; but how many will be the days of her purification, tribulation, and affliction, the Lord has kept hid from my eyes; and when I enquire concerning this subject, the voice of the Lord is: Be still, and know that I am God; all those who suffer for my name shall reign with me, and he that layeth down his life for my sake shall find it again. (TPJS, 34)[19]

•••

I preached to . . . persuade the Saints to trust in God when sick, and not in an arm of flesh, and live by faith and not by medicine, or poison; and when they were sick, and had called for the Elders to pray for them, and they were not healed, to use herbs and mild food. (TPJS, 190)[62]

•••

The way I know in whom to confide— God tells me in whom I may place confidence. (TPJS, 301)[105]

•••

The light of the latter-day glory begins to break forth through the dark atmosphere of sectarian wickedness, and their iniquity begins to roll up into view, and the nations of the Gentiles are like the waves of the sea, casting up mire and dirt, or all in commotion, and they are hastily preparing to act the part allotted them, when the Lord rebukes the nations, when He shall rule them with a rod of iron, and break them in pieces like a potter's vessel. (TPJS, 16)[9]

•••

We hope that this adversary of truth [*Mormonism Unveiled*] will continue to stir up the sink of iniquity, that the people may the more readily discern between the righteous and the wicked. (TPJS, 99)[34]

•••

The fundamental principles of our religion are the testimonies of the Apostles and Prophets, concerning Jesus Christ, . . . and the final triumph of truth. (TPJS, 121)[45]

•••

The things of God are of deep import; and time, and experience, and careful and ponderous and solemn thoughts can only find them out. Thy mind, O man! If thou will lead a soul unto salvation, must stretch as high as the utmost heavens, and search into and contemplate the darkest abyss and the broad expanse of eternity. (TPJS, 137)[47]

♦♦♦

Ignorance, superstition and bigotry . . . is oftentimes in the way of the prosperity of this Church; like the torrent rain in the mountains, that floods the most pure and crystal stream with mire, and dirt, and filthiness, and obscures everything that was clear before, and all rushes along in one general deluge; but time weathers tide; and notwithstanding we are rolled in the mire of the flood for the time being, the next surge peradventure, as time rolls on, may bring to us the fountain as clear as crystal, and as pure as snow; while the filthiness, flood-wood and rubbish is left and purged out by the way. (TPJS, 138)[47]

♦♦♦

Water, fire, truth and God are all realities. (TPJS, 139)[47]

♦♦♦

Even the least Saint may know all things as fast as he is able to bear them. (TPJS, 149)[48]

♦♦♦

The truth, like the sturdy oak, has stood unhurt amid the contending elements, which have beat upon it with tremendous force. The floods have rolled, wave after wave, in quick succession, and have not swallowed it up. . . . "The floods have lifted up their voice; but the Lord of Hosts is mightier than the mighty waves of the sea": nor have the flames of persecution, with all the influence of mobs, been able to destroy it; but like Moses' bush, it has stood unconsumed. (TPJS, 184)[59]

♦♦♦

Prejudice, with its attendant train of evil, is giving way before the force of truth whose benign rays are penetrating the nations afar off. (TPJS, 184)[59]

♦♦♦

Surely "facts are stubborn things." It will be as it ever has been, the world will prove Joseph Smith a true prophet by circumstantial evidence, in experiments, as they did Moses and Elijah. (TPJS, 267)[86]

♦♦♦

We don't ask any people to throw away any good they have got; we only ask them to come and get more. (TPJS, 275)[91]

♦♦♦

If I had not actually got into this work and been called of God, I would back out. (TPJS, 286)[99]

♦♦♦

The world is full of technicalities and misrepresentation, which I calculate to overthrow, and speak of things as they actually exist. (TPJS, 292)[101]

♦♦♦

I hope sober-thinking and sound-reasoning people will sooner listen to the voice of truth, than be led astray by the vain pretensions of the self-wise. (TPJS, 299)[104]

♦♦♦

The opinions of men, so far as I am concerned, are to me as the crackling of thorns under the pot, or the whistling of the wind. I break the ground; I lead the way. (TPJS, 304)[109]

♦♦♦

One of the grand fundamental principles of "Mormonism" is to receive truth, let it come from whence it may. (TPJS, 313)[114]

♦♦♦

Truth will cut its own way. (TPJS, 313)[114]

◆ ◆ ◆

We should gather all the good and true principles in the world and treasure them up, or we shall not come out true "Mormons." (TPJS, 316)[115]

◆ ◆ ◆

Whenever light shone, it stirred up darkness. Truth and error, good and evil cannot be reconciled. (TPJS, 325)[121]

◆ ◆ ◆

I cannot believe in any of the creeds of the different denominations, because they all have some things in them I cannot subscribe to, though all of them have some truth. I want to come up into the presence of God and learn all things; but the creeds set up stakes, and say, "Hitherto shalt thou come, and no further"; which I cannot subscribe to. (TPJS, 327)[122]

◆ ◆ ◆

One truth revealed from heaven is worth all the sectarian notions in existence. (TPJS, 338)[128]

◆ ◆ ◆

In relation to the power over the minds of mankind which I hold, I would say, It is in consequence of the power of truth in the doctrines which I have been an instrument in the hands of God of presenting unto them, and not because of any compulsion on my part. (TPJS, 341)[129]

◆ ◆ ◆

Why do not my enemies strike a blow at the doctrine? They cannot do it: it is truth, and I defy all men to upset it. (TPJS, 341)[129]

◆ ◆ ◆

I do not intend to please your ears with superfluity of words or oratory, or with much learning; but I intend to edify you with the simple truths from heaven. (TPJS, 342)[130]

◆ ◆ ◆

It will not be by sword or gun that this kingdom will roll on: the power of truth is such that all nations will be under the necessity of obeying the Gospel. (TPJS, 366)[132]

◆ ◆ ◆

I never told you I was perfect; but there is no error in the revelations which I have taught. (TPJS, 368)[132]

◆ ◆ ◆

When did I ever teach anything wrong from this stand? When was I ever confounded? (TPJS, 368)[132]

◆ ◆ ◆

The heads of the Gods appointed one God for us; and when you take [that] view of the subject, it sets one free to see all the beauty, holiness and perfection of the Gods. All I want is to get the simple, naked truth, and the whole truth. (TPJS, 372)[133]

◆ ◆ ◆

Did I build on any other man's foundation? I have got all the truth which the Christian world possessed, and an independent revelation in the bargain, and God will bear me off triumphant. (TPJS, 376)[133]

◆ ◆ ◆

It is not always wise to relate all the truth. (TPJS, 392)[145]

TRUTH-SEEKING

(See also OPEN MINDEDNESS)

Avoid contentions and vain disputes with men of corrupt minds, who do not desire to know the truth. (TPJS, 43)[20]

✦✦✦

[Many] have eyes to see, and see not, but none are so blind as those who will not see. (TPJS, 96)[34]

✦✦✦

The things of God are of deep import; and time, and experience, and careful and ponderous and solemn thoughts can only find them out. Thy mind, O man! If thou will lead a soul unto salvation, must stretch as high as the utmost heavens, and search into and contemplate the darkest abyss and the broad expanse of eternity. (TPJS, 137)[47]

✦✦✦

There are many yet on the earth among all sects, parties, denominations, who are blinded by the subtle craftiness of men, whereby they lie in wait to deceive, and who are only kept from the truth because they know not where to find it. (TPJS, 145)[47]

✦✦✦

"Mormonism" . . . is now taking a deep hold in the hearts and affections of all those, who are noble-minded enough to lay aside the prejudice of education, and investigate the subject with candor and honesty. (TPJS, 184)[59]

✦✦✦

[Some men,] . . . intelligent, learned, virtuous and lovely, walking in uprightness

and in all good conscience, so far as they have been able . . . [are left to] discern duty from the muddy stream of tradition, or from the blotted page of the book of nature. (TPJS, 192)[63]

✦✦✦

As a Church and a people it behooves us to be wise, and to seek to know the will of God, and then be willing to do it; for "blessed is he that heareth the word of the Lord, and keepeth it," say the Scriptures. (TPJS, 253)[81]

✦✦✦

I hope sober-thinking and sound-reasoning people will sooner listen to the voice of truth, than be led astray by the vain pretensions of the self-wise. (TPJS, 299)[104]

✦✦✦

One of the grand fundamental principles of "Mormonism" is to receive truth, let it come from whence it may. (TPJS, 313)[114]

✦✦✦

We should gather all the good and true principles in the world and treasure them up, or we shall not come out true "Mormons." (TPJS, 316)[115]

✦✦✦

I advise all to go on to perfection, and search deeper and deeper into the mysteries of Godliness. (TPJS, 364)[132]

UNDERSTANDING

Humble [yourselves] in a peculiar manner that God may open the eyes of [your] understanding. (TPJS, 78)[29]

◆◆◆

Men who have no principle of righteousness in themselves, and whose hearts are full of iniquity, and have no desire for the principles of truth, do not understand the word of truth when they hear it. The devil taketh away the word of truth out of their hearts, because there is no desire of righteousness in them. (TPJS, 96)[34]

◆◆◆

As females possess refined feelings and sensitiveness, they are also subject to overmuch zeal, which must ever prove dangerous, and cause them to be rigid in a religious capacity—[they] should be armed with mercy, notwithstanding the iniquity among us. (TPJS, 238)[78]

◆◆◆

All the gifts of the Spirit are not visible to the natural vision, or understanding of men; indeed very few of them are. (TPJS, 244)[80]

◆◆◆

Be virtuous and pure; be men of integrity and truth; keep the commandments of God; and then you will be able more perfectly to understand the difference between right and wrong—between the things of God and the things of men; and your path will be like that of the just, which shineth brighter and brighter unto the perfect day. (TPJS, 247)[80]

◆◆◆

It is for us to be righteous, that we may be wise and understand; for none of the wicked shall understand; but the wise shall understand. (TPJS, 253)[81]

◆◆◆

I have a key by which I understand the scriptures. . . . To ascertain [a scripture's] meaning, we must dig up the root and ascertain what it was that drew the saying out of Jesus. (TPJS, 276)[93]

◆◆◆

We never can comprehend the things of God and of heaven, but by revelation. We may spiritualize and express opinions to all eternity; but that is no authority. (TPJS, 292)[101]

◆◆◆

It is not wisdom that we should have all knowledge at once presented before us; but that we should have a little at a time, then we can comprehend it. (TPJS, 297)[103]

◆◆◆

The Lord deals with this people as a tender parent with a child, communicating light and intelligence and the knowledge of His ways as they can bear it. (TPJS, 305)[109]

◆◆◆

Never afflict thy soul for what an enemy hath put it out of thy power to do, if thy desires are ever so just. (TPJS, 317)[116]

◆◆◆

There has been a great difficulty in getting anything into the heads of this generation. . . . Even the Saints are slow to understand. (TPJS, 331)[123]

◆◆◆

If men do not comprehend the character of God, they do not comprehend themselves. (TPJS, 343)[130]

UNITY

(*See also* BROTHERHOOD; ZION)

It is needful . . . that you should be all of one heart, and of one mind, in doing the will of the Lord. (TPJS, 24)[13]

♦♦♦

We remember your losses and sorrows [Brother Peck]; our first ties are not broken; we participate with you in the evil as well as the good, in the sorrows as well as the joys; our union, we trust, is stronger than death, and shall never be severed. (TPJS, 79)[29]

♦♦♦

Zion . . . is a place of righteousness, and all who build thereon are to worship the true and living God, and all believe in one doctrine, even the doctrine of our Lord and Savior Jesus Christ. (TPJS, 80)[30]

♦♦♦

[The] Priesthood . . . may be illustrated by the figure of the human body, which has different members, which have different offices to perform; all are necessary in their place, and the body is not complete without all the members. (TPJS, 112)[41]

♦♦♦

In viewing the Church as a whole, we may strictly denominate it one Priesthood. (TPJS, 112)[41]

♦♦♦

Our circumstances are calculated to awaken our spirits to a sacred remembrance of everything, and we think . . . that nothing therefore can separate us from the love of God and fellowship one with another; and that every species of wickedness and cruelty practiced upon us will only tend to bind our hearts together and seal them together in love. (TPJS, 130)[47]

♦♦♦

How pleasing it is for the brethren to dwell together in unity! (TPJS, 174)[55]

♦♦♦

The greatest temporal and spiritual blessings which always come from faithfulness and concerted effort, never attended individual exertion or enterprise. (TPJS, 183)[58]

♦♦♦

When our brethren . . . show a unity of purpose and design, and all put their shoulder to the wheel, our care, toil, labor and anxiety is materially diminished, our yoke is made easy and our burden is light. (TPJS, 231)[76]

♦♦♦

The cause of God is one common cause, in which the Saints are alike all interested; we are all members of the one common body, and all partake of the same spirit, and are baptized into one baptism and possess alike the same glorious hope. (TPJS, 231)[76]

♦♦♦

The advancement of the cause of God and the building up of Zion is as much one man's business as another's. The only difference is, that one is called to fulfill one duty, and another another duty; "but if one member suffers, all the members suffer with it, and if one member is honored, all the rest rejoice with it, and the eye cannot say to the ear, I have no need of thee, nor the head to the foot, I have no need of thee"; party feelings, separate interests, exclusive designs should be lost sight of in the one common cause, in the interest of the whole. (TPJS, 231)[76]

♦♦♦

The Church is a compact body composed of different members, and [as] Paul . . . says, "now ye are the body of Christ and members in particular; and God hath set some in the Church, first Apostles, secondarily Prophets, thirdly Teachers, after miracles, then gifts of healing, helps, governments, diversities of tongues. Are all Teachers? Are all workers of miracles? Do all speak with tongues? Do all interpret? It is evident that they do not; yet they are all members of one body. All members of the natural [human] body are not the eye, the ear, the head or the hand—yet the eye cannot say to the ear, I have no need of thee, nor the head to the foot, I have no need of thee; they are all so many component parts in the perfect machine—the one body; and if one member suffer, the whole of the members suffer with it; and if one member rejoice, all the rest are honored with it." (TPJS, 244)[80]

◆◆◆

What if all the world should embrace the Gospel? They would then see eye to eye, and the blessings of God would be poured out upon the people, which is the desire of my whole soul. Amen. (TPJS, 275)[91]

◆◆◆

If a skillful mechanic . . . succeeds in welding together iron or steel more perfectly than any other mechanic, is he not deserving of praise? And if by the principles of truth I succeed in uniting men of all denominations in the bonds of love, shall I not have attained a good object? (TPJS, 313)[114]

◆◆◆

Christians should cease wrangling and contending with each other, and cultivate the principles of union and friendship in their midst . . . before the millennium can be ushered in and Christ takes possession of His kingdom. (TPJS, 314)[114]

◆◆◆

There is no greater love than this, that a man lay down his life for his friends. I discover hundreds and thousands of my brethren ready to sacrifice their lives for me. (TPJS, 315)[114]

◆◆◆

Friendship is like Brother Turley in his blacksmith shop welding iron to iron; it unites the human family with its happy influence. (TPJS, 316)[115]

◆◆◆

What would it profit us to come unto the spirits of the just men, but to learn and come up to the standard of their knowledge? (TPJS, 320)[118]

UNPARDONABLE SIN
(*See also* SONS OF PERDITION)

There is a superior intelligence bestowed upon such as obey the Gospel with full purpose of heart, which, if sinned against, the apostate is left naked and destitute of the Spirit of God, and he is, in truth, nigh unto cursing, and his end is to be burned. When once that light which was in them is taken from them, they become as much darkened as they were previously enlightened, and then, no marvel, if all their power should be enlisted against the truth . . . they, like Judas, seek the destruction of those who were their greatest benefactors. (TPJS, 67)[21]

◆◆◆

If men sin willfully after they have received the knowledge of the truth, there remaineth no more sacrifice for sin, but a certain fearful looking for of judgment and fiery indignation to come, which shall devour these adversaries. . . . Of how much more severe punishment suppose ye, shall he be thought worthy, who hath sold his brother, and denied the new and everlasting covenant by which he was sanctified, calling it an unholy thing, and doing despite to the Spirit of grace. (TPJS, 128)[46]

•••

All other sins are not to be compared to sinning against the Holy Ghost, and proving a traitor to the brethren. (TPJS, 156)[49]

•••

The unpardonable sin is to shed innocent blood, or be accessory thereto. (TPJS, 301)[105]

•••

If men have received the good word of God, and tasted of the powers of the world to come, if they shall fall away, it is impossible to renew them again, seeing they have crucified the Son of God afresh, and put Him to an open shame. (TPJS, 339)[128]

•••

No man can commit the unpardonable sin after the dissolution of the body, nor in this life, until he receives the Holy Ghost; but they must do it in this world. (TPJS, 357)[130]

•••

When a man begins to be an enemy to this work, he hunts me, he seeks to kill me, and never ceases to thirst for my blood. He gets the spirit of the devil—the same spirit that they had who crucified the Lord of Life—the same spirit that sins against the Holy Ghost. You cannot save such persons; you cannot bring them to repentance; they make open war, like the devil, and awful is the consequence. (TPJS, 358)[130]

•••

What must a man do to commit the unpardonable sin? He must receive the Holy Ghost, have the heavens opened unto him, and know God, and then sin against Him. . . . He has got to say that the sun does not shine while he sees it; he has got to deny Jesus Christ when the heavens have been opened unto him, and to deny the Plan of Salvation with his eyes open to the

truth of it; and from that time he begins to be an enemy. This is the case with many apostates of the Church of Jesus Christ of Latter-day Saints. (TPJS, 358)[130]

URGENCY OF THE WORK

The temple of the Lord . . . will be so constructed as to enable all the functions of the Priesthood to be duly exercised and where instructions from the Most High will be received, and from this place go forth to distant lands. Let us then concentrate all our powers, . . . and strive to emulate the action of the ancient covenant fathers, and patriarchs, in those things which are of such vast importance to this and every succeeding generation. (TPJS, 182)[57]

•••

Hasten the work in the Temple, renew your exertions to forward all the work of the last days, and walk before the Lord in soberness and righteousness. (TPJS, 326)[121]

•••

The Saints have not too much time to save and redress their dead, and gather together their living relatives, that they may be saved also, before the earth will be smitten, and the consumption decreed falls upon the world. (TPJS, 330)[122]

•••

If the whole Church should go to with all their might to save their dead, seal their posterity, and gather their living friends, and spend none of their time in behalf of the world, they would hardly get through before night would come, when no man can work. (TPJS, 330)[123]

•••

The greatest responsibility in this world that God has laid upon us is to seek after our dead. (TPJS, 356)[130]

VALIANCE

Impressed with the . . . [fact of darkness covering the earth and minds of men,] what can be the feelings of those who have been partakers of the heavenly gift and have tasted the good word of God, and the powers of the world to come? Who but those that can see the awful precipice upon which the world of mankind stands in this generation, can labor in the vineyard of the Lord without feeling a sense of the world's deplorable situation? Who but those who have duly considered the condescension of the Father of our spirits, in providing a sacrifice for His creatures, a plan of redemption, a power of atonement, a scheme of salvation, having as its great objects, the bringing of men back into the presence of the King of heaven, crowning them in the celestial glory, and making them heirs with the Son to that inheritance which is incorruptible, undefiled, and which fadeth not away—who but such can realize the importance of a perfect walk before all men, and a diligence in calling upon all men to partake of these blessings? How indescribably glorious are these things to mankind! Of a truth they may be considered tidings of great joy to all people; and tidings, too, that ought to fill the earth and cheer the heart of everyone when sounded in his ears. The reflection that everyone is to receive according to his own diligence and perseverance while in the vineyard, ought to inspire everyone who is called to be a minister of these glad tidings, to so improve his talent that he may gain other talents, that when the Master sits down to take an account of the conduct of His servants, it may be said, "Well done, good and faithful servant: thou hast been faithful over a few things; I will now make thee ruler over many things: enter thou into the joy of thy Lord." (TPJS, 47)[21]

•••

The Lord says that every man is to receive according to his works. Reflect for a moment, . . . and enquire whether you would consider yourselves worthy a seat at the marriage seat with Paul and others like him, if you had been unfaithful? Had you not fought the good fight, and kept the faith, could you expect to receive? (TPJS, 64)[21]

•••

We do not care for them that can kill the body; they cannot harm our souls. We ask no favors at the hands of mobs, nor of the world, nor of the devil, nor of his emissaries the dissenters, and those who love, and make, and swear falsehoods, to take away our lives. We have never dissembled, nor will we for the sake of our lives. (TPJS, 123)[46]

•••

As well might the devil seek to dethrone Jehovah, as overthrow an innocent soul that resists everything which is evil. (TPJS, 226)[75]

•••

If a man stands and opposes the world of sin, he may expect to have all wicked and corrupt spirits arrayed against him. (TPJS, 259)[84]

•••

He that will war the true Christian warfare against the corruptions of these last days will have wicked men and angels of devils, and all the infernal powers of darkness continually arrayed against him. (TPJS, 259)[84]

◆◆◆

Never, while the spirit of liberty, or the virtue of a Saint, hold communion in the flesh, let us hear of those who profess to be governed by the law of God, and make their garments clean in the blood of the Lamb, shrinking from the assistance of those who bear the ark of the Lord—in the hour of danger! (TPJS, 261)[85]

◆◆◆

I am bold to declare I have taught all the strong doctrines publicly, and always teach stronger doctrines in public than in private. (TPJS, 370)[133]

VANITY

All are subjected to vanity while they travel through the crooked paths and difficulties which surround them. Where is a man that is free from vanity? . . . But notwithstanding their vanity, men look forward with hope to the time of their deliverance. (TPJS, 187)[60]

VENGEANCE

Bear and forbear one with another, for so the Lord does with us. Pray for your enemies in the Church and curse not your foes without: for vengeance is mine, saith the Lord, and I will repay. (TPJS, 77)[29]

◆◆◆

I do not want to cloak iniquity—all

things contrary to the will of God, should be cast from us, but don't do more hurt than good. . . . I want the innocent to go free—rather spare ten iniquitous among you, than condemn one innocent one. . . . "Fret not thyself because of evildoers." God will see to it. (TPJS, 239)[78]

◆◆◆

The devil's retaliation is, he comes into this world, bind's up men's bodies, and occupies them himself. When the authorities come along, they eject him from a stolen habitation. (TPJS, 306)[109]

VIRTUE

Now for a man to consecrate his property, wife and children, to the Lord, is nothing more nor less than to feed the hungry, clothe the naked, visit the widow and fatherless, the sick and afflicted, and do all he can to administer to their relief in their afflictions, and for him and his house to serve the Lord. In order to do this, he and all his house must be virtuous, and must shun the very appearance of evil. (TPJS, 127)[46]

VISIONS

An open vision will manifest that which is more important. (TPJS, 161)[49]

◆◆◆

It is my meditation all the day, and more than my meat and drink, to know how I shall make the Saints of God comprehend the visions that roll like an overflowing surge before my mind. (TPJS, 296)[102]

WAR

And now I am prepared to say by the authority of Jesus Christ, that not many years shall pass away before the United States shall present such a scene of *bloodshed* as has not a parallel in the history of our nation. (TPJS, 17)[9]

◆◆◆

Exalt the standard of Democracy! Down with that of priestcraft, and let all the people say Amen! That the blood of our fathers may not cry from the ground against us. (TPJS, 117)[42]

◆◆◆

Sacred is the memory of that blood which bought for us our liberty. (TPJS, 117)[42]

◆◆◆

Nothing is a greater injury to the children of men than to be under the influence of a false spirit when they think they have the Spirit of God. Thousands have felt the influence of its terrible power and baneful effect . . . pain, misery and ruin have followed in their train; nations have been convulsed, kingdoms overthrown, provinces laid waste, and blood, carnage and desolation are habiliments in which it has been clothed. (TPJS, 205)[71]

◆◆◆

The world itself presents one great theater of misery, woe, and "distress of nations and perplexity." All, all, speak with a voice of thunder, that man is not able to govern himself, to legislate for himself, to protect himself, to promote his own good, nor the good of the world. (TPJS, 250)[81]

◆◆◆

When my enemies take away my rights, I will bear it and keep out of the way; but if they take away your rights, I will fight for you. (TPJS, 268)[87]

◆◆◆

The prediction is that army will be against army; it may be that the Saints will have to beat their ploughs into swords, for it will not do for men to sit down patiently and see their children destroyed. (TPJS, 366)[132]

WARNING

Repent, repent, is the voice of God to Zion; and strange as it may appear, yet it is true, mankind will persist in self-justification until all their iniquity is exposed, and their character past being redeemed, and that which is treasured up in their hearts be exposed to the gaze of mankind. I say to you [and what I say to you I say to all] hear the warning voice of God, lest Zion fall, and the Lord swear in His wrath the inhabitants of Zion shall not enter into His rest. (TPJS, 18)[10]

◆◆◆

I feel it my duty to drop a few hints, that perhaps the Elders traveling through the world, [may] warn the inhabitants of the earth to flee the wrath to come, and save themselves from this untoward generation. (TPJS, 79)[30]

◆◆◆

It is a day of warning, and not of many words. (TPJS, 156)[49]

◆◆◆

Satan will rage, and the spirit of the devil is now enraged. I know not how soon these [horrible] things will take place; but with a view of them, shall I cry peace? No; I will lift up my voice and testify of them. (TPJS, 161)[49]

◆◆◆

Let this [early death] . . . prove as a warning to all not to procrastinate repentance, or wait till a death-bed, for it is the will of God that man should repent and serve Him in health, and blessing and power of his mind, in order to secure his blessing, and not wait until he is called to die. (TPJS, 197)[68]

◆◆◆

We should take warning and not wait for death-bed to repent, as we see the infant taken away by death, so may the youth and middle-aged . . . be suddenly called into eternity. (TPJS, 197)[68]

◆◆◆

If [you] have done anything . . . that [you] are sorry for, or that [you] would not like to meet and answer for at the bar of God . . . let it prove as a warning to all to deal justly before God, and with all mankind, then we shall be clear in the day of judgment. (TPJS, 216)[72]

◆◆◆

And, in consequence of rejecting the Gospel of Jesus Christ and the Prophets whom God hath sent, the judgments of God have rested upon people, cities, and nations, in various ages of the world, which was the case with the cities of Sodom and Gomorrah, that were destroyed for rejecting the prophets. (TPJS, 271)[91]

◆◆◆

This [passing of Brother Barnes] has been a warning voice to us all to be sober and diligent and lay aside mirth, vanity and folly, and to be prepared to die tomorrow. (TPJS, 296)[102]

◆◆◆

Beware, O earth, how you fight against the saints of God and shed innocent blood; for in the days of Elijah, his enemies came upon him, and fire was called down from heaven and destroyed them. (TPJS, 340)[128]

◆◆◆

Why do not my enemies strike a blow at the doctrine? They cannot do it: it is truth, and I defy all men to upset it. I am the voice of one crying in the wilderness, "Repent ye of your sins and prepare the way for the coming of the Son of Man; for the kingdom of God has come unto you, and henceforth the axe is laid unto the root of the tree; and every tree that bringeth not forth good fruit, God Almighty . . . shall hew it down and cast it into the fire." (TPJS, 341)[129]

◆◆◆

Woe, woe be to that man or set of men who lift up their hands against God and His witness in these last days: for they shall deceive almost the very chosen ones! (TPJS, 365)[132]

WASHING OF FEET

The ordinance of washing of feet [of the Twelve] . . . is necessary now, as much it was in the days of the Savior; and we must have a place prepared, that we may attend to this ordinance aside from the world. . . . It was never intended for any but official members. It is calculated to unite our hearts, that we may be one in feeling and sentiment, and that our faith may be strong, so that Satan cannot overthrow us, nor have any power over us here. (TPJS, 90)[33]

WEAKNESS

The great and wise of ancient days have failed in all their attempts to promote eternal power, peace and happiness. Their nations have crumbled to pieces; their thrones have been cast down in their turn, and their cities, and their mightiest works of art have been annihilated; or their dilapidated towers, or time-worn monuments have left us but feeble traces of their former magnificence and ancient grandeur. They proclaim as with a voice of thunder, those imperishable truths—that man's strength is weakness, his wisdom is folly, his glory is his shame. (TPJS, 249)[81]

•••

I find that in the midst of business and care the spirit is willing, but the flesh is weak. (TPJS, 315)[114]

•••

I have tried a number of years to get the minds of the Saints prepared to receive the things of God; but we frequently see some of them, after suffering all they have for the work of God, will fly to pieces like glass as soon as anything comes that is contrary to their traditions: they cannot stand the fire at all. How many will be able to abide a celestial law, and go through and receive their exaltation, I am unable to say, as many are called, but few are chosen. (TPJS, 331)[123]

WEAPONS

He that arms himself with gun, sword, or pistol, except in the defense of truth, will sometime be sorry for it. I never carry any weapon with me bigger than my penknife. When I was dragged before the cannon and muskets in Missouri, I was unarmed. God will always protect me until my mission is fulfilled. (TPJS, 365)[132]

WELFARE

A man filled with the love of God, is not content with blessing his family alone, but ranges through the whole world, anxious to bless the whole human race. (TPJS, 174)[54]

•••

I love that man better who swears a stream as long as my arm, yet deals justice to his neighbors and mercifully deals his substance to the poor, than the long, smooth-faced hypocrite. (TPJS, 303)[109]

•••

Some say it is better to give to the poor than build the Temple. The building of the Temple has sustained the poor who were driven from Missouri, and kept them from starving; and it has been the best means for this object which could be devised. (TPJS, 329)[122]

WICKED SPIRITS

It would seem also, that wicked spirits have their bounds, limits and laws by which they are governed or controlled, and know their future destiny; . . . they possess a power that none but those who have the Priesthood can control. (TPJS, 208)[71]

WICKEDNESS

(See also CORRUPTION; EVIL)

Consider for a moment, brethren, the fulfillment of the words of the prophet; for we behold that darkness covers the earth, and gross darkness the minds of the inhabitants thereof—that crimes of every description are increasing among men—vices of great enormity are practices—the rising generation growing up in the fullness of pride and arrogance—the aged losing every sense of conviction, and seemingly banishing every thought of a day of retribution—intemperance, immorality, extravagance, pride, blindness of heart, idolatry, the loss of natural affection; the love of the world, and indifference toward the things of eternity increasing among those who profess a belief in the religion of heaven, and infidelity spreading itself in consequence of the same—men giving themselves up to commit acts of the foulest kind, and deeds of the blackest dye, blaspheming, defrauding, blasting the reputation of neighbors, stealing, robbing, murdering; advocating error and opposing the truth, forsaking the covenant of heaven, and denying the faith of Jesus— and in the midst of all this, the day of the Lord fast approaching when none except those who have won the wedding garment will be permitted to eat and drink in the presence of the Bridegroom, the Prince of Peace! (TPJS, 47)[21]

♦♦♦

Darkness prevails at this time as it did at the time Jesus Christ was about to be crucified. The powers of darkness strove to obscure the glorious Sun of righteousness, that began to dawn upon the world, and was soon to burst in great blessings upon the heads of the faithful. (TPJS, 90)[33]

♦♦♦

Men who have no principle of righteousness in themselves, and whose hearts are full of iniquity, and have no desire for the principles of truth, do not understand the word of truth when they hear it. The devil taketh away the word of truth out of their hearts, because there is no desire of righteousness in them. (TPJS, 96)[34]

♦♦♦

Such inhumanity, and relentless cruelty and barbarity as were practiced against the Saints in Missouri can scarcely be found in the annals of history. (TPJS, 126)[46]

♦♦♦

We think . . . that every species of wickedness and cruelty practiced upon us will only tend to bind our hearts together and seal them together in love. . . . We are driven from our homes and smitten without cause. . . . We are compelled to hear nothing but blasphemous oaths, and witness a scene of blasphemy, and drunkenness and hypocrisy, and debaucheries of every description. (TPJS, 130)[47]

♦♦♦

The time is soon coming, when no man will have any peace, but in Zion and her stakes. (TPJS, 161)[49]

♦♦♦

In the earlier ages of the world a righteous man, and a man of God and intelligence, had a better chance to do good, to be believed and received than at the present day; but in these days, such a man is much opposed and persecuted by most of the inhabitants of the earth, and he has much sorrow to pass through here. (TPJS, 196)[68]

♦♦♦

If we are not drawing towards God in principle, we are going from Him and drawing towards the devil. (TPJS, 216)[73]

♦♦♦

Monarchial, aristocratical, and republican governments of their various kinds and grades, have, in their turn, been raised to dignity, and prostrated in the dust. The plans of the greatest politicians, the wisest senators, and most profound statesmen have been exploded; and the proceedings of the greatest chieftains, the bravest generals, and the wisest kings have fallen to the ground. Nation has succeeded nation, and we have inherited nothing but their folly. History records their [childish] plans, their short-lived glory, their feeble intellect and their ignoble deeds. (TPJS, 249)⁸¹

•••

The earth is groaning under corruption, oppression, tyranny and bloodshed; and God is coming out of His hiding place. (TPJS, 253)⁸¹

•••

When I do the best I can—when I am accomplishing the greatest good, then the most evil and wicked surmisings are got up against me. (TPJS, 259)⁸⁴

•••

There will be wicked men on the earth during the thousand years. The heathen nations who will not come up to worship will be visited with the judgments of God, and must eventually be destroyed from the earth. (TPJS, 268)⁸⁸

•••

This generation is as corrupt as the generation of the Jews that crucified Christ; and if He were here today, and should preach the same doctrine He did then, they would put Him to death. (TPJS, 328)¹²²

WISDOM

We must be wise as serpents and harmless as doves. (TPJS, 36)¹⁹

•••

Why will not man learn wisdom by precept at this late age of the world, when we have such a cloud of witnesses and examples before us, and not be obliged to learn by sad experience everything we know. (TPJS, 155)⁴⁹

•••

I do not want to cloak iniquity—all things contrary to the will of God, should

be cast from us, but don't do more hurt than good. . . . I want the innocent to go free—rather spare ten iniquitous among you, than condemn one innocent one. . . , "Fret not thyself because of evildoers." God will see to it. (TPJS, 239)⁷⁸

•••

Man's strength is weakness, his wisdom is folly, his glory is his shame. (TPJS, 249)⁸¹

•••

As God governed Abraham, Isaac and Jacob as families, and the children of Israel as a nation; so we, as a Church, must be under His guidance if we are prospered, preserved and sustained. Our only confidence can be in God; our only wisdom obtained from Him; and He alone must be our protector and safeguard, spiritually and temporally, or we fall. (TPJS, 253)⁸¹

•••

It is for us to be righteous, that we may be wise and understand; for none of the wicked shall understand; but the wise shall understand. (TPJS, 253)⁸¹

•••

It is not wisdom that we should have all knowledge at once presented before us; but that we should have a little at a time, then we can comprehend it. (TPJS, 297)¹⁰³

•••

The way to get along in any important matter is to gather unto yourselves wise men, experienced and aged men, to assist in council in all times of trouble. (TPJS, 299)¹⁰³

•••

Our lives have already been jeopardized by revealing the wicked and bloodthirsty purposes of our enemies; and for the future we must cease to do so. All we have said about them is truth, but it is not always wise to relate all the truth. (TPJS, 392)[14]

WISDOM OF THE WORLD

The great designs of God in relation to the salvation of the human family, are very little understood by the professedly wise and intelligent generation in which we live. (TPJS, 218)[74]

♦♦♦

There are a great many wise men and women too in our midst who are too wise to be taught; therefore they must die in their ignorance, and in the resurrection they will find their mistake. Many seal up the door of heaven by saying . . . God may reveal and I will believe. (TPJS, 309)[113]

WIVES

Wives, submit yourselves unto your own husbands, as it is fit in the Lord. Husbands, love your wives, and be not bitter against them. (TPJS, 88)[31]

♦♦♦

[Joseph] exhorted the sisters always to concentrate their faith and prayers for, and place confidence in their husbands, whom God has appointed for them to honor, and in those faithful men whom God has placed at the head of the Church to lead His people. (TPJS, 226)[75]

♦♦♦

You need not be teasing your husbands because of their deeds, but let the weight of your innocence, kindness and affection be felt, which is more mighty than a millstone hung about the neck; not war, not jangle, not contradiction or dispute, but meekness, love, purity—these are the things that should magnify you in the eyes of all good men. (TPJS, 227)[75]

♦♦♦

Let [the Relief] Society teach women how to behave towards their husbands, to treat them with mildness and affection. (TPJS, 228)[75]

♦♦♦

When a man is born down with trouble, when he is perplexed with care and difficulty, if he can meet a smile instead of an argument or a murmur . . . if he can meet with mildness, it will calm down his soul and soothe his feelings; when the mind is going to despair, it needs a solace of affection and kindness. (TPJS, 228)[75]

♦♦♦

When you go home, never give a cross or unkind word to your husbands, but let kindness, charity and love crown your works henceforward. (TPJS, 229)[75]

WOMEN

A woman has no right to found or organize a church—God never sent them to do it. (TPJS, 212)[71]

♦♦♦

No matter who believeth, these signs, such as healing the sick, casting out devils, etc., should follow all that believe, whether male or female. (TPJS, 224)[75]

♦♦♦

[Joseph] exhorted the sisters always to concentrate their faith and prayers for, and place confidence in their husbands, whom God has appointed for them to honor, and in those faithful men whom God has placed at the head of the Church to lead His people. (TPJS, 226)[75]

♦♦♦

This is a charitable [Relief] Society, and according to your natures; it is natural for females to have feelings of charity and benevolence. You are now placed in a situation in which you can act according to those sympathies which God has planted in your bosoms. (TPJS, 226)[75]

♦♦♦

Females, if they are pure and innocent, can come in the presence of God; for what is more pleasing to God than innocence? . . . If we would come before God, we must keep ourselves pure, as He is pure. (TPJS, 227)[75]

♦♦♦

You need not be teasing your husbands because of their deeds, but let the weight of your innocence, kindness and affection be felt, which is more mighty than a millstone hung about the neck; not war, not jangle, not contradiction or dispute, but meekness, love, purity—these are the things that should magnify you in the eyes of all good men. (TPJS, 227)[75]

♦♦♦

[Joseph said that] it was according to revelation that the sick should be nursed with herbs and mild food, and not by the hand of an enemy. Who are better qualified to administer than our faithful and zealous sisters, whose hearts are full of faith, tenderness, sympathy and compassion. No one. (TPJS, 229)[75]

♦♦♦

As females possess refined feelings and sensitiveness, they are also subject to overmuch zeal, which must ever prove dangerous, and cause them to be rigid in a religious capacity—[they] should be armed with mercy, notwithstanding the iniquity among us. (TPJS, 238)[78]

WORD OF WISDOM

No official member in this Church is worthy to hold an office after having the word of wisdom properly taught him; and he, the official member, neglecting to comply with and obey it. (TPJS, 117)[43]

WORDS

(See also LANGUAGE)

The lips betray the haughty and overbearing imaginations of the heart; by his words and his deeds let him be judged. (TPJS, 137)[47]

WORLD

It is reasonable to suppose that man departed from the first teachings, or instructions which he received from heaven in the first age, and refused by his disobedience to be governed by them. Consequently, he formed such laws as best suited his own mind, or as he supposed, were best adapted to his situation. (TPJS, 57)[21]

♦♦♦

Such is the darkness and ignorance of this generation, that they look upon it as incredible that a man should have any intercourse with his Maker. (TPJS, 89)[32]

♦♦♦

I am well aware that you [the Twelve] have to sustain my character against the vile calumnies and reproaches of this ungodly generation, and that you delight in doing so. (TPJS, 89)[33]

♦♦♦

Darkness prevails at this time as it did at the time Jesus Christ was about to be crucified. The powers of darkness strove to obscure the glorious Sun of righteousness, that began to dawn upon the world, and was soon to burst in great blessings upon the heads of the faithful. (TPJS, 90)[33]

♦♦♦

Men are in the habit, when the truth is exhibited by the servants of God, of saying, All is mystery; they have spoken in parables, and therefore, are not to be understood. It is true they have eyes to see, and see not, but none are so blind as those who will not see. (TPJS, 96)[34]

• • •

Men who have no principle of righteousness in themselves, and whose hearts are full of iniquity, and have no desire for the principles of truth, do not understand the word of truth when they hear it. The devil taketh away the word of truth out of their hearts, because there is no desire of righteousness in them. (TPJS, 96)[34]

• • •

Now, dear brethren, if any men ever had reason to claim this promise "great is your reward in heaven, for so persecuted they the Prophets which were before you.," we are the men; for we know that the world not only hate us, but they speak all manner of evil of us falsely, for no other reason than that we have been endeavoring to teach the fullness of the Gospel of Jesus Christ. (TPJS, 124)[46]

• • •

Such inhumanity, and relentless cruelty and barbarity as were practiced against the Saints in Missouri can scarcely be found in the annals of history. (TPJS, 126)[46]

• • •

The time is soon coming, when no man will have any peace, but in Zion and her stakes. (TPJS, 161)[49]

• • •

The world has always mistook false prophets for true ones, and those that were sent of God, they considered to be false prophets, and hence they killed, stoned, punished and imprisoned the true prophets . . . and though the most honorable men of the earth, they banished them from their society as vagabonds, whilst they cherished, honored and supported knaves, vagabonds, hypocrites, imposters, and the basest of men. (TPJS, 206)[71]

• • •

The great designs of God in relation to the salvation of the human family, are very little understood by the professedly wise and intelligent generation in which we live. (TPJS, 218)[74]

• • •

The greatest acts of the mighty men have been to depopulate nations and to overthrow kingdoms; and whilst they have exalted themselves and become glorious, it has been at the expense of the lives of the innocent, the blood of the oppressed, the moans of the widow, and the tears of the orphans. (TPJS, 248)[80]

• • •

Monarchial, aristocratical, and republican governments of their various kinds and grades, have, in their turn, been raised to dignity, and prostrated in the dust. The plans of the greatest politicians, the wisest senators, and most profound statesmen have been exploded; and the proceedings of the greatest chieftains, the bravest generals, and the wisest kings have fallen to the ground. Nation has succeeded nation, and we have inherited nothing but their folly. History records their [childish] plans, their short-lived glory, their feeble intellect and their ignoble deeds. (TPJS, 249)[81]

• • •

The world itself presents one great theater of misery, woe, and "distress of nations and perplexity." All, all, speak with a voice of thunder, that man is not able to govern himself, to legislate for himself, to protect himself, to promote his own good, nor the good of the world. (TPJS, 250)[81]

•••

The earth is groaning under corruption, oppression, tyranny and bloodshed; and God is coming out of His hiding place. (TPJS, 253)[81]

•••

The world is full of technicalities and misrepresentation, which I calculate to overthrow, and speak of things as they actually exist. (TPJS, 292)[101]

•••

I have not the least idea, if Christ should come to the earth and preach such rough things as He preached to the Jews, but that this generation would reject Him for being so rough. (TPJS, 307)[113]

•••

There are a great many wise men and women too in our midst who are too wise to be taught; therefore they must die in their ignorance, and in the resurrection they will find their mistake. Many seal up the door of heaven by saying . . . God may reveal and I will believe. (TPJS, 309) 113

•••

I do not grudge the world all the religion they have got; they are welcome to all the knowledge they possess. (TPJS, 320)[118]

•••

That which hath been hid from before the foundation of the world is revealed to babes and sucklings in the last days. (TPJS, 321)[118]

•••

This generation is as corrupt as the generation of the Jews that crucified Christ; and if He were here today, and should preach the same doctrine He did then, they would put Him to death. (TPJS, 328)[122]

•••

I intend to lay a foundation that will revolutionize the whole world. (TPJS, 366)[132]

WORLDLINESS

The light of the latter-day glory begins to break forth through the dark atmosphere of sectarian wickedness, and their iniquity begins to roll up into view, and the nations of the Gentiles are like the waves of the sea, casting up mire and dirt, or all in commotion, and they are hastily preparing to act the part allotted them, when the Lord rebukes the nations, when He shall rule them with a rod of iron, and break them in pieces like a potter's vessel. (TPJS, 16)[9]

•••

Consider for a moment, brethren, the fulfillment of the words of the prophet; for we behold that darkness covers the earth, and gross darkness the minds of the inhabitants thereof—that crimes of every description are increasing among men— vices of great enormity are practices—the rising generation growing up in the fullness of pride and arrogance—the aged losing every sense of conviction, and seemingly banishing every thought of a day of retribution—intemperance, immorality, extravagance, pride, blindness of heart, idolatry, the loss of natural affection; the love of the world, and indifference toward the things of eternity increasing among those who profess a belief in the religion of heaven, and infidelity spreading itself in consequence of the same—men giving themselves up to commit acts of the foulest kind, and deeds of the blackest dye, blaspheming, defrauding, blasting the reputation of neighbors, stealing, robbing, murdering; advocating error and opposing the truth, forsaking the covenant of heaven, and denying the faith of Jesus— and in the midst of all this, the day of the Lord fast approaching when none except those who have won the wedding garment will be permitted to eat and drink in the presence of the Bridegroom, the Prince of Peace! (TPJS, 47)[21]

•••

"Behold, there are many called, but few are chosen. And why are they not chosen? Because their hearts are so set upon the things of this world, and aspire to the honors of men, that they do not learn this one lesson—that the rights of the Priesthood are inseparably connected with the powers of heaven, and that the powers of heaven cannot be controlled nor handled only upon the principles of righteousness. That they may be conferred upon us, it is true; but when we undertake to cover our sins, or to gratify our pride, our vain ambition, or to exercise control, or dominion, or compulsion, upon the souls of the children of men in any degree of unrighteousness, behold, the heavens withdraw themselves, the Spirit of the Lord is grieved; and when it is withdrawn, Amen to the Priesthood, or the authority of that man. Behold! Ere he is aware, he is left to himself to kick against the pricks, to persecute the saints, and to fight against God.

"We have learned by sad experience that it is the nature and disposition of almost all men, as soon as they get a little authority, as they suppose, they will immediately begin to exercise unrighteous dominion. Hence, many are called, but few are chosen. (TPJS, 142)[47]

•••

In the earlier ages of the world a righteous man, and a man of God and intelligence, had a better chance to do good, to be believed and received than at the present day; but in these days, such a man is much opposed and persecuted by most of the inhabitants of the earth, and he has much sorrow to pass through here. (TPJS, 196)[68]

•••

If any revelations are given of God, they are universally opposed by the priests and Christendom at large; for they reveal their wickedness and abominations. (TPJS, 217)[73]

•••

There are a great many wise men and women too in our midst who are too wise to be taught; therefore they must die in their ignorance, and in the resurrection they will find their mistake. Many seal up the door of heaven by saying . . . God may reveal and I will believe. (TPJS, 309)[113]

WORSHIP

When we lose a near and dear friend, upon whom we have set our hearts, it should be a caution unto us not to set our affections too firmly upon others, knowing that they may in like manner be taken from us. Our affections should be placed upon God and His work more intensely than upon our fellow beings. (TPJS, 216)[72]

WORTH OF SOULS

Souls are as precious in the sight of God as they ever were; and the Elders were never called to drive any down to hell, but to persuade and invite all men everywhere to repent, that they may become heirs of salvation. (TPJS, 77)[29]

WORTHINESS

Remember not to murmur at the dealings of God with His creatures. You are not as yet brought into as trying circumstances as were the ancient Prophets and Apostles . . . of whom the world was not worthy . . . amidst all their afflictions they rejoiced that they were counted worthy to receive persecution for Christ's sake. (TPJS, 32)[18]

♦♦♦

We know not what we shall be called to pass through before Zion is delivered and established; therefore, we have great need to live near to God, and always be in strict obedience to all His commandments, that we may have a conscience void of offense toward God and man. (TPJS, 32)[18]

♦♦♦

God has in reserve a time, or period appointed in His bosom, when He will bring all his subjects, who have obeyed his voice and kept His commandments, into His celestial rest. This rest is of such perfection and glory, that man has need of a preparation before he can, according to the laws of that kingdom, enter it and enjoy its blessings. This being the fact, God has given certain laws to the human family, which, if observed, are sufficient to prepare them to inherit this rest. This, then, we conclude, was the purpose of God in giving His laws to us. (TPJS, 54)[21]

♦♦♦

In the 22nd chapter of Matthew's account of the Messiah, we find the Kingdom of Heaven likened unto a king who made a marriage for his son. . . . This son was the Messiah . . . The Saints, or those who are found faithful to the Lord, are the individuals who will be found worthy to inherit a seat at the marriage supper . . . Let us be glad and rejoice, and give honor to Him; for the marriage of the Lamb is come, and His wife hath made herself ready. And to her was granted that she should be arrayed in fine linen, clean and white: For the fine linen is the righteousness of Saints. (TPJS, 63)[21]

♦♦♦

The Lord says that every man is to receive according to his works. Reflect for a moment, . . . and enquire whether you would consider yourselves worthy a seat at the marriage seat with Paul and others like him, if you had been unfaithful? Had you not fought the good fight, and kept the faith, could you expect to receive? (TPJS, 64)[21]

♦♦♦

The Messiah's kingdom on earth is of that kind of government, that there has always been numerous apostates, for the reason that it admits of no sins unrepented of without excluding the individual from its fellowship. (TPJS, 66)[21]

♦♦♦

The great Plan of Salvation is a theme which ought to occupy our strict attention, and be regarded as one of heaven's best gifts to mankind. No consideration whatever ought to deter us from showing ourselves approved in the sight of God. (TPJS, 68)[21]

♦♦♦

Meekly persuade and urge every one to forgive one another all their trespasses, offenses and sins, that they may work out their own salvation with fear and trembling. (TPJS, 77)[29]

♦♦♦

Live worthy of the blessings that shall follow, after much tribulation, to satiate the souls of them that hold out faithful to the end. (TPJS, 78)[29]

♦♦♦

No official member in this Church is worthy to hold an office after having the word of wisdom properly taught him; and he, the official member, neglecting to comply with and obey it. (TPJS, 117)[43]

♦♦♦

[We must] be on the alert to concentrate our energies, ... the best feelings should exist in our midst; and then, by the help of the Almighty, we shall go on from victory to victory, and from conquest to conquest; our evil passions will be subdued, our prejudices depart; we shall find no room in our bosoms for hatred; vice will hide its deformed head, and we shall stand approved in the sight of Heaven, and be acknowledged the sons of God. (TPJS, 179)[54]

•••

If you wish to go where God is, you must be like God, or possess the principles which God possesses; for if we are not drawing towards God in principle, we are going from Him and drawing towards the devil. (TPJS, 216)[73]

•••

As well might the devil seek to dethrone Jehovah, as overthrow an innocent soul that resists everything which is evil. (TPJS, 226)[75]

•••

Females, if they are pure and innocent, can come in the presence of God; for what is more pleasing to God than innocence? . . . If we would come before God, we must keep ourselves pure, as He is pure. (TPJS, 227)[75]

•••

What would it profit us to come unto the spirits of the just men, but to learn and come up to the standard of their knowledge? (TPJS, 320)[118]

YOUTH

That which hath been hid from before the foundation of the world is revealed to babes and sucklings in the last days. (TPJS, 321)[118]

ZION

(*See also* BROTHERHOOD; UNITY)

Every man lives for himself. . . . But except a man be born again, he cannot see the kingdom of God. . . . He can never come unto Mount Zion, and unto the city of the living God . . . unless he becomes as a little child, and is taught by the Spirit of God. (TPJS, 12)[8]

•••

The city of Zion spoken of by David, in the one hundred and second Psalm, will be built upon the land of America. (TPJS, 17)[9]

•••

It is needful . . . that you should be all of one heart, and of one mind, in doing the will of the Lord. (TPJS, 24)[13]

•••

It is not the will of the Lord for you to sell your lands in Zion, if means can possibly be procured for your sustenance without. (TPJS, 31)[18]

•••

You will recollect that the Lord has said, that Zion should not be removed out of her place; therefore the land should not be sold, but be held by the saints, until the Lord in His wisdom shall open a way for your return. (TPJS, 33)[18]

◆◆◆

I know that Zion, in the due time of the Lord, will be redeemed; but how many will be the days of her purification, tribulation, and affliction, the Lord has kept hid from my eyes; and when I enquire concerning this subject, the voice of the Lord is: Be still, and know that I am God. (TPJS, 34)[19]

◆◆◆

Zion . . . is a place of righteousness, and all who build thereon are to worship the true and living God, and all believe in one doctrine, even the doctrine of our Lord and Savior Jesus Christ. (TPJS, 80)[30]

◆◆◆

We want all honest men to have a chance to gather and build up a city of righteousness, when even upon the bells of the horses shall be written *"Holiness to the Lord."* (TPJS, 93)[35]

◆◆◆

We ought to have the building up of Zion as our greatest object.. (TPJS, 160)[49]

◆◆◆

The time is soon coming, when no man will have any peace, but in Zion and her stakes. (TPJS, 161)[49]

◆◆◆

The cause of God is one common cause, in which the Saints are alike all interested; we are all members of the one common body, and all partake of the same spirit, and are baptized into one baptism and possess alike the same glorious hope. (TPJS, 231)[76]

◆◆◆

The advancement of the cause of God and the building up of Zion is as much one man's business as another's. The only difference is, that one is called to fulfill one duty, and another another duty; "but if one member suffers, all the members suffer with it, and if one member is honored, all the rest rejoice with it, and the eye cannot say to the ear, I have no need of thee, nor the head to the foot, I have no need of thee"; party feelings, separate interests, exclusive designs should be lost sight of in the one common cause, in the interest of the whole. (TPJS, 231)[76]

◆◆◆

What if all the world should embrace the Gospel? They would then see eye to eye, and the blessings of God would be poured out upon the people, which is the desire of my whole soul. Amen. (TPJS, 275)[91]

◆◆◆

If a skillful mechanic . . . succeeds in welding together iron or steel more perfectly than any other mechanic, is he not deserving of praise? And if by the principles of truth I succeed in uniting men of all denominations in the bonds of love, shall I not have attained a good object? (TPJS, 313)[114]

◆◆◆

The whole of America is Zion itself from north to south, and is described by the Prophets, who declare that it is the Zion where the mountain of the Lord should be. (TPJS, 362)[131]

◆◆◆

I have received instructions from the Lord that from henceforth wherever Elders of Israel shall build up churches and branches unto the Lord . . . there shall be a stake of Zion. (TPJS, 363)[131]

ENDNOTES

Inasmuch as the material for *Joseph Speaks—Topical Quoets by the Prophet Joseph Smith* is drawn from *Teachings of the Prophet Joseph Smith* (1976 edition), credit is given to the former Church Historian Joseph Fielding Smith and his associates not only for their informational research presented in that well-known book, but for careful documentation as well. Page references are made to that source (TPJS) for each quote entered, followed by a footnote entry to the original source. The footnotes used are listed below in a convenient chronological order.

ABBREVIATIONS
DHC—Documentary History of the Church
FWR—Far West Record
E&MS—Evening and Morning Star
M&A—Messenger and Advocate
MSS—Manuscript History
TS—Times and Seasons

1. Re: Book of Mormon Title Page	DHC 1:71, 1830
2. Re: Value of Revelations	DHC 1:235–36, at Hiram, Nov. 1831
3. At an Assembly re: Perfecting Faith	FWR, 13–14, 25 Oct. 1831
4. At an Assembly re: Perfecting Faith	FWR, 16, 25 Oct. 1831
5. Re: Bible Translation	DHC 1:245, 16 Feb. 1832
6. Re: Vision as Translating Bible Scripture	DHC 1:252–253, Feb. 1832
7. Excerpts from Published Article	*Evening and Morning Star*, Aug. 1832
8. From Article Published in *E&M S*	DHC 1:282–284, Aug. 1832
9. From Letter to Newspaper Editor	DHC 1:312–316, 4 Jan. 1833
10, "Olive Leaf" Letter to W. W. Phelps in MO	DHC 1:316, 14 Jan. 1833
11. Epistle from First Pres. to Church in Ohio	DHC 1:324–5, 6 Feb. 1833
12. Re: Manner of Church Instruction	DHC 1:338–339, 13 Apr. 1833
13. First Presidency Answers to Queries	DHC 1:364–368, 4 June 1833
14. Excerpts of Writings to Brethren in Zion	DHC 1:368–370, 2 Jul. 1833
15. Letter to V. Jaques at Independence, MO	DHC 1:407–409, 4 Sep.1833
16. To M. Nickerson in Upper Canada	DHC 1:441–443, 19 Nov. 1833
17. Re: the Falling of Sidney Rigdon	DHC 1:443–444, 19 Nov. 1833
18. From Kirtland re: Land Sale in Zion	DHC 1:448–451, 5 Dec. 1833
19. From Kirtland to Exiled Saints in MO	DHC 1:453–456, 10 Dec. 1833
20. Letter to the Brethren of the Church	DHC 1:467–469, Dec. 1833
21. From Kirtland Epistle to Those Abroad	DHC 2:4–24, 22 Jan. 1834
22. Priesthood Council in Kirtland	DHC 2:25–26, 12 Feb. 1834
23. Elders' Conference re: Joel, Chapter 2	DHC 2:52, 21 Apr. 1834
24. Zion's Camp March: Kirtland to Missouri	DHC 2:71, 26 May 1834
25. Re: Holding Spiritual Powers Sacred	DHC 2:95–96, 16 Jun. 1834
26. Instruction to the Twelve	DHC 2:198–199, 27 Feb. 1835
27. Re: Calling of Apostles, O. Cowdery, Clerk	DHC 2:200, 27 Feb. 1835
28. Instruction to Twelve and the Seventy	DHC 2:220–222, 2 May 1835
29. Epistle to Saints Scattered Abroad	DHC 2:229–231, June 1835
30. Ohio Epistle to Elders, *M&A*, also	DHC 2:253–259, 1 Sept. 1835
31. Epistle to the Church Elders, *M&A*, also	DHC 2:259–264, Nov. 1835
32. Reflections on Man Receiving Revelation	DHC 2:302, 6 Nov. 1835

33. Council Meeting Remarks to Twelve — DHC 2:308–310, 12 Nov. 1835
34. *Messenger & Advocate* Article — DHC 2:264–272, Dec. 1835
35. High Council Remarks at Kirtland: Gathering — DHC 2:357, 6 Jan. 1836
36. Priesthood Meeting in Kirtland Temple — DHC 2:370, 15 Jan. 1836
37. Special Meeting of Twelve in Kirtland — DHC 2:373–374, 16 Jan. 1836
38. Re: Vision of the Celestial Kingdom — DHC 2:380–381, 21 Jan. 1836
39. Re: the Twelve as Revelators — DHC 2:417, 27 Mar. 1836
40. On Priesthood and Church Organization — DHC 2:431–432, 29 Mar. 1836
41. Solemn Assembly in Kirtland Temple — DHC 2:477–479, 6 April 1837
42. Political Motto for Church of Latter-day Saints — DHC 3:9, March 1838
43. Remarks on the Word of Wisdom — FWR, 111, 7 Apr. 1838
44. A Sunday Sermon to the Saints — DHC 3:27, 6 May 1838
45. Prophet's Answers to Sundry Questions — DHC 3:28–30, 8 May 1838
46. Letter to Church from Liberty Jail — DHC 3:226–233, 16 Dec. 1838
47. Epistle to Church from Liberty Jail — DHC 3:289–305, 25 Mar. 1839
48. The Prophet re: Various Doctrines — DHC 3:379–381, 27 Jun. 1839
49. Apostles and Seventies on way to England — DHC 3:383–392, 2 Jul. 1839
50. Admonitions to the Saints — DHC 4:11, 29 Sept. 1839
51. To Hyde and Page re: Palestine Mission — DHC 4:128–129, 14 May 1840
52. Joseph Instructs High Council re: Trials — DHC 4:154, 22 July 1840
53. Letter Welcoming W. W. Phelps Back — DHC 4:162–164, 22 July 1840
54. Conference Remarks on Priesthood — DHC 4:207–212, 5 Oct. 1840
55. Epistle to the Twelve — DHC 4:226–232, 19 Oct. 1840
56. Organization of a School of Instruction — DHC 4:260–267, 5 Jan. 1841
57. Proclamation from Nauvoo to Saints Abroad — DHC 4:269, 5–8 Jan. 1841
58. Proclamation from Nauvoo to Saints Abroad — DHC 4:272, 8 Jan. 1841
59. Nauvoo Cornerstone Ceremony: Order — DHC 4:336–339, 6 April 1841
60. Large Gathering on Meeting Ground — DHC 4:358–360, 16 May 1841
61. Principles of Godhead — MSS, 16 May 1841
62. Sermon to Large Congregation at the Stand — DHC 4:414, 5 Sept. 1841
63. A Large Congregation at the Stand — DHC 4:424–426, 3 Oct. 1841
64. Discourses to the Brethren — DHC 4:445–446, 7 Nov. 1841
65. In Council with the Twelve — DHC 4:461, 28 Nov. 1841
66. "Important Instructions" — DHC 4:478–479, 19 Dec. 1841
67. Public Meeting of Saints at Joseph's — DHC 4:485–486, 26 Dec. 1841
68. Sermon on Life and Death — DHC 4:553–557, 20 Mar. 1842
69. Sermon on Baptism for the Dead — DHC 4:568–569, 27 Mar. 1842
70. Remarks to the Relief Society — DHC 4:570, 30 Mar. 1842
71. Prophet's Editorial in the T & S; and — DHC 4:571–581, 1 Apr. 1842
72. Remarks at Funeral of Ephraim Marks — DHC 4:587, 9 Apr. 1842
73. Remarks to a General Mass of People — DHC 4:588, 10 Apr. 1842
74. The Prophet on Salvation for the Dead — DHC 4:595–599, 15 Apr. 1842
75. Remarks to Relief Society — DHC 4:602–607, 28 Apr. 1842
76. Re: Construction of Nauvoo Temple — DHC 4:608–610, 2 May 1842
77. Highest Order of Priesthood Revealed — DHC 5:1–2, 4 May 1842
78. Address to the Relief Society — DHC 5:19–21, 26 May 1842
79. Minutes of Relief Soc. Meeting at Grove — DHC 5:23–25, 9 June 1842
80. Editorial in *Times and Seasons* — DHC 5:26–32, 15 June 1842
81. Editorial on Man's Government Failures — DHC 5:61–66, 15 July 1842
82. Prophesy of the Saints Driven to Rockies — DHC 5:85, 6 Aug. 1842
83. Doctrine Expounded to the Saints — DHC 5:134–136, 27 Aug. 1842
84. Minutes on Remarks to Relief Society — DHC 5:139–141, 31 Aug. 1842
85. Editorial to the *Times and Seasons* — T&S 3:902–905, 1 Sept. 1842

86, "Facts are Stubborn Things"	T&S 3:921–922, 15 Sept. 1842
87. Re: Effects on Disobeying Counsel	DHC 5:181, 29 Oct. 1842
88. While in Conversation at Judge Adam's	DHC 5:212, 30 Dec. 1842
89. What Constitutes a Prophet	DHC 5:215–216, 30 Dec. 1842
90. Principles and Observations Related	DHC 5:217–219, 2 Jan. 1843
91. Bold, Authoritative Remarks to Saints	DHC 5:256–259, 22 Jan. 1843
92. Article in the Wasp, 28 Jan.1843, p. 3	DHC 5:260–262, 23 Jan. 1843
93. Address on Biblical Questions	DHC 5:260–262, 29 Jan. 1843
94. The Calling of a Prophet	DHC 5:265, 8 Feb. 1843
95. On Constitutional Powers	DHC 5:289–290, 25 Feb. 1843
96. Editorial Response in Chicago Express	DHC 5:290–291, 28 Feb. 1843
97. On Giving a Blessing	DHC 5:303, 14 Mar. 1843
98. A Prophesy re: Orrin Porter Rockwell	DHC 5:305, 15 Mar. 1843
99. Conference Remarks on Second Coming	DHC 5:336–337, 6 Apr. 1843
100.Guide on Meeting Courtesy	DHC 5:338–339, 7 Apr. 1843
101. Conference Expounding of Scriptures	DHC 5:339–345, 8 Apr. 1843
102. Remarks on Death of Lorenzo Barnes	DHC 5:360–363, 16 Apr. 1843
103. Remarks on Salvation	DHC 5:387–390, 14 May 1843
104. Letter to Editor of *Times and Seasons*	T&S 4:194, 15 May 1843
105. On the Eternal Marriage Covenant	DHC 5:391–392, 16 May 1843
106. On the Sure Word of Prophecy	DHC 5:392, 17 May 1843
107. Speaking on the Subject of Matter	DHC 5:392–393, 17 May 1843
108. Prophecy re: Stephen A. Douglas	DHC 5:393–394, 18 May 1843
109. Discourse on New Testament Chapter	DHC 5:401–403, 21 May 1843
110. On Forming Temperance Societies	DHC 5:404, 22 May 1843
111. Address to the Twelve	DHC 5:411, 27 May 1843
112. Sobering Observation re: Apostasy	DHC 5:412, 28 May 1843
113. At the Large Temple Stand Assembly	DHC 5:423–427, 1 June 1843
114. Remarks on Several Topics	DHC 5:498–500, 9 July 1843
115. Discourse on Burden of His Ministry	DHC 5:516–518, 3 July 1843
116. The Prophet's Own Proverbs	MSS, Historian's Office, 1843
117. Excerpts from a Sermon	MSS, Historian's Office, 3 July 1843
118. Remarks at Funeral of Judge Higbee	DHC 5:529–531, 13 Aug. 1843
119. Expounding on the Priesthood Order	DHC 5:554–556, 7 Aug. 1843
120. Instructions re: Plurality of Wives	DHC 6:46, 5 Oct. 1843
121. Remarks on the Demise of James Adams	DHC 6:50–52, 9 Oct. 1843
122. On the Constitution and the Bible	DHC 6:56–59, 15 Oct. 1843
123. On Priesthood's Sealing Power	DHC 6:183–185, 20 Jan. 1844
124. On Candidacy for U. S. Presidency	DHC 6:210–211, 8 Feb. 1844
125. Obedience Necessary for Salvation	DHC 6:223, 21 Feb. 1844
126. A Prophecy of Deliverance of the Saints	DHC 6:225, 25 Feb. 1844
127. Remarks on Political Matters	DHC 6:243–244, 7 Mar. 1844
128. On Futurity and Salvation of Man	DHC 6:249–254, 10 Mar. 1844
129. Discourse on Power of Truth	DHC 6:273, 24 Mar. 1844
130. King Follett Discourse to 20,000	T&S, 15 Aug. 1844, re: 7 Apr. 1844
131. Conf. on Zion and Temple Ordinances	DHC 6:318–320, 8 Apr. 1844
132. Address on Numerous Topics	DHC 6:363–367, 2 May 1844
133. Sermon at Grove re: Plurality of Gods	DHC 6:473–479, 16 June 1844
134. The Prophet Predicts His Death	DHC 6:545–551, 22 June 1844
135. A Tearful Parting from His Family	DHC 6:545–551, 22 June 1844
136. Reconciliation to Their Fate	DHC 6:545–551, 23 June 1844
137. The Start for Carthage	DHC 6:554–555, 24 June 1844
138. On the Way to Carthage	DHC 6:558, 24 June 1844

139. Interview with Militia Officers — DHC 6:566, 25 June 1844
140. The Prophet's Heavy Premonition — DHC 6:592–593, 26 June 1844
141. Re: Ill Treatment of Prophet's Uncle — DHC 6:597–598, 26 June 1844
142. The Last Night in Jail — DHC 6:600–601, 26 June 1844
143. Joseph's Interview w/ Governor Ford — DHC 6:579–585, 26 June 1844
144. Letter to Emma re: Reception of Gov. Ford — DHC 6:605, 27 June 1844
145. The Prophet's Acknowledgements — DHC 6:608–611, 27 June 1844
146. Letter of Request for Legal Counsel — DHC 6:613, 27 June 1844

STERLING H. REDD

Sterling H. Redd has had an identified interest in writing since one of his grandmothers pointed out this talent to him during his teen years. Following a year of active military duty during the Berlin Crisis, he finished his BS degree in Sociology and English at Brigham Young University. Upon graduation, he taught high school English in the Salt Lake area. After receiving an MSW degree at the University of Utah, he served for over thirty years as a clinical social worker and writer/editor for the Utah State Department of Health.

Sterling has served as a missionary in New Zealand, as a member of a stake mission presidency, and in subsequent years, as a stake missionary among people from several different countries. He has been a Gospel Doctrine teacher, a High Priest Group instructor, and a High Priest Group leader. Most recently he completed a mission at the LDS Employment Resource Center, assisting a widely diverse patronage in personal resume writing.

Sterling has a love of the Gospel of Jesus Christ, as well as a love of people, nature, classical music, literature, and writing. He is the father of five grown children and is currently residing with his wife, Fusako, and two cats in Salt Lake City, Utah.

Sterling is also the author of *Resource Manual for Parents of Special-needs Children in Salt Lake and Surrounding Areas, A Topical Guide for Latter-day Saints and Related Videos*, and is the editor/indexer of the latest edition of *A Story to Tell.*